OXFORD
UNIVERSITY PRESS

ACCOUNTING

for Cambridge International AS & A Level

David Austen
Jacqueline Halls-Bryan
Peter Hailstone

Oxford excellence for Cambridge AS & A Level

OXFORD

OXFORD
UNIVERSITY PRESS

Great Clarendon Street, Oxford, OX2 6DP, United Kingdom

Oxford University Press is a department of the University of Oxford. It furthers the University's objective of excellence in research, scholarship, and education by publishing worldwide. Oxford is a registered trade mark of Oxford University Press in the UK and in certain other countries

First published in 2015

British Library Cataloguing in Publication Data
Data available

9780198399711

10 9 8 7 6 5

Paper used in the production of this book is a natural, recyclable product made from wood grown in sustainable forests. The manufacturing process conforms to the environmental regulations of the country of origin.

Printed by CPI Group (UK) Ltd, Croydon CR0 4YY

Acknowledgements
The publishers would like to thank the following for permissions to use their photographs:

Cover image: Iconeer/iStock.com; p8: Tupungato / Shutterstock; p69: Imaginechina/ Rex Features; p80: Laborant / Shutterstock; p105: Club4traveler/Shutterstock; p202: Kzenon / Shutterstock; p223: momente / Shutterstock; p230: Betastock / Shutterstock; p393: Levent Konuk / Shutterstock; p269: ID1974 / Shutterstock; p332: imagedb.com / Shutterstock; p354: Aman Ahmed Khan/Shutterstock; p365: littlewormy/Shutterstock; p372: Paul Prescott/Shutterstock; p262: Arif Ali/AFP/Getty Images; p402: Yuri_Arcurs/ iStockphoto; p420: S-F/Shutterstock; p437: Dmitry Kalinovsky/Shutterstock.

Artwork by QBS Learning and OUP.

Contents

A Level

Access your support website: www.oxfordsecondary.com/9780198399711

Introduction

Welcome to your study of Accounting

The study of accounting provides an excellent introduction to understanding so many aspects of the way in which businesses and other organisations operate. For many it will give an opportunity to take the first steps necessary towards a career in some aspect of finance, accountancy, management or some related field. For some, A Level Accounting will be the first step on a pathway leading to further study such as a degree or professional qualification or both.

The purpose of this book

The intention is that this book will:

- help you to make good progress with your learning so that you enjoy your course of study and gain real satisfaction from the work you do
- provide you with the background knowledge you need to help you achieve your best at AS and/or A Level
- develop your knowledge and understanding of accounting techniques and concepts
- help you to develop your skills in recording, analysing and evaluating financial information
- provide coverage of the entire syllabus
- provide a good basis for further study of the subject.

The features of the book

To help you get the best out of this book, and to help you succeed in the subject, the book has a number of important features:

- **Key concepts** tells you the key concepts that apply to each section.
- **Learning objectives** provide a succinct summary of what you will learn in each chapter.
- **Key terms** are used to highlight important ideas. They are all collected together in the **Glossary**.
- **Illustrations** are worked examples that show you how to apply the concepts and techniques covered in each chapter.
- **Getting it right** is designed to warn you how to avoid some of the most common mistakes made by students.
- **Links** signpost connections with explanations and illustrations elsewhere in the book.

- **End-of-chapter questions** will enable you to develop the skills necessary to show you have a good understanding of the ideas and techniques covered. There is a mix of multiple-choice questions and questions requiring a longer response. Answers to all of the odd-numbered questions can be found on the website.
- **Exam-style questions** will help you to familiarise yourself with the style of questions that will be asked, and the sort of things students may be required to do.

Key concepts

Each section highlights how key concepts relate to the content of the chapter(s) in the section. These key concepts are:

- **True and fair view**: the importance of giving information to owners and other stakeholders in which they can have confidence.
- **Duality (double entry)**: the idea that every transaction affects aspects of an organisation's financial position in two different ways which are reflected in the way records are kept.
- **Consistency**: in the way accounting information is recorded, processed and reported to ensure that users can make meaningful comparisons from one period to another.
- **Business entity**: the idea that a business and the owner of the business are two separate entities; the accounting records are concerned with business's financial affairs as distinct from the personal financial affairs of the owner.
- **Money measurement**: acknowledges that accounting records are expressed in money values and so cannot record aspects of an organisation whose value cannot be determined in money.

Website

The website contains interactive resources to help you practise exam-style questions. These include:

- **Test yourself**: multiple-choice questions, which reinforce learning.
- **On your marks**: which give guidance on how to answer computational questions and those requiring a prose response.
- **Exam preparation**, which will help you prepare for success.
- **A glossary**, which contains all of the key terms you need to know for A Level Accounting.
- **Answers** to odd-numbered end-of-chapter questions and exam-style questions to help you review your progress.
- **Additional questions to develop skills in completing double-entry records**, with answers.

1 Financial accounting

Section 1.1: The accounting cycle

Key concepts

Double-entry bookkeeping is based on the idea that accounting records are required for a business and these are quite separate from the private financial records of the owner: the **business entity** concept. Double-entry records are also based on the idea that there are two aspects to every transaction which lead to the necessity of making two entries in the financial records for each transaction: the **duality (double-entry)** concept. Accounting records can only record information that has a monetary value: the **money measurement** concept.

1.1.1: An introduction to double-entry bookkeeping

Learning objectives

In this chapter you will learn:

- about the role of the bookkeeper and the role of the accountant
- about different types of business organisation
- the main types of financial statement
- about the accounting cycle
- the basic principles of the double-entry system
- the accounting equation
- how to prepare simple ledger accounts.

Note:

This chapter has been designed to help those students who have not yet studied double-entry bookkeeping. As a result this chapter has been written to introduce some important aspects of accounting. The basic principles have been outlined in a simple way in order for new students to get started on their course of study. More experienced students will probably find they can skip much of the content of this chapter.

Introduction

There is nothing new about keeping careful records of financial information. Even thousands of years ago individuals were concerned about being well informed about what they received and spent, so that they could have some idea about whether they were well off or not. Nowadays these same questions apply to individuals and organisations. In the case of businesses, the owners need to know:

- whether they are making a profit, because this is the main reason for engaging in business activity
- that they have enough money to pay all their commitments on time
- that they are making the best use of the funds they have invested in the business.

In the modern world, business activity can be on a very large scale and very complex. Even a really simple form of business organisation (e.g. a market stall) can involve a great deal of financial activity, including handling money, buying goods to sell, paying assistants, etc. Accounting is about providing accurate and comprehensive financial information to those involved in making decisions, so that businesses can survive, be successful and be run efficiently.

In order to provide this comprehensive financial information, it is necessary for the following to happen.

- All financial transactions need to be recorded in a systematic way, so that the owner of a business, and other users, can be provided with the information they need to make the right decisions. This record-keeping aspect of accounting is often called bookkeeping.
- From the bookkeeping records, which often contain vast amounts of detail, it is important to select, classify and summarise information, so that owners and other users can be given the appropriate information in the form of financial statements to help them manage the business effectively. The preparation of financial statements and providing some interpretation of what the statements reveal is often called accounting.

Key terms

Bookkeeping: recording financial information, particularly transactions, in a systematic way.

Accounting: selecting, classifying and summarising financial data in ways that provide the owners of businesses (and others) with useful information to help them assess performance and plan future activities.

Types of business organisation

What is a business? Businesses are organisations which provide goods and/or services in order to make a profit. There are a number of ways of classifying businesses.

It is possible to think about businesses by what they do, for example:

- provide raw materials through mining, farming, fishing, etc.
- manufacture goods, turning raw materials into finished products
- sell goods to the general public (retailers) or to other businesses (wholesalers)
- provide services for businesses and the general public.

It is also possible think about businesses in terms of who owns them, for example:

- **Sole trader**: where one individual owns the business. The individual controls the business. If successful, the profits made by the business belong to this individual; if unsuccessful, the individual can lose whatever has been invested and private resources too.
- **Partnerships**: where several individuals own the business. Partners jointly control the business sharing profits between them. They are also jointly responsible for the debts of the business, and can lose their private resources if the partnership is unsuccessful.
- **Limited liability companies**: these are owned by shareholders who each contribute to the funds needed to establish and run the company. Most shareholders do not take part in the day-to-day management and control of the company, but elect directors to undertake these responsibilities on their behalf. Shareholders are rewarded by receiving some of the profits made by the company if successful. Shareholders' responsibility for the debts of the company is limited to the amount they invest. Unlike sole traders and partners, shareholders are not at risk of losing their private funds if things go wrong.
- **Not-for-profit organisations**: this category includes clubs and societies which are formed by their members so that they can meet for particular activities: perhaps social or sporting activities. These organisations do not aim to make a profit, but they have to be financially viable in order to survive.

Links

There is more about financial statements in the following: (for sole traders) AS Level Section 1.4 Preparation of financial statements; AS Level Chapter 1.4.3A Partnerships: preparation of accounts; AS Level Chapter 1.4.4A Limited companies: structure and accounting for share issues; and A Level Chapter 1.1.2 Not-for-profit organisations.

What are the financial statements?

Owners, managers and other stakeholders will inspect the following financial statements.

For information about profit (or loss)

- The **income statement** is the chief source of information about profits or losses for sole traders, partnerships and limited companies.

- In the case of not-for-profit organisations, information about surpluses or deficits (these words are used instead of profit and loss) is provided by an **income and expenditure account**.

For information about ability to meet commitments on time

The **statement of financial position** provides details of the resources owned by the business which can be used to meet commitments (cash and bank balances, money to be received in the near future, etc.) and some of the commitments (e.g. amounts due to suppliers). Statements of financial position are prepared by all the organisations listed above.

For information about the efficient use of resources

The statement of financial position provides detailed information about all the resources owned by a business, and in conjunction with information about profits it can be used to reveal how successful, or otherwise, the owners and managers have been in using these resources well.

The accounting cycle

The accounting cycle is the name given to the sequence of events and processes that are used to develop the accounting records of an organisation. Briefly, the cycle is made up of the following stages:

- **Stage 1**: the collecting of source documents that provide details for the financial records.
- **Stage 2**: the listing of key details in books of prime entry. There are separate books of prime entry for different categories of transactions: credit sales, credit purchases, returns, cash and bank transactions and other miscellaneous transactions.
- **Stage 3**: 'posting' the information shown in the books of prime entry to ledger accounts. There are separate ledger accounts for each aspect of a business's finances. Bookkeeping involves the process of making two entries for every transaction in ledger accounts; this is often referred to as double-entry bookkeeping.
- **Stage 4**: checking and control systems to ensure that accounting records are arithmetically correct.
- **Stage 5**: summarising financial information periodically (and at least annually) in the form of income statements, statements of financial position, etc. These end-of-year financial statements provide the main means of judging how well a business has performed, leading to key decisions by owners, managers and others.

... and then back to the beginning; hence the idea of an accounting cycle.

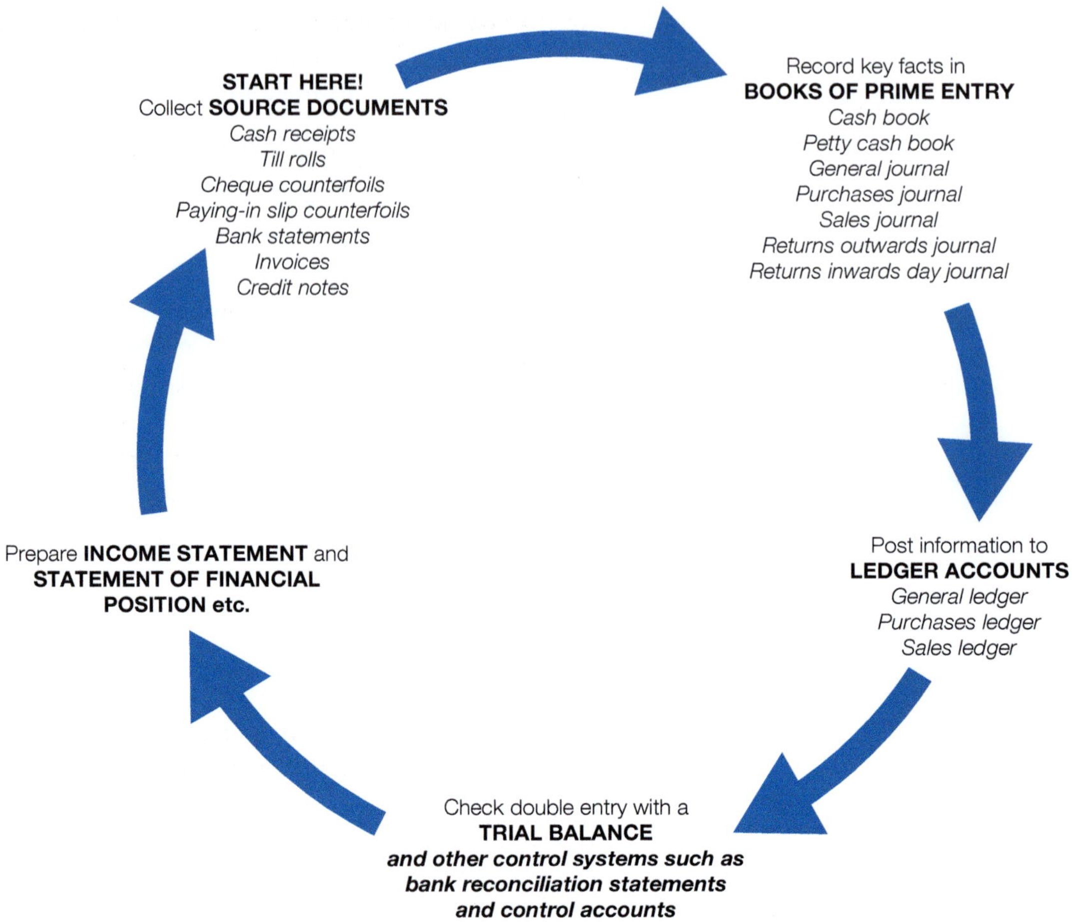

Figure 1.1.1A: The accounting cycle

Simple accounting records

Assets, liabilities, capital and the accounting equation

> **Key term**
>
> **Assets**: resources with a monetary value which are owned by a business.

All businesses own resources such as cash, vehicles, furniture, premises. These resources are known as assets. The owner of a business will have provided or purchased each asset to ensure that the enterprise can trade or provide a service effectively. Assets have a monetary value and provide a benefit to the business. Here are some more examples:

- property
- machinery
- equipment
- fittings
- inventories.

Cash is an important asset for all businesses. Usually this asset is separated into two categories as follows:

- **Cash in hand**: money in the form of notes, coins, cheques, etc. which are at the business premises (probably locked in the safe or in the cash register).

▶ **Cash at bank**: all money that has been transferred by the owner of the business to the business's bank account.

Some businesses provide goods or services on credit to their customers. This means that the customer agrees to pay for the goods or services some time after they have been sold to the customer. The amount due from credit customers is referred to as trade receivables.

What are liabilities?

Businesses often owe money to other businesses or organisations. Amounts owing to other businesses or organisations are called liabilities. For example, many businesses buy goods on credit from their suppliers. In other words, the goods are purchased but payment for them is made at some later date. The suppliers to whom the business owes money are referred to as trade payables. Here are two more examples of liabilities:

▶ bank loans

▶ bank overdrafts.

What is capital?

Businesses only exist because their owners have invested private funds in the business. As a result businesses then acquire the kinds of asset described above. Maybe other businesses and organisations also provide some finance – the liabilities also described above. The finance or investment provided by the owner is called capital.

It is usual to divide assets and liabilities into subcategories.

Non-current assets are assets that the business intends to keep and make use of for a long time (more than one year). Non-current assets include: premises, machinery, equipment, vehicles, furniture, fittings, etc.

Current assets are assets that are frequently changing in value such as inventory, trade receivables, bank and cash. So, any one item of inventory, or an amount owing from a particular trade receivable, will only be an asset for the business for a short time (less than one year).

Non-current liabilities are amounts due that are likely to be repaid in a future financial period (after more than one year). Non-current liabilities would normally include bank loans.

Current liabilities are amounts due that will be repaid within the financial period (less than one year). An example of current liabilities is trade payables.

What is the accounting equation?

There is a simple link between the three elements: assets, liabilities and capital. This link, called the accounting equation, is based on the following idea:

▶ Each business has a number of assets. These assets have either been provided by the owner of the business (capital) or by using funds provided by other businesses or organisations (liabilities).

Getting it right

You will notice that assets do *not* include employees! Assets have to be owned by the business.

Key term

Trade receivables: amounts owed by credit customers.

Key terms

Liabilities: amounts owed by a business to other businesses, organisations or individuals.

Trade payables: amounts owed by a business to suppliers.

Key terms

Capital: the investment made by the owner(s) of a business. It equates to the net value of the business.

Non-current assets: assets that should be of benefit to the business for a long time (more than one year).

Current assets: assets that are quickly turned into cash and are of benefit to the business for a short time (less than one year).

Non-current liabilities: liabilities that will be settled in the longer term (longer than one year).

Current liabilities: liabilities that will be settled in the near future (in less than one year).

Accounting equation: links the three elements that are a feature of all businesses, i.e. assets, liabilities and capital. The equation is: Assets = Capital + Liabilities.

- It follows that whatever the scale of the business: Assets = Capital + Liabilities.

Illustration 1: The accounting equation

John is the owner of a general store. The business has assets with a total value of $75 000. John provided $60 000 from his private resources to buy these assets; the other $15 000 of assets was purchased by asking for a loan from the bank.

Summary: Assets $75 000 = Capital $60 000 + Liabilities $15 000

The accounting equation can be useful for calculating otherwise unknown facts about businesses. So, if you know that business has assets of $40 000 and liabilities of $5000, it is possible to work out that the owner's capital must be $35 000. In other words:

Assets = Capital + Liabilities

$40 000 = ? + $5000

So: $40 000 = $35 000 + $5000

Key term

Duality concept: the idea that there are two aspects to every transaction which lead to the necessity of making two entries in the financial records for each transaction.

Two aspects for every transaction

Accounting records are based on the idea that for any transaction there will be two consequences, so that one transaction will lead to two entries in the accounting system. This idea is often referred to as the duality concept.

Illustration 2: Examples of transactions leading to two consequences

A business has assets of $40 000, capital of $30 000 and liabilities of $10 000, i.e. the accounting equation is:

A	=	C	+	L
40 000	=	30 000	+	10 000

a The owner of a business purchased some office furniture by cheque for $1200.

As a result of this transaction:

- **Asset** Office furniture will **increase**
- **Asset** Bank will **decrease**

Here is the effect on the accounting equation.

	A	=	C	+	L
before	40 000	=	30 000	+	10 000
transaction	+ 1 200 – 1 200				
after	40 000	=	30 000	+	10 000

b The owner of a business arranged a bank loan of $6000 with funds transferred to the business's bank account.

As a result of this transaction:

- Asset Bank will increase
- Liability Bank loan will increase

Here is the effect on the accounting equation.

	A	=	C	+	L
before	40 000	=	30 000	+	10 000
transaction	+ 6 000				+ 6 000
after	46 000	=	30 000	+	16 000

Key term

Drawings: the withdrawal of funds for private use by the owner of a business.

c The owner of a business withdrew a cheque for $500 for private use (often referred to as drawings).

As a result of this transaction:

- Asset Bank will decrease
- Capital will decrease

Here is the effect on the accounting equation.

	A	=	C	+	L
before	46 000	=	30 000	+	16 000
transaction	– 500		– 500		
after	45 500	=	29 500	+	16 000

d A motor vehicle, value $8000, was purchased on credit from Smartvans.

As a result of this transaction:

- **Asset** Motor vehicle will **increase**
- **Liability** Smartvans will **increase**

Here is the effect on the accounting equation.

	A	=	C	+	L
before	45 500	=	29 500	+	16 000
transaction	+ 8 000				+ 8 000
after	53 500	=	29 500	+	24 000

Notes:

1 The transactions demonstrate the effect of a small variety of transactions on the accounting equation.

2 The illustration includes a mixture of cash and credit transactions.

3 Whatever the transaction there are two effects.

4 Whatever the transactions the two sides of the accounting equation always agree.

Some more transactions affecting capital

Capital represents the net value of a business. Certain transactions will affect this net value. The aim of the owner(s) of every business is to increase the businesses value over a period of time. How is this done?

- In a service business (examples: a health and fitness centre, a hairdresser, a firm of accountants) the business receives money (sales) from providing a service. However, at the same time funds will be spent on running costs: electricity charges, wages, insurance, rent, etc. If receipts from sales exceed the running costs over a period of time, then the value of the business (i.e. capital) will increase; in effect the owner(s) will be wealthier.
- In a retail business (for example any of the stores in your local shopping centre) the business will receive money (sales) from selling goods. However, at the same time funds will have to be spent on the goods to be sold (purchases) and on running costs. As long as sales exceed purchases and running costs the value of the business (capital) will increase, and the owner(s) will be wealthier.

Here is a summary of these ideas using the accounting equation:

Assets = Capital (increasing for sales; decreasing for running costs) + Liabilities

Illustration 3: Further examples of effects of transactions on the accounting equation

Jason owns Ultra Fitness Centre. The business's accounting equation is as follows.

A	=	C	+	L
82 000	=	55 000	+	27 000

a During a recent week the business received money from clients totalling $4500.

As a result of this transaction:

- Asset Bank will increase
- Capital will increase because the business is now more valuable.

	A	=	C	+	L
before	82 000	=	55 000	+	27 000
transaction	+ 4 500		+ 4 500		
after	86 500	=	59 500	+	27 000

b During the same period Jason paid staff wages by cheque $2100.

As a result of this transaction:

- Asset Bank will decrease
- Capital will decrease because the business is now less valuable.

	A	=	C	+	L
before	86 500	=	59 500	+	27 000
transaction	– 2 100		– 2 100		
after	84 400	=	57 400	+	27 000

Recording transactions in accounts

Transactions are recorded in accounts. There are separate accounts to record each aspect of a transaction. So there are separate accounts for each asset, each liability, each running cost, sale, purchase, drawing, etc.

Each account has the same simple structure:

Title	
Dr	Cr

The expression 'T account' is sometimes used because of the shape of this structure.

The left-hand side of an account is called the debit side (abbreviated as Dr).

The right-hand side of an account is called the credit side (abbreviated as Cr).

The way information is recorded in accounts depends on the type of account and reflects the way the accounting equation works.

Asset	
Dr	Cr
+	–

Capital	
Dr	Cr
–	+

Liability	
Dr	Cr
–	+

This pattern has been developed to reflect that assets are on the opposite side to capital and liabilities in the accounting equation, so the accounts work in different directions as shown.

Illustration 4 shows the way accounts are set up and how they work based on this pattern.

Illustration 4: Simple examples of how transactions are recorded

a A business arranges a bank loan for $6000 and funds are transferred to the business bank account.

Asset	
Dr	Cr
+	–

Capital	
Dr	Cr
–	+

Liability	
Dr	Cr
–	+

Bank		Capital		Loan	
Dr	Cr	Dr	Cr	Dr	Cr
+	–	–	+	–	+
6 000					6 000

Notes:

1 All transactions result in a pair of entries.

2 Notice that because of the way the accounts are set up, one account has an entry on the left-hand side (a debit entry) and the other account affected has an entry on the right-hand side (a credit entry).

b The owner introduces additional capital by paying $2000 into the business bank account.

Asset		Capital		Liability	
Dr	Cr	Dr	Cr	Dr	Cr
+	–	–	+	–	+

Bank		Capital		Liability	
Dr	Cr	Dr	Cr	Dr	Cr
+	–	–	+	–	+
2 000			2 000		

Note:

Once again there is a matching pair of entries: debit and credit.

c A business receives cash (banked) from sales $700.

Asset		Capital		Liability	
Dr	Cr	Dr	Cr	Dr	Cr
+	–	–	+	–	+

Bank		Sales		Liability	
Dr	Cr	Dr	Cr	Dr	Cr
+	–	–	+	–	+
700			700		

Notes:

1 Once again there are matching debit and credit entries.

2 The entry in the sales account records the increase in the value of the business (i.e. an increase in capital).

d Rent is paid by cheque, $400.

Asset		Capital		Liability	
Dr	Cr	Dr	Cr	Dr	Cr
+	–	–	+	–	+

Bank		Rent		Loan	
Dr	Cr	Dr	Cr	Dr	Cr
+	−	−	+	−	+
	400	400			

Notes:

1 The entries record the decrease in an asset (bank) and the decrease in the value of the business (rent).

2 This again results in a matching pair of debit and credit entries.

3 It is easy to get confused: the entry in the rent account is not indicating there is less rent, it is indicating there is less capital (i.e. the business is worth less).

e The owner withdrew a cheque for $200 for private use (drawings).

Asset		Capital		Liability	
Dr	Cr	Dr	Cr	Dr	Cr
+	−	−	+	−	+

Bank		Drawings		Loan	
Dr	Cr	Dr	Cr	Dr	Cr
+	−	−	+	−	+
	200	200			

Notes:

1 As always there is a matching pair of debit and credit entries.

2 The entries record the decrease in an asset (credit entry) and the decrease in capital (because of the withdrawal of funds).

3 Again, avoid getting confused: the entry in the drawings account is not indicating there are less drawings, it is indicating there is less capital.

Detailed entries in ledger accounts

Accounts are grouped together in what is called a ledger – hence the term 'ledger accounts'. To record a transaction it is necessary to enter the:

- amount
- date of transaction
- name of the account where the matching entry is shown.

As a result ledger accounts are designed as shown:

Debit (Dr)			**Credit (Cr)**		
Date	Details	$	Date	Details	$
The date of the transaction	The account to which the other part of the transaction is posted	The amount of the transaction	The date of the transaction	The account to which the other part of the transaction is posted	The amount of the transaction

Illustration 5: Examples of entries in ledger accounts

Here are some examples of transactions recorded in ledger accounts.

Dr		**Bank**					**Cr**
Oct	1	Capital	30 000	Oct	2	Rent	1 000
	5	Sales	4 900		3	Drawings	800
	8	Bank loan	10 000		4	Purchases	5 500

Dr		**Capital**					**Cr**
				Oct	1	Bank	30 000

Dr		**Drawings**					**Cr**
Oct	3	Bank	800				

Dr		**Purchases**					**Cr**
Oct	4	Bank	5 500				

Dr		**Rent**					**Cr**
Oct	2	Bank	1 000				

Dr		**Sales**					**Cr**
				Oct	5	Bank	4 900

Dr		**Bank loan**					**Cr**
				Oct	8	Bank	10 000

Getting it right

Remember: whatever the transaction it will result in a matching debit and credit entry. So if you find yourself making two debit entries (or two credit entries) for a transaction, retrace your steps and start again!

Illustration 6: Preparing simple ledger accounts

Sahera opened a health food store on 1 February 2015. The following transactions occurred during the first two weeks of trading.

Feb	1	Sahera opened a business bank account and introduced capital of $50 000
	2	Purchased a delivery vehicle $17 000 by cheque
	3	Paid rent on shop premises by cheque for the month $600
	4	Purchased goods for resale on credit from DZX Ltd $5 600
	5	Cash sales (banked) totalled $4 900
	7	Sahera withdrew a cheque for $800 for private use (drawings)
	8	Sold goods on credit to BQY for $1 300
	11	Paid DZX Ltd by cheque $3 000
	13	Received a cheque from BQY in full settlement of the amount due

First, here is the detail of the double entry required to record these transactions.

Feb	1	Dr Bank Cr Capital	Debit bank account to record an increase in an asset Credit capital account to record an increase in capital
	2	Dr Delivery vehicle Cr Bank	Debit delivery vehicle to record an increase in an asset Credit bank to record a decrease in an asset
	3	Dr Rent Cr Bank	Debit rent to reflect the decrease in capital Credit bank to record a decrease in an asset
	4	Dr Purchases Cr Trade payable (DZX Ltd)	Debit purchases to reflect the decrease in capital Credit trade payable to record an increase in a liability
	5	Dr Bank Cr Sales	Debit bank to record an increase in an asset Credit sales to reflect the increase in capital
	7	Dr Drawings Cr Bank	Debit drawings to reflect the decrease in capital Credit bank to record a decrease in an asset
	8	Dr Trade receivable (BQY) Cr Sales	Debit trade receivable to record an increase in an asset Credit sales to reflect the increase in capital
	11	Dr Trade payable (DZX Ltd) Cr Bank	Debit trade payable to record a decrease in a liability Credit bank to record a decrease in an asset
	13	Debit Bank Credit Trade receivable (BQY)	Debit bank to record an increase in an asset Credit trade receivable to record a decrease in an asset

Here are the ledger accounts recording these details.

LEDGER ACCOUNTS

Dr					Bank		Cr
Feb	1	Capital	50 000	Feb	2	Delivery vehicle	17 000
	5	Sales	4 900		3	Rent	600
	13	BQY	1 300		7	Drawings	800
					11	DZX Ltd	3 000

Dr			Capital				Cr
				Feb	1	Bank	50 000

Dr			Delivery vehicle				Cr
Feb	2	Bank	17 000				

Dr			Drawings				Cr
Feb	7	Bank	800				

Dr			Purchases				Cr
Feb	4	DZX Ltd	5 600				

Dr			Rent				Cr
Feb	3	Bank	600				

Dr			Sales				Cr
				Feb	5	Bank	4 900
					8	BQY	1 300

Dr			Trade payable (DZX Ltd)				Cr
Feb	11	Bank	3 000	Feb	4	Purchases	5 600

Dr			Trade receivable (BQY)				Cr
Feb	8	Sales	1 300	Feb	13	Bank	1 300

Reminders:

- Every transaction must lead to a matching debit and credit entry.
- When making an entry in an account the rule is to name the other account affected by the transaction.

Note:

If you are new to keeping ledger accounts, you will find it really useful to spend some time practising preparing sets of ledger accounts. It is entirely usual for it to take some time to develop confidence and accuracy in keeping double-entry records. Further questions are contained on the CD-ROM for those of you who feel you would like a little more practice on the topics covered in this chapter.

End-of-chapter questions

1 The role of the bookkeeper and accountant

What are the differences in the role of the bookkeeper and the accountant?

2 Types of business

Describe the main features of a:

- sole trader
- partnership
- limited company
- not-for-profit organisation.

3 Purpose of financial statements

What is the purpose of the following?

a An income statement.
b A statement of financial position.

4 Terminology

Explain each of the following terms:

a non-current asset
b current asset
c non-current liability
d current liability
e capital.

5 Identifying assets, liabilities and capital

Here is a list of assets and liabilities and references to capital. Read through the list, and then identify which items are assets, liabilities, capital.

(a) Vehicle	(k) Inventory
(b) Shop fittings	(l) Trade receivables
(c) Cash at bank	(m) Bank overdraft
(d) Bank loan	(n) Trade payables
(e) Owner's investment in the business	(o) Machinery
(f) Cash in hand	(p) Loan from a friend
(g) Equipment	(q) Value of owner's stake in the business
(h) Amounts owing to suppliers	(r) Amounts owed by customers
(i) Furniture	(s) Cash at bank
(j) Land	(t) Fittings

6 Using the accounting equation

The following table shows details about some businesses' total assets, capital and total liabilities. For each business calculate the missing figure, making use of the accounting equation.

	Total assets	Capital	Liabilities
	Assets = Capital + Liabilities		
	$	$	$
Business A	80 000		20 000
Business B	42 000		11 000
Business C	57 000	24 000	
Business D	650 000	490 000	
Business E		170 000	20 000
Business F		558 000	82 000

7 Double entry

Hakim is in business selling furniture. The following transactions took place during the first week of May.

Date	Details	$
1 May	Purchased furniture for resale by cheque	2 850
2 May	Paid rent by cheque	1 500
3 May	Purchased a motor vehicle by cheque	3 500
4 May	Sold furniture for cash	200
4 May	Purchased furniture for resale on credit	4 150
5 May	Sold furniture on credit	1 140
6 May	Paid a cheque for drawings	600
7 May	Purchased furniture for resale in cash	400

Required

Detail the double entry for each of these transactions.

8 Double entry

Jack owns a business selling computers. The following transactions took place during the first week of September.

Date	Details	$
1 Sept	Introduced additional capital into the bank account	5 000
1 Sept	Purchased goods for resale on credit	3 450
3 Sept	Sold goods for cash	875
3 Sept	Sold goods on credit	2 119

4 Sept	Paid motor vehicle repairs by cheque	814
5 Sept	Purchased goods for resale by cheque	8 295
5 Sept	Paid a cheque for drawings	450
6 Sept	Purchased a new motor van by cheque	3 300

Required

State the ledger accounts to be debited and credited to record these transactions.

9 Preparing simple ledger accounts

Kisha's business opened on 1 November 2014. The business had the following assets and liabilities at that date.

	$
Furniture and fittings	18 000
Cash at bank	4 100
Cash in hand	600
Bank loan	7 000

Required

a Calculate Kisha's capital on 1 November 2014 using the accounting equation.

The following transactions occurred during November 2014.

Nov	1	Purchased goods for resale and paid by cheque $3 100
	4	Paid rent on shop premises by cheque for month $900
	7	Cash sales $2 800
	10	Purchased goods on credit from Seema Ltd $3 600
	12	Sold goods on credit to Abaxa $3 300
	15	Kisha withdrew cash for $700 for private use
	19	Sold some unwanted fittings and received a cheque for $1 000
	23	Paid staff wages in cash $1 300
	25	Received cheque from Abaxa for $2 500
	26	Made a repayment on the loan $500; the funds were transferred from the business bank account
	29	Paid Seema Ltd $1 800 by cheque

Required

b Record all of the information in suitable ledger accounts.

10 Preparing simple ledger accounts

Aziza's business opened on 1 January 2015. The business had the following assets and liabilities at that date.

	$
Shop fittings	18 000
Cash at bank	3 400
Cash in hand	900
Bank loan	4 000

Required

a Calculate Aziza's capital on 1 January 2015 using the accounting equation.

The following transactions occurred during January 2015.

Jan	2	Purchased goods for resale and paid in cash $800
	4	Paid rent on business premises by cheque for month $500
	6	Purchased goods on credit from Trez Ltd $5 800
	9	Cash sales totalled $1 700
	12	Aziza arranged an additional loan with bank for $2 000; funds were transferred to the business bank account
	14	Aziza withdrew cash $700 for private use
	19	Sold goods on credit to HLK for $4 900
	23	Purchased new shop fittings and paid by cheque $1 700
	25	Paid Trez Ltd $2 900 by cheque
	26	Paid assistants' wages in cash $1 000
	29	Received cheque from HLK in full settlement of the amount due

Required

b Record all of the information in suitable ledger accounts.

Learning objectives

In this chapter you will learn:

- about the source documents from which accounting records are prepared
- how source documents are used to prepare books of prime entry
- about the limitations of the books of prime entry.

1.1.2: Source documents and books of prime entry

Note:

This chapter has been designed to help those students who have not yet studied double-entry bookkeeping. Some more experienced students may find that they can spend less time on this chapter because they are familiar with much of the contents. It is recommended that all students feel confident in preparing double-entry records as this skill is invaluable in understanding more advanced financial accounting techniques.

Introduction

In this chapter the principle of making two entries for every transaction (the duality concept) in ledger accounts is developed further to show how information is recorded prior to the preparation of ledger accounts. Information in a business's accounting system will record information with a monetary value (money measurement concept) about that business's affairs, not those of the owner (entity concept).

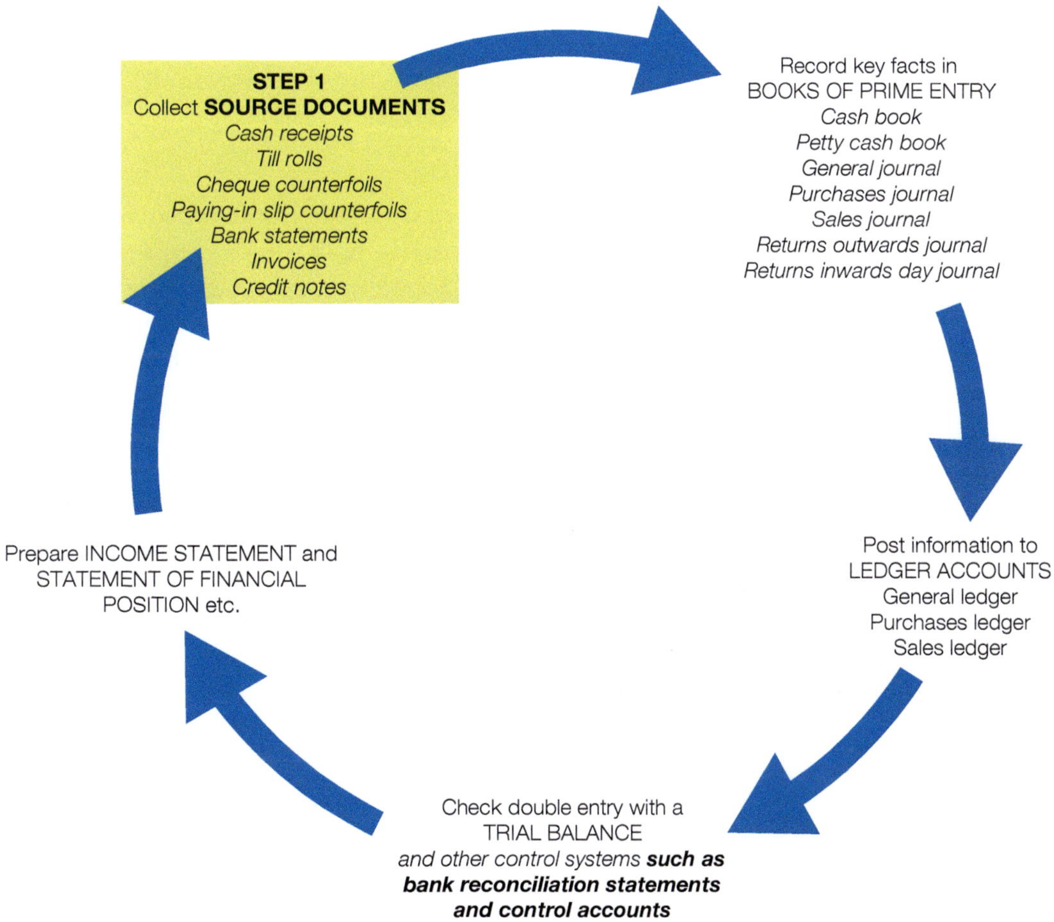

Figure 1.1.2A The accounting cycle: Step 1 ▲

Every entry in ledger accounts must be supported by evidence in the form of 'source documents'. When a source document is received it is possible to start making entries in the accounting system (step 1 in the accounting cycle, see page 25). Source documents must be carefully stored for future reference and to provide justification for an entry in the accounting system if any query is raised.

The role of different source documents

Invoices

The seller of goods or services provides an invoice for the buyer. This invoice will detail the following information:

- **Addresses:** the supplier's address, the customer's address and the delivery address (if different).
- **Dates:** the order date and the delivery date.
- **Reference:** a unique invoice number will be present, together with the customer's order number.
- **Description:** of the goods or services supplied.
- **Value:** the total amount owed by the customer.
- **Terms:** when the invoice is due for payment and any discount that is available to the customer.

The invoice informs the buyer how much is being paid for the goods or services.

Credit notes

Credit notes are sent from the supplier to the customer when an adjustment to the amount owed is required. This may, for example, be due to a calculation error, an incorrect delivery, damage to the goods, returned goods or goods lost in transit. The credit note informs the buyer how much has been deducted from the amount owed to the supplier.

Cheque counterfoils

When a cheque is written, the details are recorded on the cheque counterfoil and this becomes the source document.

The details to be recorded are:

- the date of the cheque
- the payee (the person the cheque is made payable to)
- the amount of the cheque.

Each cheque has a unique sequential number and this must be included when the details are transferred into the accounting records.

Paying-in slip counterfoils

When cash or cheques are paid into the bank, the details are recorded on the paying-in slip counterfoil and this becomes the source document.

The details to be recorded are:

- the date of the paying-in slip
- the drawers of cheques (the persons paying the organisation) or the source of cash banked
- the amount of the cheques/cash banked.

Cash receipts and till rolls

When cash or cheques are received by a business, a receipt will be issued. This receipt may take the form of a till roll or alternatively it may be a handwritten receipt. The duplicate copies of these receipts form the source document for cash and cheque receipts.

Bank statements

Payments and receipts may be debited or credited directly through the bank account. In these circumstances the bank statement itself becomes the source document for:

- Direct debits: authority is granted by the business to a third party (for example a supplier of goods or services) for fixed or variable payments to be made at the request of that third party.
- Standing orders: a fixed payment is made at regular intervals by the bank on the instructions of the business.
- **Bank interest and charges:** the bank processes its charge to the business for maintenance of the bank account or the interest on funds borrowed.
- **Credit transfers:** money has been paid direct into the bank account of the business by a third party.

Key terms

Direct debit: authority is granted by the business to a third party for fixed or variable payments to be made at the request of that third party.

Standing order: a fixed payment that is made at regular intervals by the bank on the instructions of the business.

Petty cash vouchers

When small payments are made in cash, a voucher should be made out detailing the date, the amount and what the payment was in respect of. This voucher (called a petty cash voucher) should be signed by an authorised person and, wherever possible, should have a receipt attached to it.

Key term

Petty cash voucher: an authorised voucher containing details of small cash payments made.

Other key documents

Delivery notes

A delivery note is a document detailing the goods that have been delivered by the supplier. This should be signed by the recipient and a copy returned to the supplier as proof of delivery.

Purchase orders

A purchase order is a document raised by the purchasing department used to place an order with a supplier.

Remittance advice notes

A remittance advice note is a document sent with a payment, advising the recipient which invoices etc. are being paid.

Key terms

Delivery note: a document detailing the goods that have been delivered by the supplier.

Purchase order: a document used to place an order with a supplier.

Remittance advice: a document sent with a payment, advising the recipient which invoices etc. are being paid.

Statement of account

A statement of account is a document sent to customers detailing all recent transactions and showing the total amount outstanding.

> **Key term**
>
> **Statement of account**: a document sent to customers detailing all recent transactions and informing them of the total amount outstanding.

Books of prime entry

When a source document is received the important financial details are first entered in a book of prime entry. In a full accounting system there are seven books of prime entry as follows:

- sales journal
- purchases journal
- returns outwards journal
- returns inwards journal
- cash book
- petty cash book
- general journal.

Whatever the transaction, one of these books of prime entry will be appropriate for making the first entry (Step 2 in the accounting cycle, see page 29).

> **Getting it right**
>
> It is quite a common mistake to think that the sales ledger contains the sales account, and that the purchases ledger contains the purchases account. Both these accounts appear in the general ledger.

Note: It may be useful to know that books of prime entry are sometimes referred to as 'subsidiary books' or 'books of original entry'. Sometimes journals are called 'day books'.

Posting to ledger accounts

When transactions details are recorded in a book of prime entry, information is then 'posted' (i.e. transferred) to appropriate ledger accounts (step 3 in the accounting cycle, see page 29). Most businesses organise their ledger accounts into groups as follows:

- **Sales ledger**: which includes separate accounts for each trade receivable (note: it does not include the sales account).
- **Purchases ledger**: which includes separate accounts for each trade payable (note: it does not include the purchases account).
- **General ledger**: which includes all the remaining accounts except the cash and bank accounts which form part of the cash book (see page 35).

The individual accounts of trade receivables and trade payables are often referred to as 'personal accounts'.

> **Key terms**
>
> **Sales ledger**: a part of the double-entry system that is used to keep the personal accounts of trade receivables.
>
> **Purchases ledger**: a part of the double-entry system that is used to keep the personal accounts of trade payables.
>
> **General ledger**: a part of the double-entry system that is used to keep all ledger accounts other than those of trade payables, trade receivables, cash and bank.

Preparing books of prime entry

Sales journal

The sales journal is a list of all credit sales transactions. Depending on the volume of transactions, the sales journal will be totalled daily, weekly or monthly. The usual layout for the sales journal is as follows.

> **Key term**
>
> **Sales journal**: a book of prime entry that records credit sales invoices.

Date	Customer	Invoice number	Total ($)
1 May	Jeremy	S376	214.35
2 May	Martin	S377	674.02
			888.37

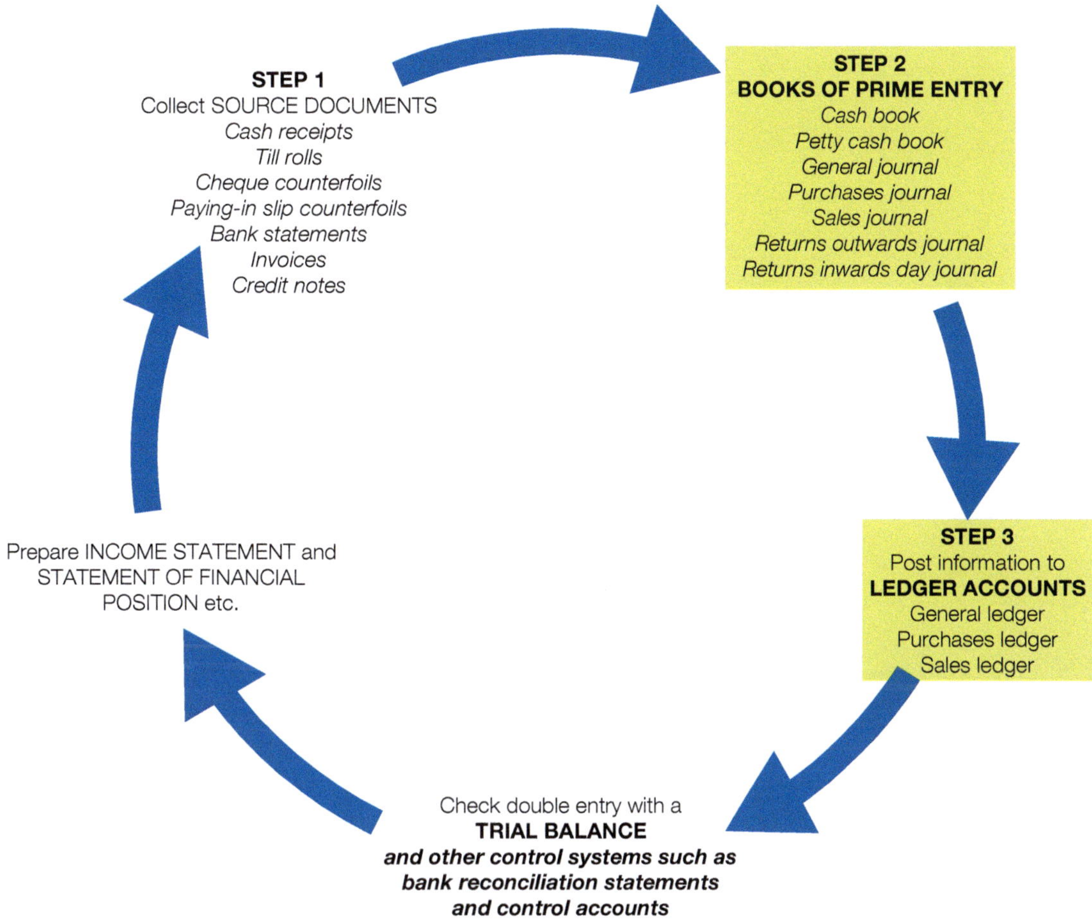

Figure 1.1.2B The accounting cycle: Steps 2 and 3 ▲

The accounts of each trade receivable will be updated immediately an invoice is recorded in the sales journal. It is important that a business has up-to-date information about amounts owed by credit customers. However, the sales account in the general ledger will be updated with the total of credit sales periodically (once a month).

The double-entry postings in the above sales journal example are:

Debit	Jeremy	$214.35
Debit	Martin	$674.02
Credit	Sales account	$888.37

The customers' accounts in the sales ledger will appear as follows, reflecting the amount owed (trade receivables) by these two businesses.

Dr		Jeremy			Cr
Date	**Details**	**$**	**Date**	**Details**	**$**
1 May	Sales journal	214.35			

Dr		Martin			Cr
Date	**Details**	**$**	**Date**	**Details**	**$**
2 May	Sales journal	674.02			

Getting it right

It is important to note that only credit sales based on information in sales invoices is recorded in the sales journal. Cash sales are recorded elsewhere (i.e. in the cash book).

Here is the sales account in the general ledger.

Dr		Sales account			Cr
Date	**Details**	**$**	**Date**	**Details**	**$**
			2 May	Sales journal	888.37

Key term

Purchases journal: a book of prime entry that records credit purchase invoices.

Purchases journal

The purchases journal is a list of all supplier invoices received in respect of credit transactions. As is the case with the sales journal, depending on the volume of transactions, this will also be totalled daily, weekly or monthly. The usual layout for the purchases journal is identical to the layout of the sales journal.

Date	Supplier	Invoice number	Total ($)
1 June	Richard	P7037	106.55
2 June	Steven	L4815	450.27
			556.82

The individual invoices are posted to the accounts of the suppliers in the purchases ledger as soon as a record is made in the purchases journal. This ensures the accounts of trade payables are up to date and show clearly the amount outstanding at any time. The total of the purchases journal is posted to the purchases account in the general ledger periodically.

The double-entry postings in the above example are:

Debit	Purchases account	$556.82
Credit	Richard	$106.55
Credit	Steven	$450.27

The suppliers' accounts in the purchases ledger will now appear as follows, reflecting the amount owing (trade payables) to these two businesses.

Dr		Richard			Cr
Date	**Details**	**$**	**Date**	**Details**	**$**
			1 June	Purchases journal	106.55

Dr		Steven			Cr
Date	**Details**	**$**	**Date**	**Details**	**$**
			2 June	Purchases journal	450.27

Getting it right

Cash purchases are not recorded in the purchases journal. They are recorded elsewhere (i.e. in the cash book).

Here is the purchases account in the general ledger.

Dr		Purchases account			Cr
Date	**Details**	**$**	**Date**	**Details**	**$**
2 June	Purchases journal	556.82			

Key term

Trade discount: a reduction in price given as a reward for buying in large quantities.

Getting it right

Remember that the amount of trade discount is *not* recorded in the accounting system – only the net amount after deducting trade discount is shown in the books of prime entry and ledger accounts. There is no such thing as a trade discount account!

Trade discount

A trade discount is the reduction in the price to be charged for goods. The following important conditions normally apply to this form of discount:

- trade discount is only offered to other businesses engaged in the same line of activity
- trade discounts are given for placing large orders
- trade discount is normally *not* available to private individuals.

Information about trade discounts will be shown on source documents, but it is important to note that only the net amount being charged is recorded in the accounting system. What matters to a business is the actual charge (not what might have been charged).

Illustration 1: Accounting records and trade discount

Lendford Wholesalers received the following invoice during September 2014.

Sept	8	Purchase invoice T2734 received from JFZ Manufacturers. The normal price of the goods was $7 500. However, the invoice showed the deduction of a 20% trade discount.

Lendford Wholesalers issued the following invoice during September 2014.

Sept	12	Sales invoice N835 sent to Amberly Stores. The normal price of the goods was $2 800. However, the invoice showed the deduction of a 10% trade discount.

Here are the invoice details.

Purchase invoice:

JFZ Manufacturers (8 September)	**$**
Goods at normal selling price	7 500
Less: 20% trade discount	1 500
AMOUNT CHARGED	6 000

Sales invoice:

Amberly Stores (12 September)	**$**
Goods at normal selling price	2 800
Less: 10% trade discount	280
AMOUNT CHARGED	2 520

Here are the purchases and sales journals.

Purchases journal				
Date		Supplier	Invoice number	$
Sept	8	JFZ Manufacturers	T2734	6 000
		Total purchases		6 000

Sales journal				
Date		Customer	Invoice number	$
Sept	12	Amberly Stores	N835	2 520
		Total sales		2 520

Note: the amounts entered in the journals are the net amount actually charged by the supplier, or charged to the customer.

Here are the transfers to the purchases, sales and general ledgers.

PURCHASES LEDGER							
Dr			JFZ Manufacturers				Cr
				Sept	8	Purchases	6 000

SALES LEDGER							
Dr			Amberly Stores				Cr
Sept	12	Sales	2 520				

GENERAL LEDGER							
Dr			Purchases				Cr
Sept	30	Purchases journal	6 000				

Dr			Sales				Cr
				Sept	30	Sales journal	2 520

Returns outwards

It is not unusual for a business to return goods to suppliers which have previously been purchased on credit. This can happen when some items in a delivery are:

- damaged or broken
- not as ordered (wrong model, wrong size, wrong colour, etc.)
- received too late (sell-by date exceeded).

Key terms

Returns outwards: goods sent back by a business to the supplier; sometimes also called purchases returns.

Returns inwards: goods sent back to a business by a customer; sometimes also called sales returns.

Credit note: the source document that records the amount to be deducted from (or allowed against) a previous invoice to avoid a business being overcharged – usually the business has returned goods to the supplier.

Returns outwards journal: the book of prime entry used to list in date order details shown on credit notes relating to goods returned to suppliers.

The return of goods to a supplier is often referred to as returns outwards or 'returns out' (as the goods are going 'out' of the business and back to the supplier), and sometimes referred to as 'purchases returns'. At the end of a financial period the total of returns outwards is deducted from the total purchases to give a net figure for purchases for the period.

Of course, it is also possible for a customer to return goods that have previously been sold on credit. This situation would be referred to as returns inwards. At the end of a financial period the total of returns inwards is deducted from the total sales to give a net figure for sales for the period.

The usual source document for returns outwards is a credit note which is sent by the supplier to the business that has received damaged or unwanted goods to the notify it of the amount that can be deducted from the invoice. Sometimes the credit note will be used to correct an overcharge in the original invoice. If a trade discount was involved in the original purchase it will also be shown on the credit note, and only the net amount will be recorded in the accounting system.

Details from credit notes received from suppliers are recorded in the returns outwards journal.

Illustration 2: Preparing and posting a returns outwards journal

Here is an example of a completed returns outwards journal that has been posted to the relevant ledger accounts.

Returns outwards journal

Date		Supplier	Credit note number	$
Sept	14	Bennett & Co	347	112
	27	Mungroo Ltd	1279	273
		Total returns outwards		385

Here are the double-entry records for these returns outwards.

PURCHASES LEDGER

Dr		Bennett & Co		Cr
Sept	14	Returns outwards	112	

Dr		Mungroo Ltd		Cr
Sept	27	Returns outwards	273	

GENERAL LEDGER				
Dr	**Returns outwards**			**Cr**
	Sept	30	Returns outwards journal	385

Notes:

1 The process for recording returns outwards is very similar to that for credit purchases and credit sales.

2 Credit notes received from suppliers are listed in date order in the returns outwards journal. The personal accounts in the purchases ledger are updated immediately.

3 At the end of the month (or more frequently if desired) the journal is totalled and the total of returns outwards is posted to the general ledger account.

Key term

Returns inwards journal: the book of prime entry used to list in date order details shown on credit notes relating to goods returned by customers.

Recording returns inwards

The accounting procedures for returns inwards follow a similar sequence to that described for returns outwards.

The basic double entry for returns inwards is:

- **Debit:** a returns inwards account
- **Credit:** the account of the trade receivable.

A business receiving back goods from a dissatisfied credit customer will make out a credit note, send the original version to the customer, and keep a copy from which the accounting records can be prepared. If a trade discount was involved in the original, it will also appear in the credit note and only the net amount will be recorded in the accounting records.

Illustration 3: Preparing and posting a returns inwards journal

Here is an example of a completed returns inwards journal that has been posted to the relevant ledger accounts.

Returns inwards journal

Date		Customer	Credit note number	$
Jan	9	Garcia Ltd	103	23
	23	Rampersad & Co	104	119
		Total returns inwards		142

Here are the double-entry records for these returns inwards.

SALES LEDGER

Dr				Garcia Ltd			Cr
				Jan	14	Returns inwards	23

Dr				Rampersad & Co			Cr
				Jan	23	Returns inwards	119

GENERAL LEDGER

Dr				Returns inwards			Cr
Jan	31	Returns inwards journal	142				

Notes:

1 Copies of credit notes issued to customers are listed in date order in the returns inwards journal. The personal accounts in the sales ledger are updated immediately.

2 At regular intervals the journal is totalled and the total of returns inwards is posted to the general ledger account.

Key terms

Three-column cash book: a book of prime entry used to record payments and receipts and to make a note of cash discounts allowed and received.

Discount allowed: a discount given as a reward for prompt payment by a business for goods sold on credit to customers.

Discount received: a discount given as a reward to a business for paying credit suppliers within a specified time.

The three-column cash book

Source documents recording money transactions are recorded in a cash book. The cash book has a double role as it also shows the ledger accounts for cash and for bank. Many businesses make use of a three-column cash book which makes it possible to record cash and bank transactions as part of the double-entry process, but also to make a note of cash discounts. Cash discounts are rewards for prompt payment. When credit customers pay the amount due within a specified time limit they may be permitted to deduct what is called a discount allowed. When a business pays its credit suppliers within a specified time it may be permitted to deduct what is called a discount received.

Illustration 4: The three-column cash book

Robin is the owner of a wholesale business. He offers his credit customers a 2 per cent cash discount for prompt payment of amounts due. Robin's suppliers also offer a cash discount of 5 per cent for prompt payment.

On 1 May 2014 Robin's cash book showed balances as follows: cash $1350, bank $7480.

The following money transactions occurred during May 2014.

Date		Source document	Transaction
May	3	Cheque counterfoil	Payment of a trade payable, Campbell Traders. The amount owed was $2 600. This amount was settled less 5% cash discount
	5	Paying-in slip counterfoil	Receipt of cheque from trade receivable, K Scott, who owed $1 600. This amount was settled less 2% cash discount
	9	Till rolls	Cash sales totalling $4 540
	16	Cheque counterfoil	Payment of a trade payable, LT Wright. The amount owed was $4 480. This amount was settled less 5% cash discount
	21	Paying-in slip counterfoil	Paid cash, $4 200, into the bank account
	28	Paying-in slip counterfoil	Receipt of a cheque from trade receivable, D Pitts, who owed $900. This amount was settled less 2% cash discount
	29	Cheque counterfoil	Rent for the month $350

Here is the three-column cash book for May.

Dr					Cash book						Cr
			Discounts allowed	Cash	Bank				Discounts received	Cash	Bank
			$	$	$				$	$	$
May	1	Balances		1 350	7 480	May	3	Campbell Traders	130		2 470
	5	K Scott	32		1 568		16	LT Wright	224		4 256
	9	Sales		4 540			21	Bank		4 200	
	21	Cash			4 200		29	Rent			350
	28	D Pitts	18		882						
			50						354		

The discount columns are totalled and the totals posted to the discount accounts in the general ledger.

GENERAL LEDGER

Dr		Discounts allowed					Cr
May	31	Cash book	50				

Dr		Discounts received					Cr
				May	31	Cash book	354

Notes:

1 The opening entry to record the starting amount in any account is called the balance.

2 An entry in the discounts allowed column is a note that a discount was given to customer – it is not a debit entry for that discount.

3 An entry in the discounts received column is a note that a discount was received from a supplier – it is not a credit entry for that discount.

Key term

Balance: the starting amount in any account.

4 Discount columns are totalled and the totals are used to make one entry per month in the discounts allowed account and discounts received account in the general ledger. These entries for discount totals replace what would otherwise have been individual debit/credit entries every time a discount was allowed or received.

5 When cash is paid into the bank account (see 21 May) or when cash is taken from the bank account, both the debit and credit entries for these transactions will appear in the cash book. These entries are sometimes referred to as 'contras'.

The petty cash book

In some businesses where there are a large number of transactions in cash, the decision is sometimes made to operate a second cash book which is used exclusively to record relatively minor cash transactions – otherwise known as petty cash transactions.

Often the task of preparing the petty cash book is given to a more junior member of the accounts team, who is sometimes called the petty cashier. Responsibility for handling the business's cash is usually tightly controlled.

- The petty cashier is only allowed to handle a specified maximum amount of petty cash at any one time. This maximum amount is sometimes called the float or imprest. The size of the float or imprest is decided by the owner or manager of the business.
- The petty cashier is only allowed to give cash to employees to reimburse them for payments they have made on behalf of the business if they can produce formal evidence, usually in the form of a receipt.

For each payment made, the petty cashier is required to complete a petty cash voucher. The voucher has to be signed by the person receiving cash as well as by the petty cashier. Other evidence of the transaction (e.g. the receipt) is attached to the voucher.

Key terms

Petty cash: small cash payments.

Imprest: a system for maintaining a petty cash book which gives the petty cashier responsibility for a petty cash float.

Illustration 5: An analysed petty cash book

The owner of a business decided to maintain a petty cash book. It was agreed that the imprest would be $150. The following transactions occurred in May 2014.

		Voucher number	
May	1		Petty cashier received $150 cash
	2	1	Stationery $32.62
	8	2	Postage $26.29
	11	3	Travel expenses $18.40
	15	4	Postage $11.83
	20	5	Purchases ledger account of D Morris, $20.70
	23	6	Stationery $11.37
	27	7	Travel expenses $19.11

Here is the petty cash book for May 2014.

PETTY CASH BOOK										
Receipts	Date		Details	Voucher number		Stationery	Postage	Travel	Purchases ledger
$					$	$	$	$	$
150.00	May	1	Cash						
		2	Stationery	1	32.62	32.62			
		8	Postage	2	26.29		26.29		
		11	Travel	3	18.40			18.40	
		15	Postage	4	11.83		11.83		
		20	D Morris	5	20.70				20.70
		23	Stationery	6	11.37	11.37			
		27	Travel	7	19.11			19.11	
					140.32	43.99	38.12	37.51	20.70

Notes:

1 In the petty cash book the receipts column is the equivalent of the debit side of the petty cash account; the payments column is the equivalent of the credit side.

2 Each payment must be cross-referenced to the relevant voucher.

3 Each payment is analysed under appropriate headings. These would be decided in advance by the owner or manager of the business. Theoretically there can be as many analysis columns as are required.

4 The analysis columns are totalled at agreed intervals, and the totals are posted to the relevant ledger accounts. This process saves much time as otherwise separate entries would have to be made in the ledger accounts of every petty cash payment however small the amount involved.

Key term

General journal: a book of prime entry used to make the first record of transactions that it would not be appropriate to record in the other books of prime entry. Sometimes this book of prime entry is referred to as the 'Journal' for convenience.

The general journal

The general journal is a book of prime entry. The general journal is used to record non-routine transactions or entries when no other book of prime entry is suitable.

A journal entry is a written record of an instruction to those who keep ledger accounts of the entries that are to be made for particular situations. In other words, a journal entry is an instruction as to which account should be debited and which account should be credited.

There is a considerable range of possible source documents for journal entries. As well as the familiar invoice (for the purchase of a non-current asset), there could be letters or emails received from other businesses or organisations, and internal notes or emails written by the owner, managers or other employees.

Illustration 6: Purchase of a non-current asset on credit

On 4 July 2014 the owner of a business purchased a new vehicle, value $32 000, for business use on credit from Blue River Motors Ltd.

The journal entry is shown below.

JOURNAL				
Date		Details	Dr	Cr
			$	$
July	4	Vehicles	32 000	
		Blue River Motors Ltd		32 000
		Purchase of new vehicle on credit, invoice number 4872		

Notes:

1. A journal entry requires the following details:
   - a date of the transaction
   - b account to be debited and the amount
   - c account to be credited and the amount
   - d a short explanation of the nature of the transaction – called the narrative.
2. It is usual to slightly indent the name of the account to be credited in the detail column.
3. Each journal entry is separated from the next one by ruling off the details column.

The journal entry should be posted through to the relevant ledger accounts as follows. (Please note: in some businesses the account of a supplier of a non-current asset on credit would be recorded in the general ledger, in order that the purchases ledger is used exclusively for the accounts of suppliers of goods for resale on credit.)

GENERAL LEDGER

Dr		Vehicles					Cr
July	4	Blue River Motors Ltd	32 000				

PURCHASES LEDGER

Dr		Blue River Motors Ltd					Cr
				July	4	Vehicle	32 000

Illustration 7: Cancelling entries

Here is another example of a situation when a journal entry would be required.

The owner of a business recently paid a trade payable, I Watson, and deducted a cash discount of $40. However, on 12 October 2014, I Watson emailed to say that the discount should not have been deducted because payment was made after the 30-day limit.

The journal entry is as follows.

JOURNAL				
Date		Details	Dr	Cr
			$	$
Oct	12	Discount received	40	
		I Watson		40
		Cancellation of discount deducted in error		

And ledger account entries are:

GENERAL LEDGER							
Dr		Discount received					Cr
Oct	12	I Watson	40				

PURCHASES LEDGER							
Dr		I Watson					Cr
				Oct	12	Discount received	40

Illustration 8: Correcting errors

It is inevitable that errors will be made in the accounts from time to time. The rule is always that errors should be corrected by making additional entries. It would never be acceptable to cross out or try to remove the wrong entries as this could look as if the accounts had been tampered with.

On 5 August 2014 a business's bookkeeper recorded the payment of rent by cheque, $345, as $354 in both the bank account and rent account.

The journal entry to record the correction of these entries is:

JOURNAL				
Date		Details	Dr	Cr
			$	$
Aug	5	Bank	9	
		Rent		9
		Correction of error in recording the amount paid for rent		

Link

There is much more about the correction of errors in AS Level Chapter 1.3.1 Verification: trial balance.

Here are the entries in the bank account and in the rent account, showing the original entries and the posting of the corrections.

Dr		CASH BOOK (Bank columns) Page 5					Cr
			Bank				Bank
			$				$
Aug	5	Rent	9	Aug	5	Rent	354

			GENERAL LEDGER				
Dr			Rent (Account number 4)				Cr
Aug	5	Bank	354	Aug	5	Bank	9

Illustration 9: Starting a business and opening ledger accounts

Salim started a business selling cameras on 1 February 2015.
He introduced a motor vehicle worth $4000, fixtures and fittings worth $2000 and cash in the bank of $5000.

JOURNAL				
Date		Details	Dr	Cr
			$	$
Feb	1	Motor vehicle	4 000	
		Fixtures and fittings	2 000	
		Cash at bank	5 000	
		Capital		11 000
		Entries to record the assets and capital on opening the books of account		

The limitations of books of prime entry

Books of prime entry are designed to ensure that all transactions are recorded in date order as soon as source documents are available. Their role in the accounting system is therefore rather limited. It is not possible to use the books of prime entry to find some of the key facts that are of interest to the owners and managers of businesses. For example, it is important to know just how much is owing to each trade payable and how much is owed by each trade receivable. For this, and for analysed information about a business's finances, it is necessary to look at ledger accounts.

End-of-chapter questions

Note:

If you are new to preparing books of prime entry, you will find it really useful to spend some time developing your skills in this area. Remember it is entirely usual for it to take some time to develop confidence and accuracy in keeping double-entry records. Further questions are contained on the CD-ROM for those of you who feel you would like a little more practice on the topics covered in this chapter.

1 Entries in the purchases journal are taken from:
- A cash receipts
- B credit notes
- C delivery notes
- D invoices

2 If you wished to check the accuracy of the returns outwards journal, which of the following should you examine, referring to copies if necessary?
- A Credit notes issued
- B Credit notes received
- C Invoices issued
- D Invoices received

3 Which of the following source documents should be used for making entries in the sales journal?
- A A credit note received from a supplier
- B An invoice sent to a customer
- C Petty cash voucher for travelling expenses
- D Statement of account sent by a supplier

4 A paying-in slip counterfoil is used to make entries in the:
- A cash book
- B petty cash book
- C purchases journal
- D sales returns journal

5 Which of these transactions should be entered in the general journal?
- A Correction of error in recording purchases returns
- B Owner's cash drawings
- C Purchase of new equipment by cheque
- D Returns of goods to a supplier

6 The owner of a business purchased a new delivery vehicle for business use. A cash deposit of 10 per cent was paid at the time of purchase; the balance is to be paid in four months' time. Which books of prime entry should be used to record this information?
- A General journal
- B General journal and cash book
- C Purchases journal
- D Purchases journal and cash book

7 The following totals were shown in the discount columns of a business's cash book.

Dr			CASH BOOK			Cr
	Discounts	**Cash**	**Bank**	**Discounts**	**Cash**	**Bank**
	610			450		

What entries should be made in the general ledger?

A	Debit discounts allowed $450	Credit discounts received $610
B	Debit discounts allowed $610	Credit discounts received $450
C	Debit discounts received $450	Credit discounts allowed $610
D	Debit discounts received $610	Credit discounts allowed $450

8 On 1 August Salma sold goods to Riaz. Riaz returned some of these goods a week later. In which order will Salma issue documents to Riaz during April?
- A Credit note, invoice, statement of account
- B Invoice, credit note, statement of account
- C Invoice, statement of account, credit note
- D Statement of account, invoice, credit note

9 Adam is responsible for keeping a petty cash book for his employer. The monthly imprest is $200. During January the following petty cash payments were made: travel expenses $82; postage $45; office cleaning $39.

How much should Adam receive at the end of January to restore the imprest?

A $34
B $166
C $200
D $366

10 A retailer purchased $2000 of goods from a supplier on the following terms: 25 per cent trade discount, 10 per cent cash discount if the invoice is paid within 30 days.

The retailer paid the invoice 20 days after receipt. How much should the retailer pay?

A $1300
B $1350
C $1500
D $1800

11 Preparing a purchases journal and posting to ledger accounts

Becky owns a shoe shop. During May 2014 she received the following purchase invoices.

May	3	Invoice 2730	Purchase invoice received from Whiteford Ltd for $1 230
	11	Invoice 9702	Purchase invoice received from P Sackley for $2 720
	24	Invoice 1818	Purchase invoice received from A Hereton for $990
	27	Invoice 2823	Purchase invoice received from Whiteford Ltd for $2 440

Prepare the following accounting records to record these transactions:

- purchases journal
- trade payable accounts in the purchases ledger
- purchases account in the general ledger.

12 Recording credit sales in a sales journal and posting to ledger accounts

Stephen owns a shop selling the latest music technology. During August 2014 he issued the following sales invoices to customers.

Aug	5	Invoice T339	Sales invoice sent to Bartford Ltd for goods $1 480
	10	Invoice T340	Sales invoice sent to J Williams for goods $920
	23	Invoice T341	Sales invoice sent to Bartford Ltd for goods $2 840
	28	Invoice T342	Sales invoice sent to J Williams for goods $1 550

Prepare the following accounting records to record these transactions:

- sales journal
- trade receivable accounts in the sales ledger
- sales account in the general ledger.

13 Recording purchases and sales where there is a trade discount

James and Alvo Ltd are wholesalers of bicycles.

The company buys goods from a number of bicycle manufacturers. Manufacturers offer trade discounts for large orders.

During October 2014 the following invoices were received.

Oct	12	Purchase invoice received from Melfin Ltd for 20 bicycles with a normal price of $160 each. The invoice showed the deduction of a trade discount of 25%
	28	Purchase invoice received from Harvey Bikes for 15 bicycles with a normal price of $430 each. The invoice showed the deduction of a trade discount of 33⅓%

James and Alvo Ltd sell bicycles to many retailers.

During October 2014 the following invoices were issued.

Oct	7	Sales invoice sent to W Gifford for 6 cycles with a normal price of $400 each. The invoice showed the deduction of a trade discount of 20%
	26	Sales invoice sent to T Perry for 8 cycles with a normal price of $330 each. The invoice showed the deduction of a trade discount of 15%

Prepare the following accounting records in the books of James and Alvo Ltd:

- purchases journal
- sales journal
- purchases ledger accounts
- sales ledger accounts
- appropriate general ledger accounts.

14 Recording returns outwards

Kerron owns a shop supplying fishing tackle. During March 2014 he returned goods to suppliers that had previously been purchased on credit.

March	11	Credit note 242	Goods returned to Scott Ltd with a value of $275
	18	Credit note 375	Goods returned to Taylor & Sons with a value of $328

	29	Credit note 247	Goods returned to Scott Ltd. These goods had been invoiced at $550 less a trade discount of 20%

Prepare the following accounting records to record these transactions:

- returns outwards journal
- trade payable accounts in the purchases ledger
- returns outwards account in the general ledger.

15 Recording returns inwards

Mikhail is the owner of a business supplying car accessories to local garages and car dealers. During June 2014 credit customers returned goods that had been sold to them on credit.

June	11	Credit note 454	Goods returned by Parsed Garages Ltd with a value of $220
	13	Credit note 455	Goods returned by Beretta Car Dealers with a value of $507
	24	Credit note 456	Goods returned by Parsed Garages Ltd. These goods had been invoiced at $1 500 less a trade discount of 33⅓%

Prepare the following accounting records to record these transactions:

- returns inwards journal
- trade receivable accounts in the sales ledger
- returns inwards account in the general ledger.

Note: Students requiring further practice at this point should turn to additional questions 1, 2 and 3 on the CD-ROM.

16 Preparing a three-column cash book and discount accounts

The following balances were extracted from the books of Apex Universal, a wholesaler, on 1 November 2014.

	$
Cash in hand	2 190
Cash at bank	7 330
Trade payables:	
TM Davis	1 600
Ryan & Co	2 300
Trade receivables:	
Fray Ltd	900
VK Watson	650

Trade payables give a cash discount of 5 per cent if accounts are settled within 30 days.

Apex Universal gives a cash discount of 2 per cent to its credit customers who settle their accounts within 30 days. During November 2014, the following transactions occurred.

Date		Source document	Transaction
Nov	5	Cheque counterfoil	Payment of amount due to TM Davis on 1 November less 5% cash discount
	8	Paying-in slip counterfoil	Cheque received from Fray Ltd in full settlement of their account on 1 November less 2% cash discount
	14	Till roll	Cash sales totalling $1 420
	17	Paying-in slip counterfoil	Transfer of cash to bank $1 250
	21	Cheque counterfoil	Payment of amount due to Ryan & Co on 1 November less 5% cash discount
	24	Paying-in slip counterfoil	Cheque received from VK Watson in full settlement of their account on 1 November less 2% cash discount

Prepare the business's three-column cash book for November 2014. Total the discount columns on this date. Post the totals of the discount columns to the discount accounts in the general ledger.

17 Preparing a three-column cash book and discount accounts

The following balances were extracted from the books of Sophia's business on 1 June 2014.

	$
Cash in hand	450
Cash at bank	2 720
Trade payables:	
N Singh	3 200
Zamran Stores	1 500
Trade receivables:	
K Gobin	600
QR Pulchan Ltd	2 080

Trade payables give a cash discount of 5 per cent if accounts are settled within 30 days.

Sophia gives a cash discount of 5 per cent to its credit customers who settle their accounts within 30 days.

During June 2014, the following transactions occurred.

Date		Source document	Transaction
June	5	Cheque counterfoil	Payment of amount due to N Singh on 1 June less 5% cash discount
	8	Paying-in slip counterfoil	Cheque received from K Gobin in full settlement of their account on 1 June less 5% cash discount
	14	Till roll	Cash sales totalling $3 920
	17	Paying-in slip counterfoil	Transfer of cash to bank $3 800
	21	Cheque counterfoil	Payment of amount due to Zamran Stores on 1 June less 5% cash discount
	24	Paying-in slip counterfoil	Cheque received from QR Pulchan Ltd in full settlement of their account on 1 June less 5% cash discount

Prepare the business's three-column cash book for June 2014. Total the discount columns on this date. Post the totals of the discount columns to the discount accounts in the general ledger. Prepare the customer and supplier accounts recording the opening balances and the transactions in June 2014.

18 Preparing a petty cash book

Jamal's business makes use of a petty cash book. On 1 February 2014 the balance of petty cash in hand was $14.55. The petty cash book operates with an imprest of $220 and with the following analysis columns:

- postage
- stationery
- vehicle expenses
- casual labour
- office expenses
- purchase ledger accounts.

During February 2014 the following petty cash transactions occurred.

		Voucher number	
Feb	1		Petty cashier received cash to restore the imprest
	2	141	Stationery $9.70
	8	142	Vehicle fuel $35.50
	10	143	Postage $11.10
	13	144	Casual labour $38.25
	15	145	Office expenses $8.42
	18	146	Trade payable, Ryan & Co Ltd, $17.11
	21	147	Vehicle fuel $34.22
	23	148	Trade payable, BY Scott, $9.28
	25	149	Postage $8.56
	26	150	Casual labour $21.80

Prepare the petty cash book for February 2014 and total the analysis columns.

19 Selecting the correct book of prime entry

Renea is the owner of a retail unit. Her business's accounting system includes all seven books of prime entry as part of her books of account. The following transactions were among those that occurred during September 2014. In each case decide which book of prime entry should be used to make the first record of the transaction.

Sept	3	Received an invoice for some new equipment for business use
	6	Cheque stub showed the payment of rent for the month
	11	Entries were made to correct a mistake made by the bookkeeper
	14	Invoice was issued for the sale of goods on credit
	15	Credit note was issued for the return of goods by a customer
	20	A voucher showed the purchase of postage stamps
	23	Invoice was received for goods for resale
	25	Some of the new equipment was found to be faulty and was returned to the supplier

20 Selecting the correct book of prime entry

During the month of February 2015, the following transactions occurred affecting the accounts of Rishi, a trader. Rishi maintains all seven books of prime entry as part of his books of account. In the case of each transaction, decide which book of prime entry should be used to make the first entry in the accounting system.

Feb	4	Received an invoice for goods for resale
	7	Paid a trade payable by cheque
	11	A voucher showed the payment of travel expenses in cash
	15	Received a credit note from a trade payable for goods damaged in transit
	17	Cancelled the entries for a cash discount that had been incorrectly deducted by a customer when settling their account
	18	A cheque was drawn for the payment of wages
	22	Received an invoice for a new vehicle for business use
	24	Issued a credit note to a trade receivable for goods returned as unsuitable
	28	Corrected a mistake in the accounts where the wrong amount had been debited and credited in the ledger accounts

21 Preparing journal entries

Prepare journal entries to record the following.

July	3	Purchases new equipment, $3 600, for business use on credit from J Rajah Ltd – invoice number 7361
	10	A customer, Gobin Ltd, had claimed a cash discount of $380 when settling their account and this had been recorded in the accounting records. However, it has now been decided that the customer was not entitled to the discount and the entries are to be cancelled
	14	It was noticed that the bookkeeper had made a mistake when recording the sale of goods, $780, on credit to TM Williams. The correct entry had been made in the sales account, but the account of T Williams Ltd had been debited in error. Entries were made to correct this mistake
	19	Some of the equipment purchased from J Rajah Ltd on 3 July was returned to the supplier as it was damaged in transit. The supplier sent a letter agreeing to the deduction of $520 from the amount due

Show how all the journal entries would be posted to ledger accounts.

22 Preparing journal entries

Prepare journal entries to record the following.

May	1	The owner of a business opened the books of account with the following: bank $5 000, fixtures and fittings $23 000, bank loan $8 000 and capital $20 000
	12	An error was made when the purchase of stationery for $105 was posted to the debit side of the purchases account rather than the debit side of the administration expenses account. This mistake was corrected
	15	Some fixtures, $1 050, were purchased for business use on credit from Albo Shelving Ltd, invoice number 3088
	30	A cash discount of $100 had been deducted when settling the account of a trade payable, TX Singh Ltd. However, this supplier has written to say that this discount should be cancelled as the payment had been made after the specified time limit. Entries were made to cancel the discount

Show how all the journal entries would be posted to ledger accounts.

Learning objectives

In this chapter you will learn:

- how to prepare ledger accounts from the books of prime entry
- how to prepare a trial balance
- how to balance accounts.

1.1.3: Preparing the books of account

Note:

This chapter has been designed to help those students who have not yet studied double-entry bookkeeping. Some more experienced students may find that they can spend less time on this chapter because they are familiar with much of the contents. It is recommended that all students feel confident in preparing double-entry records as this skill is invaluable in understanding more advanced financial accounting techniques.

Introduction

The three fundamental concepts associated with double-entry bookkeeping are applied in this chapter: entity, duality, money measurement.

In the previous chapter it was shown how source documents provide evidence for making the first entries in an accounting system by recording key financial details in the seven books of prime entry. It is now possible to provide an illustration showing how this process leads to the posting of information to ledger accounts. It will also be possible to show a simple process for checking the arithmetical accuracy of the double-entry records (a trial balance), i.e. that every transaction has led to matching debit and credit entries. It is useful if each account is summarised at some point to show the net amount left in the account; this is referred to as balancing accounts.

Preparing the double-entry records

Illustration 1: Preparing double-entry records from source documents

On 1 January 2015 Carmen opened a new business with the following.

	$
Cash at bank	3 500
Vehicle	36 000
Equipment	19 000
Capital	58 500

Carmen has decided to maintain the following books of prime entry:

- general journal
- three-column cash book
- sales journal
- purchases journal
- returns inwards journal
- returns outwards journal.

During January the following transactions occurred.

Date		Source document	Details
Jan	4	Invoice (302)	From MJT Ltd for goods for resale $6 400 less 25% trade discount
	7	Till rolls	Cash sales totalled $1 240
	10	Cash receipt	Operating expenses $280
	11	Paying-in slip counterfoil	Banked cash $800
	14	Credit note (478)	Received from MJT Ltd for goods returned as damaged, $200, less 25% trade discount
	15	Invoice (478)	Additional equipment for business use from Bridge Products, $880
	16	Invoice (001)	To Geeta Stores for goods $1 200, less 15% trade discount
	19	Credit note (227)	From Bridge Products for some equipment returned as not as ordered, $90
	22	Credit note (001)	Issue to Geeta Stores for goods $100 less 15% trade discount
	24	Cheque counterfoil	Paid MJT Ltd in settlement of their account at this date less 2% cash discount
	29	Paying-in slip counterfoil	Received a cheque from Geeta Stores in full settlement of their account at this date, less a cash discount of $24

Step 1: Rule up the six books of prime entry required for Carmen's books of account.

Step 2: Rule up three sets of ledger accounts: a general ledger (11 accounts are required); a sales ledger (just one account required) a purchases ledger (just one account required).

Step 3: Take each transaction in date order and make entries in the relevant book of prime entry (the first entry is in the general journal to record the assets and capital of the business on opening). As each transaction is recorded in the book of prime entry post information through to the relevant ledger accounts.

Step 4: At the end of the month total the discount columns in the cash book and post these to the general ledger; total the sales, purchases, returns inwards, returns outwards journals and post these totals to the relevant accounts in the general ledger.

▶ The completed books of prime entry are as shown below.

JOURNAL

Date		Details	Dr	Cr
			$	$
Jan	1	Bank	3 500	
		Vehicle	36 000	
		Equipment	19 000	
		Capital		58 500
		entries to open books of account		
	15	Equipment	880	
		Bridge Products*		880
		purchase of equipment for business use on credit,		
		invoice number 478		
	19	Bridge Products*	90	
		Equipment		90
		return of equipment purchased on credit		

* The account of Bridge Products has been recorded in the general ledger. Many businesses use their purchases ledger exclusively for the accounts of suppliers of goods in which the business trades.

CASH BOOK

Dr			Discounts allowed	Cash	Bank				Discounts received	Cash	Bank Cr
			$	$	$				$	$	$
Jan	1	Balance			3 500	Jan	10	Operating exp		280	
	7	Sales		1 240			11	Bank		800	
	11	Cash			800		24	MJT Ltd	93		4 557
	29	Geeta Stores	24		911						
			24						93		

Purchases journal

Date		Details	Invoice no	$
Jan	4	MJT Ltd	302	4 800
		Total purchases		4 800

Sales journal

Date		Details	Invoice no	$
Jan	16	Geeta Stores	001	1 020
		Total sales		1 020

Returns outwards journal

Date		Details	Credit note no	$
Jan	14	MJT Ltd	073	150
		Total returns outwards		150

Returns inwards journal

Date		Details	Credit note no	$
Jan	22	Geeta Stores	001	85
		Total returns inwards		85

PURCHASES LEDGER

MJT Ltd

Dr							Cr
Jan	14	Returns outwards	150	Jan	4	Purchases	4 800
	24	Bank	4 557				
	24	Disc received	93				

SALES LEDGER

Geeta Stores

Dr							Cr
Jan	16	Sales	1 020	Jan	22	Returns inwards	85
					29	Bank	911
					29	Disc allowed	24

GENERAL LEDGER

Dr		Bridge Products						Cr
Jan	19	Equipment	90	Jan	15	Equipment	J1	880

Dr		Equipment				Cr
Jan	1	Balance	19 000	Jan	19	Bridge Products	90
	15	Bridge Products	880				

Dr		Capital				Cr
				Jan	1	Balance	58 500

Dr		Discounts allowed				Cr
Jan	31	Cash book	24			

Dr		Discounts received				Cr
				Jan	31	Cash book	93

Dr		Operating expenses				Cr
Jan	10	Cash	280			

Dr		Purchases				Cr
Jan	31	Purchases journal	4 800			

Dr		Returns inwards				Cr
Jan	31	Returns inwards journal	85			

Dr		Returns outwards				Cr
				Jan	31	Returns outwards journal	150

Dr		Sales				Cr
				Jan	7	Cash	1 240
					31	Sales journal	1 020

Dr		Vehicle				Cr
Jan	1	Balance	36 000			

Key term

Trial balance: a summary of the balances on all the accounts in a business's books of account that provides a check on the arithmetical accuracy of the double entry.

The trial balance

A trial balance provides a quick check on the accuracy of the double-entry records. It is based on the idea that for every debit entry there should be a matching credit, so that if all has gone well, total debit entries should equal total credit entries. It is often said that a trial balance checks the arithmetical accuracy of the double-entry records. Preparing a trial balance forms part of Step 4 in the accounting cycle.

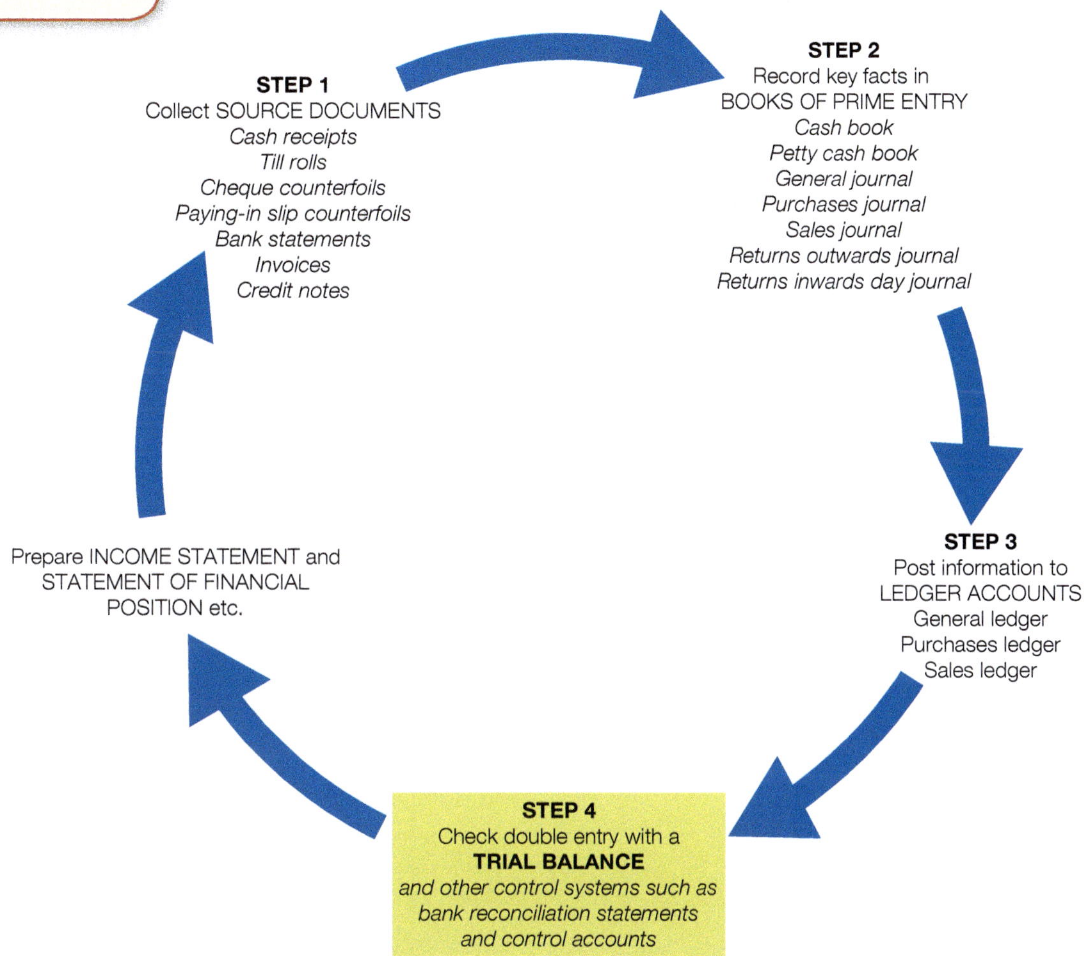

Figure 1.1.3A The accounting cycle: Step 4 ▲

Getting it right

Preparing a set of books even on a small scale is a skilful task. It is easy to overlook a transaction, for example. A common error is to forget to total discount columns in the cash book and post the totals to the ledger accounts. It is also easy to forget to post the totals of the sales, purchases and returns journals.

Illustration 2: The idea behind a trial balance

Here is a very simple set of accounts which have been correctly maintained using the rules of double entry.

Dr			**Bank**				**Cr**
Jan	1	Balance	13 000	Jan	4	Trade payable	2 000
	10	Sales	4 000				

Dr			**Capital**				**Cr**
				Jan	1	Balance	11 400

Dr			Trade payable				Cr
Jan	3	Bank	2 000	Jan	1	Balance	2 000
					7	Purchases	3 000

Dr			Purchases				Cr
Jan	7	Bank	3 000				

Dr			Sales				Cr
				Jan	10	Bank	4 000

There are very few entries, so it is fairly easy to see that total debit entries are $22 000 and total credit entries are also $22 000. So, because total debit entries equals total credit entries, it appears that the rules of double entry have been followed. You can check the detail here.

Account	Total of debit entries $	Total of credit entries $
Bank	17 000	2 000
Capital	–	11 000
Trade payable	2 000	5 000
Purchases	3 000	–
Sales	–	4 000
Totals	22 000	22 000

A trial balance also provides a quick check on double entry but also provides some useful information for those using the accounts. Here is a trial balance based on these accounts.

Trial balance at 10 January 2015		
	Dr $	Cr $
Bank	15 000	
Capital		11 000
Trade payable		3 000
Purchases	3 000	
Sales		4 000
	18 000	18 000

Instead of showing total debit entries and total credit entries for each account, a trial balance shows the *net amount* in each account. The reason is that a trial balance is also used to provide anyone who is interested with a quick update on each account in the system, as well as providing a check on the whether double-entry procedures have been followed correctly.

Illustration 3: Preparing a trial balance at 31 January 2015 for Carmen's business

Here is the trial balance for Carmen's business based on the accounts shown in Illustration 1.

Trial balance at 31 January 2015

	Dr	Cr
	$	$
Cash	160	
Bank	654	
Bridge Products		790
Vehicle	36 000	
Equipment	19 790	
Capital		58 500
Discounts allowed	24	
Discounts received		93
Operating expenses	280	
Purchases	4 800	
Returns inwards	85	
Returns outwards		150
Sales		2 260
	61 793	61 793

Notes:

1 The correct title for a trial balance is always 'trial balance at [date]'.

2 The totals of the trial balance agree, which would appear to confirm that the double-entry records are correct.

The trial balance is a very useful accounting technique, not least because it provides a brief summary of what is in the accounting system. However, it is important to note that there could still be errors in the accounts. For example, it could now be revealed that another invoice received from Carmen's supplier MJT Ltd had been overlooked. Types of error and how to correct them will be explored in a later chapter.

Key terms

Balancing accounts: the process of working out the net amount left in an account and clearly stating this as a debit or credit balance at the beginning of the next accounting period.

Closing accounts: the process of finishing off an account that does not have a balance.

Balancing accounts

Over a period of time many of the ledger accounts you have been preparing could grow to a very large size. Even the smallest business will have hundreds – possibly thousands – of transactions to record over a period of a few months.

In this chapter you will learn about balancing or closing accounts. This process is important because it has the following benefits:

- It breaks up each record into more manageable segments based on time periods.

Getting it right

It is a very common weakness to find that students do not balance accounts correctly. Even some of the most experienced students fail to follow the very precise rules for balancing accounts. These rules are set out here.

- It brings many accounts to a neat conclusion with a clear statement or update on the net value shown in the account (the balance).
- It brings some other accounts to a neat conclusion by clearly showing that there is no balance and that the account is now closed.
- It provides summary information for the preparation of the trial balance and other financial statements.

The owner of a business could balance and close the accounting records at any time. In practice balancing accounts will occur at regular intervals. This could be monthly for many accounts, possibly weekly for others. All accounts should be balanced or closed at the end of the financial year.

Accounts are balanced following a precise set of rules or steps which can be applied to almost every account that has some net value at a particular date.

Illustration 4: Balancing an ASSET account

Here is a typical set of entries in the account of a trade receivable.

Dr			Trade receivable: XJX Ltd				Cr
Sept	1	Balance	1 800	Sept	6	Returns inwards	300
	14	Sales	8 000		10	Bank	7 800
	22	Sales	5 300		10	Discount allowed	200

In order to balance the account the following steps are necessary.

Step 1: Calculate the balance. Here the total debit entries are $15 100 and the total credit entries are $8300. So the balance is $6800 (i.e. $15 100 less $8300).

Step 2: Start the balancing process by recording the balance on the side of the account which has the 'smaller total value'.

Dr			Trade receivable: XJX Ltd				Cr
Sept	1	Balance	1 800	Sept	6	Returns inwards	300
	14	Sales	8 000		10	Bank	7 800
	22	Sales	5 300		10	Discount allowed	200
							6 800

Now label this entry with the date (30 September) and the narrative balance c/d. The abbreviation c/d means 'carry down'.

Dr			Trade receivable: XJX Ltd				Cr
Sept	1	Balance	1 800	Sept	6	Returns inwards	300
	14	Sales	8 000		10	Bank	7 800
	22	Sales	5 300		10	Discount allowed	200
					30	Balance c/d	6 800

Step 3: By making the credit entry for $6800, the two sides of the account now total the same amount ($15 100). The next step is to record this total on each side of the account.

Dr		Trade receivable: XJX Ltd					Cr
Sept	1	Balance	1 800	Sept	6	Returns inwards	300
	14	Sales	8 000		10	Bank	7 800
	22	Sales	5 300		10	Discount allowed	200
					30	Balance c/d	6 800
			15 100				15 100

You will notice that the totals appear on the same line and that the next available line has been used.

Step 4: As you know, you cannot make a credit entry in the accounts without also having a matching debit entry. So to complete the balancing process, make a matching debit entry in the trade receivables account for the balance. This time label the balance 'b/d' (brought down) and for the date use the first day of the next month (here 1 October).

Dr		Trade receivable: XJX Ltd					Cr
Sept	1	Balance	1 800	Sept	6	Returns inwards	300
	14	Sales	8 000		10	Bank	7 800
	22	Sales	5 300		10	Discount allowed	200
					30	Balance c/d	6 800
			15 100				15 100
Oct	1	Balance b/d	6 800				

You will see that the trade receivables account is now ready for use during October, and that all of September's transactions have been neatly summarised by stating the net value at the end of September.

Illustration 5: Balancing a LIABILITY account

Here is a typical liability account.

Dr		Trade payable: DTQ					Cr
June	10	Bank	2 400	June	1	Balance	3 300
					22	Purchases	500

Following the same four steps:

Step 1: The balance on the account is $3800 less $2400 = $1400

Step 2: The balance c/d (dated 30 June) will appear on the debit side because this is the side with the smaller total value.

Step 3: Record the totals on both sides of the account.

Step 4: Make a matching entry for the balance – in this case a credit entry. The balance b/d should be dated 1 July.

Dr			Trade payable: DTQ				Cr
June	10	Bank	2 400	June	1	Balance	3 300
	30	Balance c/d	1 400		22	Purchases	500
			3 800				3 800
				July	1	Balance b/d	1 400

Balancing an account where ENTRIES ARE ALL ON ONE SIDE

Before balancing:

Dr			Trade receivable: Broqif				Cr
April	1	Balance	6 000				
	13	Sales	2 000				
	27	Sales	1 000				

After balancing:

Dr			Trade receivable: Broqif				Cr
April	1	Balance	6 000	April	30	Balance c/d	9 000
	13	Sales	2 000				
	27	Sales	1 000				
			9 000				9 000
May	1	Balance b/d	9 000				

Sometimes accounts have entries that are all on one side. Here the only transactions affecting receivables have been additional sales on credit. You will notice that the step-by-step balancing technique can be followed in the same way as in all the previous examples.

Accounts where there is only ONE ENTRY

Before balancing:

Dr			Vehicles				Cr
March	1	Balance	24 500				

After balancing:

Dr			Vehicles				Cr
March	1	Balance	24 500				

Nothing needs to be done with an account with just one entry! Some accounts rarely have entries made in them. Do not be tempted to waste time balancing an account with just one entry – you will only end up where you started!

Getting it right

Do not forget to bring down balances. This is the most common mistake made when balancing accounts.

Getting it right

Remember that the discounts allowed and discounts received columns are not balanced, they are totalled.

Balancing a three-column cash book

Here is Carmen's cash book (from Illustration 1) showing the cash and bank columns balanced at the end of the month. Exactly the same balancing procedures have been applied here.

Dr				CASH BOOK							Cr
			Discounts allowed	Cash	Bank				Discounts received	Cash	Bank
			$	$	$				$	$	$
Jan	1	Balance			3 500	Jan	10	Operating exp		280	
	7	Sales		1 240			11	Bank		800	
	11	Cash			800		24	MJT Ltd	93		4 557
	29	Geeta Stores	24		911		31	Balances c/d		160	654
			24	1 240	5 211				93	1 240	5 211
Feb	1	Balances b/d		160	654						

End-of-chapter questions

1 **Preparing a business's books of account**

Kimberly Watson opened a business on 1 September 2014. On that date her business's assets and liabilities were as follows.

	$
Cash in hand	1 380
Cash at bank	1 750
Non-current assets	86 500
Bank loan	15 000
Capital	74 630

During September the following transactions occurred.

Date		Source document	Transaction
Sept	4	Purchase invoice (2361)	From TM Bennett Ltd for goods $2 800 less 25% trade discount
	6	Cash receipt	Paid general expenses in cash $180
	7	Credit note received (G09)	From TM Bennett Ltd for goods not as ordered, $240 less 25% trade discount
	12	Till roll	Cash sales totalling $1 090
	14	Cheque counterfoil	Paid TM Bennett Ltd in full settlement of their account at this date less 5% cash discount
	15	Sales invoice (0001)	To KS Maharaj for goods $2 000 less 20% trade discount
	19	Cheque counterfoil	Rent for three months $2 480
	21	Paying-in slip counterfoil	Transfer of cash to bank $730
	23	Cash receipt	Kimberly withdrew cash $280 for her private use
	26	Credit note issued (01)	To KS Maharaj for damaged items sold on 15 September, $125, less 20% trade discount
	28	Paying-in slip counterfoil	Cheque received from KS Maharaj in full settlement of their account at this date less 2% cash discount
	30	Bank statement	Bank charges for the month totalled $70

Prepare the following books of prime entry for September 2014:

- general journal
- three-column cash book
- purchases journal
- sales journal
- returns outwards journal
- returns inwards journal.

Post the entries in the books of prime entry to the purchases, sales and general ledgers.

The discount columns in the cash book should be totalled and posted to the general ledger.

2 Preparing a trial balance

On 31 March 2015 the owner of a business extracted the following list of balances from the accounting system.

	$
Capital	13 700
Cash at bank	600
Cash in hand	100
Trade payables	2 500
Trade receivables	1 400
Drawings	2 200
Electricity	300
Furniture	14 900
Loan interest	500
Purchases	7 700
Salaries	11 200
Sales	22 700

Prepare a trial balance at 31 March 2015.

3 Preparing a trial balance

Prepare a trial balance dated 30 September 2014 for the business owned by Kimberley Watson based on the answer to Question 1.

4 Preparing a business's books of accounts starting with a trial balance and including the preparation of a final trial balance

Omar owns a wholesale business supplying computer accessories to retailers in the region. His business's trial balance on 1 November was as follows.

Trial balance at 1 November 2014

	Dr $	Cr $
Bank overdraft		1 480
Capital		103 560
Cash	440	
Discounts allowed	1 320	
Discounts received		1 890
Drawings	37 320	
Furniture and equipment	180 000	
Operating expenses	45 360	
Purchases	578 270	
Returns inwards	4 890	
Returns outwards		5 130
Sales		732 340
Trade payables		
LDZ Ltd		4 500
M Chin Ltd		3 200
Trade receivables		
Oldbridge Retail Unit	2 800	
Peterson Stores	1 700	
	852 100	852 100

During November 2014 the following transactions occurred.

Date		Source document	Details
Nov	1	Cash receipt	for operating expenses $380
	3	Invoice	from LDZ Ltd (number 891) for goods for resale, $4 500 less 33⅓% trade discount
	7	Paying-in slip counterfoil	cheque received from Oldbridge Retail Unit in settlement of their account at this date less 5% cash discount
	8	Credit note	received from LDZ Ltd (number 223) for goods purchased on 3 November, not as ordered, $330 less 33⅓% trade discount
	12	Till roll	cash sales totalling $2 460
	13	Cheque counterfoil	Omar withdrew $720 for private use

14	Letter	copy of letter sent to Oldbridge Retail Unit stated that the discount claimed by them when making payment on 7 November was cancelled because payment had been made after specified time limit
17	Invoice	sent to Peterson Stores (number 407) for goods $2 450 less 20% trade discount
18	Paying-in slip counterfoil	Banked cash $1 800
20	Invoice	for additional equipment for business use, $1 460, received from Deva Office Supplies (invoice number 2789)
22	Credit note	sent to Peterson Stores (number 082) for goods damaged in transit, $150 less 20% trade discount
25	Cheque counterfoil	paid M Chin Ltd the amount due at this date less 5% cash discount
29	Paying-in slip counterfoil	cheque received from Peterson Stores in settlement of their account at this date less a cash discount of $110

Prepare the following:

- general journal
- three-column cash book
- purchases journal
- sales journal
- returns outwards journal
- returns inwards journal
- purchases ledger accounts
- sales ledger accounts
- general ledger accounts
- trial balance dated 30 November 2014.

5 Balancing accounts

Make a copy of the following accounts.

Dr		Motor vehicles					Cr
Aug	1	Balance	7 000	Aug	12	Bank	7 000
	14	Bank	9 500				

Dr		Bank loan					Cr
Aug	31	Bank	3 200	Aug	1	Balance	39 400

Dr		Premises					Cr
Aug	1	Balance	74 000				

Dr		Trade receivable: DBQ Ltd					Cr
Aug	1	Balance	3 600				
	26	Sales	1 700				

Dr			Trade payable: Zexton & Co				Cr
				Aug	1	Balance	2 100
					11	Purchases	800
					25	Purchases	1 300

Balance each account as appropriate.

6 Balancing accounts

Make a copy of the following accounts.

Dr			Equipment				Cr
Jan	1	Balance	3 240	Jan	11	Bank	1 050
	15	Bank	4 360				

Dr			Trade payable: UVY Ltd				Cr
				Jan	1	Balance	4 150
					16	Purchases	2 040

Dr			Bank loan				Cr
Jan	31	Bank	1 320	Jan	1	Balance	11 000

Dr			Fittings				Cr
Jan	1	Balance	14 900				

Dr			Equipment				Cr
Jan	1	Balance	4 980				
	18	Bank	3 070				

Balance each account as appropriate.

Note: Students requiring further practice at this point should turn to additional questions 1, 2 and 3 on the CD-ROM.

Learning objectives

In this chapter you will learn:

- the meaning of capital expenditure
- the meaning of revenue expenditure
- the importance of the differences between the two types of expenditure.

Key terms

Capital expenditure: money spent on the long-term purchase or improvement of non-current assets.

Revenue expenditure: money spent on the short-term day-to-day running of a business.

1.1.4: Capital and revenue expenditure

Introduction

It is very important to recognise the difference between capital expenditure and revenue expenditure.

Capital expenditure is money spent that has a long-term benefit to the business (more than one year). In practice, this usually means money spent on buying non-current assets.

Revenue expenditure is money spent that has a short-term benefit to the business (less than one year). For example, the running costs of the business.

Capital expenditure

Any money spent on buying, altering or improving a non-current asset is classed as capital expenditure. Non-current assets are intended for continuing, long-term use in the business; they are not intended for resale. Examples include:

- premises
- motor vehicles
- plant and machinery
- fixtures and fittings.

Money spent on acquiring, improving or adding to a non-current asset is also classed as capital expenditure. Examples include:

- an extension to a property
- sign writing on a van
- legal expenses when purchasing a property.

Revenue expenditure

Money spent on the day-to-day running costs of a business is classed as revenue expenditure. Examples include:

- purchase of raw materials
- staff wages
- maintenance or repair of non-current assets
- rent, rates, light and heat
- stationery
- advertising.

One feature of revenue expenditure is that it is recurring: in other words, it is not usually a one-off payment.

Illustration 1: Revenue expenditure

A business purchases a new motor van and incurs the following costs.

	$
Cost price of the van	22 100
Sign writing the company name on the van	300
Fitting shelves into the van	550
Van insurance	650
Fuel	85

The capital expenditure is the cost price of the van, the sign writing and fitting the shelves: a total of $22 950. These are permanent, one-off items of expenditure.

The revenue expenditure is the recurring costs of insurance and fuel: a total of $735.

Why the distinction between the two is important

Capital expenditure appears on the statement of financial position of a business, listing all assets and liabilities of a business. Revenue expenditure appears on the income statement of a business and is deducted from revenue to calculate the profit or loss for a period.

If an error is made by incorrectly classifying expenditure under the wrong heading, the result would be as follows:

- The profit or loss for the period shown on the income statement would be either understated or overstated.
- The value of the business shown by the statement of financial position would be incorrect.

Both of these errors may result in the owners of a business drawing incorrect conclusions from the information and possibly making wrong decisions about the business as a result. In addition, the errors could result in an incorrect taxation liability being assessed.

End-of-chapter questions

1 Capital expenditure
Explain the term 'capital expenditure' and give two examples of it.

2 Revenue expenditure
Explain the term 'revenue expenditure' and give two examples of it.

3 Capital and revenue expenditure
If revenue expenditure was incorrectly treated as capital expenditure, what would be the effect on the business's profit for the year?

4 Capital and revenue expenditure
If capital expenditure was incorrectly treated as revenue expenditure, what would be the effect on the business's profit for the year?

5 Capital and revenue expenditure
For each of the following items of expenditure, state whether they are capital expenditure or revenue expenditure.

a Repairs to plant and machinery.
b Legal fees on the purchase of new premises.
c Computer repairs.
d Annual maintenance contract on computer systems.

6 Capital and revenue expenditure
For each of the following items of expenditure, state whether they are capital expenditure or revenue expenditure.

a Motor vehicle repairs.
b Extension to business premises.
c Redecorating the office premises.
d Sign writing on a new van.

7 Capital and revenue expenditure
George has had new machinery installed in his factory. The total expenditure was as follows.

	$
Cost price of the machinery	45 600
Alterations to the machinery to make it fit for purpose	1 570
Maintenance contract	1 200
Lubricant for the machine	260
Installation costs of the new machinery	300
Strengthening the factory floor prior to installation	650

Required

Calculate the total capital expenditure and total revenue expenditure for the new machinery.

1.1.5: Accounting concepts and principles

Learning objectives

In this chapter you will learn:

- how to explain the purpose of accounting concepts and principles
- how to explain the rule covered by each concept and the reason for the rule
- how to apply each concept to a variety of situations.

Introduction

Various accounting principles, concepts and conventions underlie the accounting process and you will find it much easier to understand new techniques if you are familiar with all of these. The purpose of the rules is to ensure that everyone treats a particular situation in the same way. This ensures that the financial statements will be the same, no matter who has prepared them.

Going concern

The concept of going concern states that it should be assumed that the business is going to continue to trade for the foreseeable future (at least one year). A result of this concept is that assets should be valued on the basis of cost, not on what they would fetch if sold today. The reason is clear: assets are to help the business trade, they are not for sale.

Key term

Going concern: this concept states that it should be assumed that the business will continue to trade for the foreseeable future.

Illustration 1: Going concern concept

Baahir owns specialised machinery that helps to produce his products. He has been advised that although the machinery has a value of $8000 on his statement of financial position, if he was forced to sell it, it would only realise $2000.

Because Baahir intends to continue in business producing his products, the value to his business is $8000 and it should remain on the statement of financial position at that value. If he intended to close the business down, then the value should be written down to the realisable value of $2000.

Accruals

The accruals concept (sometimes referred to as the matching concept) states that costs and revenues should be matched to the same accounting period. This matching of costs and revenues considers whether or not monies have been paid or received. This concept is the reason why financial statements make adjustments for accruals, prepayments and closing inventory.

Key term

Accruals: this concept states that costs and revenues should be matched to the same accounting period.

Link

There is more about adjustments in AS Level Chapter 1.4.1 Adjustments to financial statements.

Illustration 2: Accruals concept

Hadeel is in business selling ladies' clothes. She has purchased inventory for $5000 but at the year end has only sold $2000 of that inventory. Although she has bought and paid for all the inventory, the financial statements should be adjusted by reducing purchases by the closing inventory of $3000 that will be carried forward into the next accounting period.

Hadeel has not yet received an invoice for some advertising taken out last month. Although this has not yet been paid for, it relates to this year's accounts and should be provided for by increasing this year's advertising cost with an accrual.

Key term

Consistency: this concept states that accounting policies should not be changed without a specific and valid reason.

Consistency

The consistency concept states that when a business adopts a particular policy in recording its transactions, it should continue to use the same policy for future financial statements. This means that year-on-year figures can be directly compared in the knowledge that the same policies have been applied.

Link

There is more about depreciation in AS Level Chapter 1.2.1 Accounting for non-current assets.

Illustration 3: Consistency concept

Kamal has always depreciated his non-current assets at 25 per cent each year. This year he feels that his profit looks rather low and he wants to change the depreciation rate to 10 per cent to make the business look more profitable.

He is advised that unless there is a specific business reason for making the change, he should not do so since the accounts would not be comparable on a like-for-like basis and would mislead users of the information.

Key term

Materiality: this concept states that financial statements should not take account of items that are trivial or may be misleading.

Materiality

The concept of materiality states that the financial statements should not take account of items that are trivial or may be misleading. In other words, the information in the accounts should be significant to the users of those accounts.

Illustration 4: Materiality concept

Layla purchases a new calculator for her office for $6. She thinks that the calculator will last for three years. Although it could be regarded as a non-current asset, the amount involved is so small that there would be no benefit in depreciating the calculator over its three-year life, so it should be written off to the income statement in the year of purchase.

Key term

Prudence: this concept states that losses should be provided for as soon as they are anticipated; profits should not be recognised until they are realised.

Prudence

The concept of prudence states that losses should be provided for as soon as they are anticipated, but profits should not be recognised until they are realised. The basic reason behind this concept is that if the owners of a business were to be over-optimistic, then profits may be overstated and be misleading to the users of financial statements.

Link

There is more about debts in AS Level Chapter 1.4.1 Adjustments to financial statements.

Illustration 5: Prudence concept

Nabeel sold goods to a customer for $120 and has been waiting for payment for six months. On the grounds of prudence, Nabeel should write off the amount as an irrecoverable debt, since it is becoming increasingly unlikely that he will be paid.

Key term

Business entity: this concept states that only those matters affecting the financial position of the business should be recorded in the accounting records.

Business entity

The business entity concept states that only those matters that affect the financial position of a business should be recorded in the accounting records. Any private financial transactions of the owners of a business should be disregarded.

Illustration 6: Business entity concept

Dalal purchased a computer using her business funds. The computer was actually for her own private use at home. Since there was to be no benefit to the business, the computer should have been purchased using her own money rather than that of the business. In these circumstances, the amount should be debited to Dalal's drawings.

Key term

Historical cost: this concept states that all transactions should be recorded using the original actual cost of purchase.

Historical cost

The concept of historical cost states that all transactions should be recorded using the original actual cost of purchase. The basis behind the concept is that it avoids the necessity of using someone's opinion as to the value of an asset.

Illustration 7: Historical cost concept

Jamal purchased machinery some years ago for $9000. He has been told that it may now cost $14 000 to replace the machinery and he wonders whether he should adjust the cost of the machinery in his financial statements.

Jamal should leave the machinery in his financial statements at the historical cost of $9000, because the actual replacement cost of the machinery would vary depending on a variety of factors.

Key term

Realisation: this concept states that revenue should only be recorded either when cash has been received or when an invoice has been issued.

Realisation

The realisation concept states that revenue should only be recorded in the books of account either when cash has been received or when a receivable recognised by the issue of an invoice has been processed.

Illustration 8: Realisation concept

Rafiq has completed work worth $1500 for a customer but has not yet invoiced him. The $1500 should not be recorded in the books of account until the invoice has been produced and sent to the customer. Until this happens, there is no obligation for the customer to pay.

Key term

True and fair view: a principle stating that the income statement should show a 'true and fair view' of the profit or loss; the statement of financial position should show a 'true and fair view' of the business's financial position.

True and fair view

The true and fair view principle states that the income statement should show a 'true and fair view' of an organisation's profit or loss and that the statement of financial position should show a 'true and fair view' of the organisation's financial position. This means that the financial statements should be factually accurate wherever possible and should show reasonable, accurate estimates only if necessary.

Key term

Money measurement: a concept stating that financial statements should only record information that has a monetary value.

Money measurement

The principle states that financial statements should only record information that has a monetary value. Some aspects of a business cannot be recorded in monetary terms, for example the location of the business, its customer base, the loyalty of its employees, etc.

Illustration 9: The money measurement principle

James has owned a supply business for a number of years. The business has many regular and reliable customers and loyal staff who have worked for him since the business started. Although both of these facts are assets to the business, it is not possible to place a monetary value on them and as such, they will not appear in James's financial statements.

Duality

The principle states that every business transaction has two aspects leading to making two entries for each transaction in the accounting records.

Illustration 10: The duality concept

Luke purchased new machinery by cheque for $2000. The duality concept recognises both aspects of this transaction. Firstly, the value of non-current assets has increased by $2000 therefore machinery is debited with $2000. The second aspect of this transaction is that the current asset of cash at the bank reduces so that account is credited with $2000.

Key term

Substance over form: a principle stating that information should show the substance of a transaction rather than the legal form.

Substance over form

The principle states that information shown in the financial statements should reflect the underlying realities of accounting transactions rather than the legal form in which they appear.

Illustration 11: The substance over form principle

Thomas purchases a new motor van on hire purchase. The legal position is that the van remains the property of the seller until the final payment has been made. However, Thomas has full use of the motor van in exactly the same way as all of his other non-current assets that have not been bought on hire purchase. This is the substance of the transaction, and even though legally Thomas does not own the motor van, it will appear as a non-current asset on his financial statements.

End-of-chapter questions

1 **Accounting concepts**

The owner of a business purchased a new television for his own use and charged the amount to his drawings account. Which accounting concept is this an example of?

A Accruals
B Business entity
C Consistency
D Prudence

2 **Accounting concepts**

The owner of a business had paid two months' rent in advance at her year end and deducted the payment from her expenses. Which accounting concept is this an example of?

A Accruals
B Consistency
C Prudence
D Realisation

3 **Accounting concepts**

Identify the appropriate accounting concept to be applied to the following:

a Trade receivables include a figure of $1000 that the owner knows is an irrecoverable debt. He wishes to leave this figure in trade receivables to show the highest value of current assets possible.

b The owner of a successful business is planning for next year. She is considering showing her non-current assets at the cost of replacement in order to show the highest value of non-current assets possible.

c The owner of a business wishes to change the rate of depreciation applied to his non-current assets in order to increase his profit for the year.

d A business has not yet received an invoice for rent for the last three months of the year. The owner wishes to ignore this in order to increase her reported profit for the year.

4 **Accounting concepts**

Identify the appropriate accounting concept to be applied to the following:

a A trader uses the reducing-balance method of depreciation for all of his non-current assets. He is considering changing to the straight-line method in order to deduct fewer expenses from his income statement.

b A business purchases computer software for $96. The owner of the business wishes to class this as a non-current asset as he says it will last for many years.

c On the last day of his financial year, Jake sells goods to a customer for $4500 but does not produce the invoice until one week later. He wishes to show the sale in the current financial year.

d A business has a financial year end of 31 December 2014. At the year end, the owner of the business has not received an invoice for rent for the final two months of the year. She wishes to ignore this as it would reduce her profit for the year.

Section 1.2: Accounting for non-current assets

Key concepts

The key concept that is of greatest importance in accounting for non-current assets is the **duality (double-entry)** concept. This concept requires two entries to be made for every transaction to reflect that there are two aspects to every transaction.

In addition, it is important that the other key concepts are also applied. For example, the owners and managers of a business must always ensure that they present a **true and fair view** of the business's non-current assets. This is particularly important when assessing depreciation changes.

Furthermore, accounting policies (e.g. depreciation methods) must always be applied **consistently** in each accounting year to ensure that meaningful comparisons of a business's results can be made.

Learning objectives

In this chapter you will learn:

- the difference between capital and revenue expenditure and receipts
- what a non-current asset is
- how to record the purchase of a non-current asset
- the nature of depreciation
- how to depreciate a non-current asset
- how depreciation is calculated
- how to record the sale of a non-current asset
- how to deal with part exchange.

Key terms

Capital receipts: revenue from the sale of non-current assets or from investment in the business.

Revenue receipts: receipts arising from normal business activities.

1.2.1: Accounting for non-current assets

Capital and revenue expenditure and receipts

As discussed previously, it is very important to recognise the difference between capital expenditure and revenue expenditure and receipts.

Capital expenditure is money spent that has a long-term benefit to the business (more than one year). In practice, this usually means money spent on buying or improving non-current assets.

Revenue expenditure is money spent that has a short-term benefit to the business (less than one year), for example the day-to-day running costs of the business.

Capital receipts arise from the sale of non-current assets or capital being invested in the business from either the owners or outside lenders.

Revenue receipts are receipts that arise from normal business activities. Examples include rent received, commission received, etc.

Capital receipts

Any money received that is not from normal trading activities is classed as a capital receipt. Examples include:

- sale proceeds from the disposal of non-current assets
- receipt of loan finance from banks or other lenders
- capital introduced into the business by the owners.

Capital receipts do not appear on the income statement but are accounted for on the statement of financial position.

Revenue receipts

Revenue receipts arise from the normal business activities, for example the sale of goods or services. They may also be incidental to the main business activity.

Examples include:

- rents received
- commission received
- interest received.

Revenue receipts are credited to the income statement.

Illustration 1: Capital and revenue receipts

The receipts of a business during the month included the following.

Cash received from the sale of a motor van	$4 000
Rent received from a tenant	$450
Bank loan received into the business bank account	$8 000

The capital revenue is the cash received from the sale of a motor van and the receipt of the bank loan. Both of these items are one-off receipts of funds.

The revenue receipt is the rent received from a tenant. This is the cash received in the normal course of business; it is a recurring receipt.

Recording the purchase of a non-current asset

The purchase of a non-current asset that is paid for immediately will be recorded in the cash book. The purchase of a non-current asset on credit will be recorded in the general journal.

Illustration 2: Recording the purchase of a non-current asset

George purchased:

- a new property for $45 000 and paid $1200 legal fees, paying by cheque
- some machinery for $82 000 on credit from QDP Ltd.

The entries in the books of prime entry are as follows.

Dr	Cash book (bank columns)	Cr
		$
	Property	45 000
	Property (legal fees)	1 200

Journal		
	Dr	Cr
	$	$
Machinery	82 000	
QDP Ltd		82 000
purchase of machinery on credit		

The non-current asset accounts appear as follows.

GENERAL LEDGER

Dr	Machinery		Cr
QDP Ltd	82 000		

Dr	Property		Cr
Bank	45 000		
Bank	1 200		

Depreciating a non-current asset

Key terms

Useful economic life: the expected useful lifetime of an asset.

Depreciation: the spreading of the cost of an asset over its useful economic life.

Most non-current assets do not last forever, they have what is known as a useful economic life. This will vary from asset to asset. For example, a property may last for 100 years or more, but a computer may have a useful life of only two or three years.

The reasons for this limited useful life are as follows:

- Most assets will lose value through wear and tear and eventually they will wear out.
- As technology changes over time, assets will become outdated and will no longer meet the business's needs.
- As the business grows, machinery may become inadequate to meet the increased capacity and needs of the business.

To account for this loss in value, non-current assets are depreciated over their useful economic life. As an example, if a non-current asset is purchased for $30 000 and sold five years later for $10 000, then it has depreciated $20 000 over the five years it has been owned. This total amount of depreciation must be spread over the lifetime of the asset in accordance with the accruals concept. Providing for depreciation is also an application of the prudence concept. If the cost of using an asset was not included in the income statement then profits would be overstated. The annual charge for depreciation appears as an expense on the income statement.

Key terms

Residual value: the expected value of an asset at the end of its useful economic life.

Straight-line method of depreciation: the cost of the asset less the expected residual value, spread equally over the estimated useful life of the asset.

Reducing-balance method of depreciation: a fixed percentage of the net book value of the asset is charged as depreciation each year.

Revaluation method of depreciation: the annual depreciation charge is based on the difference between the estimated value of a group of non-current assets at the end of the year and the estimated value at the start of the year.

How depreciation is calculated

In order to calculate depreciation, the following information is needed:

- The purchase price of the asset.
- The estimated useful economic life of the asset.
- The estimated residual value (how much the asset will be worth at the end of its useful economic life).

There are three main methods of calculating depreciation: the straight-line method, the reducing-balance method and the revaluation method.

The straight-line method of depreciation

The straight-line method involves depreciating the asset by the same amount each year. It is calculated as follows:

$$\text{The annual depreciation charge} = \frac{\text{Cost of the asset} - \text{Net residual value}}{\text{Estimated useful life of the asset}}$$

Illustration 3: Straight-line method of depreciation

Bushra purchased a new machine for \$14 000. She estimates that its useful economic life will be six years and that the machine will have a residual value of \$2000 at the end of the six years.

Calculate the annual depreciation charge for the machine.

$$\text{The annual depreciation charge} = \frac{\$14\,000 - \$2000}{6 \text{ years}} = \$2000 \text{ per annum.}$$

The straight-line method of depreciation has the advantage that it is very straightforward to calculate and it results in the same depreciation charge to the income statement each year.

Key term

Net book value (NBV): the value of an asset less the depreciation shown in the books of account.

The reducing-balance method of depreciation

The reducing-balance method of depreciation calculates the annual depreciation charge as a fixed percentage of the net book value (NBV) of the asset.

Illustration 4: Reducing-balance method of depreciation

Bushra purchased a motor vehicle for \$20 000. She depreciates her motor vehicles at 25 per cent per annum using the reducing-balance method.

Calculate the annual depreciation charge for the motor vehicle for the first two years.

Year 1	\$20 000 × 25% = \$5000
Year 2	\$20 000 – \$5000 = NBV \$15 000. Annual depreciation = \$15 000 × 25% = \$3750

The NBV of the motor vehicle to carry forward into Year 3 is therefore \$15 000 – \$3750 = \$11 250.

The reducing-balance method of depreciation is more complicated to calculate, but it may be more realistic because as the asset reduces in value, so the annual depreciation charge will also reduce.

The revaluation method of depreciation

The revaluation method of depreciation is based on comparing the estimated value of a group of non-current assets at the end of the year with the estimated value of the same group of non-current assets at the start of the year. The difference in this value is charged as depreciation for the year in the income statement.

Illustration 5: Revaluation method of depreciation

A building contractor uses many small loose tools that are added to or replaced regularly. At the start of the financial year, the owner of the business valued these loose tools at $3600. During the year, new loose tools were purchased for $1600. At the end of the financial year, the estimated value was $3900.

The depreciation charge for the year is the difference between the closing and opening valuations after taking account of the additional tools purchased.

Opening valuation	$3 600
Additions	$1 600
	$5 200
Closing valuation	$3 900
Depreciation charge for the year	$1 300

Choosing the right method of depreciation

As providing for depreciation is an application of the accruals concept, what should be considered before deciding which method of depreciation is appropriate for a particular non-current asset?

The straight-line method will be most appropriate when the asset is expected to earn revenue for the business evenly over its useful life or where the asset has a clearly defined fixed life. Motor vehicles are frequently depreciated using this method.

The reducing-balance method will be most appropriate when the earning power of the asset is expected to diminish with age. Most items of plant and machinery are depreciated using the reducing-balance method.

The revaluation method will be most appropriate where, due to the nature of the asset, it may be unreasonable to keep detailed records. For example, the assets may individually be of limited value, but taken together their value may be significant. The most common example of assets being depreciated using the revaluation method are loose tools in a building or construction environment.

Accounting entries for depreciation

It is important to remember that the depreciation on a non-current asset is not recorded in the asset account, it is credited to a separate account called provision for depreciation. A business must keep a separate provision for depreciation account for each class of asset. As a result, the amount recorded in the provision for depreciation account will increase each year until such time as the asset is sold.

In the financial statements, the balance on the provision for depreciation account appears under non-current assets on the statement of financial position, reducing the value of the non-current asset to its net book value.

Illustration 6: Journal entry for depreciation

In Illustration 4, the journal entry for depreciation in Year 1 would be:

Details	Dr ($)	Cr ($)
Depreciation (income statement)	5 000	
Provision for depreciation: motor vehicles		5 000

Illustration 7: Ledger entries for depreciation

Kamal purchased a new machine on 1 January 2012 for $18 000. The machine is depreciated at 10 per cent per annum using the reducing-balance method.

Record the purchase of the machine and the depreciation for each of the first three years in Kamal's records.

Step 1: Record the purchase of the machine in the non-current asset account.

Step 2: Calculate the annual depreciation charge for each of the first three years.

Step 3: Record the entries for depreciation in the provision for depreciation account.

Machinery at cost account

2012	Details	$	2012	Details	$
1 Jan	Bank	18 000			

Bank account

2012	Details	$	2012	Details	$
			1 Jan	Machinery	18 000

Provision for depreciation machinery account

2012	Details	$	2012	Details	$
31 Dec	Balance c/d	1 800	31 Dec	Income statement	1 800
2013			**2013**		
31 Dec	Balance c/d	3 420	1 Jan	Balance b/d	1 800
			31 Dec	Income statement	1 620
		3 420			3 420
2014			**2014**		
31 Dec	Balance c/d	4 878	1 Jan	Balance b/d	3 420
			31 Dec	Income statement	1 458
		4 878			4 878
			31 Dec	Balance b/d	4 878

The net book value of the machinery at 31 December 2014 is $18 000 – $4878 = $13 122.

Key term

Accumulated depreciation: the total depreciation charged on an asset to date.

How to record the sale of a non-current asset

When a non-current asset is sold, it is necessary to do the following:

- Open a disposal of non-current assets account.
- Transfer the cost of the asset sold from the debit of the asset cost account to the credit of the asset disposal account.
- Transfer the accumulated depreciation on the asset sold from the credit of the provision for depreciation account to the debit of the asset disposal account.
- Record the amount received for the asset in the credit of the asset disposal account.

It is then necessary to assess whether a profit or a loss has been made on the sale of the asset. If the sale proceeds are more than the net book value of the asset, then a profit has been made; if the sale proceeds are less than the net book value of the asset, a loss has been made.

If the balance on the asset disposal account is a debit, then a loss has been made; if the balance on the asset disposal account is a credit, then a profit has been made.

The resulting balance on the asset disposal account (i.e. the profit or the loss) is then transferred to the income statement at the end of the financial period.

Illustration 8: Ledger entries for sale of a non-current asset

Kamal sold the machine that was purchased in Illustration 7 on 31 December 2014 for $13 000.

Record the sale of the machine in Kamal's records.

Step 1: Open a disposal of non-current assets account.

Step 2: Transfer the cost of the machine sold to the disposal of non-current assets account.

Step 3: Transfer the accumulated depreciation on the machine to the disposal of non-current assets account.

Step 4: Transfer the balance on the disposal of non-current assets account to the income statement.

Machinery at cost account

2012	Details	$	2014	Details	$
1 Jan	Bank	18 000	31 Dec	Disposals account	18 000

Bank account

2014	Details	$	2014	Details	$
31 Dec	Disposals account	13 000			

Provision for depreciation machinery account

2012	Details	$	2012	Details	$
31 Dec	Balance c/d	1 800	31 Dec	Income statement	1 800
2013			**2013**		
31 Dec	Balance c/d	3 420	1 Jan	Balance b/d	1 800
			31 Dec	Income statement	1 620
		3 420			3 420
2014			**2014**		
31 Dec	Disposal account	4 878	1 Jan	Balance b/d	3 420
			31 Dec	Income statement	1 458
		4 878			4 878

Disposal of non-current assets account

2014	Details	$	2014	Details	$
31 Dec	Cost	18 000	31 Dec	Depreciation	4 878
			31 Dec	Bank	13 000
			31 Dec	Income statement	122
		18 000			18 000

The machine was sold at a loss of $18 000 – ($4878 + $13 000) = $122.

Key term

Part exchange: when part of the purchase price of a new non-current asset is satisfied by exchanging an old non-current asset.

Purchase of non-current assets on part-exchange basis

Occasionally, a business may purchase a new non-current asset and part exchange a non-current asset that it wishes to dispose of, as part of the purchase price. The part-exchange value of the asset being disposed of is debited to the non-current asset cost account and credited to the disposal account.

Illustration 9: Purchase of a motor vehicle using part exchange

On 30 November 2014, Yannick purchased a new motor vehicle at a total cost of $35 000. He paid for the vehicle with a cheque of $28 000 and part exchanged his old vehicle for the balance. The old vehicle had originally cost $26 000 and had been depreciated by $20 000.

Record this transaction in Yannick's records.

Step 1: Open the motor vehicles at cost account with an opening balance of $26 000 for the old vehicle.

Step 2: Open the motor vehicles provision for depreciation account with an opening balance of $20 000 for the old vehicle.

Step3: Transfer the cost of the old motor vehicle that is being part exchanged to the disposal of non-current assets account.

Step 4: Transfer the part-exchange value of the old motor vehicle that is being part exchanged to the disposal of non-current assets account (debit motor vehicles at cost account and credit disposal of non-current assets account).

Step 5: Transfer the accumulated depreciation on the old vehicle to the disposal of non-current assets account.

Step 6: Record the amount of the cheque paid in the motor vehicles at cost account and in the bank account.

Step 7: Transfer the balance on the disposal of non-current assets account to the income statement.

Motor vehicle at cost account

2014	Details	$	2014	Details	$
30 Nov	Balance b/d	26 000	30 Nov	Disposal account	26 000
30 Nov	Disposal account	7 000	30 Nov	Balance c/d	35 000
30 Nov	Bank account	28 000			
		35 000			35 000
1 Dec	Balance b/d	35 000			

Motor vehicle provision for depreciation account

2014	Details	$	2014	Details	$
30 Nov	Disposal account	20 000	30 Nov	Balance b/d	20 000

Disposal of non-current assets account

2014	Details	$	2014	Details	$
30 Nov	Motor vehicle cost account	26 000	30 Nov	Motor vehicles depreciation a/c	20 000
30 Nov	Income statement	1 000	30 Nov	Motor vehicles cost account	7 000
		27 000			27 000

Bank account

2014	Details	$	2014	Details	$
			30 Nov	Motor vehicles cost account	28 000

End-of-chapter questions

1 **Depreciation calculation and journal entry**
Kate purchased new machinery for her business at a cost of $69 000. She estimates that the machinery will have a useful economic life of eight years and that it will have a residual value of $9000. Kate uses the straight-line method of depreciation.

a Calculate the annual charge for depreciation of the machinery.

b State the journal entry required to include the depreciation in the financial statements for the first year.

2 **Depreciation calculation and entries in the books of account**
Holly purchased a new motor vehicle for her business for $24 000. Holly depreciates motor vehicles at 25 per cent per annum using the reducing-balance method of depreciation.

a Calculate the annual charge for depreciation of the motor vehicle for each of the first three years of ownership.

b Complete the motor vehicle at cost account to record the purchase of the motor vehicle. Complete the provision for depreciation for the motor vehicle account to show the annual charge for depreciation.

3 **Calculation of profit or loss on disposal**
Patrice has sold machinery for $2000. The machinery was purchased two years ago for $3600. Patrice depreciates his machinery at 20 per cent per annum using the reducing-balance method of depreciation.

Calculate the profit or loss on the sale of the machinery.

4 **Calculation of profit or loss on disposal**
Anais has sold a motor vehicle for $8500. She purchased the motor vehicle three years ago for $18 000 and estimated that it would have a useful economic life of four years. She estimated that the residual value at the end of four years would be $4000. Anais depreciates her motor vehicles using the straight-line method of depreciation.

Calculate the profit or loss on the sale of the motor vehicle.

5 **Depreciation and disposal entries in the books of account**
Rahul purchased machinery on 1 January 2011 for $64 000. He estimated that it would have a useful economic life of five years and that the residual value at the end of that time would be $34 000. Rahul sold the machinery on 31 December 2014 for $41 000. Rahul depreciates machinery using the straight-line method of depreciation. The business's financial year end is 31 December.

Complete the following accounts in Rahul's books of account.

a Machinery at cost account.
b Machinery provision for depreciation account.
c Disposal of non-current assets account.

6 **Depreciation and disposal entries in the books of account**
Bernard purchased a new motor van on 1 April 2011 for $32 000. Motor vans are depreciated at 25 per cent per annum using the reducing-balance method of depreciation. The motor van was sold on 31 March 2014 for $12 000. The business's financial year end is 31 March. Bernard's policy is to provide a full year's depreciation in the year of purchase and the year of sale.

Complete the following accounts in Bernard's books of account.

a Motor van at cost account.
b Motor van provision for depreciation account.
c Disposal of non-current assets account.

7 **Purchase involving part exchange**
Lee purchased a new motor vehicle for $25 000. The cost of the vehicle was settled by the payment of $21 000 by cheque and the part exchange of his old motor vehicle for the balance. The old motor vehicle had originally cost $15 000 and had been depreciated by $12 000 at the date of part exchange.

Complete the following accounts in Lee's books of account.

a Motor vehicle at cost account.
b Motor vehicle provision for depreciation account.
c Disposal of non-current assets account.

8 **Purchase involving part exchange**
A business purchased new plant and machinery for $38 000. The cost was settled by the payment of $34 000 by cheque and the part exchange of two items of plant and machinery for the balance. The two items part exchanged had cost $14 000 and $8000 originally and had net book values of $5000 and $1000.

The following were the balances of the plant and machinery account in the business's books of account at the date of the part exchange:

Cost $160 000, Provision for depreciation $96 000, Net book value $64 000.

Complete the following accounts in the business's books of account.

a Plant and machinery at cost account.
b Plant and machinery provision for depreciation account.
c Disposal of non-current assets account.

Section 1.3: Reconciliation and verification

Key concepts

It is vital that accounting records provide a **true and fair view** of a business's financial position. It follows, therefore, that entries in the books of account must be checked for accuracy. The concept of **duality** is applied in making corrections to errors.

Learning objectives

In this chapter you will learn:

- the purpose of the trial balance
- the presentation of the trial balance
- errors that will be revealed by the trial balance
- errors that will not be revealed by the trial balance
- the presentation of the suspense account
- the effect of errors on the profit for the year
- how to assess the effect of errors on the profit for the year.

1.3.1: Verification: trial balance

Introduction

The trial balance is a listing of all the general ledger balances at a given date. As already discussed, the basic rule of double-entry bookkeeping is that for every debit there must be equal and corresponding credit(s). Provided that the double entry has been accurately carried out, the total of all the debits will equal the total of all the credits and the trial balance will balance.

The purpose of the trial balance

The main purpose of the trial balance is to check the arithmetical accuracy of the accounting records. It is important to remember that because the trial balance totals agree, it does not necessarily mean that all of the accounts are correct. As we shall see later, there is the possibility of errors in the records that do not show up in the trial balance. The trial balance only verifies the arithmetical accuracy of the accounting records.

The secondary purpose of the trial balance is to assist in the preparation of the financial statements. The trial balance acts as a link between the bookkeeping records and the income statement and statement of financial position.

What if the trial balance does not balance?

If the trial totals do not agree, you will need to check for one or more errors. Firstly, check for the following:

- Are the additions in the trial balance itself correct?
- Have all of the general ledger balances been included in the trial balance?
- Have all of the balances been copied onto the trial balance correctly?
- Have all of the balances been entered on the correct side of the trial balance?

Errors that will be revealed by the trial balance

If the trial balance totals do not agree, you know there must be at least one error present. The possible errors are:

- **Transposition error**: This occurs when two figures are transposed. For example, $78 is incorrectly transposed and posted as $87. A clue to a transposition error is that the difference will always divide by 9.
- **Addition error**: This may be on the trial balance itself or perhaps in the general ledger account.

- **Posting error:** This occurs when one side of the transaction is posted to the wrong side of the account.
- **Partial omission error:** This occurs when one side of the transaction has not been posted.
- **Unequal posting error:** This occurs when the debit side of the posting does not equal the credit side.

> **Getting it right**
> Remember, if the difference on a trial balance divides by 9, check whether figures have been transposed.

Errors that will not be revealed by the trial balance

Even if the trial balance totals agree, it does not mean that the financial statements are going to be correct as it is still possible that there may be errors present. These are as follows.

- **Error of omission:** This occurs when both sides of the transaction, both the debit and the credit, have been omitted from the records.
- **Compensating error:** This occurs when errors on the debit side are the same amount as errors on the credit side and they cancel each other out.
- **Error of commission:** This occurs when an amount is posted to an incorrect account of the same class. For example, an invoice for $100 is posted to the account of M. Khan when it should actually have been posted to the account of A. Khan.
- **Error of principle:** This occurs when an amount is posted to an incorrect class of account. For example, an invoice for motor repairs (an expense) is posted in error to the motor vehicles account (an asset).
- **Error of original entry:** This occurs when an error is made transferring an amount from the original source document (for example the invoice) into the book of prime entry (for example the purchases journal).
- **Error of reversal:** This occurs when the account that should have been debited has been credited and the amount that should have been credited has been debited.

Errors and the suspense account

What is a suspense account?

When the trial balance totals do not agree, until such time as the error is identified and corrected, the difference may be entered into a suspense account to temporarily ensure the trial balance totals agree. Remember, the suspense account is only a temporary account until errors are found and corrected.

> **Key term**
> **Suspense account:** a temporary account holding a trial balance difference until the cause is found.

Illustration 1: Suspense account with a known balance

Azzam & Co has extracted a trial balance at 30 November. The total of the debit column is $85 900 while the total of the credit column is $85 990. The difference of $90 has been posted to the debit of a suspense account.

It is discovered that the difference was caused by a posting error. A cheque for purchases of $870 had been posted to the purchases account as $780.

To correct the error, $90 ($870 – $780) must be removed from the suspense account and transferred to the purchases account, which is where it should have been posted.

The journal entry to correct this will be:

Debit	Purchases	$90
Credit	Suspense account	$90

As a result of this transfer, the suspense account now has a zero balance and is no longer required and the purchases account now shows the correct balance.

Getting it right

Remember, the entry in the suspense account will be the opposite of that in the correct nominal account. For example if you wish to increase (credit) sales by $100, the entry in the suspense account will be a debit.

Making entries in the suspense account

Occasionally, more than one error will have affected the balancing of the trial balance.

Illustration 2: Suspense account – balance unknown

Misbah has extracted a trial balance at 30 September. The trial balance totals do not agree and he has now discovered the following errors:

- Due to an addition error, the balance of the purchases account had been overstated by $200.
- The trade receivables total included an amount of $450 that had been written off.
- A discount received of $300 had been incorrectly entered on the debit side of that account.
- A cheque for $500 payable to Yousef had been entered in the account of Wakim in error.

Required

Make any necessary entries in the suspense account to correct these errors and show the opening balance. You are not told the opening balance of the suspense account, so in order to answer this type of question you must take each error in turn to assess the effect on the suspense account.

Step 1: As the balance of the purchases account has been overstated by $200, you need to credit the purchases account to reduce the balance and debit the suspense account.

Step 2: The trade receivables balance has been overstated by $450 as the debt had already been written off. To correct the error, you must credit trade receivables with $450 to reduce the balance and debit the suspense account.

Step 3: A discount received of $300 has been entered on the debit side of that account whereas it should have been entered on the credit side. As a result, the correction has to be for $600, i.e. $300 to cancel the debit entry and a further $300 to place the entry on the credit side of the discount received account. Therefore, the correcting entry should be to debit the suspense account and credit the discounts received account with $600.

Step 4: The final error does not affect the suspense account at all. The cheque for $500 has been correctly posted, just into the wrong person's account. While it must be transferred from Wakim's account into Yousef's account, it will have no effect on the suspense account.

The journal entries to correct the first three errors are as follows.

Details	Dr ($)	Cr ($)
Suspense account	200	
Purchases		200
Suspense account	450	
Trade receivables		450
Suspense account	600	
Discounts received		600

The completed suspense account will be as follows.

Details	Dr ($)	Details	Cr ($)
Purchases	200	Opening balance	1 250
Trade receivables	450		
Discounts received	600		
	1 250		1 250

Assuming that all of the errors have been discovered, the opening balance on the suspense account is $1250 credit, the figure required to balance that account.

Assessing the effect of errors on profit

Errors will often affect the calculation of profit. This could apply to errors that do affect the trial balance or, indeed, errors that do not affect the trial balance.

Examination questions may concentrate on the effect that errors have on the calculation of profit and require the calculation of an amended profit.

Illustration 3: Calculating the amended profit

Dion has prepared a draft income statement for his business for the year ended 30 April 2014 that shows a profit for the year of $36 420. He then discovers the following errors:

- The purchases journal has been overcast by $600.
- A payment of $350 for light and heat has been completely omitted from the accounts.
- The closing inventory has been recorded in the income statement as $27 800. The correct figure for the closing inventory was $26 800.
- A cheque for $480 received from P. Richards had been incorrectly posted to the account of P. Richardson.
- Discount received of $1450 had been charged as an expense in the income statement.
- The cost of repairs to machinery of $1300 had been debited to the plant and machinery account.

Required

Calculate the amended profit for the year. Show clearly whether each adjustment is added to the profit, deducted from the profit or has no effect on the profit for the year.

Corrected profit for the year ended 30 April 2014

	$
Profit for the year as calculated	36 420
1. Purchases overcast	
2. Light and heat omitted	
3. Closing inventory	
4. Error of commission	
5. Discount received	
6. Machinery repairs	

Approach

Take each point in turn and decide firstly whether it has any effect on the profit for the year and secondly what that effect is.

Step 1: The purchases journal has been overcast by $600. As a result, purchases have been overstated by the same amount. Decreasing purchases will increase the profit for the year.

Step 2: Correcting the error of omission of $350 for light and heat will increase expenses and, therefore, reduce the profit for the year.

Step 3: Closing inventory has been overstated by $1000. Since closing inventory is deducted from the cost of sales, too much has been taken away. Correcting this error will increase the cost of sales by $1000 and therefore reduce the profit for the year.

Step 4: Posting an amount to the wrong sales ledger account is an error of commission that must be corrected through the sales ledger. The amount has been processed through the correct ledger, just the incorrect account, so this will have no effect on the profit for the year.

Step 5: Discount received had been charged as an expense in the income statement, but it should be shown as income. Correcting the error will increase the profit for the year by $2900: firstly by $1450 to cancel the expense and, secondly, by a further $1450 to process the income.

Step 6: The cost of repairs to machinery has been debited to the plant and machinery account. Since plant and machinery are non-current assets, correcting the error will increase the expense of repairs by $1300 and therefore reduce the profit for the year.

Correction of all of the above errors will result in the following.

Corrected profit for the year ended 30 April 2014

	$
Profit for the year as calculated	36 420
1. Purchases overcast	600
2. Light and heat omitted	(350)
3. Closing inventory	(1 000)
4. Error of commission	–
5. Discount received	2 900
6. Machinery repairs	(1 300)
	37 270

Getting it right

When answering a question of this nature, ask yourself what effect, if any, the correction of the error will have on expenses or income. If expenses will increase or income will decrease, then the profit for the year will decrease. If expenses will decrease or income will increase, then the profit for the year will increase.

End-of-chapter questions

1 **Debit or credit balance**

Which of the following accounts would normally have a credit balance?

A Discount allowed
B Motor expenses
C Purchases returns
D Sales returns

2 **Debit or credit balance**

Which of the following accounts would normally have a debit balance?

A Capital account
B Discount received
C Drawings
D Returns outwards

3 Types of error

A cheque received from a customer, A. Sobers, has been incorrectly posted to the account of G. Sobers. What type of error is this?

A Compensating error
B Error of commission
C Error of original entry
D Error of principle

4 Types of error

A payment for a new motor vehicle has been incorrectly posted to the motor expenses account. What type of error is this?

A Compensating error
B Error of commission
C Error of original entry
D Error of principle

5 Errors not affecting profit

Which one of the following errors will not affect the profit for the year?

A An accrual for light and heat was omitted.
B An invoice for a new motor van was incorrectly posted to motor expenses.
C An invoice for travel expenses was incorrectly posted to motor expenses.
D Closing inventory had been overstated.

6 Errors affecting profit

Which one of the following errors will affect the profit for the year?

A A cheque received from a credit customer had been completely omitted from the books.
B An invoice for new machinery was incorrectly posted to fixtures and fittings.
C A sales invoice to Peters had been incorrectly posted to Peterson's account.
D A sales credit note had been completely omitted from the records.

7 Errors revealed by the trial balance

State and explain three errors that will be revealed by the trial balance.

8 Errors not revealed by the trial balance

State and explain three errors that will not be revealed by the trial balance.

9 Prepare a trial balance

Yasmin has extracted the following balances from her books of account at 30 November 2014.

	$
Cash at bank	21 536
Capital account	29 493
Drawings	18 600
Inventory at 1 December 2013	21 700
Non-current assets at cost	43 210
Motor and travel expenses	3 748
Property rental (expense)	18 500
Purchases	72 100
Revenue	196 840
Staff wages	14 240
Sundry expenses	7 970
Trade payables	21 804
Trade receivables	26 533

Required

Prepare Yasmin's trial balance at 30 November 2014.

10 Prepare a trial balance

Jane runs a business selling ladies clothes. She has extracted the following balances from her books of account at 31 January 2014.

	$
Bank overdraft	11 276
Capital account	16 983
Carriage outwards	652
Discounts allowed	417
Discounts received	1 058
Drawings	9 420
Inventory at 1 February 2013	22 030
Non-current assets at cost	37 200
Purchases	65 152
Rent payable	12 600
Returns inwards	325
Returns outwards	1 458
Revenue	159 238
Sundry expenses	12 049
Trade payables	10 309
Trade receivables	14 140
Wages and salaries	26 337

Required

Prepare Jane's trial balance at 31 January 2014.

11 Prepare a trial balance

Salim runs a business selling books. He has extracted a trial balance at 30 April 2014 but has not yet included the following balances.

	$
Carriage inwards	1 036
Discounts received	614
Drawings	12 455
Fixtures and fittings at cost	54 180
Returns outwards	1 412
Trade receivables	11 150
Wages and salaries	8 557

Required

Complete the trial balance below. Enter any difference as 'bank balance'.

Details	Dr ($)	Cr ($)
Capital account		54 652
Carriage inwards		
Carriage outwards	894	
Discounts allowed	1 290	
Discounts received		
Drawings		
Fixtures and fittings at cost		
Inventory at 1 May 2013	37 200	
Purchases	83 660	
Rent and rates	12 420	
Returns inwards	1 715	
Returns outwards		
Revenue		186 994
Sundry expenses	18 206	
Trade payables		7 526
Trade receivables		
Wages and salaries		
Bank balance		

12 Prepare a trial balance

Steve runs a business selling beds. He has extracted a trial balance at 31 March 2014 but has not yet included the following balances.

	$
Capital account	65 183
Carriage inwards	1 882
Computer equipment at cost	27 115
Discounts received	1 881
Drawings	18 240
Inventory at 1 April 2013	45 750
Returns inwards	945
Trade payables	16 705

Required

Complete the trial balance below. Enter any difference as 'bank balance'.

Details	Dr ($)	Cr ($)
Capital account		
Carriage inwards		
Carriage outwards	1 270	
Computer equipment at cost		
Discounts allowed	2 538	
Discounts received		
Drawings		
Fixtures and fittings at cost	24 625	
Inventory at 1 April 2013		
Purchases	96 512	
Rent and rates	17 400	
Returns inwards		
Returns outwards		1 216
Revenue		279 546
Sundry expenses	21 043	
Trade payables		
Trade receivables	14 298	
Wages and salaries	52 381	
Bank balance		

13 Suspense account

Harry has extracted a trial balance from his books of account at 30 April 2014. The totals do not agree. He has posted the difference to a suspense account.

Harry has found the following errors:

a The revenue account was undercast by $400.

b A payment for rent of $1250 had been correctly entered in the cash book but had not been posted to the rent account.

c Trade receivables account should have included an amount of $75 that had been written off as an irrecoverable debt.

Required

Complete the suspense account correcting the above errors. Balance the suspense account.

Suspense account	Dr ($)	Cr ($)
Trial balance difference	775	

14 Suspense account

Cherie has extracted a trial balance from her books of account at 31 March 2014. The trial balance totals do not agree and the difference has been posted to a suspense account.

Cherie has found the following errors:

- **a** Purchases account had been overcast by $20.
- **b** A payment of $270 to a supplier, A. Davies, was posted to the account of P. Davies in error.
- **c** Cherie had taken drawings of $800. This was entered correctly in the cash book but had not been posted to the drawings account.
- **d** A receipt of $250 from Bernard, a customer, had been correctly entered in the cash book but had been posted to the wrong side of his account.
- **e** The debit balance on the stationery account of $2378 had been brought down as $2387.

Required

Make any necessary entries in the suspense account to correct these errors and show the opening balance on the suspense account.

15 Calculate the amended profit

Talpur has prepared a draft income statement for his business for the year ended 31 January 2015 that shows a profit for the year of $42 910. He then discovers the following errors:

- **a** The sales journal had been undercast by $350.
- **b** Repairs to a motor vehicle of $520 had been completely omitted from the records.
- **c** Rent paid of $1800 had been incorrectly posted to the light and heat account.
- **d** A purchases credit note of $845 had been completely omitted from the records.
- **e** Closing inventory had been overstated by $500.
- **f** A sales invoice of $2300 for Johns had been incorrectly posted to the account of Johnson.

Required

Calculate the amended profit for the year. Show clearly whether each adjustment increases the profit, decreases the profit or has no effect on the profit.

16 Calculate the amended profit/loss

James has prepared a draft income statement for his business for the year ended 31 December 2014 that shows a profit for the year of $4970. He then discovers the following errors:

- **a** Closing inventory had been understated by $1200.
- **b** Discount received of $240 had been entered on the debit side of that account.
- **c** The debit balance on the insurance account of $734 had been brought down as $743.
- **d** A purchase invoice of $5840 had been completely omitted from the records.
- **e** The rents received account had been overcast by $600.
- **f** An invoice of $125 for cleaning expenses had been incorrectly posted to wages.

Required

Calculate the amended profit or loss for the year. Show clearly whether each adjustment increases the profit, decreases the profit or has no effect on the profit.

17 Calculate the amended profit/loss

Kate has prepared a draft income statement for her business for the year ended 28 February 2015 that shows a loss for the year of $1060. She then discovers the following errors:

- **a** Rent payable of $1250 had been paid in advance. This had not been recorded in the rent account.
- **b** Discounts allowed of $480 had been incorrectly credited to the discounts received account.
- **c** Returns outwards of $280 had been incorrectly credited to the purchases account.
- **d** An item of inventory of $960 had been omitted from the closing inventory.
- **e** Plant and machinery depreciation had been overstated by $750.
- **f** The credit balance on rents received of $1890 had been brought down as $1980.

Required

Calculate the amended profit or loss for the year. Show clearly whether each adjustment increases the loss, decreases the loss or has no effect on the loss for the year.

1.3.2: Verification: bank reconciliation

Learning objectives

In this chapter you will learn:

- the purpose of the bank reconciliation
- the reasons for differences between the cash book balance and the bank statement balance
- how to present a bank reconciliation statement
- how to prepare a bank reconciliation statement
- the importance of the bank reconciliation statement.

Key terms

Unpresented cheque: a cheque drawn and entered in the cash book but not yet presented to the bank for payment.

Uncredited banking: money paid into the bank and entered in the cash book, but not yet appearing on the bank statement. This is also referred to as 'outstanding banking'.

Introduction

The bank reconciliation statement reconciles the balance as per the cash book with the balance as per the bank statement. As a result of this, internal records (the cash book) can be reconciled with external records (the bank statement).

The differences between the two

Unpresented cheques

Unpresented cheques are cheques drawn and recorded in the cash book, but not yet presented to the bank for payment.

Uncredited bankings

Uncredited bankings are cash or cheques that have been received, paid into the bank and recorded in the cash book but have not yet appeared on the bank statement. These are also referred to as 'outstanding bankings'.

Direct debits

A direct debit is authority granted by a business to a third party for fixed or variable payments to be made at the request of that third party.

Standing orders

A standing order is a fixed payment made at regular intervals by the bank on the instructions of the business account holder.

Bank charges and bank interest

Periodically, the bank will make charges for running the bank account and these will be debited to the business's bank account. Similarly, any interest due to either the bank or the bank account holder will be debited or credited to the business's bank account.

Errors

There may be errors in recording transactions in the cash book or errors made by the bank.

The presentation of the bank reconciliation statement

The bank reconciliation may be presented in one of two ways:

- Commencing with the balance as per the cash book and reconciling to the balance as per the bank statement.
- Commencing with the balance as per the bank statement and reconciling to the balance as per the cash book.

Balance as per cash book		XXX
Add: unpresented cheques	XXX	
	XXX	
	XXX	XXX
		XXX
Less: outstanding bankings	XXX	
	XXX	(XXX)
Balance as per bank statement		XXX

Alternative presentation:

Balance as per bank statement		XXX
Less: unpresented cheques	XXX	
	XXX	
	XXX	(XXX)
		XXX
Add: outstanding bankings	XXX	
	XXX	XXX
Balance as per cash book		XXX

How the bank reconciliation statement is prepared

Step 1: Tick all items that appear on the bank statement and also in the cash book.

Step 2: Any items that appear on the bank statement but not in the cash book should be entered in the cash book.

Step 3: Balance the bank columns of the cash book and carry down the closing balance.

Step 4: Start the bank reconciliation statement by entering the closing balance as per the cash book.

Step 5: Any unticked payments in the cash book are unpresented cheques. Enter these onto the bank reconciliation statement.

Step 6: Unticked receipts in the cash book are outstanding bankings. Enter these onto the bank reconciliation statement.

Step 7: Calculate the closing balance on the bank reconciliation statement. This should agree with the balance as per the bank statement.

Getting it right

Remember that the bank statement is a record of the customer's account in the books of the bank. As a result, the entries are the opposite of the entries in the customer's cash book.

- The debit column of the bank statement contains payments out of the bank. The credit column of the bank statement contains receipts into the bank.
- A credit balance on the bank statement indicates a balance of cash in the bank. A debit balance on the bank statement indicates an overdrawn balance.

Illustration 1: Preparing a bank reconciliation statement

Jacob has received his latest bank statement dated 31 May 2014. The statement shows a closing credit balance of $4320. Jacob's cash book shows a closing debit balance of $3875.

Jacob discovers that there are unpresented cheques totalling $845 and an uncredited banking of $400.

Jacob's bank reconciliation statement at 31 May 2014 would be as follows.

	$
Balance as per cash book	3 875
Add: unpresented cheques	845
	4 720
Less: outstanding bankings	(400)
Balance as per bank statement	4 320

Key term

Bank overdraft: a loan where the bank allows the business to withdraw more money from its account than it has in the account.

A bank reconciliation with a bank overdraft

Preparing a bank reconciliation with a bank overdraft is a very similar process to that shown previously, but care must be taken in adding and subtracting amounts.

Illustration 2: Preparing a bank reconciliation with an overdrawn balance

Jacob has now received his bank statement dated 30 June 2014. The statement shows a closing debit balance of $3610. Jacob's cash book shows a closing credit balance of $3475. Jacob discovers that there are unpresented cheques totalling $515 and an uncredited banking of $650.

Jacob's bank reconciliation statement at 30 June 2014 would be as follows.

	$
Balance as per cash book	(3 475)
Add: unpresented cheques	515
	(2 960)
Less: outstanding bankings	(650)
Balance as per bank statement	(3 610)

Updating the cash book and preparing a bank reconciliation statement

Part of the process of preparing a bank reconciliation statement is making sure that transactions that have been entered straight onto the bank statement, such as direct debits and bank charges, are entered into the cash book.

Illustration 3: Update cash book and reconcile

Nadia has received the following bank statement for her business account.

Date	Details	Dr ($)	Cr ($)	Balance ($)
1 May 2014	Balance b/f			2 553.20 Cr
2 May 2014	Cheque 565287	512.25 ✓		2 040.95 Cr
2 May 2014	Credit		455.80 ✓	2 496.75 Cr
3 May 2014	Direct debit: Jacobson	42.65		2 454.10 Cr
3 May 2014	Cheque 565285	108.96 ✓		2 345.14 Cr
4 May 2014	Bank charges	88.42		2 256.72 Cr
4 May 2014	Credit transfer: Sandhu		519.78	2 776.50 Cr
4 May 2014	Cheque 565286	360.31 ✓		2 416.19 Cr
5 May 2014	Credit		1 227.42 ✓	3 643.61 Cr
5 May 2014	Bank interest		135.60	3 779.21 Cr
5 May 2014	Balance c/f			3 779.21 Cr

The following is Nadia's cash book as at 5 May 2014.

Dr			Cash book		Cr
2014	**Details**	**$**	**2014**	**Details**	**$**
1 May	Balance b/d	2 553.20	1 May	565285 Abdul	108.96 ✓
1 May	West Ltd	455.80 ✓	1 May	565286 Booth	360.31 ✓
5 May	Chaudhury	1 227.42 ✓	1 May	565287 Salim	512.25 ✓
			3 May	565288 Mohammad	624.75

Required

Complete Nadia's cash book and prepare a bank reconciliation statement at 5 May 2014.

Step 1: Tick all amounts that appear on both the bank statement and in the cash book.

Step 2: Enter all unticked amounts on the bank statement into the cash book and balance the cash book.

The cash book will now appear as follows.

Dr			Cash book		Cr
2014	**Details**	**$**	**2014**	**Details**	**$**
1 May	Balance b/d	2 553.20	1 May	565285 Abdul	108.96
1 May	West Ltd	455.80	1 May	565286 Booth	360.31
5 May	Chaudhury	1 227.42	1 May	565287 Salim	512.25
4 May	Credit transfer: Sandhu	519.78	3 May	565288 Mohammad	624.75
5 May	Bank interest	135.60	3 May	Direct debit: Jacobson	42.65
			4 May	Bank charges	88.42
			5 May	Balance c/d	3 154.46
		4 891.80			4 891.80
6 May	Balance b/d	3 154.46			

As you will see, the cash book balance still does not reconcile with the bank statement balance. The reason for this is that the cash book payment on 3 May, cheque number 565288, to Mohammad has not been ticked. This is therefore an unpresented cheque.

Nadia's bank reconciliation statement at 5 May 2014 is as follows.

	$
Balance as per cash book	3 154.46
Add: unpresented cheques	624.75
	3 779.21
Less: outstanding bankings	–
Balance as per bank statement	3 779.21

The balance as per the bank statement now agrees with the reconciled balance as per the cash book.

The importance of the bank reconciliation statement

- It identifies any errors in the cash book and enables them to be corrected.
- It identifies any errors on the bank statement enabling them to be investigated and notified to the bank for correction.
- It enables any missing entries in the cash book to be accounted for.
- It identifies any out-of-date cheques (cheques over six months old) and enables them to be cancelled in the cash book.
- It identifies dishonoured cheques and enables action to be taken to recover amounts due.
- It acts as a deterrent to fraud. The bank statement is an independent external record prepared by the bank.

Key term

Dishonoured cheque: a cheque that the bank has refused to pay, usually due to insufficient funds being available.

End-of-chapter questions

1 Unpresented cheques and direct debits

Explain what these terms mean.

a Unpresented cheque

b Direct debit

2 Uncredited bankings and standing orders

Explain what these terms mean.

a Uncredited banking

b Standing order

3 Prepare a bank reconciliation statement

Prepare a bank reconciliation statement from the following information, clearly identifying the balance as per the bank statement.

	$
Debit balance as per cash book	1 898.34
Unpresented cheques	537.44
Uncredited bankings	914.57

4 Prepare a bank reconciliation statement

Prepare a bank reconciliation statement from the following information, clearly identifying the balance as per the bank statement.

	$
Credit balance as per cash book	1 912.86
Unpresented cheques	277.10
Uncredited bankings	463.28

5 Prepare a bank reconciliation statement

Prepare a bank reconciliation statement from the following information, clearly identifying the balance as per the cash book.

	$
Credit balance as per bank statement	259.03
Unpresented cheques	719.55
Uncredited bankings	672.28

6 Prepare a bank reconciliation statement

Prepare a bank reconciliation statement from the following information, clearly identifying the balance as per the cash book.

	$
Debit balance as per bank statement	916.05
Unpresented cheques	161.33
Uncredited bankings	304.85

7 Update the cash book and prepare a bank reconciliation statement

The cash book of Nafisah shows a debit balance of $3849.30 at 6 January 2015. The balance shown on the bank statement at the same date did not agree with the cash book balance.

The following errors have now been found:

a A cheque paid for travel expenses of $456 on 31 December 2014 had been entered in the cash book as $465.

b On 6 January 2015, the bank had debited the bank account with $92.20 for bank charges and credited the account with $125.70 for bank interest. Neither of these amounts had been entered in the cash book.

c The receipts from Marwat and Bharti had not yet appeared on the bank statement.

d The payment to PR Travel had not yet appeared on the bank statement.

Required

Update the cash book below and prepare a bank reconciliation statement at 6 January 2015.

Dr		Cash book			Cr
2015	**Details**	**$**	**2015**	**Details**	**$**
1 Jan	Balance b/d	4 392.16	1 Jan	102380 Salim	816.35
1 Jan	Akram	1 724.15	1 Jan	102381 Khan	492.22
4 Jan	Hussain	844.50	1 Jan	102382 Mahmood	1 552.13
6 Jan	Marwat	1 272.05	1 Jan	102383 Butt	390.44
6 Jan	Bharti	509.49	1 Jan	102384 Mushtaq	1 272.36
			1 Jan	102385 PR Travel	369.55

8 Update the cash book and prepare a bank reconciliation statement

Sadiq has received the following bank statement for his business account.

Date	Details	Dr ($)	Cr ($)	Balance ($)
1 Jan	Balance b/d			2 880.12 Cr
2 Jan	Credit		1 435.60	4 315.72 Cr
2 Jan	Credit transfer James		312.00	4 627.72 Cr
3 Jan	Cheque 271012	730.85		3 896.87 Cr
4 Jan	Cheque 271013	416.56		3 480.31 Cr
4 Jan	Bank charges	132.40		3 347.91 Cr
4 Jan	Bank interest		209.55	3 557.46 Cr
5 Jan	Direct debit Green	110.50		3 446.96 Cr
5 Jan	Credit		702.16	4 149.12 Cr
6 Jan	Cheque 271016	1 138.74		3 010.38 Cr
6 Jan	Balance c/f			3 010.38 Cr

Sadiq's cash book entries as at 6 January were as follows.

Dr		Cash book			Cr
2015	**Details**	**$**	**2015**	**Details**	**$**
1 Jan	Balance b/d	2 880.12	2 Jan	271012 Evans	730.85
1 Jan	Andrews	1 435.60	2 Jan	271013 Swann	416.56
4 Jan	Portland	702.16	2 Jan	271014 Morris	1 552.13
6 Jan	Wright	1 272.05	3 Jan	271015 Friar	390.44
			3 Jan	271016 Dawson	1 138.74

Required

Complete Sadiq's cash book below and prepare a bank reconciliation statement at 6 January 2015.

Learning objectives

In this chapter you will learn:

- the purpose of control accounts
- the presentation of control accounts
- how to produce a sales ledger control account and a purchases ledger control account
- errors that will be revealed by the control account
- errors that will not be revealed by the control account
- the benefits and limitations of control accounts.

Link

There is more about irrecoverable debts written off in AS Level Chapter 1.4.1 Adjustments to financial statements.

1.3.3: Verification: ledger control accounts

The purpose of control accounts

A control account is a master total account and its purpose is to verify the accuracy of entries made in the sales ledger and the purchases ledger.

It is important to remember that control accounts do not form part of the double-entry system: they are effectively memorandum accounts.

When individual postings are made to the suppliers' accounts in the purchases ledger and the customers' accounts in the sales ledger, the totals of these postings may be transferred to the purchases ledger control account and the sales ledger control account respectively.

In this way, the balance on the two control accounts should agree with the totals of all the individual balances in the respective ledgers.

Types of control account and how they are presented

Sales ledger control account

The structure of a typical sales ledger control account is as follows.

Dr		Sales ledger control account			Cr
Date	**Details**	**$**	**Date**	**Details**	**$**
1 May	Balance b/d	72 000	31 May	Bank	127 000
31 May	Sales journal	135 000	31 May	Discounts allowed	1 500
31 May	Returned cheques	200	31 May	Sales returns journal	2 000
			31 May	Contras	1 500
			31 May	Irrecoverable debts written off	1 200
			31 May	Balance c/d	74 000
		207 200			207 200
1 June	Balance b/d	74 200			

If all of the individual balances in the sales ledger were added together they should total $74 200, proving the arithmetical accuracy of the postings. This does not, of course, prove that all entries have been made into the correct accounts.

Guidance notes

- **Balance b/d:** The total of all the individual customer account balances at 1 May.
- **Sales journal:** The total column of the sales journal representing all invoices sent to customers in respect of credit sales.

Getting it right

It is only credit transactions that appear on a control account, not cash transactions.

Key terms

Returned cheque: a cheque received from a customer that has been paid into the bank, but not honoured by the drawer's bank (usually due to lack of funds in the account).

Contra: a bookkeeping entry to set off a balance in the sales ledger with a balance in the purchases ledger when a business both buys from and sells to the same business.

- **Returned cheques:** The total of all cheques returned unpaid by the customers' banks.
- **Balance b/d:** The total of all the individual supplier account balances at 1 May.
- **Bank:** The total of all customer cheques and cash received in respect of credit sales only from the cash book.
- **Discounts allowed:** The total of the discounts allowed column from the debit side of the cash book.
- **Sales returns journal:** The total column of the sales returns journal representing all credit notes sent to credit customers.
- **Contras:** The total of all amounts set off against customers' purchases ledger accounts.
- **Irrecoverable debts written off:** The total of all customer accounts balances that have been written off as irrecoverable debts in the period.
- **Balance c/d:** The total of all individual customer account balances at 31 May.

Note that if any customers' accounts have a credit balance rather than a debit balance, the total of all the credit balances will be shown separately in the control account.

The key to successfully preparing a sales ledger control account is to ask yourself 'what effect does this transaction have on the balance owed by the customer?'

Remember that trade receivables are assets, so the opening balance owed by customers will be a debit in the control account. Selling more goods to the customer will increase the amount owed by customers (therefore debit). Receiving a cheque from the customer or writing off an irrecoverable debt will reduce the amount owed by customers (therefore credit).

Purchases ledger control account

The structure of a typical purchases ledger control account is as follows.

Dr		Purchases ledger control account			Cr
Date	**Details**	**$**	**Date**	**Details**	**$**
31 May	Bank	92 000	1 May	Balance b/d	66 000
31 May	Discounts received	2 000	31 May	Purchases journal	95 000
31 May	Purchases returns journal	1 200	31 May	Cancelled cheques	1 000
31 May	Contras	1 500			
31 May	Balance c/d	65 300			
		162 000			162 000
			1 June	Balance b/d	65 300

Guidance notes

- **Balance b/d:** The total of all the individual supplier account balances at 1 May.
- **Purchases journal:** The total column of the purchases journal representing all invoices received from suppliers in respect of credit purchases.
- **Cancelled cheques:** The total of all cheques drawn in favour of suppliers, but either withdrawn or not accepted by the bank in the period.
- **Bank:** The total of all supplier cheques and cash paid in respect of credit purchases only, from the cash book.
- **Discounts received:** The total of the discounts received column from the credit side of the cash book.
- **Purchases returns journal:** The total column of the purchases returns journal representing all credit notes received from suppliers.
- **Contras:** The total of all amounts set off against suppliers' sales ledger accounts.
- **Balance c/d:** The total of all individual supplier account balances at 31 May.

Key term

Cancelled cheque: a cheque drawn by the business but then either withdrawn or not accepted by the bank before payment is made.

Note that if any suppliers' accounts have a debit balance rather than a credit balance, the total of all the debit balances will be shown separately in the control account.

The key to successfully preparing a purchases ledger control account is to ask yourself 'what effect does this transaction have on the balance owed to suppliers?'

Remember that trade payables are liabilities so the opening balance owed to suppliers will be a credit in the control account. Buying more goods from the supplier will increase the amount owed to suppliers (credit). Paying a cheque to the supplier or receiving a credit note will reduce the amount owed to suppliers (debit).

Illustration 1: Sales ledger control account

The following information has been extracted from the books of Razia for the month of June 2014. Prepare a sales ledger control account for the month of June 2014.

	$
Sales ledger (debit) balances at 1 June 2014	47 247
Total of sales journal for June 2014	68 220
Total of sales returns journal for June 2014	1 036
Cheques received from credit customers	64 490
Discount allowed	1 539
Irrecoverable debts written off	314
Customers' cheques returned	192
Contras to purchases ledger	568

Dr	Sales ledger control account				Cr
Date	Details	$	Date	Details	$
1 June	Balance b/d	47 247	30 June	Bank	64 490
30 June	Sales journal	68 220	30 June	Discounts allowed	1 539
30 June	Returned cheques	192	30 June	Sales returns journal	1 036
			30 June	Contras	568
			30 June	Irrecoverable debts written off	314
			30 June	Balance c/d	47 712
		115 659			115 659
1 July	Balance b/d	47 712			

Errors in control accounts

If the balance on the control account does not agree with the list of balances extracted from the sales ledger or purchases ledger, then an error has been made either in the ledger itself or in the control account.

As is the case with the trial balance, some errors will be identified by the control account, while some will not.

Key terms

Overcast: an addition error where the calculated total is more than the correct total.

Undercast: an addition error where the calculated total is less than the correct total.

Errors that will be revealed by the control account

- **Addition error:** This may be in one of the journals, in the customer or supplier ledger account or in the control account itself. If the correct figure is less than the incorrect figure, it is known as an overcast. If the correct figure is more than the incorrect figure, it is known as an undercast.
- **Transposition error:** This occurs when two figures are transposed (for example $450 has been posted as $540). This could have happened when posting to the individual ledger account or when transferring figures to the control account.
- **Partial omission error:** This occurs when an entry has been made in the individual ledger account but has not been recorded in the control account. An example is when an irrecoverable debt has been written off in the ledger account but omitted from the control account.

Errors that will not be revealed by the control account

- **Error of commission:** If an invoice for M. Khan is incorrectly posted to the account of A. Khan, the error will not be revealed by the control account.
- **Error of omission:** If a transaction is completely omitted from the records, the error will not be revealed by the control account. An example would be the complete omission of an invoice.

- **Error of original entry:** If an error is made transferring an amount from the source document to the book of prime entry, this error will not be revealed by the control account. An example would be if an invoice for $250 was entered in the sales journal as $25 and posted to the ledger as $25.

Illustration 2: Correcting errors in a control account

Waqar has prepared the following sales ledger control account for November 2014.

Dr		Sales ledger control account			Cr
Date	**Details**	**$**	**Date**	**Details**	**$**
1 Nov	Balance b/d	43 566	30 Nov	Bank	67 525
30 Nov	Sales journal	62 108	30 Nov	Sales returns journal	570
30 Nov	Returned cheques	612	30 Nov	Balance c/d	38 191
		106 286			106 286
1 Dec	Balance b/d	38 191			

The following errors have now been found.

- The sales journal has been overcast by $300.
- An irrecoverable debt of $410 has been written off the customer's ledger account but has not been entered in the control account.
- A contra for $845 has been processed through the purchases ledger and the sales ledger but has been omitted from the control account.
- An invoice for $2210 to K. Choudhury has been incorrectly posted to the account of C. Choudhury.
- Discounts allowed of $1329 have been omitted from the control account.

Required

Prepare a corrected sales ledger control account for November 2014. Each error must be taken in turn to decide what effect, if any, it has on the sales ledger control account.

Step 1: The sales journal has been overcast by $300 so the $300 must be deducted from the sales journal total of $62 108, leaving a total of $61 808.

Step 2: The irrecoverable debt has been written off in the ledger, so $410 should be entered on the credit side of the control account to reduce the value of trade receivables.

Step 3: The contra has been omitted from the control account, so $845 should be entered on the credit side of the control account to reduce the value of trade receivables.

Step 4: The invoice that has been posted to the wrong person's account does not affect the control account. An adjustment should be made in the sales ledger to transfer the amount into the correct person's account.

Step 5: Discounts allowed have been omitted from the control account, so $1329 should be entered on the credit side of the control account to reduce the value of trade receivables.

The corrected sales ledger control account should now appear as follows.

Dr		Sales ledger control account			Cr
Date	**Details**	**$**	**Date**	**Details**	**$**
1 Nov	Balance b/d	43 566	30 Nov	Bank	67 525
30 Nov	Sales journal	61 808	30 Nov	Sales returns journal	570
30 Nov	Returned cheques	612	30 Nov	Irrecoverable debts written off	410
			30 Nov	Contra	845
			30 Nov	Discounts allowed	1329
			30 Nov	Balance c/d	35 307
		105 986			105 986
1 Dec	Balance b/d	35 307			

The benefits and limitations of control accounts

Benefits

The main benefits of preparing control accounts are:

- **Accuracy:** A balanced control account verifies the arithmetical accuracy of the ledger.
- **Prevention of fraud:** Control accounts should be maintained by a member of staff other than the ledger clerk responsible for a particular ledger. Separating this duty acts as a deterrent to fraud and makes the discovery of fraud much easier.
- **Management information:** Managers are able to view the total amount owing from customers or owing to suppliers at any time without totalling all of the individual accounts.
- **Preparation of financial accounts:** Having a control account enables financial statements to be drawn up faster.

Limitations

As detailed above, the limitation of control accounts is that they only verify the arithmetical accuracy of the ledgers, that does not mean there are no other errors.

End-of-chapter questions

1 **Calculate closing sales ledger balance**
Renee has extracted the following information from her books of account for March 2015.

	$
Sales ledger balances at 1 March 2015	33 672
Cheques received from credit customers	29 224
Discounts allowed	1 536
Credit sales for the month	26 905
Irrecoverable debt written off	115
Sales returns for the month	560

What is the figure for closing sales ledger balances at 31 March 2015?

A $29 142
B $29 372
C $30 492
D $33 780

2 **Calculate closing purchases ledger balance**
Garry has extracted the following information from his books of account at 31 January 2015.

	$
Purchases ledger balances at 1 January 2015	58 116
Cheques paid to credit suppliers	32 043
Discounts received	1 353
Credit purchases for the month	31 427
Cancelled cheque	413
Purchases returns for the month	348

What is the figure for closing purchases ledger balances at 31 January 2015?

A $56 082
B $56 212
C $56 908
D $58 918

3 **Errors and the control account**
Control accounts are used to help identify errors in the bookkeeping system. How does this happen?

4 **Errors not identified by the control account**
State two types of error that would not be identified by preparing a sales ledger control account.

5 **Errors identified by the control account**
State two types of error that would be identified by preparing a sales ledger control account.

6 **Prepare a sales ledger control account**
Prepare a sales ledger control account from the following information for January 2015.

	$
Sales ledger balances (debit) at 1 January 2015	42 356
Total of sales journal for January 2015	68 902
Total of sales returns journal for January 2015	1 442
Cheques received from credit customers	62 837
Discounts allowed	840
Irrecoverable debts written off	225
Contra to purchases ledger	532

7 **Prepare a purchases ledger control account**
Prepare a purchases ledger control account from the following information for January 2015.

	$
Purchases ledger balances (credit) at 1 January 2015	33 549
Total of purchases journal for January 2015	52 807
Total of purchases returns journal for January 2015	1 163
Cheques paid to credit suppliers	54 280
Discounts received	714
Cheque paid to a supplier cancelled	1 250
Contra to sales ledger	393

8 **Prepare a sales ledger control account with corrections**
Dean has prepared the following sales ledger control account for December 2014.

Dr		Sales ledger control account			Cr
Date	Details	$	Date	Details	$
1 Dec	Balance b/d	37 185	31 Dec	Bank	72 313
31 Dec	Sales journal	75 605	31 Dec	Sales returns journal	814
31 Dec	Returned cheque	112	31 Dec	Balance c/d	39 775
		112 902			112 902
1 Jan	Balance b/d	39 775			

The following errors and omissions have been found:

a Irrecoverable debts of $882 had been written off customers' ledger accounts in December.
b The sales returns book had been undercast by $100.
c Discounts of $634 were allowed to customers during December.
d The customer's returned cheque was for $121, not $112.
e The opening balance brought down should have been $37 485.
f A cheque for $475 received from A. Patel had been incorrectly posted to the account of P. Patel.

Required

Prepare a correct sales ledger control account for December 2014.

9 **Prepare a sales ledger control account and a purchases ledger control account**

The following information has been extracted from the books of Smith Ltd for the month of February 2015.

	$
Purchases ledger balances (credit) at 1 February 2015	56 407
Sales ledger balances (debit) at 1 February 2015	83 359
Irrecoverable debt written off customer account	185
Cheques paid to credit suppliers	52 131
Cheques received from credit customers	85 460
Contra (debit balance in sales ledger set off against purchases ledger)	249
Customer cheque dishonoured	1 036
Discounts allowed	1 360
Discounts received	858
Cheque paid to a supplier cancelled	264
Total cash purchases for February 2015	880
Total cash sales for February 2015	2 367
Total of purchases journal for February 2015	62 042
Total of purchases returns journal for February 2015	1 553
Total of sales journal for February 2015	99 842
Total of sales returns journal for February 2015	2 460

Required

Prepare a sales ledger control account and a purchases ledger control account at 28 February 2015.

Note:

You are asked to prepare both a sales ledger control account and a purchases ledger control account in this question.

Step 1: Decide which entries should be part of the sales ledger control account and which entries should be part of the purchases ledger control account.

Step 2: Decide if there are any entries that should not appear in either control account.

Section 1.4: Preparation of financial statements

Key concepts

All of the key concepts apply to the preparation of financial statements:

- **True and fair view:** to ensure that interested parties are not misled by the statements.
- **Duality:** as the financial statements are connected to the everyday accounting records by means of double entry.
- **Consistency:** to ensure that the users of financial statements can make valid comparisons of a business's performance using those statements.
- **Business entity:** to ensure that the financial statements record the business's affairs quite separately to those of the owner(s).
- **Money measurement:** as the financial statements can only record information that has a monetary value.

1.4.2A: Sole traders: preparation of accounts

Learning objectives

In this chapter you will learn:

- to prepare an income statement from a trial balance
- to prepare a statement of financial position from a trial balance.

Preparing financial statements

The starting point for preparing the financial statements is the trial balance. The income statement calculates the profit or loss for the year. The statement of financial position details the financial state of the business at a given date.

The income statement

Breakdown

The income statement is effectively split into two separate sections:

- The first section (the trading account) starts with sales and deducts the cost of sales to produce the gross profit.
- The second section deducts all of the expenses of running the business to produce the profit for the year.

Calculating the gross profit

The first part of the income statement will appear as follows.

	$	$	$
Revenue			XXX
Less: returns inwards			(XXX)
			XXX
Cost of sales			
Opening inventory		XXX	
Purchases	XXX		
Less: returns outwards	(XXX)		
	XXX		
Add: carriage inwards	XXX	XXX	
		XXX	
Less: closing inventory		(XXX)	(XXX)
Gross profit			XXX

Key terms

Cost of sales: total purchases plus carriage inwards adjusted for opening and closing inventory

Carriage inwards: the cost of carriage charged to the business by the supplier.

Gross profit: the difference between sales and the cost of sales.

Adjustments for inventory

The value of inventory appearing in the trial balance is always the opening inventory from the beginning of the accounting period. The value of closing inventory will appear as additional information after the trial balance.

As we saw earlier, to maintain the principles of double entry, every debit must have an equal credit. The adjustment for closing inventory, therefore, is:

- **Debit**: Current assets in the statement of financial position (inventory is an asset that the business holds at the end of the accounting period).
- **Credit**: Income statement (inventory still held by the business reduces the cost of goods sold).

Calculating the profit for the year

Once the gross profit for the year has been calculated, the final profit for the year can be calculated by adding any other income to that gross profit (discounts received, rents received, etc.) before deducting all of the expenses of running the business during the year.

If the income is greater than the expenses, there is a profit for the year. If the expenses are greater than the income, there is a loss for the year.

The final part of the income statement will appear as follows.

Gross profit		XXX
Add: discounts received		XXX
		XXX
Less: expenses	XXX	
Carriage outwards	XXX	
Discounts allowed	XXX	
Motor expenses	XXX	
Office expenses	XXX	
Sundry expenses	XXX	
Depreciation	XXX	(XXX)
Profit for the year		XXX

Key terms

Carriage outwards: the cost of carriage for goods sold by the business.

Profit for the year: the final profit after deducting all expenses of running the business.

The statement of financial position

The statement of financial position is a statement prepared at the end of the accounting period, summarising the capital account of the owner of the business and detailing the assets and liabilities representing that capital investment at the statement of financial position date.

It is very important to analyse assets and liabilities under the correct subheadings.

- **Non-current assets:** These are intended to be held for more than one financial year. They are not purchased with the intention of being resold; the intention is that they should be held to generate profits for the business.
- **Current assets:** These are cash or assets that will be turned into cash within the next 12 months. Current assets should be listed in reverse order of liquidity on the statement of financial position, starting with the least liquid (inventory) and finishing with the most liquid (cash).
- **Current liabilities**: These are amounts owed by the business in the short term that will be paid back within the next 12 months.
- **Net current assets/liabilities (working capital)**: This is the difference between current assets and current liabilities.
- **Non-current liabilities:** These are amounts owed by the business that are not due to be paid within the next 12 months (bank loans, mortgages, etc.).
- **Capital account:** This is the amount of the investment in the business made by the owner. It is increased by the profit for the year and reduced by drawings.

Key terms

Order of liquidity: the order in which current assets are able to be turned into cash, starting with the least liquid.

Net current assets/liabilities (working capital): the difference between current assets and current liabilities.

Capital account: the amount of the investment in the business by the owner.

The closing balance on the capital account will always be equal to and represented by the excess of assets over liabilities. This conforms to the accounting equation discussed in AS Level Chapter 1.1.1 An introduction to double-entry bookkeeping:

$$\text{Assets} = \text{Capital} + \text{Liabilities}$$

A typical statement of financial position for a sole trader will be presented as follows.

	$	$
Non-current assets		
Motor vehicles at cost	XXX	
Less: accumulated depreciation	(XXX)	XXX
Current assets		
Inventory	XXX	
Trade receivables	XXX	
Other receivables (prepayments etc.)	XXX	
Bank account	XXX	
Cash account	XXX	XXX
Total assets		XXX
Capital account		
Balance brought forward	XXX	
Add: profit for the year	XXX	
	XXX	
Deduct: drawings	(XXX)	XXX
Non-current liabilities		
(Loans repayable after more than 12 months)		XXX
Current liabilities		
Trade payables	XXX	
Other payables (accruals etc.)	XXX	XXX
Total capital and liabilities		XXX

The following is how the statement of financial position used to be shown. You may see this format in the course of your studies but it should *not* be used in your examination. You should always use the format shown above.

	$	$
Non-current assets		
Motor vehicles at cost	XXX	
Less: accumulated depreciation	XXX	XXX
Current assets		
Inventory	XXX	
Trade receivables	XXX	
Other receivables (prepayments etc.)	XXX	
Bank account	XXX	
Cash account	XXX	
	XXX	
Less: Current liabilities		
Trade payables	XXX	
Other payables (accruals etc.)	XXX	
	XXX	
Net current assets (working capital)		XXX
Non-current liabilities		
(Loans repayable after more than 12 months)		(XXX)
		XXX
Capital account		
Balance brought forward		XXX
Add: profit for the year		XXX
		XXX
Deduct: drawings		(XXX)
		XXX

Preparing financial statements from a trial balance

When preparing the financial statements from a trial balance, the first step is to decide which items go in the income statement and which go in the statement of financial position.

Items of a revenue nature, such as sales, purchases (adjusted for opening and closing inventory) and expenses, belong in the income statement. Assets, liabilities, capital and drawings belong in the statement of financial position.

In the following illustration, a note has been made next to each amount showing which part of the financial statements each item should appear in.

Illustration 1: Preparing financial statements

A. Raina
Trial balance at 31 January 2015

Account	Dr ($)	Cr ($)	Working
Bank account	5 128		Statement of financial position
Capital account		33 643	Statement of financial position
Carriage inwards	612		Income statement
Carriage outwards	1 103		Income statement
Depreciation	4 000		Income statement
Discounts allowed	1 280		Income statement
Discounts received		994	Income statement
Drawings	18 432		Statement of financial position
Inventory at 1 February 2014	26 110		Income statement
Light and heat	2 734		Income statement
Motor expenses	2 681		Income statement
Motor vehicles at cost	18 450		Statement of financial position
Motor vehicles – provision for depreciation		8 000	Statement of financial position
Office expenses	6 033		Income statement
Printing and stationery	876		Income statement
Property rental	16 440		Income statement
Purchases	76 551		Income statement
Repairs and renewals	1 058		Income statement
Returns inwards	764		Income statement
Returns outwards		1 219	Income statement
Revenue		163 140	Income statement
Sundry expenses	2 456		Income statement
Trade payables		16 535	Statement of financial position
Trade receivables	26 780		Statement of financial position
Wages	12 043		Income statement
Totals	**223 531**	**223 531**	

Additional information:
Closing inventory was valued at $27 400.

Required
Prepare an income statement for the year ended 31 January 2015 and a statement of financial position at that date.

Remember that the income statement is prepared in two parts. Revenue, purchases, returns, inventory and carriage inwards form part of the gross profit calculation. The remaining items form part of the profit for the year calculation.

A. Raina
Income statement for the year ended 31 January 2015

	$	$	$
Revenue			163 140
Less: returns inwards			(764)
			162 376
Cost of sales			
Opening inventory		26 110	
Purchases	76 551		
Less: returns outwards	(1 219)		
	75 332		
Add: carriage inwards	612	75 944	
		102 054	
Less: closing inventory		(27 400)	(74 654)
Gross profit			87 722
Add: discounts received			994
			88 716
Less: expenses			
Carriage outwards		1 103	
Discounts allowed		1 280	
Light and heat		2 734	
Motor expenses		2 681	
Office expenses		6 033	
Printing and stationery		876	
Property rental		16 440	
Repairs and renewals		1 058	
Sundry expenses		2 456	
Depreciation		4 000	
Wages		12 043	50 704
Profit for the year			38 012

A. Raina Statement of financial position at 31 January 2015		
	$	$
Non-current assets		
Motor vehicles at cost		18 450
Less: provision for depreciation		(8 000)
		10 450
Current assets		
Inventory	27 400	
Trade receivables	26 780	
Bank	5 128	
		59 308
Total assets		69 758
Financed by		
Capital account		
Balance at 1 February 2014		33 643
Add: profit for the year		38 012
		71 655
Less: drawings		(18 432)
		53 223
Current liabilities		
Trade payables		16 535
Total capital and liabilities		69 758

End-of-chapter questions

1 Income statement or statement of financial position

Which one of the following items will appear on the income statement for the year ended 31 March 2015?

A Bank balance
B Computers at cost
C Drawings
D Returns inwards

2 Income statement or statement of financial position

Which one of the following items will appear on the statement of financial position at 31 March 2015?

A Carriage inwards
B Inventory at 1 April 2014
C Machinery repairs
D Trade payables

3 Prepare an income statement to calculate gross profit

The following is an extract from Richard's trial balance at 28 February 2015.

	Dr ($)	Cr ($)
Carriage inwards	914	
Discounts allowed	1 502	
Inventory at 1 March 2014	23 240	
Purchases	89 378	
Returns inwards	1 602	
Returns outwards		1 006
Revenue		165 442

Additional information:

Inventory at 28 February 2015 was valued at $24 100.

Required

Prepare an extract from Richard's income statement for the year ended 28 February 2015 to show the gross profit for the year.

4 Prepare an income statement to calculate gross profit

Harris has extracted the following balances from his books of account at 31 March 2015.

	$
Advertising	2 449
Carriage inwards	1 280
Carriage outwards	1 032
Discounts allowed	1 416
Discounts received	2 827
Inventory at 1 April 2014	34 500
Motor expenses	3 460
Purchases	92 345
Repairs and maintenance	2 724
Returns inwards	1 750
Returns outwards	1 240
Revenue	204 308
Sundry expenses	5 534
Wages	67 237

Additional information:

Inventory at 31 March 2015 was valued at $32 100.

Required

Prepare an extract from Harris's income statement for the year ended 31 March 2015 to show the gross profit for the year.

5 Prepare an income statement

David has extracted the following balances from his books of account at 31 December 2014.

	$
Carriage inwards	815
Carriage outwards	1 227
Cleaning expenses	548
Depreciation	1 500
Discounts allowed	1 282
Discounts received	1 901
Inventory at 1 January 2014	52 800
Motor expenses	5 350
Motor vehicles at cost	43 800
Motor vehicles – provision for depreciation	3 000
Purchases	127 385
Rent and rates	27 557
Returns inwards	1 557
Returns outwards	904
Revenue	289 446
Stationery and advertising	1 559
Sundry expenses	7 715
Trade payables	15 207
Trade receivables	22 319
Wages and salaries	42 161

Additional information:

Inventory at 31 December 2014 was valued at $54 350.

Required

Prepare an income statement for David for the year ended 31 December 2014.

6 Prepare an income statement and statement of financial position

Kumar has extracted the following balances from his books of account at 31 January 2015.

	$
Bank overdraft	5 640
Bank loan (repayable 2021)	9 700
Capital account	55 346
Carriage outwards	1 508
Depreciation	2 000
Discounts allowed	1 216
Drawings	28 824
Inventory 1 February 2014	36 700
Motor expenses	6 143
Motor vehicles at cost	34 200
Motor vehicles – provision for depreciation	6 840
Plant and machinery at cost	52 734
Plant and machinery – provision for depreciation	12 200
Printing and stationery	5 526
Property rental (expense)	28 500
Property repairs	1 112
Purchases	74 454
Returns inwards	2 060
Returns outwards	1 593
Revenue	273 582
Sundry expenses	3 319
Trade payables	7 241
Trade receivables	16 737
Wages	77 109

Additional information:

Inventory at 31 January 2015 was valued at $32 650.

Required

Prepare an income statement for Kumar for the year ended 31 March 2015 and a statement of financial position at that date.

7 Prepare an income statement and statement of financial position

Majid has extracted the following balances from his books of account at 30 November 2014.

	$
Balance at bank	14 225
Bank loan (repayable 2020)	5 880
Capital account	70 833
Carriage outwards	2 154
Computers at cost	8 420
Depreciation	3 200
Discounts allowed	1 508
Drawings	34 116
Inventory 1 December 2013	42 300
Motor expenses	5 527
Motor vehicles at cost	18 610
Motor vehicles – provision for depreciation	4 000
Plant and machinery at cost	42 745
Plant and machinery – provision for depreciation	8 200
Purchases	92 330
Rent and rates	12 850
Repairs and maintenance	2 207
Returns inwards	2 060
Returns outwards	1 593
Revenue	235 358
Stationery and advertising	4 852
Sundry expenses	2 920
Trade payables	15 352
Trade receivables	27 075
Wages and salaries	24 117

Additional information:

Inventory at 30 November 2014 was valued at $39 240.

Required

Prepare an income statement for Majid for the year ended 30 November 2014 and a statement of financial position at that date.

Learning objectives:

In this chapter you will learn:

- how to process adjustments to the financial statements in respect of: accruals, prepayments, irrecoverable debts and provision for doubtful debts.

1.4.1: Adjustments to financial statements

The types of adjustment that may need to be made

The financial statements produced so far have all been produced directly from the closing balances from the general ledger, which are found in the trial balance. However, because accounts are drawn up on a cash basis, adjustments will need to be made for accruals and prepayments. There will also be times when irrecoverable debts need to be written off or a provision for doubtful debts needs to be made.

These adjustments will ensure that the financial statements show a true profit for the year and also show a true and fair view of the state of the business at the date of the statement of financial position.

Accrual of expenses

An accrual is a liability for services that have already been used, but that have not yet been invoiced to the business.

To account for accruals in the financial statements:

- increase the expense charge from the trial balance by the amount of the accrual
- include the amount of the accrual in the statement of financial position as a current liability.

Accruals are referred to as 'other payables.' on a statement of financial position.

Key term

Other payables: a current liability arising from expense accruals and income received in advance.

Illustration 1: Adjustment for accruals

Elaine has produced the following trial balance at 31 March 2015.

	Dr ($)	Cr ($)
Electricity charges	2 742	

Elaine has used $250 of electricity that has not yet been billed.

If the additional electricity that has been used was ignored, the total cost of electricity for the year would be understated and the financial statements would not be accurate.

We therefore have to provide an accrual for the unbilled amount of $250. This will increase the charge for electricity by $250 and make provision for an accrual (a current liability) on the statement of financial position.

Since this accrual will be carried forward into the next accounting period until the electricity bill is received, the ledger account will appear as follows.

Dr	Electricity charges				Cr
Date	Details	$	Date	Details	$
31 March	Balance b/d	2 742	31 March	Income statement	2 992
31 March	Balance c/d	250			
		2 992			2 992
			1 April	Balance b/d	250

Prepayment of expenses

Key term

Prepayment: an expense relating to the next accounting period that has been paid in advance.

A prepayment arises when an expense is paid in advance and all or part of the payment relates to the next accounting period.

To account for prepayments in the financial statements:

- reduce the expense charge from the trial balance by the amount of the prepayment
- include the amount of the prepayment in the statement of financial position as a current asset.

Prepayments are recorded as 'other receivables' on a statement of financial position.

Illustration 2: Adjustment for prepayments

Elaine has produced the following trial balance at 31 March 2015.

	Dr ($)	Cr ($)
Property rental	33 600	

Elaine paid $7200 for three months' rent on 1 March 2015. At 31 March 2015, two months' rent has been paid in advance. The amount of the prepayment is therefore:

($7200 ÷ 3 months) × 2 months = $4800.

If the prepaid property rental was ignored, the total cost of property rental for the year would be overstated and the financial statements would not be accurate.

We therefore have to provide a prepayment for the two months paid in advance of $4800. This will reduce the charge for property rental by $4800 and make provision for a prepayment (a current asset) on the statement of financial position.

Since this prepayment will be carried forward into the next accounting period, the ledger account will appear as follows.

Dr	Property rental				Cr
Date	Details	$	Date	Details	$
31 March	Balance b/d	33 600	31 March	Balance c/d	4 800
			31 March	Income statement	28 800
		33 600			33 600
1 April	Balance b/d	4 800			

Irrecoverable debts written off

As was explained in Chapter 1.3.3, there will be times when a trade receivable is unable to pay what is owing to the business. The trade receivable may dispute the amount owing or simply not be in a position to pay the debt. These debts are then written off the customer's account in the sales ledger. This write-off is an expense to the business and must, therefore, be charged to the income statement so that the financial statements reflect the correct position.

If we fail to write off a debt that is not going to be recovered, the effect will be twofold:

- The profit will be overstated by the amount of the irrecoverable debt.
- The statement of financial position will not reflect the correct position: trade receivables will be overstated by the amount of the irrecoverable debt.

To account for irrecoverable debts in the financial statements:

- Increase expenses in the income statement by the amount of the irrecoverable debt written off.
- Reduce trade receivables by the amount of the irrecoverable debt written off.

Illustration 3: Adjustment for irrecoverable debt written off

One of Elaine's customers is bankrupt and owes Elaine $600. As Elaine knows that she will not receive this amount, she wishes to write it off as an irrecoverable debt.

The entry will be as follows.

Include irrecoverable debts written off as cost in the income statement	$600
Reduce trade receivables in the statement of financial position	$600

The effect of this entry will be to show the correct profit for the year and also the correct state of the business in the statement of financial position.

Provision for doubtful debts

Businesses have a duty to present a true and fair view of the position of the business. As such, on the grounds of prudence, if the business anticipates that all of its debts will not be paid, some provision should be made for this in the financial statements. If this were not the case, trade receivables could be overstated.

The provision will usually be based on the past experiences of the business and will usually be represented as a percentage of the total receivables.

To account for a provision for doubtful debts in the financial statements:

- Increase expenses in the income statement by the amount of the increase in the provision for doubtful debts.
- Show the provision for doubtful debts on the statement of financial position as a reduction in the amount of trade receivables.

Illustration 4: Adjustment for provision for doubtful debts

Elaine is of the view that based on past experience, 2 per cent of her trade receivables may never pay the amounts due to her, and so she wishes to make a provision for doubtful debts of 2 per cent of her total trade receivables.

Elaine's total trade receivables at 31 March 2015 are $42 400. The provision for doubtful debts will be $42 400 × 2% = $848.

Include provision for doubtful debts as a cost in the income statement	$848
Reduce trade receivables in the statement of financial position by the amount of the provision for doubtful debts	$848

The statement of financial position entry after this adjustment will be as follows.

Current assets	$	$
Trade receivables	42 400	
Less: provision for doubtful debts	848	41 552

To increase a provision for doubtful debts

Once a provision for doubtful debts has been made, it is important that this is reviewed at subsequent period ends. When the provision for doubtful debts is to be increased the following entry should be made:

Debit Increase in provision for doubtful debts (income statement).

Credit Provision for doubtful debts (statement of financial position).

Illustration 5: Increase in provision for doubtful debts

Elaine already has a provision for doubtful debts in her accounts for $848. If her trade receivables for the following year increase to $53 700 and she wishes to retain a 2 per cent provision, the following action should be taken.

Trade receivables total $53 700. The total provision should therefore be $53 700 × 2% = $1074. Since Elaine already has a provision of $848, the increase required in the provision is $1074 – $848 = $226.

The accounting entry required is:

Debit	Increase in provision for doubtful debts (income statement)	$226	
Credit	Provision for doubtful debts (statement of financial position)		$226

In this way, the total provision is adjusted to the required figure of $1074.

To decrease a provision for doubtful debts

If the provision for doubtful debts needs to be decreased, the reverse of the above entry should be processed:

Debit Provision for doubtful debts (statement of financial position).

Credit Decrease in provision for doubtful debts (income statement).

Illustration 6: Decrease in provision for doubtful debts

Elaine now has a provision for doubtful debts in her accounts for $1074. If her trade receivables for the following year decrease to $48 600 and she wishes to retain a 2 per cent provision, the following action should be taken.

Trade receivables total $48 600. The total provision should therefore be $48 600 × 2% = $972. Elaine now has a provision of $1074, so the decrease in the provision will be $1074 – $972 = $102.

The accounting entry required is:

Debit	Provision for doubtful debts (statement of financial position)		$102
Credit	Decrease in provision for doubtful debts (income statement)	$102	

The provision is therefore reduced to the required figure of $972 and the decrease in the provision will be added to the gross profit in the income statement.

End-of-chapter questions

1 **Calculate charge involving a payment in advance**
Rent of $35 300 has been paid during the year; $3300 has been paid in advance. What is the amount of rent to appear in the income statement for the year?

A $3300
B $32 000
C $35 300
D $38 600

2 **Calculate charge involving an accrual**
Wages of $83 630 have been paid during the year. Accrued wages at the year end were $1200. What is the value of wages to appear in the income statement for the year?

A $1200
B $82 430
C $83 630
D $84 830

3 Journal entries to account for accruals

Ahmed has extracted a trial balance from his books of account at 30 November 2014 that includes the following entries.

	Dr ($)	Cr ($)
Rent and rates	14 120	
Electricity charges	4 113	

You are told that one month's rent of $1100 is still outstanding and that Ahmed has used $630 of electricity that has not yet been billed to him.

Required

Detail the journal entries to include these amounts in the financial statements.

4 Journal entries to account for payments in advance

James has extracted a trial balance from his books of account at 31 December 2014 that includes the following entries.

	Dr ($)	Cr ($)
Property rental	2 000	
Hotel expenses	3 550	

You are told that the property rental shown in the trial balance is for a period of 14 months, so two months are paid in advance. Included in the hotel expenses is an amount of $400 that relates to expenses for the following accounting period.

Required

Detail the journal entries to include these amounts in the financial statements.

5 Journal entries to account for provision for doubtful debts

Simon is preparing his financial statements for the year ended 31 December 2014. The trade receivables total $84 350 and he wishes to make a provision for doubtful debts of 3 per cent.

Required

Detail the journal entry to include the provision in the financial statements.

6 Prepare an income statement and statement of financial position

Daniel has extracted the following trial balance from the books of account at 31 March 2015.

	Dr ($)	Cr ($)
Bank account		2 274
Bank loan account (repayable 2019)		8 400
Capital account		88 022
Carriage inwards	1 280	
Carriage outwards	2 345	
Discount allowed	1 076	
Discount received		1 452
Drawings	31 180	
Inventory at 1 April 2014	10 250	
Light and heat	3 109	
Motor expenses	6 846	
Motor vehicles		
– cost at 1 April 2014	54 600	
– provision for depreciation at 1 April 2014		23 888
Office expenses	8 309	
Professional fees	2 400	
Property rental	33 600	
Purchases	109 690	
Returns inwards	1 251	
Returns outwards		1 036
Revenue		212 520
Stationery and advertising	2 884	
Trade payables		9 354
Trade receivables	35 870	
Wages	42 256	
Totals	346 946	346 946

Additional information:

- Provide for depreciation for the year on motor vehicles at 25 per cent per annum using the reducing-balance method.
- Property rental is paid at $2400 per month. Two months have been paid in advance.
- Daniel has used $520 worth of light and heat that has not yet been billed to him.
- Daniel wishes to create a provision for doubtful debts amounting to 2 per cent of trade receivables at 31 March 2015.
- Inventory at 31 March 2015 was valued at $12 440.

Required

Prepare an income statement for the year ended 31 March 2015 and a statement of financial position at that date taking account of the additional information.

7 Prepare an income statement and statement of financial position

Adele has extracted the following balances from her books of account at 31 December 2014.

	$
Advertising	5 143
Bank overdraft	12 027
Bank loan account (repayable 2021)	18 370
Capital account	90 283
Carriage inwards	914
Discount allowed	2 194
Drawings	52 496
Inventory at 1 January 2014	47 200
Legal expenses	2 310
Light and heat	12 952
Motor expenses	11 380
Motor vehicles	
– cost at 1 January 2014	64 200
– provision for depreciation at 1 January 2014	21 680
Office expenses	12 275
Plant and equipment	
– cost at 1 January 2014	18 240
– provision for depreciation at 1 January 2014	6 480
Printing and stationery	1 849
Property rental	48 000
Provision for doubtful debts at 1 January 2014	1 025
Purchases	137 604
Returns inwards	1 459
Returns outwards	1 337
Revenue	354 440
Trade payables	15 807
Trade receivables	42 300
Wages	55 817
Workshop expenses	5 116

Additional information:

- Inventory at 31 December 2014 was valued at $43 450.
- Advertising costs of $580 relate to an advertising campaign to be launched in 2015.
- Property rental currently costs $3200 per month. Two months have been paid in advance.
- Light and heat worth $600 has been used but not yet invoiced.
- Depreciation for the year should be provided on the following basis.

Motor vehicles	25% per annum using the reducing-balance method
Plant and equipment	10% per annum using the straight-line method

- Adjust the provision for doubtful debts to 3 per cent of trade receivables at 31 December 2014.

Required

Prepare an income statement for the year ended 31 December 2014 and a statement of financial position at that date taking account of the additional information.

1.4.2B: Final accounts from incomplete records

Learning objectives

In this chapter you will learn:

- what incomplete records are
- how to prepare a statement of affairs from incomplete records
- how to calculate a profit or loss from information about changes in capital and drawings
- how to prepare an income statement, including how to calculate the missing figures required
- how to prepare a statement of financial position, including how to calculate the missing figures required.

Key term

Incomplete records: these are where an organisation (usually a small business or a not-for-profit organisation) has anything less than a full double-entry accounting system.

Getting it right

It is important to realise that, whichever method is used, a business will have the same income statement and statement of financial position, regardless of whether it maintains its books by single entry or double entry.

What are incomplete records?

A sole trader or partnership often does not have the time or the expertise to keep a double-entry bookkeeping system. However, preparing accounting statements is essential for tax purposes and for making effective management decisions. How can the owner of a business know how well the business is performing if profits cannot be calculated due to inadequate bookkeeping records?

Many businesses, especially sole traders, will not even have a cash book and will do little more than collect all their receipts and bank statements, which they then pass to an accountant at the end of the year. Many other small businesses operate a single-entry system around a cash book, which records all their payments and receipts in one location. A record may be kept elsewhere of any trade receivables or trade payables, but this will not be part of a double-entry system.

Although operating a single-entry system may suit the owners of many small businesses, it will still be important to keep track of drawings, and the owner will need to know how much capital expenditure takes place so that depreciation can be calculated. Adjustments also need to be made for prepaid and accrued income and expenses.

A single-entry system of bookkeeping can be simply converted to a double-entry system by recording in a new ledger the 'other entries' for those already made in the cash book. For example, a credit entry for the payment of wages within the cash book only needs a wages account within the general ledger where the corresponding debit entry can be made.

Both single-entry and almost non-existent records are referred to as incomplete records.

Preparing a statement of affairs

In order to calculate the capital of a business at the beginning of the financial year, a statement of affairs is drawn up. This statement lists all the assets and liabilities of a business on a certain date so that the accounting equation can be used:

Assets = Capital + Liabilities

Illustration 1: Preparing a statement of affairs from incomplete records

B. Khan owns a clothes shop. He has been so busy that he has not kept complete accounting records.

He has the following information available at 30 April 2014.

	$
Vehicles	12 000
Machinery	6 000
Trade payables	11 500
Trade receivables	14 000
Bank overdraft	3 500
Prepayments	2 500
Accruals	4 000
Short-term loan	8 500
Inventory	16 500

Here is B. Khan's statement of affairs at 30 April 2014, which has been produced by dividing the available information into assets and liabilities, with the capital calculated at the end.

	$	$
Assets		
Vehicles		12 000
Machinery		6 000
Trade receivables		14 000
Prepayments		2 500
Inventory		16 500
Total assets		51 000
Liabilities		
Trade payables	11 500	
Accruals	4 000	
Bank overdraft	3 500	
Short-term bank loan	8 500	
Total liabilities		(27 500)
Capital		23 500

Calculating the profit or loss for the year

Drawings

If you calculate the capital for both the beginning of the financial year and the end of it, the difference will be the profit (or loss) for the year once any drawings have been taken into account.

	$
Capital at end of financial year	XX
Less capital at start of financial year	(XX)
Plus drawings for the year	XX
Profit for the year	XX

When calculating profit (or loss) using this method, it is important to notice that any drawings are added. This is because drawings represent the removal of profit by the owner, and you are trying to establish what the profit was before the drawings occurred.

The following illustration shows that a profit can be calculated without producing an income statement, although it is not normally considered accurate enough for management or taxation purposes.

Illustration 2: Using a statement of affairs to calculate profit or loss

B. Khan wishes to know what his profit or loss amount is for the year ended 30 April 2014. He withdrew $6200 as drawings during the year, and capital at 1 May 2013 was $19 100.

The profit for the year would therefore be:

	$
Capital at 30 April 2014	23 500
Less capital at 1 May 2013	(19 100)
Plus drawings for the year	6 200
Profit for the year	10 600

By deducting the opening capital from the closing capital, it can be established that capital has increased by $4400. This change in capital is after the owner removed some of the profit in the form of drawings. Add back the drawings to find the profit for the year of $10 600.

Additional capital

Sometimes the owner of a business will introduce extra amounts of capital during the year. This usually takes the form of extra money from private funds being placed in the business's bank account, but the owner could also introduce additional assets of other kinds from private resources. When extra capital is introduced, the profit (or loss) calculation has an additional stage.

	$
Capital at end of financial year	XX
Less capital at start of financial year	(XX)
Plus drawings for the year	XX
Less additional capital introduced during the year	(XX)
Profit for the year	XX

Note: Additional capital is deducted when calculating the profit. This is because otherwise the amount of profit would include an amount that had nothing to do with the trading activities of the business.

Missing information and the income statement

Often a business will have very few records except for a cash book and receipts for purchases and sales. Cash sales and cash purchases can easily be calculated by adding up these receipts, but it is more difficult to calculate credit sales and purchases. In this instance, more workings have to be completed before a set of accounts can be produced.

Credit sales

The following information is the minimum required to calculate credit sales for a period:

- opening receivables at the start of the period
- closing receivables at the end of the period
- cash received during the period from credit customers.

A sales ledger control account is used to calculate the amount of credit sales for a period.

Illustration 3: Calculating credit sales for a period using a sales ledger control account

Dara owns a small factory that makes leather goods. She has been so busy that she has not had time to maintain full accounting records. She is able to provide the following information for the year ended 31 March 2015.

	$
Amounts due from trade receivables at 1 April 2014	12 100
Amounts due from trade receivables at 31 March 2015	11 400
Cash received from credit customers during the year	142 500

The sales ledger control account based upon this information is:

Dr	Sales ledger control account		Cr
Opening balance of receivables	12 100	Cash received from credit customers	142 500
Credit sales for period	141 800	Closing balance of receivables c/d	11 400
	153 900		153 900
Balance b/d	11 400		

The process for calculating the missing credit sales figure is to follow the normal procedure for preparing a trade receivables account or sales ledger control account up to the point of finding the missing figure.

The sales ledger control account can also include discounts allowed, irrecoverable debt and returns inwards accounts.

Getting it right

Remember that the amount recorded for sales in the income statement will include both the credit and cash sales for the period.

Credit purchases

The following information is the minimum required to calculate credit purchases for a period:

- opening trade payables at the start of the period
- closing trade payables at the end of the period
- cash paid during the period to credit suppliers.

A purchases ledger control account is used to calculate the amount of credit purchases for a period.

Illustration 4: Calculating a missing figure for credit purchases for a period

Dara is able to provide the following information for the year ended 31 March 2015.

	$
Amounts due to trade payables at 1 April 2014	9 900
Amounts due to trade payables at 31 March 2015	10 600
Cash paid to credit suppliers during the year	121 800

Here is the purchases ledger control account based on this information.

Dr		Purchases ledger control account	Cr
Payments to credit suppliers	121 800	Opening balance of payables	9 900
Closing balance of payables c/d	10 600	Credit purchases for period	122 500
	132 400		132 400
		Balance b/d	10 600

The process for calculating the missing credit purchases figure is to follow the normal procedure for preparing a trade payables account or purchases ledger control account up to the point of finding the missing figure.

The purchase ledger control account can also include discounts received and returns outwards.

Getting it right

Remember that the amount recorded for purchases in the income statement will include both the credit and cash purchases for the period.

Missing figures within the financial statements

Mark-up and margin

Many businesses use a simple mark-up on cost to calculate their selling prices so that they know that they are achieving a profit margin on everything they sell:

$$\text{Cost} + (\text{Mark-up} \times \text{Cost}) = \text{Selling price}$$

For example, Dara has calculated that each leather bag costs $24 to make. She has a policy to mark up all products by 25 per cent to achieve a selling price, so each leather bag sells for $24 + ($24 × 0.25) = $24 + $6 = $30

Dara's profit on each leather bag is $30 – $24 = $6 (the amount of the mark-up).

The gross profit margin is worked out as follows:

$$\text{Gross profit margin} = \frac{\text{Profit}}{\text{Selling price}} \times 100$$

$$\text{Dara's gross profit margin is } \frac{\$6}{\$30} \times 100 = 20\%$$

Key term

Mark-up: the percentage added to the cost to calculate the selling price, namely the amount of gross profit in cents added to each $1 of cost of sales.

Link

There is more about mark-up and gross profit margin in AS Level Chapter 1.5.1 Analysis and communication of accounting information to stakeholders.

Illustration 5: Using mark-up to calculate a missing revenue figure

Owen is a sole trader who sells computer games at a mark-up on cost of 50 per cent. His year end was 31 December 2014. At that date the following information was available.

	$
Inventory at 1 January 2014	8 600
Inventory at 31 December 2014	9 200
Purchases for the year	46 000

The revenue can be calculated by preparing a summarised trading section of an income statement.

Owen		
Summarised income statement (trading section) for the year ended 31 December 2014		
	$	**$**
Revenue		?
Opening inventory	8 600	
Purchases	46 000	
	54 600	
Closing inventory	(9 200)	
Cost of sales		(45 400)
Gross profit (must be 50% of cost of sales)		22 700

The revenue must be the cost of sales + the gross profit: $68 100.

Illustration 6: Using gross profit margin to calculate a missing cost of sales figure

Dwight has a marketing business. His sales for the year ended 30 June 2014 were $162 800. He has a gross profit margin of 20 per cent.

His cost of sales can, therefore, be calculated using the following arithmetical process:

Sales × Margin = Gross profit

Gross profit = $162 800 × 0.2
= $32 560

Sales – Gross profit = Cost of sales

Cost of sales = $162 800 – $32 560
= $130 240

> **Key term**
>
> **Inventory turnover**: the amount of times a year that inventory needs to be replaced.

> **Link**
>
> There is more about the rate of inventory turnover in AS Level Chapter 1.1.1 An introduction to double-entry bookkeeping.

Rate of inventory turnover

A business can also use the rate of inventory turnover to calculate sales and purchases.

The rate of inventory turnover is calculated as: $\dfrac{\text{Cost of sales}}{\text{Average inventory}}$

where average inventory is $\dfrac{(\text{Opening inventory} + \text{Closing inventory})}{2}$

Illustration 7: Using rate of inventory turnover to complete the trading section of an income statement

Jacqueline runs a shop selling a range of confectionery items. The following information is available for the year ended 31 May 2014.

	$
Inventory at 1 June 2013	4 200
Inventory at 31 May 2014	3 800
Revenue for the year	192 000
Rate of inventory turnover is 40 times	

With these few facts, it is still possible to prepare a complete trading section. The process is to create the trading section with the known figures, then to calculate the cost of sales and thus the purchases.

Jacqueline
Summarised income statement (trading section)
for the year ended 31 May 2014

	$	$
Revenue		192 000
Opening inventory	4 200	
Purchases (see note 2)	159 600	
	163 800	
Closing inventory	(3 800)	
Cost of sales (see note 1)		(160 000)
Gross profit		32 000

Note 1: The cost of sales figure is found using the business's rate of inventory turnover:

$$\text{Cost of sales} \div \frac{(4200 + 3800)}{2} = 40$$

$$\text{Cost of sales} \div 4000 = 40$$

Therefore, the cost of sales is $160 000.

Note 2: Once the cost of sales figure is known, the purchases figure can be found.

- If the cost of sales is $160 000 and the closing inventory is $3800, then the subtotal immediately before closing inventory must be $163 800.
- If the subtotal of opening inventory ($4200) and purchases is $163 800, the figure for purchases must be $159 600.

Missing information and the statement of financial position

When a business does not keep complete accounting records or records are lost, there are several techniques available to find the missing information.

Missing cash

If a business believes that cash has been stolen, the easiest way to calculate the missing amount is to prepare a cash account by recording receipts on the debit side and payments on the credit side. The balance on the cash account can then be compared to the actual amount of cash held and the missing figure will give the amount of stolen cash.

This technique could also be used if the owner of a business had not kept a careful record of cash drawings during a period.

Illustration 8: Calculating missing or stolen cash

Penelope runs a busy grocer's shop. She often does not have time to bank the money at the end of the day and instead keeps it in her coat pocket at the shop until the money is then banked with the next day's proceeds. At the beginning of October, she took on a new part-time assistant. Unfortunately, she has begun to suspect that money is being taken out of her coat pocket before she can bank it. The following information is available for the month ended 31 October 2014.

	$
Opening cash balance at 1 October	260
Closing cash balance at 31 October	140
Cash takings for the month	4 120
Cash banked during the month	2 150
Expenses paid in cash	2 000

Here is the cash account based on this information.

Dr			Cash				Cr
			$				$
Oct	1	Opening balance	260	Oct		Cash banked	2 150
		Cash takings	4 120			Cash expenses	2 000
						Missing/stolen cash	90
					31	Closing balance c/d	140
			4 380				4 380
Nov	1	Balance b/d	140				

The process to calculate the amount of missing cash is to complete a cash account as normal. The opening and closing balances should be entered. If the sides do not balance and there is a difference on the credit side ($90 in this example), then it is due to cash going missing, perhaps lost or stolen.

Trade receivables

The sales ledger control account can be used to calculate the closing trade receivables figure if the sales ledger is not complete or is lost. This figure will then be recorded as a current asset within the statement of financial position.

The following information is the minimum required to calculate the closing trade receivables:

- opening trade receivables at the start of the period
- credit sales for the period
- cash received during the period from credit customers.

Illustration 9: Calculating a missing figure for closing trade receivables

Simeon owns a small souvenir shop on the beachfront in a coastal town. He does not know how to maintain full accounting records. He is able to provide the following information for the year ended 31 August 2014.

	$
Amounts due from trade receivables at 1 September 2013	7 100
Cash received from credit customers during the year	42 500
Discounts allowed during the year	1 750
Irrecoverable debt written off	125
Returns inwards during the year	7 125
Credit sales during the year	52 300

Here is the sales ledger control account showing the missing figure for the closing balance of trade receivables.

Dr		Sales ledger control account					Cr
			$				$
Sept	1	Opening balance	7 100	Aug	31	Cash received	42 500
Aug	31	Credit sales	52 300			Discounts allowed	1 750
						Irrecoverable debts written off	125
						Returns inwards	7 125
						Closing receivables c/d	7 900
			59 400				59 400
Sept	1	Balance b/d	7 900				

The process for calculating the closing trade receivables figure is to complete the sales ledger control account as normal. The difference between the two sides is the balance brought down for the missing trade receivables ($7900).

Trade payables

The same approach can be used to calculate the missing closing trade payables balance, but this time the purchases ledger control account is used. The balance calculated is then recorded as a current liability in the statement of financial position.

Capital figures

If the opening capital figure is missing, it can be calculated using the statement of affairs. In the following illustration, the opening capital is, therefore, calculated as total assets less total liabilities on 1 December 2013.

Illustration 10: Calculating opening capital using the statement of affairs

Rakesh is a builder's merchant. He has been so busy that he has not had time to keep proper financial records but he is able to provide the following information for the year ended 30 November 2014.

Dr		Summarised bank account					Cr
			$				$
Dec	1	Opening balance	4 300			Trade payables	112 600
		Trade receivables	128 100			Expenses	28 000
		Loan	20 000			Loan repayment	400
						Purchase of new vehicle	4 000
				Nov	30	Closing balance c/d	7 400
			152 400				152 400
Dec	1	Balance b/d	7 400				

The list of other balances at 1 December 2013 and 30 November 2014 is:

	1 Dec 2013	30 Nov 2014
	$	$
Premises at NBV	160 000	152 000
Vehicles at NBV	14 000	16 200
Inventory	58 300	58 800
Trade receivables	29 500	26 000
Prepaid electricity	2 700	3 000
Accrued wages	5 900	4 100
Loan	10 200	28 300
Trade payables	23 400	24 500

Here is the statement of affairs at 1 December 2013 based on this information.

Rakesh		
Statement of affairs at 1 December 2013		
Assets		
Premises	160 000	
Vehicles	14 000	
Inventory	58 300	
Trade receivables	29 500	
Prepaid electricity	2 700	
Bank	4 300	
		268 800
Liabilities		
Accrued wages	5 900	
Loan	10 200	
Trade payables	23 400	
		(39 500)
Opening capital		229 300

Getting it right

One of the common errors that students make when calculating the opening capital using the statement of affairs is to omit the bank balance. This will often not be shown among the list of assets and liabilities, but must still be included in the calculation.

Depreciation

It is likely that direct information about depreciation charges will not be available when dealing with incomplete records. In the illustration above, the non-current assets have changed their net book value. This has either arisen through a sale or a purchase of a non-current asset, or depreciation.

Illustration 11: Calculating a depreciation charge for the year

Rakesh has the following information for non-current assets.

	At 1 Dec 2013	At 30 Nov 2014
	$	$
Premises	160 000	152 000
Vehicles – NBV	14 000	16 200

During the year, there was the purchase of a van for $4000. There were no disposals of non-current assets.

Getting it right

The question may not state that there has been a purchase of a non-current asset other than in the cash book where the cost of the new asset is recorded. Do not, of course, record this cost as an expense (it is capital expenditure); use it in the calculation of the depreciation charge for the year to be entered in the income statement.

The calculation of the depreciation charge for the non-current assets is as follows.

	Premises	Vehicles
	$	$
NBV at 1 December 2013	160 000	14 000
Plus cost of purchases of non-current assets	–	4 000
Less NBV at 30 November 2014	(152 000)	(16 200)
Depreciation charge for the year	8 000	1 800

Incomplete expenses

Often the information about expenses is contained within the bank account and the list of balances used to produce a statement of affairs. The amount within the bank account is purely the amount paid during the year and not the amount that is recorded for the expense within the income statement. This is because it does not take account of the amounts prepaid or accrued at the year end, and possibly also at the beginning of the year. The closing balances will be stated on the statement of financial position but, along with the cash paid and the opening balances, can be used to calculate the amount to be recorded within the income statement.

Illustration 12: Calculating expenses to be charged to the income statement

In the previous example, Rakesh had the following information available for electricity.

	At 1 Dec 2013	At 30 Nov 2014
	$	$
Prepaid expenses	2 700	3 000

During the year, Rakesh had paid $18 000 for his electricity.

The calculation for electricity charges for the year is as follows.

	$
Cash paid for electricity	18 000
Less electricity prepaid at 30 November 2014	(3 000)
Plus electricity prepaid at 1 December 2013	2 700
Electricity charges for income statement	17 700

Rakesh also had the following information available for wages.

	At 1 Dec 2013	At 30 Nov 2014
	$	$
Accrued wages	5 900	4 100

During the year, Rakesh had paid $10 000 for his wages.

The calculation for wages for the year is as follows.

	$
Cash paid for wages	10 000
plus wages accrued at 30 November 2014	4 100
less wages accrued at 1 December 2013	(5 900)
Wages expense for income statement	8 200

The table below is useful to remember this process.

	At start of year	At end of year
Prepaid expenses	+	–
Accrued expenses	–	+

End-of-chapter questions

1 Calculating the opening capital

Bert does not keep complete records. He can, however, provide the balances of his assets and liabilities at 1 April 2015.

	$
Premises – cost	300 000
Machinery – cost	46 200
Vehicles – cost	16 600
Trade payables	62 400
Trade receivables	19 000
Bank	6 500
Other receivables	12 800
Other payables	11 200
Loan	60 000
Inventory	66 000
Premises – provision for depreciation	42 000
Machinery – provision for depreciation	19 400
Vehicles – provision for depreciation	2 000

Calculate the capital at 1 April 2015 by producing a statement of affairs.

2 Calculating profit/loss for the year

Doreen has capital of $64 500 on 1 January 2014. At 31 December 2014, the closing capital for the year was $51 000 after an additional investment by Doreen of $10 000. During the year, Doreen has also taken $7000 cash from the business for her own use and taken home materials worth $5000 that had been purchased for business use.

What is the value of profit or loss for the year?

3 Calculating profit or loss for the year

P. Ramish is a car mechanic operating from a small garage. He has been so busy that he has not had time to keep proper financial records.

He is able to provide the following information.

	1 Jun 2013	31 May 2014
	$	$
Premises	260 000	225 200
Vehicles	24 000	20 400
Machinery	24 100	26 600
Inventory	38 300	28 800
Trade receivables	39 500	36 000
Other receivables	3 700	4 000
Other payables	6 900	5 100
Loan	11 200	29 300
Trade payables	13 400	44 500
Bank overdraft		5 700
Cash at bank	10 600	

P. Ramish also notes that during the year his drawings totalled $30 800, but that he did invest an extra $20 000 of capital during the year.

Prepare statement of affairs at 1 June 2013 and 31 May 2014 to calculate the opening and closing capital. Calculate the profit or loss for the year ended 31 May 2014.

4 **Calculating profit or loss for the year**
Robin does not keep a full set of accounting records but is able to provide the following information.

	1 Jan 2014	31 Dec 2014
	$	$
Premises	160 000	155 000
Vehicles	14 000	12 000
Machinery	4 500	6 000
Inventory	18 000	16 500
Trade receivables	19 000	14 000
Other receivables	1 200	2 500
Other payables	4 000	3 000
Loan	9 300	7 600
Trade payables	11 500	12 900
Bank overdraft	3 500	
Bank balance		8 500

During the year, Robin's drawings totalled $32 000. However, on 1 August 2014, Robin transferred $15 500 from his private account to the business's bank account.

Prepare statements of affairs at 1 January and 31 December 2014 to calculate the opening and closing capitals. Calculate the profit or loss for the year ended 31 December 2014.

5 **The statement of affairs**
To what is a statement of affairs similar?

A A bank reconciliation statement
B A bank statement
C A cash book
D A statement of financial position

6 **Business information**
A retailer has never kept books of account, but has asked you to tell her how much her business is worth. In order to give her the information, what should you provide?

A A cash book
B A statement of financial position
C An income and expenditure account
D An income statement

7 **Calculating the business profit**
Miquel was able to produce the following information concerning his business.

	$
Capital 1 January 2014	100 000
Capital 31 December 2014	170 000
Drawings during year	34 000

What was the business's profit for the year?

A $36 000
B $70 000
C $104 000
D $236 000

8 **Calculating the business profit**
The following information is available for a retailer.

1 January 2014	Capital $150 000
31 December 2014	Capital $290 000

Drawings for the year amounted to $20 000. The retailer paid $70 000 into his business's bank account during the year as additional capital.

What was the profit for the year?

A $50 000
B $90 000
C $120 000
D $230 000

9 **Calculating the business profit**
Bobby is in business as a market stallholder. He has not kept full accounting records.

His statement of affairs at 1 April 2014 showed his capital was $86 000; his statement of affairs at 31 March 2015, however, showed his capital was $106 000. During the year his drawings were $28 000 and he introduced $24 000 as extra capital.

What was his profit for the year?

A $16 000
B $20 000
C $24 000
D $28 000

10 **Calculating credit sales using a sales ledger control account**
Mary-Anne owns a shop that sells jewellery. She does not know how to keep full accounting records, but is able to provide the following information for the year ended 31 December 2014.

	$
Amounts due from trade receivables at 1 January 2014	16 200
Amounts due from trade receivables at 31 December 2014	15 900
Cash received from credit customers during the year	81 400
Discounts allowed during the year	1 600
Irrecoverable debts	200
Returns inwards during the year	3 700
Amounts due to trade payables at 1 January 2014	28 100
Amounts due to trade payables at 31 December 2014	23 500
Cash paid to credit suppliers during the year	254 300
Discounts received during the year	13 400
Returns outwards during the year	42 200

Calculate the value of credit sales and credit purchases for the year.

11 Preparing the trading section of an income statement using rate of inventory turnover

Faye is a florist. The following information is available for the year ended 30 November 2014.

	$
Inventory at 1 December 2013	3 200
Inventory at 30 November 2014	4 800
Revenue for the year	150 000
Rate of inventory turnover is 30 times	

Prepare the trading section of an income statement for the year ended 30 November 2014.

12 Using mark-up to calculate revenue and calculating the amount of missing cash

Alvin runs a music store but does not keep a full set of accounting records. He marks up his goods by 50 per cent. All sales are on a credit basis and all takings are banked at the end of the day. Alvin believes that some cash was stolen from the till on 31 December 2014 when he was unable to get to the bank because it closed early.

He can provide the following details.

	$
Cash banked	165 100
Inventory at 1 January 2014	24 500
Inventory at 31 December 2014	23 100
Purchases	111 600
Trade receivables at 1 January 2014	23 200
Trade receivables at 31 December 2014	21 400

Calculate the amount of cash missing from the till using the following procedure:

- **a** Prepare the trading section of the income statement for the year ended 31 December 2014 to find the credit sales for the year.
- **b** Prepare the total receivables account to find the money received from receivables.
- **c** Compare your answer in b to the cash banked to give the figure for missing cash.

13 Using gross profit margin to calculate cost of sales and calculating the amount of stolen cash

Seeta runs a food store but does not keep a full set of accounting records. Her gross profit margin is 20 per cent. All takings are banked at the end of the day. Seeta believes that some cash was stolen from the till by her assistant on 31 October 2014 when Seeta was at the wholesalers.

She can provide the following details.

	$
Cash paid to suppliers	42 200
Inventory at 1 November 2013	14 600
Inventory at 31 October 2014	13 400
Sales	50 600
Trade payables at 1 November 2013	9 200
Trade payables at 31 October 2014	8 400

Calculate the amount of cash missing from the till by using the following procedure:

- **a** Prepare the total payables account to find credit purchases for the year.
- **b** Prepare the trading section of the income statement for the year ended 31 October 2014 to find the correct figure for total sales.
- **c** Compare this sales figure with the figure given in the question to calculate the missing cash.

14 Preparing the income statement and statement of financial position from incomplete records

K.D. Green has a shop selling carpets. He has been so busy that he has not had time to keep proper financial records, but he is able to provide the following information for the year ended 30 June 2014.

Dr		Summarised bank account					Cr
			$				$
July	1	Opening balance	2 300			Trade payables	32 400
		Trade receivables	48 100			Rent	6 000
		Loan	5 000			Loan repayment	500
						Advertising costs	2 000
						Purchase of new vehicle	6 000
						Drawings	8 300
				June	30	Closing balance c/d	200
			55 400				55 400
July	1	Balance b/d	200				

List of other balances at 1 July 2013 and 30 June 2014:

	1 July 2013	30 June 2014
	$	$
Premises at NBV	64 000	54 000
Vehicles at NBV	8 000	12 200
Inventory	8 500	8 800
Trade receivables	7 500	6 200
Prepaid rent	500	400
Accrued advertising costs	200	100
Loan	5 500	10 000
Trade payables	3 900	4 700

a Calculate the sales for the year ended 30 June 2014.

b Calculate the purchases for the year ended 30 June 2014.

c Calculate the amount to be included in the income statement for the year for rent and advertising costs.

d Prepare an income statement for the year ended 30 June 2014 and a statement of financial position at that date.

15 Preparing the income statement and statement of financial position from incomplete records

Maurice has two gift shops. He does not keep full accounting records but is able to provide the following information for the year ended 31 March 2015.

The list of balances at 1 April 2014 and 31 March 2015 is:

	1 Apr 2014	31 Mar 2015
	$	$
Premises at NBV	264 000	260 000
Vehicles at NBV	28 000	22 200
Fixtures and fittings at NBV	36 100	38 200
Inventory	10 500	9 700
Trade receivables	11 300	8 400
Prepaid insurance	300	700
Accrued business wages	400	200
Bank balance	2 100	–
Bank overdraft	–	3 600
Trade payables	6 200	5 900

Maurice has provided the following additional information.

Dr		Summarised bank account					Cr
			$			$	
Apr	1	Opening balance	2 100			Trade payables	132 800
		Trade receivables	168 500			Business expenses	21 300
		Cash banked	32 100			Wages	45 000
Mar	31	Balance c/d	3 600			Purchase of new fixtures	6 000
						Insurance	1 200
			206 300				206 300
				Apr	1	Balance b/d	3 600

The cash takings for the year were $41 850. Before paying this money into the bank, Maurice used some of the cash received to pay for casual staff wages of $400 per month and personal drawings of $300 per month. Unfortunately, Maurice believes that some cash has been stolen during March but does not know how much.

a Prepare the cash account to calculate the amount of stolen cash.

b Prepare the sales ledger control account to calculate the amount of credit sales during the year.

c Prepare the purchases ledger control account to calculate the amount of purchases during the year.

d Prepare an income statement for the year ended 31 March 2015 and a statement of financial position at that date.

16 Calculating business purchases

A sole trader did not keep proper books of account. The following information is available about 2014.

	$
Payments to suppliers of goods	175 000
Cash discounts received	15 000
Purchases returns	9 000
Opening trade payables	25 000
Closing trade payables	49 000

What were the business's purchases for 2014?

A $166 000
B $205 000
C $214 000
D $223 000

17 Calculating business credit sales

The following information has been supplied by the owner of a business who has not kept full accounting records.

	$
Trade receivables, 1 June 2013	33 400
Trade receivables, 31 May 2014	31 600
Discounts allowed	2 100
Receipts from trade receivables	74 300

What were the business's credit sales for the year ended 31 May 2014?

A $70 400
B $74 000
C $74 600
D $78 200

18 Calculating purchases

The following information is available about a business's transactions with its suppliers of goods for resale.

	$
Owed to suppliers at beginning of year	14 000
Owed to suppliers at end of year	17 000
Paid to suppliers during the year	38 000
Discounts received from suppliers during the year	1 000
Cash purchases	5 000

What was the total value of purchases of goods for resale during the year?

A $34 000
B $40 000
C $41 000
D $47 000

19 Calculating profit

A business started trading on 1 June 2013. The owner has not kept full accounting records. The following information is available for the year ended 31 May 2014.

Dr	Cash book (summary)		Cr
	$		$
Sales	157 000	Purchases	103 000
		Expenses	28 000
		Balance	26 000
	157 000		157 000

All purchases are made for cash and there was no inventory. At 31 May 2014, trade receivables totalled $7000; expenses due but unpaid amounted to $3000.

What was the profit for the year ended 31 May 2014?

A $26 000
B $30 000
C $33 000
D $36 000

20 Calculating trade receivables

A retailer has not maintained full accounting records. The following information was available for the business's financial year ended on 30 April 2014.

	$
Cheques received from trade receivables	83 400
Discounts allowed	900
Trade receivables, 30 April 2014	4 800
Credit sales for the year	85 000

What was the value of the business's trade receivables at 1 May 2013?

A $3200
B $4100
C $6200
D $7300

21 The method of calculating credit sales

The owner of a business that has limited financial records is trying to calculate the business's credit sales for the year.

Which of the following items should be ignored when making this calculation?

A Irrecoverable debts
B Cheques received from credit customers that were dishonoured
C Discounts allowed
D Returns outwards

22 Calculating stolen inventory

The owner of a business reports that some inventory has been stolen. The business does not have complete financial records. However, the following information is available.

Income statement (extract)
for the month ended 31 March 2015

	$	$
Revenue		80 000
Opening inventory	48 000	
Purchases	62 000	
	110 000	

The inventory at 31 March was valued at $45 000. The business's policy is to obtain a gross profit margin of 25 per cent on all sales.

What was the value of the stolen inventory?

A $2000
B $5000
C $7000
D $9000

1.4.3A: Partnerships: preparation of accounts

Learning objectives

In this chapter you will learn:

- about the advantages and disadvantages of partnerships
- about the content of a deed of partnership
- how to prepare fixed and fluctuating capital accounts and current accounts
- how to prepare a partnership's financial statements
- how to prepare an appropriation account to show how profits or losses are shared among partners
- how to prepare a statement of financial position
- how to record a new partner entering the partnership or a partner leaving the partnership, including accounting for goodwill within the accounts
- how to adjust for changes in the profit-sharing ratio.

What is a partnership?

A partnership is a form of business ownership in which there are at least two owners (partners) who share the profits or losses made by the business. The technically correct definition of a partnership is 'the relationship between persons carrying on a business in common with the intention of making a profit'.

Key term

Partnership: a form of business ownership when two or more individuals work together with the intention of making a profit.

The advantages and disadvantages of partnerships

A partnership enjoys several advantages that do not apply to a sole trader:

- There is the opportunity to raise more capital than would normally be possible if there was just one owner.
- The specialist skills and expertise of each partner can be brought together for the benefit of the business.
- With more than one owner, it may be easier to manage the business because the workload can be shared.

However, there are also some potential disadvantages to a partnership:

- In almost every case, each partner will have unlimited liability for the debts of the business. This is exactly the same disadvantage that is experienced by a sole trader. (The only exception is limited partnerships, discussed below.)
- Decision-making can be more difficult, or take longer, because all the partners will be required to agree on key aspects of running the business. Sometimes a good idea will not be implemented because one of the partners does not support it.
- Each partner is bound by the agreements made by all the partners.
- All the partners are jointly responsible for the debts of the partnership, even if an individual partner played no direct part in incurring the debt.
- A partnership business may be somewhat short-lived, because it may have to close on the retirement or death of one of the partners.
- There has to be a high level of trust between the partners, so good relationships have to be maintained for a partnership to be successful. This may not always be easy with the everyday worries of running a business.

What is a limited partnership?

Key term

Limited partnership: where one or more of the partners has limited liability for the debts of the business.

It is possible to establish a partnership business where one or more of the partners enjoy 'limited liability' for the debts of the business; this is referred to as a limited partnership. This means that limited partners could only lose their capital contribution to the business in the event of the business failing. There are, however, certain conditions that must be fulfilled:

- Limited partners cannot take part in the day-to-day running or management of the business.
- Limited partners cannot withdraw any part of their capital contribution while the business is a going concern.
- There must be a least one partner who is not a limited partner, often referred to as a 'general partner'.
- The business has to be formally registered as a limited partnership, otherwise it would be considered to be a 'general partnership' in the eyes of the law.

What extra accounting records do partnerships require?

In most partnerships, the partners prefer to keep a separate record of their main capital contributions (often called fixed capitals), their drawings and their shares of profits or losses, as well as a statement setting out how the profits and losses have been allocated for the financial statements.

So the usual arrangement is as follows:

- **Capital account**: This records the main capital contribution of each partner and any additions or withdrawals of capital. Changes to a partner's fixed capital would be an unusual event and would normally have to be agreed by all the partners.
- **Drawings account**: This records each partner's drawings during the year. This account is closed at the year end and the total drawings transferred to the partner's current account.
- **Current account**: This records each partner's total drawings for the year and allocations of profits or losses at the year end. The balance of the current account can be credit (indicating that the partner is 'owed' money by the partnership) or debit (indicating that the partner 'owes' money to the partnership).
- **Appropriation account**: This is prepared annually as part of the financial statements and it records the profit or loss for the year (transferred from the income statement), setting out the details of how the profit or loss is shared among the partners following the agreed wishes of the partners.

Key terms

Fixed capitals: an arrangement whereby each owner's (partner's) capital contribution remains unchanged unless all owners (partners) agree to an alteration.

Drawings account: this records all of the resources withdrawn from the business by each partner for private use.

Current accounts: a record of a partner's drawings and shares of profits or loss.

Appropriation account: a part of the end-of-year financial statements of a partnership recording how the profit or loss for the year is shared between the partners.

The content of a deed of partnership

Normally partners make an agreement about how they intend to share the profits (or losses) made by the business and other key matters that could affect their relationship with each other. It is usually considered wise for partners to have a formal written agreement. However, this is not essential as the partners could just make an oral agreement.

> **Key term**
>
> **Deed of partnership**: the formal agreement between partners that states how profit and losses will be shared and the rules under which the partners will work together.

The formal written document drawn up by partners stating how they will work together and share profits and losses is called a deed of partnership.

Partners will often agree:

- the profit- and loss-sharing agreement between the partners
- the responsibilities each partner will have in the management and running of the business
- a limit on each partner's drawings
- the amount of capital to be invested in the business by each partner. In many partnerships, partners agree that the capital invested should be fixed, so that individual partners cannot increase or decrease their capital contribution without the agreement of the other partners.

It is quite common for partners to make arrangements within the partnership agreement to ensure that partners are fairly rewarded for the ways in which they have contributed to the business or penalised for the amount of drawings they have taken from the business. The agreement contains, therefore:

- any salary to be received by a partner
- any interest to be credited on capital contributions to the partnership and charged on drawings from the partnership.

Appropriation account

The appropriation account for a partnership is an extension of the income statement. The profit or loss of a partnership is calculated in exactly the same way as that of a sole trader. The resultant profit or loss is then appropriated between the partners in accordance with their agreement.

Adjustments are made to the profit or loss to take account of:

- interest on drawings
- interest on capital
- partners' salaries.

The remaining profit or loss is then divided between the partners in their agreed profit-sharing ratio.

An appropriation account for a partnership with two partners, A and B, will appear as follows.

Profit/loss for the year		XXX
Add: interest on drawings		
Partner A	XXX	
Partner B	XXX	XXX

Less: interest in capital		
Partner A	XXX	
Partner B	XXX	(XXX)
Less: partners' salaries		
Partner A	XXX	
Partner B	XXX	(XXX)
		YYY
Residual profit divisible		
Partner A	XXX	
Partner B	XXX	YYY

Rewards and penalties

Sharing profits and losses

Key term

Profit- and loss-sharing ratio: the ratio that is used to share any residual profit (or loss) of the partnership.

Partners can make the profit/loss-sharing arrangement very straightforward by simply agreeing to split profit or losses equally or in some other ratio. This is called the profit- and loss-sharing ratio.

Illustration 1: Sharing profits

Sally and Tom have agreed to form a partnership. They have drawn up a deed of partnership which states that:

- Sally is to contribute $90 000 as her capital
- Tom is to contribute $60 000 as his capital
- Sally and Tom will jointly manage the day-to-day running of the business
- neither partner is permitted to withdraw more than $25 000 per annum from the partnership for personal use
- profits or losses are to be shared in the ratio Sally to Tom, 3 : 2.

In the first year of operation, the partnership made a profit of $82 000.

In accordance with their agreement, this profit was shared in the following way:

- Sally: $\frac{3}{5} \times \$82\,000 = \$49\,200$
- Tom: $\frac{2}{5} \times \$82\,000 = \$32\,800$

Interest on capital

Key term

Interest on capital: a reward for each partner in the form of a share of profits that is related to the amount of capital they have contributed.

Each partner may be allocated a share of profits based on the size of his or her capital contributions. This is achieved by giving each partner interest on capital at an agreed rate per annum. Therefore, the partner who has made the largest capital contribution receives a greater reward than the other partners, who have contributed less.

Illustration 2: Interest on capital

Anna and Bob are in partnership, sharing profits and losses in the ratio 4 : 3. The partners' capital contributions are as follows.

	$
Anna	100 000
Bob	160 000

The partners have also agreed to allow interest on capitals at 10 per cent per annum.

During the year ended 31 December 2014, the partnership made a profit of $75 000.

Following the terms of their agreement, Anna and Bob will share the profit of $75 000 in the following way.

	Anna	Bob
	$	$
Profit to be shared = $75 000		
Interest on capitals (10% × capital)	10 000	16 000
Residual profit (profit less interest on capital) = $75 000 – $26 000 = $49 000, shared in ratio 4 : 3	28 000	21 000
Total share of profits	38 000	37 000

Key term

Residual profit (or loss): the profit (or loss) of the partnership after all agreed rewards have been allocated to partners.

Partnership salary

A partner who has taken on a particular role in the business, and has therefore contributed more to the management and running of the partnership than the others, can be allocated an agreed amount of profit each year called a partnership salary.

The partnership salary is a means of allocating some profit to a partner.

This is not the same as an employee's salary, which would be charged as an expense in the income statement.

Key term

Partnership salary: a reward in the form of a share of profits for any partner who has particular responsibilities in the business.

Illustration 3: Partner's salary

Rakesh and Stacy are in partnership, sharing profits and losses in the ratio 2 : 1.

Stacy takes the most responsibility for managing the business and so the partners have agreed that Stacy should receive a partnership salary of $15 000 per annum.

During the year ended 31 October 2014, the partnership made a profit of $84 000.

Rakesh and Stacy will, therefore, share the profit of $84 000 in the following way.

	Rakesh	Stacy
	$	$
Profit to be shared = $84 000		
Salary		15 000
Residual profit (profit less salary) = $84 000 – $15 000 = $69 000	46 000	23 000
Total share of profits	46 000	38 000

Interest on drawings

Key term

Interest on drawings: a penalty whereby a partner is charged interest on drawings. The interest takes account of the amount of the drawings and the timing.

As well as rewarding partners for their contributions towards the success of the business, a partnership agreement can penalise partners for actions that could have had an adverse effect. Some agreements, therefore, contain a clause that charges each partner interest on drawings at a specified rate per annum. The charge is based on the time that a partner has deprived the business of cash, so that drawings taken early in the year are penalised more heavily than drawings taken later in the year.

Illustration 4: Interest on drawings

Leo and Mala are in partnership, sharing profits and losses in the ratio 3 : 2. The partnership agreement states that interest is charged on drawings at the rate of 10 per cent per annum.

During the year ended 31 December 2014, each partner's drawings were:

- Leo: $6000 on 31 March 2014 and $6000 on 30 September 2014
- Mala: $3000 on 30 April 2014 and $9000 on 31 October 2014.

During the year ended 31 December 2014, the partnership made a profit of $74 050.

The interest on drawings for each partner is calculated as follows.

Leo		
Details	**Calculation**	**$**
31 March 2014: drawings of $6 000	$6 000 × 9 months (3/4 year remaining) × 10%	450
30 September 2014: drawings of $6 000	$6 000 × 3 months (1/4 year remaining) × 10%	150
	Total	600

Mala		
Details	**Calculation**	**$**
30 April 2014: drawings of $3 000	$3 000 × 8 months (2/3 year remaining) × 10%	200
31 October 2014: drawings of $9 000	$9 000 × 2 months (1/6 year remaining) × 10%	150
	Total	350

Leo and Mala will, therefore, share the profit of $74 050 in the following way.

	Leo	Mala
	$	$
Profit to be shared = $74 050		
Interest on drawings	(600)	(350)
Residual profit (profit plus interest on drawings = $74 050 + $950 = $75 000	45 000	30 000
Total share of profits	44 400	29 650

- Interest on drawings can be complicated to calculate, because the total interest is built up of charges on each of the partner's withdrawals, and there could be many individual withdrawals during a year.
- In some questions, the amount of each partner's interest on drawings is stated.
- *Interest on drawings is added to profit* for the year. In the earlier illustrations, all 'rewards' for partners reduced the profit available for sharing. It follows that, as interest on drawings is a 'penalty' (rather than a reward), the reverse should apply, so it is added to profit.

Sharing profits and losses where there is no agreement

In some partnerships, the partners do not make any formal written agreement about sharing profits and losses. This may not cause any problems as long as the partners can come to some spoken agreement. However, there is always the risk of a dispute in these situations. Where partners cannot agree, the correct procedure is to implement the terms of the Partnership Act of 1890, which requires:

- profits and losses to be shared equally between partners
- no appropriations of profit to be made, such as interest on capital, salary, etc.
- no interest to be charged on drawings.

In addition, the Act makes provision for any partner who has made a loan to the partnership to receive interest at 5 per cent per annum.

Interest on a partner's loan should be treated in the same way as any other interest charge, that is, it should be charged as an expense in the income statement. It would not be correct to deduct the interest in the appropriation account.

Key term

Interest on a partner's loan: an agreed amount of interest is paid on any loans above the partner's capital contribution. Where there is no agreement, interest is payable at 5 per cent per annum. The interest is charged as an expense.

Illustration 5: Sharing profits and losses where there is no agreement

Jarel, Kisha and Leela are in partnership. They have no formal agreement about how to share profits or losses.

Kisha made a loan to the partnership of $40 000 some years ago. There is no agreement between the partners about the interest to be provided on this loan.

During the year ended 31 December 2014 the partnership made a profit of $92 000 before allowing for interest on Kisha's loan.

The partners cannot agree how to share the profit for the year ended 31 December 2014.

Step 1: Calculate the profit for the year having allowed for interest (at 5 per cent per annum) on Kisha's loan: $92 000 less interest of $2000 (5% × $40 000) = $90 000.

Step 2: Divide the profit for the year of $90 000 equally between the partners, so Jarel, Kisha and Leela will each receive $30 000.

Fluctuating capital accounts

Key term

Fluctuating capital account: this is where each owner (partner) has just one account to record that partner's capital contribution, drawings and shares of profits and losses.

In some partnerships, the partners decide that it is unnecessary to keep separate current accounts and drawings accounts, and instead all transactions affecting the partners are recorded in one capital account for each partner. This arrangement – usually referred to as a fluctuating capital account – can apply where the partners do not think it likely that any individual partner will make any significant change to his or her capital contributions. It is also a possibility where the partnership agreement is relatively simple, and does not include any provision concerning interest on capital, since this would be very difficult to calculate with frequent changes in capital balances.

Illustration 6: Fluctuating capital accounts

Sean, Tamara and Urban are in partnership, sharing profits and losses in the ratio 3 : 2 : 5. The partners do not have any agreement about fixed capitals and so maintain just one account to record the affairs of each partner.

On 1 January 2014 the balances on the partners' capital accounts were:

	$
Sean	248 550
Tamara	172 365
Urban	495 600

During the year ended 31 December 2014, the partners' drawings were:

	$
Sean	34 360
Tamara	48 490
Urban	62 850

The partnership agreement provides that Tamara should be given a partnership salary of $40 000 per annum for managing the business.

The partnership made a profit of $148 000 during the year ended 31 December 2014.

The partnership's appropriation account and fluctuating capital accounts are as follows.

Sean, Tamara and Urban Appropriation account for the year ended 31 December 2014		
	$	**$**
Profit for the year	148 000	
Less salary, Tamara	(40 000)	
		108 000
Shares of residual profit:		
Sean	32 400	
Tamara	21 600	
Urban	54 000	
		(108 000)

Dr				**Capital accounts**							**Cr**
			Sean	Tamara	Urban				Sean	Tamara	Urban
Dec	31	Drawings	34 360	48 490	62 350	Jan	1	Balances	248 550	172 365	495 600
	31	Balances c/d	246 590	184 475	487 250	Dec	31	Salary		40 000	
							31	Share of profits	32 400	21 600	54 000
			280 950	233 965	549 600				280 850	233 965	549 600
						Jan	1	Balances b/d	246 950	184 475	487 250

- If preferred, each partner could have a separate capital account rather than the columnar version shown in the illustration.
- With fluctuating capital accounts, it is not easy to tell whether any partner has withdrawn more than their share of profits during the year. This could be considered a disadvantage of this method.

Partnerships formed by sole traders

Quite often a partnership is formed when two (or more) sole traders agree to amalgamate their businesses into one. Where this is the case, each sole trader needs to close his or her books of account, and then open a new set of books for the partnership in which the combined assets, liabilities and the appropriate capital contributions of each partner are recorded.

The formal process should make use of journal entries.

Illustration 7: Sole traders agreeing to form a partnership

Monique and Nigel have agreed to form a partnership that will begin trading on 1 July 2014. Monique and Nigel each own their own businesses.

Monique's statement of financial position prior to the formation of the partnership was:

Monique
Statement of financial position at 30 June 2014

	$
Premises	320 000
Vehicle	30 000
Inventory	20 000
Trade receivables	25 000
Bank	12 000
	407 000
Capital	372 000
Bank loan	35 000
	407 000

Nigel's statement of financial position prior to the formation of the new partnership was:

Nigel
Statement of financial position at 30 June 2014

	$
Equipment	18 000
Inventory	14 000
Trade receivables	8 000
Bank	5 000
	45 000
Capital	37 000
Trade payables	8 000
	45 000

A journal entry will be prepared in the new partnership's books to record Monique's contribution.

Journal

Date		Details	Dr	Cr
			$	$
July	1	Premises	320 000	
		Vehicle	30 000	
		Inventory	20 000	
		Trade receivables	25 000	
		Bank	12 000	

		Bank loan		35 000
		Capital (Monique)		372 000
		Entries to record Monique's contributions to the business		

The journal entry to record Nigel's contribution will be:

Journal				
Date		Details	Dr	Cr
			$	$
July	1	Equipment	18 000	
		Inventory	14 000	
		Trade receivables	8 000	
		Bank	5 000	
		Trade payables		8 000
		Capital (Nigel)		37 000
		Entries to record Nigel's contributions to the business		

The first (summarised) statement of financial position of the new partnership will be:

Monique and Nigel Summarised statement of financial position at 1 July 2014	
	$
Premises	320 000
Vehicle	30 000
Equipment	18 000
Inventory	34 000
Trade receivables	33 000
Bank	17 000
	452 000
Capital accounts	
Monique	372 000
Nigel	37 000
Bank loan	35 000
Trade payables	8 000
	452 000

Preparing a partnership's end-of-year financial statements

A partnership's end-of-year financial statements will consist of the following:

- an income statement (which will be very similar to that of a sole trader, but remember that the interest on a partner's loan should be included in the income statement as an expense)
- an appropriation account
- a statement of financial position.

Illustration 8: Preparing a partnership appropriation account

Gary, Huanna and Iris entered into partnership on 1 January 2014. The partners' fixed capitals were:

	$
Gary	150 000
Huanna	180 000
Iris	120 000

They have agreed that:

- partners should be charged interest on drawings at 12 per cent per annum
- partners should be entitled to interest on capitals at 10 per cent per annum
- Huanna should receive a salary of $16 000 per annum for taking a leading role in managing the business
- remaining profits or losses are to be shared in the ratio Gary, Huanna, Iris 2 : 2 : 1.

During the year ended 31 December 2014, the partnership made a profit of $94 000. Partners' drawings totalled:

	$
Gary	32 000
Huanna	38 000
Iris	27 000

Interest on drawings has been calculated and amounted to the following.

	$
Gary	2 400
Huanna	3 800
Iris	800

The appropriation account is as follows.

Gary, Huanna and Iris
Appropriation account for the year ended 31 December 2014

	$	$
Profit for the year		94 000
Add: interest on drawings		

Gary	2 400	
Huanna	3 800	
Iris	800	7 000
		101 000
Less: interest on capital		
Gary ($150 000 × 10%)	15 000	
Huanna ($180 000 × 10%)	18 000	
Iris ($120 000 × 10%)	12 000	(45 000)
		56 000
Less: partner's salary		
Huanna		(16 000)
		40 000
Share of residual profit		
Gary (2/5)	16 000	
Huanna (2/5)	16 000	
Iris (1/5)	8 000	(40 000)

The capital accounts of the partners are as follows.

Dr				Capital accounts							Cr
			Gary	Huanna	Iris				Gary	Huanna	Iris
			$	$	$				$	$	$
						Jan	1	Balances	160 000	180 000	120 000

During the year each partner's drawings would be debited to the drawings account. At the year end, the drawings account is closed off and the total drawings for the year are transferred to the current accounts.

These are the drawings accounts of the partners.

Dr			Drawings accounts					Cr
		Gary	Huanna	Iris			Gary	Huanna	Iris
		$	$	$			$	$	$
Jan–Dec	Bank	32 000	38 000	27 000	Dec 31	Current accounts	32 000	38 000	27 000

- The debit entries for drawings shown here are the totals of what are likely to be many individual withdrawals of cash by each partner spread throughout the year.
- At the end of the year, the sharing of profits and losses between the partners is set out in detail as part of the financial statements. It is important to follow the terms of the partnership agreement.

The current accounts of each partner now need to be prepared, showing not only the profit shares allocated to each partner, but also each partner's total drawings for the year.

Dr	Current accounts								Cr
		Gary	Huanna	Iris			Gary	Huanna	Iris
		$	$	$			$	$	$
Dec 31	Drawings	32 000	38 000	27 000	Dec 31	Interest on capitals	15 000	18 000	12 000
31	Interest on drawings	2 400	3 800	800	31	Salary		16 000	
31	Balance c/d		8 200		31	Residual profits	16 000	16 000	8 000
					31	Balances c/d	3 400		7 800
		34 800	50 000	27 800			34 800	50 000	27 800
Jan 1	Balances b/d	3 400		7 800	Jan 1	Balance b/d		8 200	

- Total drawings are transferred from the drawings account at the year end.
- Interest on drawings is transferred from the appropriation account and debited to the current accounts so that each partner is penalised.
- Interest on capitals, partners' salaries and residual profit shares are credited to the current accounts so that each partner is rewarded.
- Huanna has a credit balance on her current account because her drawings have been less than her total share of profits. Huanna is 'owed' $8200 by the partnership.
- Gary and Iris have debit balances on their current accounts because their drawings have exceeded their profit shares. Gary and Iris owe $3400 and $7800 respectively to the partnership.
- Once a partnership is established each partner's current account will start with either a debit or credit balance brought forward from the previous year.
- In some partnerships, the partners may choose to have separate current accounts for each partner. However, it is recommended that the multi-column style of presentation is adopted.

Getting it right

Remember to provide a full and correct title for all final accounting statements, for example:

'Appropriation account for the year ended 31 December 2014'.

Also, remember to bring down balances on current accounts as shown in the illustration.

It is easy to forget that interest on drawings is an addition to the profit for the year in the appropriation account. Unfortunately, many students make the common mistake of deducting this item.

A partnership's statement of financial position will record assets and liabilities in exactly the same way as that of a sole trader. However, the capital section will need to reflect the fact that there are a number of owners and that each partner may have a capital account and a current account.

Illustration 9: Preparing a partnership statement of financial position

Francis and Geeta are in partnership. Their summarised information at 31 October 2014 is:

	$
Non-current assets	640 000
Current assets	50 000
Non-current liability:	
Loan from Francis	20 000
Current liabilities	25 000

Capital accounts:	
Francis	400 000
Geeta	240 000
Current accounts:	
Francis	4 000 (Dr)
Geeta	9 000 (Cr)

The current accounts of the partners are shown as follows.

Dr		Current accounts					Cr
		Francis	Geeta			Francis	Geeta
		$	$			$	$
Oct 31	Drawings	105 000	55 000	Nov 1	Balances	11 000	15 000
31	Balance c/d		9 000	Dec 31	Interest on capitals	40 000	24 000
				31	Residual profits	50 000	25 000
				31	Balances c/d	4 000	
		105 000	64 000			105 000	64 000
Jan 1	Balances b/d	4 000		Jan 1	Balance b/d		9 000

The statement of financial position of the partnership will appear as follows.

Francis and Geeta
Statement of financial position at 31 October 2014

	$	$	$
Non-current assets			640 000
Current assets			50 000
Total assets			690 000
	Francis	Geeta	Total
Capital accounts	400 000	240 000	640 000
Current accounts			
Opening balance	11 000	15 000	
Interest on capital	40 000	24 000	
Residual profits	50 000	25 000	
	101 000	64 000	
Less: drawings	105 000	55 000	
	(4 000)	9 000	5 000
Non-current liabilities			
Loan from Francis			20 000
Current liabilities			25 000
Total capital and liabilities			690 000

In this version of the statement of financial position, the current accounts are shown in detail. Where this is required, provide each partner with a column and start the details with the opening balance (which could of course be negative). The column should end with the current account balance at the statement of financial position date.

An alternative presentation of the statement of financial position may be required, where only the final balances of the current accounts are shown. In this version, the second part of the statement of financial position would appear as follows.

	$	$	$
Capital accounts	Francis	Geeta	
	400 000	240 000	640 000
Current accounts	(4 000)	9 000	5 000

The version of the statement of financial position that just shows the final balances should be used as it saves time.

- It is important to keep the capital accounts and the current accounts of the partners distinct in the second part of the statement of financial position.
- Use brackets to indicate negative figures.

The introduction of a new partner into the partnership

When a partner joins an established partnership, he or she brings extra capital and in return receives a share in the partnership. At this point the original partners may decide to value the business so that a fair share of its worth is allocated to the new partner.

Key term

Goodwill: an intangible asset that represents the reputation built up by the partnership.

For example, the assets may be revalued and a value may be given to the reputation of the partnership. This reputation is known as goodwill and is an intangible non-current asset. Goodwill reflects the success of the business and is based on the previous levels of profits or the difference between the net assets and the amount the business could be sold for.

The treatment of goodwill within the partnership is either to:

- **Option 1: Keep goodwill within the accounts**

DEBIT intangible non-current assets with the total value of goodwill

CREDIT each original partner with his or her share of the goodwill in the capital account in the *old* profit-sharing ratio or

▶ **Option 2: Write off goodwill within the accounts**

DEBIT each remaining partner with the removal of goodwill in the capital account in the *new* profit-sharing ratio

CREDIT each original partner with his or her share of the goodwill in the capital account in the *old* profit-sharing ratio.

Illustration 10: The introduction of a new partner and recording goodwill

Using Illustration 9, Francis and Geeta admit Henry as a new partner on 1 November 2014. Henry is introducing $160 000 cash as capital. In return, the new profit-sharing ratio is to be 3 : 2 : 1 and goodwill is valued at $60 000.

Option 1: Goodwill is kept in the accounts and the capital account is as follows.

Dr			Capital accounts						Cr
		Francis	Geeta	Henry			Francis	Geeta	Henry
		$	$	$			$	$	$
					Nov 1	Balances	400 000	240 000	
						Capital introduced			160 000
Nov 1	Balances c/d	440 000	260 000	160 000		Goodwill OLD profit-sharing ratio (2 : 1)	40 000	20 000	
		440 000	260 000	160 000			440 000	260 000	160 000
					Nov 1	Balances b/d	440 000	260 000	160 000

Option 2: Goodwill is written off in the accounts and the capital account is as follows.

Dr			Capital accounts						Cr
		Francis	Geeta	Henry			Francis	Geeta	Henry
		$	$	$			$	$	$
Nov 1	Goodwill NEW profit-sharing ratio (3 : 2 : 1)	30 000	20 000	10 000	Nov 1	Balances	400 000	240 000	
						Capital introduced			160 000
Nov 1	Balances c/d	410 000	240 000	150 000		Goodwill OLD profit-sharing ratio (2 : 1)	40 000	20 000	
		440 000	260 000	160 000			440 000	260 000	160 000
					Nov 1	Balances b/d	410 000	240 000	150 000

Getting it right

Remember to include goodwill as an intangible non-current asset in the statement of financial position in Option 1.

Remember that goodwill is *not* recorded in the books of account in Option 2 and so does not appear anywhere in the financial statements.

The departure of a partner from the partnership

When a partner decides to leave a partnership, perhaps due to retirement, the other partners must decide how to pay the leaving partner for his or her share of the partnership. This can be done either in cash or by creating a loan within the partnership if limited funds are available.

Illustration 11: Preparing the accounts when a partner leaves the partnership

Following on from Illustration 6 where Sean, Tamara and Urban shared profits and losses 3 : 2 : 5, on 1 January 2015 Sean decides to leave the partnership. At that date goodwill was valued as $50 000. The remaining partners decide to share profits and losses equally after Sean leaves and to not maintain goodwill within the accounts. Of the monies due to Sean, $150 000 is to be paid in cash and the rest is be held as a loan to the partnership.

Dr	Capital accounts								Cr
		Sean	Tamara	Urban			Sean	Tamara	Urban
Jan 1	Goodwill NEW profit-sharing ratio (equally)		25 000	25 000	Jan 1	Balances b/d	246 590	184 475	487 250
	Loan	111 590				Goodwill OLD profit-sharing ratio (3 : 2 : 5)	15 000	10 000	25 000
	Cash	150 000							
	Balances c/d		169 475	487 250					
		261 590	194 475	512 250			261 590	194 475	512 250
					Jan 1	Balances b/d		169 475	487 250

In the statement of financial position, the bank balance will therefore be reduced by $150 000 and a new liability of a loan of $111 590 will be shown.

In this illustration the partnership has fluctuating capital accounts and so does not use current accounts. If the partnership had used current accounts then Sean's current account should have been closed down and the balance transferred to the capital account, so that any money due to him within the current account was also paid out or included in the loan.

Changes in the profit-sharing ratio

In the previous illustrations the profit ratio changed when a new partner entered or an old partner left a partnership. However, there does not need to be this movement in partners for there to be a change in the profit-sharing ratio. For example, some partners may decide to reduce their working commitment to the partnership and so their share of profits will be reduced. The change can occur at any point in the year, not necessarily at the year end.

Illustration 12: A change in the profit-sharing ratio during the year

Azamat, Gawain and Louis are in partnership, sharing profits and losses in the ratio 3 : 2 : 1. The partners had capital invested of $90 000, $60 000 and $30 000 respectively. Interest on capital was 10 per cent per annum. On 1 April 2014 Azamat reduced his work commitment to the partnership due to ill health. At this date it was agreed that the new profit-sharing ratio would be 2 : 2 : 1 and Gawain would receive a salary of $6000 per annum. For the year ended 31 December 2014 the partnership made a profit of $66 000 which is assumed to accrue evenly throughout the year.

The appropriation account for the partnership for the year ended 31 December 2014 is as follows.

		1 Jan to 31 March 2014		1 April to 31 December 2014	
		$	$	$	$
Profit for the year (3/12 and 9/12)			16 500		49 500
Salary (9/12 × $6 000)	Gawain			4 500	
Interest on capital (3/12 and 9/12)	Azamat	2 250		6 750	
	Gawain	1 500		4 500	
	Louis	750	(4 500)	2 250	(13 500)
Profit after appropriations			12 000		36 000
Share of residual profit	Azamat	6 000		14 400	
	Gawain	4 000		14 400	
	Louis	2 000	(12 000)	7 200	(36 000)

All of the appropriations are recorded in the current account as normal.

Dr			Current accounts						Cr
		Azamat	Gawain	Louis			Azamat	Gawain	Louis
		$	$	$			$	$	$
					Jan 1	Balances b/f	X	X	X
					Mar 31	Interest on capital	2 250	1 500	750
Mar 31	Balances c/d	X	X	X		Share of residual profit	6 000	4 000	2 000
		XX	XX	XX			XX	XX	XX
	Drawings	X	X	X	Apr 1	Balances b/d	X	X	X
Dec 31	Balances c/d	X	X	X	Dec 31	Salary		4 500	
						Interest on capital	6 750	4 500	2 250
						Share of residual profit	14 400	14 400	7 200
		XX	XX	XX			XX	XX	XX
					Jan 1	Balances b/d	X	X	X

Getting it right

The important thing to remember is that all appropriations are apportioned to a time period. For example, although the salary for Gawain is $6000 per annum, this only relates to the period of time from the date when the agreement changed, 1 April 2014. It is a common error to include a whole year instead of apportioning the amount.

It is also important that a clear layout is used so that workings can easily be followed through.

End-of-chapter questions

1 **Calculating profit shares**

Jennifer, Kim and Lewis are planning to enter into partnership. They have not yet decided what profit/loss-sharing ratio they should adopt. They have considered the following possibilities:

a Equal shares.

b Jennifer, Kim, Lewis in the ratio of 6 : 3 : 1.

c Jennifer, Kim, Lewis in the ratio of 2 : 3 : 7.

They expect to make a profit of $84 000 during the first year.

Calculate each partner's share of the profit for each of these three profit-sharing arrangements.

2 **Calculating profit shares when there is interest on capitals**

Robin, Sharla and Tom are in partnership, sharing profits and losses in the ratio 3 : 2 : 1, respectively. The partners have agreed that each partner should be entitled to interest on capital at 8 per cent per annum. The partners' capitals are:

	$
Robin	200 000
Sharla	360 000
Tom	240 000

Calculate each partner's share of the profit for the year ended 31 October 2014, when the partnership made a profit of $198 000.

3 **Calculating profits shares when there is a partnership salary**

Cindy, David and Fitz are in partnership, sharing profits and losses in the ratio 3 : 3 : 2. Fitz is entitled to a partnership salary of $34 000 per annum for taking responsibility for the day-to-day running of the business.

Calculate each partner's share of the profit for the year ended 31 January 2015, when the partnership made a profit of $274 000.

4 **Sharing profit and losses when there is a residual loss**

Yvonne and Zara are in partnership, sharing profits and losses in the ratio 2 : 1. Their partnership agreement also states that:

- partners should receive interest on their capitals at 8 per cent per annum
- Yvonne should receive a partnership salary of $51 000 per annum.

The partners' capitals are:

	$
Yvonne	420 000
Zara	360 000

The partnership made a small profit of $54 000 during the year ended 31 October 2014.

Calculate each partner's share of the profit for the year ended 31 October 2014.

5 **Preparing partners' accounts, interest on drawings given**

Jackie and Kerri entered into partnership on 1 April 2014. The partners agreed that:

- interest should be allowed on fixed capitals at 10 per cent per annum
- Jackie should receive a salary of $60 000 per annum
- remaining profits and losses should be shared between Jackie and Kerri in the ratio 3 : 2, respectively.

Additional information:

	Fixed capitals	Drawings for the year ended 31 March 2015	Interest on drawings for the year ended 31 March 2015
	$	$	$
Jackie	360 000	38 500	4 620
Kerri	600 000	58 500	7 020

The partnership made a profit of $216 000 during the year ended 31 March 2015.

Prepare:

a the partners' capital accounts

b the partners' drawing accounts

c the appropriation account for the year ended 31 March 2015

d the partners' current accounts.

6 **Sole traders agreeing to form a partnership**

Rajiv and Sharla are sole traders. They have agreed to form a partnership that will start trading on 1 May 2014.

The statements of financial position of each business are shown below.

Rajiv Statement of financial position at 30 April 2014	
	$
Premises	290 000
Furniture and fittings	38 000
Inventory	29 000
Bank	22 000
	379 000
Capital	342 000
Bank loan	25 000
Trade payables	12 000
	379 000

Sharla Statement of financial position at 30 April 2014	
	$
Premises	75 000
Furniture and fittings	28 000
Inventory	17 000
Trade receivables	9 000
	129 000
Capital	104 000
Bank loan	10 000
Bank overdraft	8 000
Trade payables	7 000
	129 000

It was agreed that all the assets and liabilities of each business should be transferred to the new partnership, which would begin trading on 1 May 2014.

Prepare:

a a journal entry to record Rajiv's contribution to the partnership on 1 May 2014

b a journal entry to record Sharla's contribution to the partnership on 1 May 2014

c the opening statement of financial position of the new partnership on 1 May 2014.

7 Preparing partners' accounts, including the calculation of interest on drawings

Ryan, Sonya and Tara are in partnership. The partners made an agreement that profits and losses should be shared as follows:

- Interest should be charged on drawings at 12 per cent per annum.
- Interest should be allowed on capitals at 8 per cent per annum.
- Ryan should receive a salary of $33 000 per annum for managing the business.
- Tara should receive a salary of $15 000 per annum for being responsible for promoting the business.
- Partners' drawings during the year ended 31 July 2014 were:
  - Ryan: $24 000 on 30 November 2013 and $39 000 on 31 March 2014
  - Sonya: $51 000 on 31 December 2013 and $36 000 on 31 May 2014
  - Tara: $39 000 on 31 January 2014 and $39 000 on 30 June 2014.
- Remaining profits and losses should be shared equally.

The profit for the year ended 31 July 2014 was far lower than the partners had expected and amounted to $87 390.

Additional information:

	Fixed capitals	Current account balances 1 August 2013
	$	$
Ryan	660 000	5 300 Dr
Sonya	540 000	8 100 Cr
Tara	300 000	2 700 Dr

Prepare:

a the profit and loss appropriation account for the year ended 31 July 2014

b the partners' capital accounts

c the partners' drawings accounts

d the partners' current accounts.

8 Preparing fluctuating capital accounts

Jenny and Keith are in partnership, sharing profits and losses in the ratio 2 : 3. The partners have agreed not to maintain separate current accounts.

On 1 August 2013 the balances on the partners' capital accounts were:

	$
Jenny	284 570
Keith	345 830

During the year ended 31 July 2014, the partners' drawings were:

	$
Jenny	55 490
Keith	62 440

The partners have agreed that Jenny is entitled to a partnership salary of $33 000 per annum and Keith a partnership salary of $18 000 per annum.

During the year ended 31 July 2014, the partnership made a loss of $25 000.

Prepare:

a an appropriation account for the year ended 31 July 2014

b the partners' capital accounts.

9 Partnerships with no profit/loss-sharing agreement

Bryan and Stacey are in partnership with fixed capitals of $200 000 and $150 000, respectively. The partners do not have a formal agreement about how to share profits and losses, although salaries for each have been agreed, as well as interest on capital of 5 per cent per year.

During the year ended 31 December 2014, the partnership was profitable and Bryan made an attempt to show Stacey how he thought the profits should be shared. The following statement was prepared by Bryan:

Statement of profit shares for the year ended 31 December 2014

	$	$
Profit for the year (before interest on loan)	135 000	
Less interest on Bryan's loan of $80 000	(8 000)	
Profit after interest on loan		127 000
Less salaries:		
Bryan	20 000	
Stacey	30 000	
		(50 000)
		77 000
Less shares of residual profit:		
Bryan (in proportion to fixed capital)	44 000	
Stacey (in proportion to fixed capital)	33 000	
		(77 000)

Stacey does not agree with Bryan's ideas about how the profits should be shared.

Assuming Bryan and Stacey cannot agree, calculate how the profit for the year ended 31 December 2014 should be shared between the partners.

10 End-of-year financial statements of a partnership

Gaynor, Henry and Irvin are in partnership, sharing profits and losses as follows: Gaynor 20 per cent; Henry 40 per cent; Irvin 40 per cent. The following trial balance was extracted from the business's books of account on 31 August 2014, the last day of the partnership's financial year.

Trial balance at 31 August 2014

	Dr	Cr
	$000	$000
Bank overdraft		12
Capital accounts:		
Gaynor		260
Henry		310
Irvin		370
Current accounts:		
Gaynor	6	
Henry		8
Irvin	9	
Discounts	11	15
Drawings:		
Gaynor	44	
Henry	61	
Irvin	52	
Furniture and equipment		
Cost	220	
Provision for depreciation, 1 September 2013		66
General expenses	19	
Gross profit		291
Inventory, 31 August 2014	68	
Premises at cost	660	
Provision for doubtful debts, 1 September 2013		6
Insurance	27	
Trade payables		18
Trade receivables	40	
Wages and salaries	139	
	1 356	1 356

Additional information:

- Insurance: $3000 was prepaid at 31 August 2014.
- Wages and salaries due but unpaid totalled $12 000 at 31 August 2014.

- Depreciation should be provided on furniture and fittings at 20 per cent per annum using the straight-line method.
- The provision for doubtful debts should be maintained at 5 per cent of trade receivables.

The partnership agreement includes the following terms:

- Interest should be charged on drawings. Interest charged on drawings for the year ended 31 August 2014 was: Gaynor $4000, Henry $5000, Irvin $7000.
- Gaynor is entitled to receive a partnership salary of $28 000 per annum.
- Partners are entitled to receive interest on capitals at the rate of 10 per cent.

Prepare:

a an income statement for the year ended 31 August 2014

b an appropriation account for the year ended 31 August 2014

c partners' current accounts for the year ended 31 August 2014

d a statement of financial position at 31 August 2014; this should show only the balances on the partners' current accounts at this date.

11 End-of-year financial statements of a partnership

Ishaka and Joshua are in partnership, sharing profits and losses as follows: Ishaka 60 per cent and Joshua 40 per cent.

At the end of the financial year, 30 September 2014, the following balances were extracted from the books of the partnership after calculation of the gross profit for the year.

Trial balance at 30 September 2014

	Dr	Cr
	$	$
Capital accounts:		
Ishaka		240 000
Joshua		200 000
Cash at bank	31 000	
Current accounts:		
Ishaka	4 000	
Joshua		7 000
Drawings:		
Ishaka	47 000	
Joshua	35 000	
Gross profit		237 000
Inventory	63 000	
Loan account (Ishaka)		40 000
Non-current assets:		
Cost	820 000	
Provision for depreciation at 1 October 2013		340 000
Operating expenses	68 000	
Trade payables		24 000
Trade receivables	20 000	
	1 088 000	1 088 000

Additional information:

- Non-current assets should be depreciated by 20 per cent per annum using the reducing-balance method.
- Operating expenses due but unpaid at 30 September 2014 totalled $5000.
- The partners have decided that it is necessary to create a provision for doubtful debts amounting to 5 per cent of trade receivables at 30 September 2014.
- The partnership agreement includes the following terms:
  - Ishaka is entitled to interest of 10 per cent per annum on her loan.
  - Interest is charged on drawings. Interest on drawings for the year ended 30 September 2014 was: Ishaka $6000 and Joshua $4000.
  - Joshua is to receive a partnership salary of $28 000 per annum.

Prepare:

a an income statement for the year ended 30 September 2014

b an appropriation account for the year ended 30 September 2014

c partners' current accounts for the year ended 30 September 2014

d a statement of financial position at 30 September 2014; the statement of financial position should show only the balances on the partners' current accounts at this date.

12 A new partner

Marion and Nina are in partnership. Their summarised information at 31 October 2014 is:

	$
Non-current assets	520 000
Current assets (including bank)	70 000
Non-current liability:	
Loan from Francis	30 000
Current liabilities	15 000
Capital accounts:	
Marion	300 000
Nina	240 000
Current accounts:	
Marion	4 000 (Dr)
Nina	9 000 (Cr)

Currently profits and losses are shared in the ratio 5:4. On 1 November they admit Oliver as a partner. Oliver contributes capital of $60 000 cash. At that date goodwill is valued at $90 000 and it is agreed that the new profit-sharing ratio will be 5:4:1.

Prepare:

a a statement of financial position at 1 November 2014 after the admission of Oliver as a partner assuming goodwill is to remain in the books of account

b a statement of financial position at 1 November 2014 after the admission of Oliver as a partner assuming goodwill is *not* to remain in the books of account.

13 The retirement of a partner

Ron, Stan and Frank are in partnership, sharing profits and losses equally. Their summarised statement of financial position at 31 March 2014 was:

Statement of financial position at 31 March 2014		
	$	$
Non-current assets		470 000
Current assets		50 000
		520 000
Capital accounts:		
Ron	150 000	
Stan	150 000	
Frank	150 000	450 000
Current accounts:		
Ron	40 000	
Stan	15 000	
Frank	(5 000)	50 000
		500 000
Current liabilities		20 000
		520 000

Frank decides to retire on 1 April 2014. At that date goodwill is valued at $30 000 but goodwill will not be maintained in the books of account. After Frank leaves, Ron and Stan will share profits and losses equally. The partnership does not have enough cash to pay Frank when he leaves. The money due will, therefore, be repaid over five years.

Prepare:

a the capital accounts of the partnership to record the retirement of Frank

b the statement of financial position at 1 April 2014 to show how the balance due to Frank is recorded.

14 Change in partnership profit-sharing ratio

Walter and Vera are in partnership. The following trial balance is available at 31 August 2014.

Trial balance at 31 August 2014		
	Dr	Cr
	$000	$000
Bank overdraft		8
Capital accounts		
Walter		200
Vera		250
Current accounts:		
Walter		5
Vera	12	
Drawings:		
Walter	34	
Vera	44	
Furniture and equipment		
Cost	160	
Provision for depreciation, 1 September 2013		80
General expenses	20	
Gross profit		135
Inventory, 31 August 2014	33	
Premises at cost	270	

Insurance	12	
Trade payables		12
Trade receivables	42	
Wages and salaries	63	
	690	690

Additional information:

- Depreciation on furniture and equipment is charged at 10 per cent per annum on cost.
- The partnership agreement originally stated that all profits and losses were to be shared equally. However, this agreement was changed on 1 January 2014 due to Walter's ill health. On this date it was agreed that Vera would receive a salary of $9000 per annum, and interest on capital was to be charged at 6 per cent per annum. Residual profits or losses should be shared equally.

Prepare an income statement for the year ended 31 August 2014, an appropriation account for the year ended 31 August 2014 and a statement of financial position at 31 August 2014. (Assume profits arose evenly throughout the year.)

15 Profit share

Mala and Norris are in partnership, with capitals of $240 000 and $120 000, respectively. The partners are entitled to interest on capitals at 10 per cent per annum and remaining profits are shared equally. For the year ended 31 December 2014, the business made a profit of $144 000.

What is Mala's share of the residual profit for the year ended 31 December 2014?

A $54 000
B $72 000
C $78 000
D $96 000

16 Calculating the closing balance in a current account

Xavier and Yvonne are partners in a business. Xavier's current account has been prepared by an inexperienced bookkeeper.

	$		$
Interest on capital	36 000	Balance b/d	1 500
Salary	45 000	Drawings	75 000
Balance c/d	85 500	Profit	90 000
	166 500		166 500

Assuming that Xavier's opening balance was correctly recorded, what should the closing balance on his current account be?

A $25 500
B $67 500
C $82 500
D $97 500

17 Content of a partnership appropriation account

What should a partnership appropriation account include?

A Shares of residual loss, partnership salaries, drawings, interest on partners' loans
B Shares of residual loss, partnership salaries, interest on partners' loans
C Shares of residual profit, partnership salaries, drawings, interest on capitals
D Shares of residual profit, partnership salaries, interest on drawings, interest on capitals.

18 Double entry for interest on drawings

In the books of a partnership, what should the ledger entries for interest on drawings be?

A Debit: appropriation account
Credit: partners' current accounts

B Debit: partners' current accounts
Credit: appropriation account

C Debit: partners' current accounts
Credit: partners' drawings accounts

D Debit: partners' current accounts
Credit: partners' current accounts

19 Interest on drawings

In the books of a partnership, what should interest on drawings be debited to?

A The appropriation account
B The bank account
C The partners' current accounts
D The partners' drawings accounts

20 An individual partner's capital contribution

Renea and Stephen agreed to go into partnership. Renea was a sole trader and her business's statement of financial position before the formation of the partnership was:

Renea Statement of financial position			
	$		$
Premises	330 000	Capital	374 000
Vehicle	29 000	Bank loan	40 000
Inventory	40 000	Trade payables	20 000
Bank	35 000		
	434 000		434 000

Renea is to transfer her business's assets and liabilities to the partnership, subject to the following conditions:

- Renea should discharge the payables using her business's funds.
- She should keep the business's vehicle for her private use.
- The premises should be valued at $450 000.

What was Renea's capital contribution to the new partnership?

A $445 000
B $465 000
C $474 000
D $494 000

21 Capital account balance

Urban and Victoria are in partnership. They do not maintain separate current accounts.

The following information is available concerning Urban for the year ended 31 December 2014.

	$
Capital account balance 1 January 2014	65 000
Drawings for the year	32 000
Interest on drawings	4 000
Salary	28 000
Share of profit for the year	8 000

What is the balance of Urban's capital account at 31 December 2014?

A $51 000
B $59 000
C $63 000
D $65 000

22 Sharing loss without a partnership agreement

Julie and Keith do not have a partnership agreement. The following information is available.

	Julie	Keith
	$	$
Fixed capital	160 000	80 000
Loan		40 000

The partnership made a loss of $60 000 during the year ended 30 September 2014. Loan interest had been ignored in arriving at this figure.

What is Keith's share of the residual loss?

A $20 000
B $29 000
C $30 000
D $31 000

1.4.3B: Dissolution of partnerships

Learning objectives

In this chapter you will learn:

- about the possible reasons behind a partnership dissolution
- how to record the effects of asset and liability revaluation on the date of dissolution
- how to prepare a realisation account on the date of dissolution
- how to prepare the ledgers to record the dissolution and close down the books of the partnership.

Reasons for partnership dissolution

Before beginning this chapter, it is recommended that you review Chapter 1.4.3A Partnerships: preparation of accounts.

A partnership dissolution is the closure or cessation of a partnership. This may arise for the following reasons:

- The partnership is no longer profitable and there is no longer any reason to carry on trading.
- The partners disagree on how to run the partnership and can no longer work together.
- A partner has died, retired or been declared bankrupt and the remaining partners agree to close the partnership.

Key term

Partnership dissolution: the closure or cessation of a partnership.

The dissolution process

According to the Partnership Act 1890, the partnership stops trading at dissolution and:

- the assets are disposed of
- the liabilities are paid to everyone other than the partners
- the partners are repaid any investment above their capital and current balances
- the current account balances are transferred to the capital accounts
- the partners are paid any amounts due to them on their capital accounts.

The disposal of assets

The assets can be disposed of in a variety of ways. They can be:

- sold for cash
- sold to a limited company for shares, debentures or a combination of cash, shares and debentures
- taken over by an existing partner for an agreed value. Cash is not paid under these circumstances, but instead the partner's capital account is charged (debited) with the agreed value.

Link

The purchase of a business using shares, debentures and cash is discussed in A Level Chapter 1.2.1 Business purchase and merger.

The realisation account

In order to carry out the process of dissolution, a realisation account is used. This is used to calculate whether there has been a profit or a loss on dissolution, which is then shared to the partners' capital accounts in their profit-sharing ratio.

Key term

Realisation account: the account used to calculate the profit or loss on dissolution of a partnership.

The contents of a realisation account are as follows.

Realisation account	
Debit	**Credit**
The book value of non-current assets	Value of assets taken over by the partners
The book value of current assets except for cash and cash equivalents	The book value of current and non-current liabilities
Payments for current and non-current liabilities	Receipts from the sale of non-current and current assets
Costs of dissolution	Other income and benefits
Profit on dissolution	Loss on dissolution

An alternative way to present the account is *not* to record both the trade receivables and trade payables within the assets/liabilities and their receipts/payments, but instead to just record the discounts allowed on the trade receivables (debit) side and discounts received on the trade payables (credit) side on dissolution.

The profit on dissolution is credited to the partners' capital accounts in the profit-sharing ratio. The loss on dissolution is debited to the partners' capital accounts in the profit-sharing ratio.

Illustration 1: A simple example of a partnership dissolution

Raj and Seema are in partnership, sharing profits in the ratio 3 : 1. They decide to dissolve the partnership on 31 December 2014. The statement of financial position at that date is:

Raj and Seema Statement of financial position at 31 December 2014		
	$	**$**
Non-current assets at book value		120 000
Current assets		
Inventory	14 500	
Trade receivables	32 000	
Cash and cash equivalents	1 500	48 000
Total assets		168 000
Capital accounts		
Raj	82 000	
Seema	59 000	141 000
Current liabilities		
Trade payables		27 000
Total capital and liabilities		168 000

Additional information:

- The non-current assets were sold for $101 000, except for a motor car. This had a book value of $3000 and was taken over by Raj at this value.

- The inventory was sold for $14 000, the trade receivables paid $30 000 and trade payables were paid $24 500.
- The costs of dissolution were $4000.

The entries to dissolve the partnership are, therefore, as follows.

Realisation account

	$		$
Non-current assets	120 000	Trade payables	27 000
Inventory	14 500	Bank: receipts from non-current assets	101 000
Trade receivables	32 000	Motor car taken over by Raj	3 000
Bank: trade payables	24 500	Bank: inventory	14 000
Bank: costs of dissolution	4 000	Bank: trade receivables	30 000
		Loss on dissolution: Raj (3/4)	15 000
		Loss on dissolution: Seema (1/4)	5 000
	195 000		195 000

Capital accounts

	Raj	Seema		Raj	Seema
	$	$		$	
Motor car	3 000		Balance b/d	82 000	59 000
Loss on dissolution	15 000	5 000			
Cash and cash equivalents	64 000	54 000			
	82 000	59 000		82 000	59 000

Cash and cash equivalents

	$		$
Balance b/d	1 500	Trade payables	24 500
Receipts from non-current assets	101 000	Costs of dissolution	4 000
Inventory	14 000	Capital account: Raj	64 000
Trade receivables	30 000	Capital account: Seema	54 000
	146 500		146 500

Remember that the cash/bank balance is *not* split in the profit-sharing ratio but is allocated according to the amounts due or payable in the capital accounts.

In this instance, the discounts allowed are not shown, but instead the trade receivables book value and the receipts from the trade receivables are both shown. The same applies to the trade payables and the discounts received.

The alternative approach for the realisation account is shown below (either approach is acceptable).

Getting it right

A common mistake is to record both the trade receivables and the discounts allowed in the realisation account, plus the trade payables and the discounts received in the realisation account. This is incorrect as the net effect is doubled as the amounts are entered twice.

Realisation account

	$		$
Non-current assets	120 000	Bank: receipts from non-current assets	101 000
Inventory	14 500	Motor car taken over by Raj	3 000
Bank: costs of dissolution	4 000	Bank: inventory	14 000
Discounts allowed (note 1)	2 000	Discounts received (note 2)	2 500
		Loss on dissolution: Raj (3/4)	15 000
		Loss on dissolution: Seema (1/4)	5 000
	140 500		140 500

Note 1: Discounts allowed are calculated as $32 000 – $30 000 = $2000

Note 2: Discounts received are calculated as $27 000 – $24 500 = $2500

The important thing to remember is that, whichever method is used, the profit/loss on dissolution will be the same for each partner. All the entries in the capital accounts and cash/bank accounts remain the same.

If the ledgers have been drawn up correctly, then the balances on the cash and cash equivalents account will balance the capital accounts. There should be no final balances to bring down as the partnership has ceased to trade.

Illustration 2: A more complex example of a partnership dissolution

Ali and Bobir are in partnership, sharing profits in the ratio 2 : 1. They decide to dissolve the partnership on 31 October 2014. The statement of financial position at that date is as follows.

Ali and Bobir
Statement of financial position at 31 October 2014

	$	$
Non-current assets		
Premises at book value		250 000
Motor vehicles at book value		21 000
		271 000
Current assets		
Inventory	35 600	
Trade receivables (less provision for doubtful debts $1 400)	56 200	91 800
Total assets		362 800
Capital accounts		
Ali	150 000	
Bobir	70 000	220 000

Current accounts		
Ali	66 500	
Bobir	(29 300)	37 200
Current liabilities		
Trade payables	77 000	
Cash and cash equivalents	28 600	105 600
Total capital and liabilities		362 800

Additional information:

- The premises are sold for $260 000.
- The trade receivables paid $52 200 after irrecoverable debts and discounts allowed and the trade payables settled at $76 500 after discounts received.
- The motor vehicles are taken over by the partners: Ali $7000 and Bobir $12 000.
- Bobir also takes over the inventory at a value of $39 000. No cash is paid.
- The costs of dissolution were $4000.

The entries to dissolve the partnership are, therefore, as follows.

Realisation account

	$		$
Premises	250 000	Trade payables	77 000
Motor vehicles	21 000	Motor car taken over by Ali	7 000
Inventory	35 600	Motor car taken over by Bobir	12 000
Trade receivables	56 200	Bank: receipts from non-current assets	260 000
Bank: trade payables	76 500	Inventory taken over by Bobir	39 000
Bank: costs of dissolution	4 000	Bank: trade receivables	52 200
Profit on dissolution: Ali	2 600		
Profit on dissolution: Bobir	1 300		
	447 200		447 200

Current accounts

	Ali	Bobir		Ali	Bobir
	$	$	$	$	
Balance b/d		29 300	Balance b/d	66 500	
Capital account	66 500		Capital account		29 300
	66 500	29 300		66 500	29 300

Capital accounts

	Ali	Bobir		Ali	Bobir
	$	$	$	$	
Current account		29 300	Balance b/d	150 000	70 000
Motor vehicle	7 000	12 000	Current account	66 500	

Inventory		39 000	Profit on dissolution	2 600	1 300
Cash and cash equivalents	212 100		Cash and cash equivalents		9 000
	219 100	80 300		219 100	80 300

Cash and cash equivalents

	$		$
Receipts from non-current assets	260 000	Balance b/d	28 600
Trade receivables	52 200	Trade payables	76 500
Capital account: Bobir	9 000	Costs of dissolution	4 000
		Capital account: Ali	212 100
	321 200		321 200

In this illustration, both partners receive a profit on dissolution: this amount is transferred to the credit of their capital accounts. If there had been a loss on dissolution, then the amount would have been transferred to the debit side of their capital accounts.

The current accounts are closed down with the balances transferred to the capital accounts. In this illustration, Bobir had a debit balance on his current account as he had withdrawn more than he was entitled to from the appropriations over the years.

As well as a motor vehicle, Bobir also took the inventory at an agreed value.

At the end of the dissolution, Ali is due $212 100 but Bobir has put $9000 cash into the partnership as he has a debit balance on his capital account.

End-of-chapter questions

1 **Sharing out the bank balance**
Tapiwa and Rufaro are in partnership, sharing profits in the ratio 4 : 1, respectively. They have decided to dissolve the partnership. Tapiwa believes that any closing balance in the bank account, after all the assets have been sold and the liabilities paid off, will be shared 80 per cent : 20 per cent.

Explain why this is not necessarily true and how the closing balance will be shared.

2 **Preparing the realisation account on dissolution of a partnership**
Onai and Mazrita are in partnership, sharing profits in the ratio 2 : 1, respectively. They decide to dissolve the partnership on 31 March 2015 due to repeated disagreements about the running of the partnership.

	Book value at 31 March 2015	On dissolution
Inventory	$12 000	$9 200
Machinery	$16 200	$15 400
Trade receivables	$7 400	$6 800
Trade payables	$12 000	$11 400
Vehicles (2)	$24 000	$9 200 taken over by Onai $12 400 taken over by Mazrita

The cost of dissolution was $3000.

a Prepare the realisation account to show the profit or loss on dissolution. Do not record the discounts received or allowed as separate items.

b Prepare the realisation account to show the profit or loss on dissolution. Record the discounts allowed and the discounts received as separate items.

3 Preparing the ledgers on the dissolution of a partnership

The statement of financial position for Sara and Tracey at 30 November 2014 was as follows.

Sara and Tracey Statement of financial position at 30 November 2014		
	$	$
Non-current assets at book value		180 000
Current assets		
Inventory	24 500	
Trade receivables	42 600	
Cash at bank	4 600	71 700
Total assets		251 700
Capital accounts		
Sara	110 000	
Tracey	114 000	224 000
Current liabilities		
Trade payables		27 700
Total capital and liabilities		251 700

Sara and Tracey share profits and losses equally. They have agreed to dissolve the partnership as Sara has decided to move abroad. Tracey will buy most of the assets as she wishes to continue to trade but as a sole trader.

The non-current assets are taken over by Tracey at a value of $210 000. She also takes over the inventory at a value of $23 000.

The trade receivables pay $41 000 and the trade payables are paid $26 000. The cost of dissolution is $4400.

Prepare the ledger accounts necessary to record the dissolution.

4 Preparing the ledgers on the dissolution of a partnership

Jane and John are in partnership, sharing profits and losses in the ratio 5 : 3, respectively. They decided to dissolve the partnership on 31 December 2014.

Jane and John Statement of financial position at 31 December 2014		
	$	$
Non-current assets at book value		
Premises	250 000	
Machinery	64 200	
Fixtures and fittings	43 800	
Motor vehicles	22 000	380 000
Current assets		
Inventory	29 600	
Trade receivables (less provision for doubtful debts $1 400)	42 200	71 800
Total assets		451 800
Capital accounts		
Jane	225 000	
John	135 000	360 000
Current accounts		
Jane	68 100	
John	(27 100)	41 000
Current liabilities		
Trade payables	36 600	
Cash and cash equivalents	14 200	50 800
Total capital and liabilities		451 800

Additional information:

- At dissolution the premises were sold for $256 000, the machinery for $59 200, the fixtures and fittings for $38 400. The motor vehicles were taken over by the partners: Jane $9000 and John $11 000.
- The inventory was sold for $26 400.
- The trade receivables paid $39 800 and the trade payables are paid on $32 600.
- The cost of dissolution was $8000.

Required

Prepare the ledger accounts to record the dissolution.

5 Recording the distribution of the bank balance at dissolution

A partnership has been dissolved and $15 000 is left in the bank.

How should this be distributed between the partners?

A According to the last agreed balances on their capital accounts

B According to the last agreed profit-sharing ratio

C According to the last agreed total balances on their capital and current accounts

D Equally.

6 Identifying the ledger to be used at dissolution

Which ledger account is to be used on the dissolution of a partnership?

A Disposal account

B Dissolution account

C Realisation account

D Revaluation account.

Learning objectives

In this chapter you will learn:

- what a limited company is
- what the characteristics of a limited company are
- about the capital and the reserves of a limited company
- about the different types of shares a limited company may issue
- the difference between bonus issues and rights issues of shares
- how to prepare the journal entries to record the issue of shares and debentures
- how to prepare ledger accounts to record the issue of different types of shares
- how to calculate and deal with dividends paid
- how to describe the sources of finance for a limited liability company, including shares and debentures.

Key terms

Limited liability company: an organisation owned by its shareholders, whose liability is limited to the amount of individually owned fully paid-up shares.

Shareholders: the owners of the share capital of a limited company.

Limited liability: the liability of any shareholder to the debts of the company is limited to the amount of their fully paid-up shares.

Directors: officials appointed by the shareholders to manage the company for them. A director can, but does not have to, be a shareholder.

1.4.4A: Limited companies: structure and accounting for share issues

What is a limited company?

A limited liability company is an organisation owned by its shareholders, whose liability is limited to its share capital. In other words, a limited liability company is a business whose owners' liability for the business's debts is limited to the amount of money that they invested in shares in the business, so their personal possessions cannot be lost. The owner of a company is, therefore, a shareholder.

The following table shows the differences between a sole trader, a partnership and a limited company.

Sole trader	Partnership	Limited company
One owner (sole trader)	Two or more owners (partners)	Unlimited ownership (shareholders)
Unlimited liability	Unlimited liability	Limited liability
Sole trader is entitled to all of the profits	The profits are shared among the partners	Shareholders receive a dividend as their share of profits
Sole trader has all the risk	Risk is shared between the partners according to their partnership agreement	Risk is limited to the amount invested in shares
Sole trader does not have separate legal entity	Partnership does not have separate legal entity	Limited company has separate legal entity to its owners
Sole trader is not required to have an audit or publish accounts	Partnership is not required to have an audit or publish accounts	Limited company must have an audit and publish accounts
Sole trader has full responsibility for running the business	Responsibility of running partnership divided between the partners	Company run by directors who are not necessarily the shareholders
Internal capital is from sole trader	Internal capital is from each partner; each new partner brings extra capital	Capital is raised on the issue of shares
Ideas and workload are limited to the sole trader	Ideas and workload are shared among partners	Directors are appointed by shareholders to have the ideas and to take on the workload

The characteristics of a limited company

A limited company has a separate legal identity from its members. What this means is that a limited company can, for example, sue and be sued in its own name.

The effect of this separate legal identity is best explained by looking at a sole trader compared to a limited company. If a sole trader, John Smith, owes money to a supplier, the supplier can sue John for the amount owing and if he is unable to pay, he could be made bankrupt. If John Smith forms a limited company, John Smith Limited, and the limited company owes money to a supplier, the supplier would sue John Smith Limited. Under these circumstances, if the limited company was unable to pay the debt, the limited company could be liquidated, but John Smith himself would be protected due to the separate legal identity.

A limited company is run and managed by the directors, but is owned by the shareholders. The shareholders invest in a limited company by buying shares in that company and their personal liability is limited to the amount they have paid for their shares.

All limited companies must file a memorandum of association and articles of association with the Registrar of Companies. The memorandum of association details the company's external relationship with the outside world. It gives details of the company name, address and registered office, the company's share capital and the company's objectives. The articles of association contain the rules governing the internal organisation of the company detailing directors' powers, voting rights, conduct of meetings, etc.

Key terms

Memorandum of association: details the company's external relationship with the outside world.

Articles of association: contain the rules governing the internal organisation of the company.

There are two main types of limited company:

- a public limited company
- a private limited company.

Public limited company names end with the abbreviation 'plc' and these companies are able to offer their shares to members of the public. The shares can then be traded on a recognised stock exchange. A public limited company in the UK must have share capital of at least $50 000, at least two shareholders and at least two directors.

Private limited company names end with the abbreviation 'Ltd' and these companies are not allowed to offer their shares to members of the public. In the UK a private limited company must have at least one shareholder and at least one director. There is no minimum requirement for issued share capital.

The reserves of a limited company

Limited companies rarely distribute all of their profits to the shareholders in the form of dividends. Many companies will retain part of their profit for the year in the form of reserves for the future.

Revenue reserves

Revenue reserves are those reserves that are created by transfer from profits made by the company. Revenue reserves may be created for a specific purpose, such as the replacement of non-current assets or major repair work that the directors are aware of. Alternatively, a general reserve may be maintained that has no specific use, but retains profits in the company. Retained earnings themselves are a revenue reserve.

Key term

Revenue reserves: created by transfer from the profits of a company.

> **Key term**
> **Capital reserves**: created as a result of non-trading activities.

Capital reserves

Capital reserves are created as a result of non-trading activities and are not available for distribution to the shareholders in the form of dividends. They cannot be transferred to the income statement. Capital reserves are often represented by unrealised gains, the most common being the revaluation reserve.

The other common capital reserves are:

- the share premium account
- the revaluation reserve.

Share premium account

Shares may be issued at a price above their nominal value if the directors of the company are confident that there will be a demand for the shares or if the shares are already trading on a stock exchange at a price above their nominal value. When this happens, the shares are said to be issued at a premium.

For example, if shares with a nominal value of $1 are issued at a price of $1.50, $1 is credited to the share capital account and the remaining $0.50 is credited to the share premium account. The share premium account is a reserve of the company that is shown separately to the share capital in the equity section of the statement of financial position.

> **Key terms**
> **Share premium account**: created when shares are issued at a value over their nominal value.
> **Debentures**: long-term loans.

The Companies Acts permit only very limited uses of the share premium account as follows:

- To issue bonus shares to shareholders.
- To pay premiums on the redemption of debentures.
- To write off any expenses incurred in the formation of the company.
- To write off any expenses incurred in the issue of shares or debentures.

Shares

The capital of a limited company is divided into small units called shares. The value of a share in a limited company could be as low as $0.50, but $1 shares are more typical, and shares with other nominal values are possible. To be a member (owner) of a limited company, a person must become a shareholder by buying one or more of the available shares.

> **Key terms**
> **Shares**: the capital of a limited company is split into small units called shares.
> **Nominal value**: the price description of an issued share under the company's constitution.

Private companies (Ltd) sell shares to known individuals, such as family and friends, whereas public limited companies (plc) sell their shares to the general public. Public limited companies tend to be larger than private limited companies as they can raise more funds from a wider range of people.

If a company loses all of its assets, shareholders will lose their investment. If shareholders have paid in full for their shares then their liability is limited to what they have paid, whereas shareholders who have not yet paid in full for their shares can only be asked to pay any balance outstanding. This is called limited liability.

The return shareholders receive on their investment is called a dividend. A dividend can be paid at some point during the financial year (called an interim dividend) and/or declared at the end of the financial year, once profits are known (a final dividend).

Alternatively, many people invest in shares not for the dividend, but for capital growth. If shares are issued at their nominal value, they are referred to as issued at par. If shares are issued at a higher price than their nominal value, a share premium is created. Both the nominal value and share premium are shown in the financial statements. The market price of a share can fluctuate daily, depending on what individuals are willing to pay for shares, and this is not shown in the financial statements. Capital growth is achieved if the shares are sold for a higher market price than their original purchase price.

Types of shares

Ordinary shares are the most common type of share issued. An ordinary shareholder receives a variable dividend based on the level of profit, but if there is insufficient cash or profit, or both, then dividends do not have to be paid.

Each share represents one vote at the annual general meeting (AGM), so the more shares a shareholder owns, the greater the control. Various decisions are voted on at the AGM, including the rate of dividend. Ordinary shareholders receive their dividend out of profits after preference shareholders. There is generally thought to be more risk associated with ordinary shares as their dividend is not guaranteed and is paid last, so many ordinary shareholders invest in shares for capital growth only.

Holders of preference shares have a preferential right to dividends over ordinary shareholders and so receive their dividend first. As they are more likely to receive a dividend, they are seen as holding the shares with the lower risk. However, the amount of dividend that they receive is at a fixed percentage of the nominal value of their investment, so in periods of high profits it is possible that their dividend will be lower than that paid to an ordinary shareholder.

Preference shareholders are not entitled to vote at the AGM and are therefore seen as having less control than ordinary shareholders. The shares will be either cumulative preference shares or non-cumulative preference shares. If dividends are not paid in one year due to a lack of funds or profits, then in the case of cumulative preference shares the shareholders carry forward their right to the dividend to the next year,

Key terms

Dividend: the amount given to shareholders as their share of the profits of the company.

Capital growth: this arises when shares are sold by a shareholder for a value greater than their original purchase cost.

Share issued at par: a share issued at its nominal (face) value.

Share premium: the difference between the nominal value of shares and the price at which they are issued.

Ordinary share: the most common type of share with voting rights. There is no guarantee of dividend payment as each share has a variable rate of dividend dependent on the level of profit.

Preference share: a share entitled to a fixed rate of dividend that is appropriated ahead of any ordinary share dividend. Normally, preference shares are seen as low risk and do not carry voting rights.

Cumulative preference share: a share where, if a company fails to pay the preference dividend in any year, then the dividend arrears are carried forward until profits are large enough to pay the arrears.

Non-cumulative preference share: a share where, if a company fails to pay the preference dividend in any years, then the dividend arrears are *not* carried forward until profits are large enough to pay the arrears.

Key terms

Redeemable preference shares: these issued shares can be bought back by the company at a future date.

Authorised share capital: the maximum amount of share capital that a limited company is allowed to issue under its constitution.

Issued share capital: the amount of share capital that the company has actually issued to shareholders, which cannot exceed the authorised amount.

and so on until the accumulating dividend rights can be paid. Non-cumulative preference shares do not have this advantage.

* Redeemable preference shares can be bought back by the company if allowed by the Articles of Association (e.g. 8 per cent redeemable preference shares 2016 can be bought back by 2016).

The issue of shares

When a company is formed, the maximum number of shares that can be issued is referred to as the authorised share capital, whereas the number of shares actually issued is referred to as the issued share capital.

The amount received for the shares when they are first issued depends on the market price of the shares. The market price may be higher than the nominal (face) value of the share. In the accounting records of a limited company, it is important to record the nominal (face) value of shares separately from any extra value (the share premium) gained when the shares are issued.

Illustration 1: Preparing the journal entries required to record the issue of shares

A limited company has authorised share capital of 200 000 ordinary shares of $1 each and 100 000 8 per cent preference shares of $2 each.

The company decided to issue 100 000 ordinary shares at $1.30 and 50 000 8 per cent preference shares at $2.20. These shares are fully subscribed and paid up.

Required

1 Record the issue of ordinary shares.

Step 1: Work out how much money will be raised:

100 000 × $1.30 = $130 000

Step 2: Separate the nominal value of the shares from the share premium:

Nominal value: 100 000 × $1 nominal value = $100 000

Share premium: 100 000 shares × $0.30 premium = $30 000

2 Record the issue of the 8 per cent preference shares.

Step 1: Work out how much money will be raised:

50 000 × $2.20 = $110 000

Step 2: Separate the nominal value of the shares from the share premium:

Nominal value: 50 000 shares × $2 nominal value = $100 000

Share premium: 50 000 shares × $0.20 = $10 000

The journal needed to record this issue of shares is as follows.

Journal		
	Dr ($)	Cr ($)
Bank	240 000	
Issued share capital		
Ordinary shares		100 000
Preference shares		100 000
Share premium		40 000
Issue of ordinary and preference shares at a premium		

- Share capital (always at nominal value) and share premium are recorded in the equity section of the statement of financial position.
- The money received for the issue is recorded within the bank account in current assets.

Illustration 2: Completing the equity section in the statement of financial position

The issue of ordinary and preference shares detailed in Illustration 1 would be recorded in the equity section of the company's statement of financial position as shown.

Equity	$
Issued share capital:	
100 000 ordinary shares of $1 each	100 000
50 000 8% preference shares of $2 each	100 000
Share premium	40 000
Reserves	XX
Retained earnings	XX
Total equity	XX

Using a bonus or rights issue of shares to increase capital

Limited companies often choose to increase their issued share capital by making either a bonus issue or a rights issue to existing shareholders.

Bonus issue

Companies may use their reserves to issue bonus shares to their ordinary shareholders in the ratio of their existing shareholding. These shares are issued with no payment required by the shareholders since they already own the reserves of the company. A bonus issue is a way of releasing reserves to the shareholders without the impact on cash flow that would occur if a dividend were declared, since no cash flows into or out of the company.

Either capital reserves or revenue reserves can be used to issue bonus shares, but companies will use capital reserves first, as this is one of the few uses allowed for capital reserves.

The effect of issuing bonus shares is that the share capital will increase on the statement of financial position by the amount of shares issued, while reserves will decrease by the same amount. The rest of the statement of financial position will remain the same as before the issue.

Illustration 3: Bonus issue of shares

A company's statement of financial position at 31 December 2014 is:

	$000
Non-current assets	1 550
Net current assets	250
	1 800
Equity	
Ordinary shares of $1 each	1 000
Share premium	400
General reserve	250
Retained earnings	150
	1 800

The directors decide to issue bonus shares on the basis of one share for every two ordinary shares held. The statement of financial position of the company after the issue of the bonus shares will be:

	$000
Non-current assets	1 550
Net current assets	250
	1 800
Equity	
Ordinary shares of $1 each	1 500
General reserve	150
Retained earnings	150
	1 800

Note that $400 000 of the bonus issue reduces the share premium account (a capital reserve) to a zero balance. The remaining $100 000 is taken off the general reserve (a revenue reserve). The ordinary shares in issue increase by $500 000 of the bonus issue.

Rights issue

Unlike the bonus issue of shares, the purpose of a rights issue is to raise further finance for the company. A rights issue offers existing shareholders the opportunity to purchase additional shares at a price slightly below the current market price. As is the case with a bonus issue, shareholders are offered the additional shares in proportion to their current shareholding. The shareholder has the option of either taking up and paying for the shares offered or, alternatively, selling the rights on the stock market.

Illustration 4: Rights issue of shares

A company's statement of financial position at 31 December 2014 is:

	$000
Non-current assets	1 100
Net current assets	100
	1 200
Equity	
Ordinary shares of $1 each	600
General reserve	350
Retained earnings	250
	1 200

The directors wish to raise additional finance and offer shareholders a rights issue of one additional ordinary share for every three shares held at a price of $1.25 (the current market price is $1.30).

Assuming that all shareholders take up the rights issue, the statement of financial position on completion will be:

	$000
Non-current assets	1 100
Net current assets	350
	1 450
Equity	
Ordinary shares of $1 each	800
Share premium	50
General reserve	350
Retained earnings	250
	1 450

The fact that the shares have been sold at a premium of $0.25 means that a share premium account is created for the total premium received of $50 000 (200 000 shares × $0.25). Net current assets increase by the total cash received of $250 000 and share capital increases by the nominal value of shares sold (200 000).

The calculation of dividends

Ordinary shares

The dividends to be paid on ordinary shares can be calculated in different ways.

Illustration 5: Calculating dividends on ordinary shares using a percentage

A limited company has 100 000 ordinary shares of $1 each. A dividend is declared at 6 per cent.

A shareholder with 1000 shares would receive a dividend of 6 per cent of the nominal value of the shareholder's investment = 1000 × (6 ÷ 100) = $60

Illustration 6: Calculating dividends on ordinary shares using a rate per share

A limited company has 100 000 ordinary shares of $1 each. A dividend is declared at $0.08 per share.

A shareholder with 1000 shares would receive a dividend of:

1000 × $0.08 = $80

Illustration 7: Calculating dividends on ordinary shares with a nominal value of less than $1

A limited company has raised $200 000 from issuing ordinary shares with a nominal value of $0.50 each. A dividend is declared at $0.02 per share.

The number of issued shares is ($200 000 ÷ $0.50) = 400 000 shares.

The total dividend is 400 000 × $0.02 = $8000.

Preference shares

Illustration 8: Calculating dividends on preference shares

A limited company has 200 000 8 per cent preference shares of $1 each. A dividend is declared.

A shareholder with 1000 shares would receive a dividend of:

1000 × (8 ÷ 100) = $80

Summary

Share details	Rate	Calculation of dividend
20 000 $1 ordinary shares	$0.05 per share	20 000 × $0.05 = $1 000
40 000 $1 preference shares	4%	40 000 × (4 ÷ 100) = $1 600
500 000 $2 ordinary shares	$0.02	500 000 × $0.02 = $10 000
100 000 $0.50 preference shares	5%	(100 000 ÷ 2) × (5 ÷ 100) = $2 500

Interim and final dividends

Preference shareholders receive a fixed rate of dividend. The total amount paid to preference shareholders cannot exceed the fixed rate, so it does not matter to a preference shareholder if there is an interim dividend as well as a final dividend because these two dividends will equal the fixed rate. However, an ordinary shareholder can receive two dividend payments that are totally independent of each other and for which there is no maximum.

Illustration 9: Calculating interim and final dividends on preference shares and ordinary shares

A limited company has issued share capital consisting of 100 000 ordinary shares of $2 each and 50 000 6 per cent preference shares of $1 each.

During the financial year, an interim dividend of $0.05 per share is paid on the ordinary shares as well as a final dividend of $0.10 per share. An interim dividend of $1500 is paid to the preference shareholders with the remainder paid as a final dividend at the end of the year.

The dividend calculations are:

	Interim dividend	Final dividend	Total dividend
	$	$	$
Preference shares	1 500	1 500	$50 000 × 6% = 3 000
Ordinary shares	100 000 × $0.05 = 5 000	100 000 × $0.10 = 10 000	15 000

Note: The maximum amount of dividend that the preference shareholders can receive in this example is $3000. The directors have decided to divide the total dividend into two payments of equal amounts. Ordinary shareholders have no maximum or minimum amount of dividend, as their dividend depends on the level of profitability.

Debentures

Debentures are long-term loans, usually redeemable (repayable) at a specific date and carrying a fixed rate of interest. A limited company receives money on loan and in return issues certificates called debentures to the lender. These certificates stipulate the amount of interest to be paid.

Debenture interest is paid out of profits and before dividends on any type of share. The amount of interest paid is the same every year and is not optional, as it must be paid regardless of the level of profit or availability of cash. Usually, debentures are secured against the value of assets so that if the company defaults on an interest payment then the assets can be taken as payment instead. These are called 'mortgage debentures'. Debentures without such security are referred to as 'simple' or 'naked' debentures.

Getting it right

Do not confuse debenture holders with shareholders. Debenture holders are not the owners of the company and have no say in how the company is run. Debenture interest payments are a running cost of the company.

It is also important to remember that debentures appear as non-current liabilities on the statement of financial position (unless they are to be redeemed within the coming 12 months) and do not appear in the equity section.

Illustration 10: Calculating interest on debentures

A limited company has 400 000 7 per cent debentures 2014–2016.

These debentures have a 7 per cent rate of interest, so the total interest to be paid is: 400 000 × 0.07 = $28 000.

The debentures must be redeemed between 2014 and 2016.

Debentures are issued for cash.

Illustration 11: Creating the journal entry required to record the issue of debentures

A limited company issued $300 000 8 per cent debentures.

The journal to record this issue is:

Journal		
	Dr ($)	**Cr ($)**
Bank	300 000	
Debentures		300 000
Debentures issued for cash		

- Debentures are recorded in the non-current liabilities section in the statement of financial position.
- The interest paid and payable on debentures is recorded as an expense in the income statement.
- Any interest outstanding is recorded as an accrual in the current liabilities section in the statement of financial position.

End-of-chapter questions

1 Calculating the amount of ordinary and preference dividends

A limited company has issued share capital of:

- 300 000 ordinary shares of $2 each
- 200 000 6 per cent preference shares of $1 each.

During the financial year ended 31 December 2014, a dividend of $0.05 per share was paid on the ordinary shares as well as the dividend on the preference shares.

Calculate how much the company paid out as dividends during the year ended 31 December 2014.

2 Calculating the amount of ordinary and preference dividends

A limited company has authorised share capital of:

- 500 000 ordinary shares of $0.50 each
- 200 000 5 per cent preference shares of $1 each.

The company had actually issued 80 per cent of its ordinary shares and 50 per cent of its preference shares.

During the year ended 31 March 2014, the company declared and paid an ordinary dividend of $0.02 per share and the preference dividend due.

Calculate the amount of dividends paid by the company during the year.

3 **Preparing the journal to record the issue of ordinary shares**
Fox Ltd, a limited company, has authorised share capital of 200 000 ordinary shares of $1 each.

The company decided to issue 100 000 ordinary shares at $1.30. These shares were fully subscribed and paid up.

Prepare the journal to record the issue of ordinary shares.

4 **Preparing the journal to record the issue of preference shares and debentures**
Fox Ltd has also authorised share capital of 500 000 preference shares of $0.20 each.

The company decided to issue all of the preference shares at $0.45 each, as well as 8 per cent debentures to the value of $200 000.

Prepare the journal to record the issue of preference shares and the debentures.

5 **Preparing the journal to record the issue of shares and the payment of a dividend**
S. Green Ltd has authorised share capital of 100 000 ordinary shares of $1 each.

The company decided to issue 50 000 ordinary shares at $1.50 each. These shares were fully subscribed and paid up. After six months, the company paid a dividend of $0.05 per share.

Prepare the journal entries to record the issue of ordinary shares and the payment of the dividend.

6 **Preparing the journal to record the issue of debentures and the payment of interest**
Roses in Bloom Ltd issued $200 000 6 per cent debentures on 1 January 2014. Interest was paid for the year on 31 December 2014.

Prepare the journal entries to record the issue of the debenture and the payment of interest.

7 **Calculation of ordinary share dividend**
What do limited companies calculate their ordinary share dividend as being a percentage of?

A Nominal value of authorised capital
B Nominal value of issued capital
C Total assets
D Total reserves.

8 **Authorised share capital**
What is a limited company's authorised capital?

A Capital that has been authorised to be put into reserves
B Capital that has been authorised to be spent on non-current assets
C The number of shares that only company directors are allowed to own
D The number of shares that the company is allowed to issue.

9 **Share issue**
To which of the following is the difference credited when a limited company sells shares at more than their nominal value?

A Retained earnings
B The income statement
C The ordinary share capital account
D The share premium account.

10 **Preference share dividends**
TJZL Ltd has an authorised capital that includes 200 000 10 per cent $1 preference shares, of which 160 000 are issued. These shares are currently being sold for $2 each.

Assuming that the company makes sufficient profits, what will the dividend payment to preference shareholders in any one year be?

A $4000
B $16 000
C $20 000
D $32 000

11 **Calculation of dividends**
A limited company's records show the following.

	$
Authorised capital	1 000 000
Issued capital	700 000
10% debentures	500 000

If the directors declare a 10 per cent dividend, what will shareholders receive?

A $50 000
B $70 000
C $100 000
D $220 000

12 **Calculation of dividends**
A limited company has an authorised capital of 400 000 ordinary shares of $0.50 each. The issued capital is $150 000. The directors declare a dividend of $0.10 per share.

What will the dividend amount be?

A $10 000
B $20 000
C $30 000
D $40 000

13 Rights issue

A company has an issued share capital of 500 000 ordinary shares of $1 each. The company makes a rights issue of one ordinary share for every two shares held at $1.20 per share. What will the effect be on the share capital account and on the share premium account?

A Share capital increases by $250 000. Share premium account increases by $50 000
B Share capital increases by $300 000. Share premium account increases by $50 000
C Share capital increases by $250 000. Share premium account is unchanged
D Share capital increases by $300 000. Share premium account is unchanged.

14 Bonus issue

A company has an issued share capital of 500 000 ordinary shares of $1 each. The company makes a bonus issue of one ordinary share for every two shares held. What will the effect be on the share capital account and on the net current assets?

A Share capital increases by $250 000. Net current assets increase by $300 000
B Share capital increases by $250 000. Net current assets are unchanged
C Share capital increases by $300 000. Net current assets increase by $50 000
D Share capital increases by $300 000. Net current assets are unchanged.

15 Revenue reserves

Which one of the following reserves is a revenue reserve?

A Capital redemption reserve
B General reserve
C Revaluation reserve
D Share premium account.

16 Bonus and rights issue

A company has an issued share capital of 100 000 ordinary shares of $1 each. On 1 June, the company makes a bonus issue of one ordinary share for every four shares held. On 1 September, the company makes a rights issue of one ordinary share for every five shares held at $1.20. The rights issue is fully subscribed.

What is the issued share capital of the company as a result of the bonus issue and the rights issue?

A $120 000
B $125 000
C $150 000
D $155 000

Learning objectives

In this chapter you will learn:

- how to prepare the income statement of a limited company
- how to prepare the statement of changes in equity of a limited company
- how to prepare the statement of financial position of a limited company.

Link

The statement of cash flows is discussed in A Level Chapter 1.1.3 Limited liability companies.

1.4.4B: Limited companies: financial statements

The financial statements of a limited company

The financial statements of a limited company should comprise:

- the income statement
- the statement of changes in equity
- the statement of financial position
- the statement of cash flows.

The income statement

The income statement of a limited company is very similar to the income statement of a sole trader as shown in Chapter 1.4.2A. The main difference is that the limited company income statement is in a more abbreviated format.

Illustration 1: Income statement

AB Limited trades as a retailer of motor vehicles. The following is an example of its income statement for the year ended 31 March 2015.

AB Limited
Income statement for the year ended 31 March 2015

	$000	$000
Revenue		9 000
Cost of sales		(4 000)
Gross profit		5 000
Overheads:		
Distribution costs (note 1)	(7 00)	
Administrative expenses (note 2)	(2 400)	
		(3 100)
Profit from operations		1 900
Finance costs (note 3)		(400)
Profit for the year (note 4)		1 500

Explanatory notes

1 Distribution costs include all costs of advertising goods for sale, selling goods and distributing them to the customers.

2 Administrative expenses include all other overheads, including payments made to the directors.

3 Finance costs include all interest costs to banks, and dividends paid to preference shareholders.

4 Profit for the year is taken to the statement of changes in equity.

Expenses specific to limited companies

There are some expenses that do not occur in any business or organisation other than in a limited company, as discussed below.

Auditors' fees

Auditors are appointed by the directors to verify the accuracy of the records and financial statements. They are independent and are appointed to report back to the shareholders at the annual general meeting (AGM) on whether the accounts are true and fair. Their fees are recorded as an expense in the income statement and, if unpaid and owing for that financial period, are shown as a current liability in the statement of financial position.

Directors' remuneration

Directors are appointed by the shareholders to manage the business on their behalf. They have a stewardship role. Not all directors are shareholders and only a few shareholders are directors. All monies paid to directors (fees, salaries, etc.) are referred to as their remuneration and are recorded as an expense in the income statement. If any remuneration is outstanding and unpaid at the year end, it is recorded in the current liabilities in the statement of financial position.

Debenture interest

Debentures are loans that bear a fixed rate of interest. This interest is an expense and should be recorded in the income statement. Again, if all or part of the interest remains unpaid it should be recorded as an accrual in the current liabilities section of the statement of financial position. The debentures are recorded as a non-current liability.

The statement of changes in equity

The statement of changes in equity shows how changes have taken place in the shareholders' stake in the company and shows both realised gains and losses, such as:

- increases or decreases in retained earnings
- equity dividends paid
- unrealised gains such as transfers to revaluation reserves.

Illustration 2: Statement of changes in equity

The following is an example of the statement of changes in equity of AB Limited for the year ended 31 March 2015.

Link

There is more on auditors and directors in A Level Chapter 1.1.5 Auditing and stewarding of limited companies.

Key terms

Auditors: external independent checkers of the accounting information used to prepare the financial statements.

Annual general meeting (AGM): an annual meeting that all companies hold, to which all shareholders are invited.

Stewardship: the idea that managers, directors, etc. are responsible to the owners of a business for the efficient use of a business's resources.

Getting it right

It is important to remember that debenture holders are not the owners of the limited company and, therefore, the interest payable is treated as an expense. A common error is to treat debenture holders as shareholders.

Profit is then either shared out to stakeholders, such as to the shareholders in the form of dividends, or retained by the company for future use as reserves. Profit for the year is then taken to the statement of changes in equity.

AB Limited				
Statement of changes in equity for the year ended 31 March 2015				
	Total	**Share capital**	**Retained earnings**	**Revaluation reserve**
	$000	**$000**	**$000**	**$000**
Balance at 1 April 2014	3 670	2 000	1 450	220
Profit for the year	900		900	
Dividends paid	(120)		(120)	
Revaluation of property	80			80
Balance at 31 March 2015	4 530	2 000	2 230	300

The closing balances on the statement of changes in equity will form part the equity (capital and reserves) section of the statement of financial position at 31 March 2015.

The statement of financial position

The statement of financial position of a limited company takes exactly the same structure as that of a sole trader, except the capital account of a sole trader is replaced by the capital and reserves of a limited company.

Illustration 3: The statement of financial position

The following is an example of the statement of financial position of AB Limited at 31 March 2015.

AB Limited Statement of financial position at 31 March 2015		
	$000	**$000**
Non-current assets		
Goodwill		200
Property, plant and equipment		3 400
		3 600
Current assets		
Inventory	1 800	
Trade and other receivables	1 400	
Cash and cash equivalents	100	3 300
Total assets		6 900
Equity		
Issued ordinary share capital		2 000
Revaluation reserve		300
Retained earnings		2 230
		4 530
Non-current liabilities		
Bank loans	50	

6% debentures (2019–2021)	150	200
Current liabilities		
Trade and other payables	900	
Taxation	600	
Cash and cash equivalents	670	2 170
Total equity and liabilities		6 900

Dividends

Dividends are the share of the company's distributable profits that the directors decide to distribute to the ordinary shareholders as a return on their investment. The amount of the dividend will depend on the level of profits: occasionally, the directors will declare no dividend at all.

A company may declare an interim dividend based on the half-year results of the company. This will be paid during the current financial year. At the end of the financial year, the directors will then decide on the amount, if any, of the final dividend to be paid. This will be paid after the end of the financial year.

Dividends may be presented in two different ways:

- As an amount per ordinary share (for example $0.15 per share).
- As a percentage of the nominal value of each ordinary share (for example 15 per cent).

Only those dividends that are actually paid during the financial year will be shown in the company's financial statements. The total amount of dividends paid will be shown as part of the statement of changes in equity. Where the directors have declared a final dividend for the year, a note to the accounts will be made, but no provision is made in the accounts themselves.

Preparing the financial statements of a limited company

Illustration 4: Limited company accounts

The following trial balance has been extracted from the books of account of Source Ltd at 31 March 2015.

	$000	$000
Revenue		620 500
Purchases	332 000	
Inventory at 1 April 2014	85 000	
Distribution costs	74 000	

Administration expenses	62 000	
Finance costs	18 000	
Taxation	2 000	
Freehold property at cost	110 000	
Motor vehicles at cost	84 000	
Motor vehicles provision for depreciation		36 000
Plant and equipment at cost	102 000	
Plant and equipment provision for depreciation		81 600
8% debenture 2019/2020		40 000
Trade receivables	26 000	
Trade payables		22 000
50 000 ordinary shares of $1 each		50 000
40 000 5% preference shares of $1 each		40 000
Share premium account		15 000
General reserve		10 000
Retained earnings		9 400
Ordinary shares dividends paid	7 500	
Preference shares dividends paid	1 000	
Cash and cash equivalents	21 000	
Totals	**924 500**	**924 500**

Additional information:

1 Inventory at 31 March 2015 is valued at $90 000.

2 Debenture interest for the six months ended 31 March 2015 is outstanding.

3 The preference share dividend for the six months ended 31 March 2015 is outstanding.

4 Depreciation for the year ended 31 March 2015 is to be provided as follows:

   a Motor vehicles 25 per cent reducing balance charged to administration expenses.

   b Plant and machinery 10 per cent straight-line charged to cost of sales.

5 The directors wish to transfer $4000 to the general reserve.

6 The directors wish to make a provision for taxation of $30 000.

7 There have been no changes to share capital during the year.

8 The authorised ordinary share capital of Source Ltd is $100 000.

Required

Prepare the following for Source Ltd.

a An income statement for the year ended 31 March 2015.

b A statement of changes in equity for the year ended 31 March 2015.

c A statement of financial position as at 31 March 2015.

Solution

Source Ltd Income statement for the year ended 31 March 2015		
	$000	**$000**
Revenue		620 500
Cost of sales (85 + 332 – 90 + 10.200)		(337 200)
Gross profit		283 300
Overheads:		
Distribution costs	(74 000)	
Administrative expenses (62 + 12)	(74 000)	(148 000)
Profit from operations		135 300
Finance costs (18 + 1.6 + 1 + 1)		(21 600)
Profit before tax		113 700
Taxation (2 + 30)		(32 000)
Profit for the year		81 700

Source Ltd Statement of changes in equity for the year ended 31 March 2015					
	Total	**Share capital**	**Share premium**	**General reserve**	**Retained earnings**
	$000	**$000**	**$000**	**$000**	**$000**
Balance at 1 April 2014	84 400	50 000	15 000	10 000	9 400
Profit for the year	81 700				81 700
Dividends paid	(7 500)				(7 500)
Transfer general reserve	–			(4 000)	(4 000)
Balance at 31 March 2015	158 600	50 000	15 000	14 000	79 600

Source Ltd Statement of financial position as at 31 March 2015			
	$000	**$000**	**$000**
Non-current assets			
Freehold property	110 000	–	110 000
Motor vehicles	84 000	48 000	36 000
Plant and equipment	102 000	91 800	10 200
	296 000	139 800	156 200
Current assets			
Inventory		90 000	
Trade and other receivables		26 000	
Cash and cash equivalents		21 000	137 000
Total assets			293 200

Equity			
Issued ordinary share capital			50 000
Share premium			15 000
5% preference share capital			40 000
General reserve			14 000
Retained earnings			79 600
			198 600
Non-current liabilities			
8% debenture (2019/2020)			40 000
Current liabilities			
Trade and other payables (22 + 1 + 1.6)		24 600	
Taxation		30 000	54 600
Total equity and liabilities			293 200

Simple statements of cash flow

A company's income statement, statement of changes in equity and statement of financial position will provide owners and other interested groups with a great deal of information about profitability. However, users also need to be well informed about how well the company's cash resources have been used. Many otherwise profitable concerns have failed because this aspect of a business's affairs has not been well managed. To this end, it is possible to prepare a statement that summarises the sources from which a business has obtained cash (cash inflows) and that also shows how these cash resources have been used during a financial period (cash outflows). As a result those using the accounting statements will be able to focus on some important aspects of business management, for example:

- Has enough cash been raised to sustain the business?
- Has the company raised enough cash to pay off its debts as they fall due?
- Has the company been able to ensure investment in key resources (for example non-current assets)?

A simple statement of cash flow will identify the main cash inflows:

- Profit for the year, i.e. the cash inflow that has resulted from revenue less the costs of running the business. However, it is necessary to adjust the figure for profit to remove the effect of depreciation as this business cost has no impact on cash resources.
- Issuing shares and debentures or arranging loans.
- Receipts from the sale of non-current assets.
- Improvements to the cash position by reducing inventories or trade receivables, or by increasing the amount owed to trade payables.

Link

There is more about statements of cash flows in A Level Chapter 1.1.3 Limited liability companies. In this chapter the requirements of the relevant international accounting standard IAS 7 will be explained as well as the treatment of other more complex matters in the preparation of statements of cash flow.

Key term

Statement of cash flow: a statement that details a business's cash inflows and cash outflows during a financial period, highlighting key management decisions.

The statement will also identify the main cash outflows:

- repaying loans and debentures
- purchasing non-current assets
- paying dividends to shareholders and paying interest on debentures and other loans
- reductions to cash caused by increasing inventories, increasing trade receivables, or making payments to reduce trade payables.

It is possible to identify cash inflows and outflows for a financial year by comparing the statements of financial position at the beginning and end of the period. With additional information from the income statement and statement of changes in equity, a list of cash inflows and cash outflows can be compiled which explain any change in the company's balance of cash and cash equivalents.

Illustration 5: Preparing a simple statement of cash flows

Here are two comparative statements of financial position for Quadrone Ltd. In addition there is some information from the company's income statement and statement of changes in equity.

The notes alongside the statements of financial position explain the significance of changes for the company's balance of cash and cash equivalents.

Statements of financial position at 31 December			**Notes (figures in $000)**
	2014	***2013***	
	$000	*$000*	
Non-current assets			
Cost	480	*390*	The company purchased additional non-current assets $90
Depreciation	142	*127*	Depreciation charges during 2014 must have been $15
	338	*263*	
Current assets			
Inventory	45	*39*	An additional investment in inventory has been made $6
Trade receivables	25	*30*	The company has managed to reduce the amount owed by $5
Cash and cash equivalents	11	*4*	
	419	*336*	

Equity and reserves			
Ordinary shares of $1 each	250	*210*	There has been an issue of shares from which $40 received
Share premium	50	*30*	plus a share premium of $20
Retained earnings	102	*72*	Profit for the year after dividends has been $30
Current liabilities			
Trade payables	17	*24*	The company has paid out more to reduce trade payables $7
	419	*336*	

Additional information:

1 The company did not dispose of any non-current assets during 2014.

2 Dividends of $42 000 were paid to shareholders during 2014.

3 The company's income statement showed a profit for the year of $72 000.

Step 1: *Identifying cash inflows and cash outflows*

By comparing the two statements of financial position it is possible to identify the cash inflows and cash outflows (see the notes alongside the statement of financial position). The additional information includes details of some other items affecting cash and cash equivalents.

When the cash inflows and cash outflows are listed they should explain why the balance of cash and cash equivalents has increased by $7 000 from $4 000 at 31 December 2013 to $11 000 at 31 December 2014.

Here is the summary (all figures in $000).

Cash inflows	**$000**	
Profit for the year ($72* but add back depreciation $15 as this		
does not affect cash)	87	
Issue of shares at a premium (nominal value $40 plus premium $20)	60	
Decrease in trade receivables	5	
Total cash inflows		152
Cash outflows		
Purchase of non-current assets	90	
Dividends paid	42	
Increase in inventory	6	
Decrease in trade payables	7	
Total cash outflows		145
Net cash inflow		7

*The profit for the year, $72 000, was given in the additional information. This figure could also have been calculated by taking the increase in retained earnings ($30 000) revealed by the statements of financial position and adding back the dividends paid ($42 000).

Step 2: *Reorganising the information to show details under different headings*

It is useful to provide the information about cash inflows and cash outflows under separate headings. This will help users to focus their attention on key aspects of the management of the company's cash resources.

The sub headings in a simple statement of cash flows are:

- Profit (i.e. normal trading activities)
- Investing activities (i.e. changes in non-current assets)
- Financing activities (i.e. changes in the long-term finance of the company).

The cash inflows are shown as positive figures in this improved format and cash outflows are shown as negative figures (i.e. in brackets).

Quadrone Ltd
Simple statement of cash flows for the year ended 31 December 2014

	$000	$000
Arising from profits		
Profit for the year	87	
Increase in inventory	(6)	
Decrease in trade receivables	5	
Decrease in trade payables	(7)	
		79
Investing activities		
Purchase of non-current assets		(90)
Financing activities		
Issue of ordinary shares	60	
Payment of dividends	(42)	
		18
Increase in cash and cash equivalents		7
Balance of cash and cash equivalents at 31 December 2013		4
Balance of cash and cash equivalents at 31 December 2014		11

This simple statement of cashflows highlights information for the user of financial statements which would not be at all obvious from looking at the statement of financial position etc. Users can now see more clearly that:

- a considerable investment was made in non-current assets
- a substantial amount of cash was generated from normal trading activities (profit); more than enough to finance the payment of dividends
- the investment in non-current assets was partly financed by a share issue, but also from the company's profits
- the company's usual cash position was maintained – in fact it was slightly improved.

End-of-chapter questions

1 Dividend payment

AB plc has an authorised share capital of 50 000 ordinary shares of $0.50 each. The issued share capital is $100 000. The directors declare a dividend of $0.15 per ordinary share. What is the total amount of the dividend payment?

- **A** $15 000
- **B** $30 000
- **C** $75 000
- **D** $150 000

2 Dividend payment

CD plc has an authorised share capital of 500 000 ordinary shares of $0.25 each; 80 000 shares have been issued. The directors declare a dividend of 4 per cent. What is the total amount of the dividend payment?

- **A** $200
- **B** $500
- **C** $800
- **D** $1250

3 Equity section

Which of the following will not appear in the equity section of a limited company statement of financial position?

- **A** 5 per cent debenture
- **B** General reserve
- **C** Retained earnings
- **D** Share premium

4 Income statement

Which of the following will not be part of the income statement of a limited company?

- **A** Debenture interest
- **B** Ordinary share dividend
- **C** Preference share dividend
- **D** Taxation

5 Income statement

Which of the following is shown in the income statement of a limited company?

- **A** Asset replacement reserve
- **B** Auditors' fees
- **C** Dividends paid
- **D** Share premium

6 Auditors

Who appoints the auditors of a company?

- **A** The directors
- **B** The employees
- **C** The registrar of companies
- **D** The shareholders

7 Operating profit

A limited liability company's gross profit for the year ended 31 December 2014 was $260 000. The company's expenses were: directors' fees $80 000; administration expenses $20 000; debenture interest $30 000; depreciation charges $50 000. The company's profit from operations was:

- **A** $80 000
- **B** $110 000
- **C** $150 000
- **D** $180 000

8 Equity

A limited liability company's statement of financial position includes the following:

Authorised share capital	$300 000
Issued share capital	$160 000
General reserve	$20 000
Retained earnings	$10 000

Based on this information, the company's total equity is:

- **A** $30 000
- **B** $160 000
- **C** $180 000
- **D** $190 000

9 Preparing an income statement and statement of changes in equity for a limited company

The following balances have been extracted from the books of account of Owen Ltd at 31 March 2015.

	Dr ($000)	Cr ($000)
Administration expenses	3 660	
Cost of sales	41 650	
Distribution costs	3 710	
Dividends paid: ordinary shares	1 500	
Dividends paid: preference shares	300	
General reserve		6 000

Loan interest paid	1 040	
Ordinary $1 shares		150 000
5% preference shares		5 000
Retained earnings		12 620
Revenue		75 100
Share premium		12 500

Additional information (figures in $000):

- The directors propose to transfer $2000 to a general reserve.
- Administration expenses of $120 have been prepaid.

Required

Prepare an income statement and a statement of changes in equity for Owen Ltd for the year ended 31 March 2015.

10 Preparing an income statement and statement of changes in equity for a limited company

The following balances have been extracted from the books of account of Lightowler Ltd at 30 April 2015.

	Dr ($000)	Cr ($000)
Administration expenses	1 100	
Auditors' fees	2 200	
Cost of sales	44 500	
Debenture interest	100	
Directors' remuneration	2 600	
Dividends paid: ordinary shares	2 200	
Dividends paid: preference shares	800	
Premises: cost	54 000	
Premises: provision for depreciation		6 400
Retained earnings		16 200
Rental income		500
Revenue		92 000
Vehicles: cost	2 000	
Vehicles: provision for depreciation		1 600
Wages and salaries	2 600	

Additional information:

- Premises should be depreciated by $540 000.
- Vehicles should be depreciated by $200 000.
- A preference share dividend of $800 000 is outstanding.
- The directors propose to transfer $2 000 000 to a general reserve.

Required

Prepare an income statement and a statement of changes in equity for Lightowler Ltd for the year ended 30 April 2015.

11 Preparing a statement of financial position for a limited company

The following is an extract from the trial balance of Ramteet Ltd at 31 December 2014 after the preparation of the income statement and statement of changes in equity for the year ended on that date.

	Dr	Cr
10% debentures 2020–2022		30 000
Cash and cash equivalents		18 100
Expenses prepaid	8 200	
Fixtures and fittings: net book value	82 000	
General reserve		40 000
Inventory at 31 December 2014	44 900	
Issued share capital		
8% preference shares of $2 each		160 000
Ordinary shares of $1 each		200 000
Premises: net book value	410 000	
Rental income owing	2 100	
Retained earnings		63 900
Share premium		40 000
Trade payables		32 100
Trade receivables	36 900	
Totals	584 100	584 100

Required

Prepare the statement of financial position for Ramteet Ltd at 31 December 2014.

12 Preparing a statement of financial position for a limited company

The following balances have been extracted from the books of Bendon Ltd at 31 October 2014.

	Dr	Cr
10% debentures 2020–2022		50 000
Auditors' fees accrued		15 000
Cash and cash equivalents	15 300	
Prepayments	5 200	
Fixtures and fittings: cost	50 000	
Fixtures and fittings: provision for depreciation		10 000

General reserve		20 000
Inventory at 31 October 2014	38 100	
Issued share capital: ordinary shares of $1 each		100 000
Premises: cost	160 000	
Premises: provision for depreciation		40 000
Retained earnings		46 100
Share premium		30 000
Trade payables		42 400
Trade receivables	56 900	
Vehicles: cost	36 000	
Vehicles: provision for depreciation		8 000
Totals	361 500	361 500

Required

Prepare the statement of financial position of Bendon Ltd at 31 October 2014.

13 Preparing an income statement for a limited company

The following is an extract from the trial balance of Tiger plc at 31 January 2015.

	Dr ($000)	Cr ($000)
Revenue		1 527
Purchases	615	
Inventory at 1 February 2014	102	
Distribution costs	38	
Administration expenses	68	
Finance costs	115	
Plant and machinery: cost	120	
Plant and machinery: provision for depreciation		72
Motor vehicles: cost	160	
Motor vehicles: provision for depreciation		40
Ordinary share dividend paid	60	
6% debenture		80
Issued ordinary shares of $0.50 each		100
8% preference shares		50

Additional information:

- Inventory at 31 January 2015 was valued at $110 000.
- Depreciation is to be provided as follows:
  - Plant and machinery: 10 per cent per annum on a straight-line basis, charged to cost of sales.
  - Motor vehicles: 25 per cent per annum on a reducing-balance basis charged to administrative expenses.
- The interest on the 6 per cent debenture has been paid up to 31 July 2014.
- The preference share dividend is paid in two equal instalments. The preference share dividend for the six months ended 31 January 2015 has not yet been paid.
- The directors have recommended an ordinary share dividend of $0.10 per share.

Required

Prepare an income statement for Tiger plc for the year ended 31 January 2015.

14 Preparing an income statement for a limited company

The following is an extract from the trial balance of Airlie plc at 31 March 2015.

	Dr ($000)	Cr ($000)
Revenue		2 245
Purchases	983	
Inventory at 1 April 2014	65	
Distribution costs	145	
Administration expenses	102	
Finance costs	275	
Ordinary shares interim dividend paid	20	
Plant and machinery: cost	540	
Plant and machinery: provision for depreciation		324
Motor vehicles: cost	250	
Motor vehicles: provision for depreciation		90
Ordinary share dividend paid	85	
8% debenture 2019–2021		150
Issued ordinary shares of $0.25 each		500
10% preference shares		80

Additional information:

- Inventory at 31 March 2015 was valued at $75 000.
- Administration expenses of $2000 have been paid in advance.
- Distribution costs of $4000 are outstanding.
- Depreciation is to be provided as follows:
  - Plant and machinery: 10 per cent per annum on a straight-line basis, charged to cost of sales.

- Motor vehicles: 20 per cent per annum on a reducing-balance basis, charged to distribution expenses.
- The interest on the 8 per cent debenture has been paid up to 31 December 2014.
- The preference share dividend is paid in two equal instalments. The preference share dividend for the six months ended 31 March 2015 has not yet been paid.
- The directors have recommended a final ordinary share dividend of $0.15 per share.

Required

Prepare an income statement for Airlie plc for the year ended 31 March 2015.

15 Preparing an income statement, statement of changes in equity and statement of financial position for a limited company

The following trial balance has been extracted from the books of account of Robins plc at 31 March 2015.

	Dr ($000)	Cr ($000)
Revenue		3 790
Purchases	1 636	
Inventory at 1 April 2014	110	
Distribution costs	662	
Administration expenses	452	
Finance costs	810	
Ordinary shares interim dividend paid	70	
Plant and machinery: cost	410	
Plant and machinery: provision for depreciation		287
Motor vehicles: cost	350	
Motor vehicles: provision for depreciation		70
Freehold property: cost	750	
Freehold property: provision for depreciation		135
10% debenture 2019–2021		340
Issued ordinary shares of $0.25 each		400
Trade receivables	519	
Trade payables		265
Cash and cash equivalents	427	
Retained earnings		869
Share premium		40
	6 196	6 196

Additional information:

- Inventory at 31 March 2015 was valued at $125 000.
- Administration expenses of $4000 have been paid in advance.
- Depreciation is to be provided as follows:
  - Freehold property: 2 per cent per annum on a straight-line basis, charged to administration expenses.
  - Plant and machinery: 10 per cent per annum on a straight-line basis, charged to cost of sales.
  - Motor vehicles: 20 per cent per annum on a reducing-balance basis, charged to distribution expenses.
- The interest on the 10 per cent debenture has been paid up to 30 September 2014.
- The directors have recommended a final ordinary share dividend of $0.10 per share.

Required

Prepare the following for Robins plc.

a An income statement for the year ended 31 March 2015.

b A statement of changes in equity for the year ended 31 March 2015.

c A statement of financial position as at 31 March 2015.

16 Preparing an income statement, statement of changes in equity and statement of financial position for a limited company

The following trial balance has been extracted from the books of account of Ionians plc at 30 April 2014.

	Dr ($000)	Cr ($000)
Revenue		5 528
Purchases	2 619	
Inventory at 1 May 2013	136	
Distribution costs	714	
Administration expenses	613	
Finance costs	956	
Ordinary shares final dividend paid (2013)	60	
Ordinary shares interim dividend paid (2014)	30	
Plant and machinery: cost	820	

Plant and machinery: provision for depreciation		328
Motor vehicles: cost	645	
Motor vehicles: provision for depreciation		373
Freehold property: cost	900	
10% debenture 2020–2023		200
Issued ordinary shares of $0.25 each		800
Trade receivables	850	
Trade payables		342
Cash and cash equivalents	108	
Retained earnings		680
Revaluation reserve		150
Share premium		50
	8 451	8 451

Additional information:

- Inventory at 30 April 2014 was valued at $148 000.
- Depreciation is to be provided as follows:
  - Plant and machinery: $82 000, charged to cost of sales.
  - Motor vehicles: $68 000, charged to distribution expenses.
- The interest on the 10 per cent debenture has been paid up to 31 October 2013.
- The directors have recommended a final ordinary share dividend of $0.15 per share.
- During the year, the company had issued 200 000 ordinary shares of $0.25 at a premium of $0.10.
- The directors wish to revalue the freehold property by $50 000.

Required

Prepare the following for Ionians plc.

a An income statement for the year ended 30 April 2014.

b A statement of changes in equity for the year ended 30 April 2014.

c A statement of financial position as at 30 April 2014.

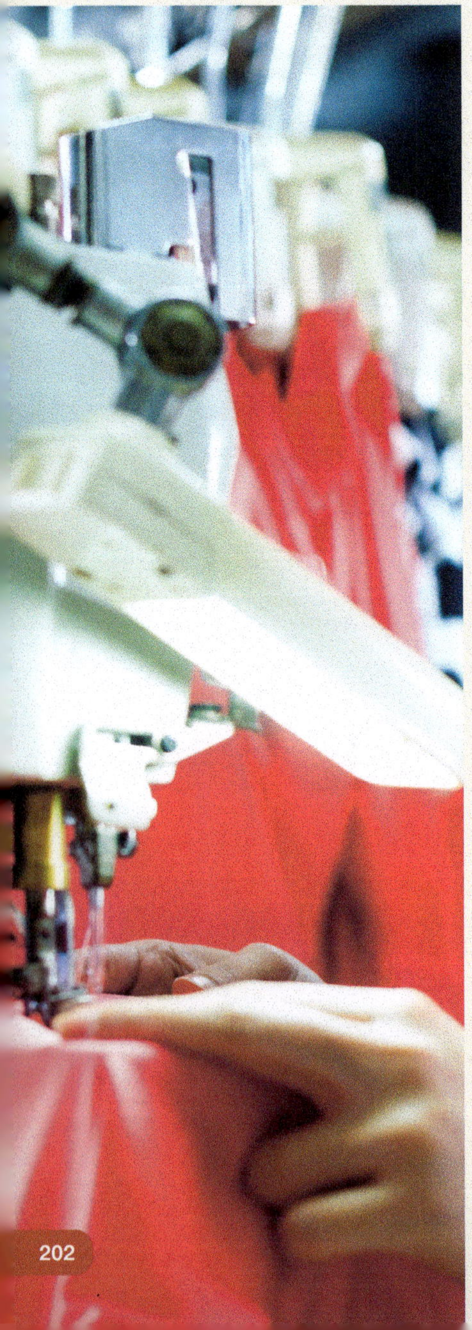

Section 1.5: Analysis and communication of accounting information to stakeholders

Key concepts

Stakeholders rely on financial statements to present a **true and fair view** of a business's affairs and to be prepared on a **consistent** basis so that they can make a valid assessment of the business's performance. Stakeholders also need to be aware that financial statements are based on the **money measurement** concept and so do not show other significant aspects of a business's performance (e.g. the quality of the management team).

1.5.1: Analysis and communication of accounting information to stakeholders

Learning objectives

In this chapter you will learn:

- about the various stakeholders in a business and the interest they have in the financial statements
- about a range of ratios that can be used to analyse the performance of a business and the formula used to calculate each one
- how to calculate ratios based on the end-of-year financial statements of a business
- what each accounting ratio can tell you about a business
- how to make judgments about the strengths and weaknesses of a business's performance
- how to make recommendations that will enable a business's performance to improve.

Key term

Ratio analysis: a method of analysing the financial results of a business in order to measure its performance.

Ratio analysis

Ratio analysis is used to interpret the information contained within financial statements in order to assess the strengths and the weaknesses of a business.

These ratios are used to:

- compare results from year to year to establish the individual company's trends
- compare one year's results to those of other companies within the same industry, using the industry average ratios to evaluate the individual company's performance
- evaluate the company's performance and provide information for interested stakeholders.

The table below shows the stakeholders in a business.

Stakeholder	Reason for interest
Managers or directors	To evaluate business performance for future decision-making, such as setting budgets for future activities and identifying areas requiring improvement.
Bank manager or other lenders	To assess whether to give finance to the business and whether the loans can be paid back with interest.
Suppliers	To assess the likelihood of receiving payment for supplies.
Customers	To be assured that the business will continue to provide goods or services.
Shareholders	To assess whether to continue as a shareholder, buy more shares or sell their current shareholding. Also, to assess the level of return and the security of their investment.
Owners/partners	To assess whether to continue in business, invest more or close the business down. Also, to assess the level of return and the security of their investment.
Potential investors	To compare the performance of one business with that of another business in order to identify the best investment.
Employees and trade unions	To check on the financial prospects of the business for job security, pay rises and wage negotiations, bonuses, training and working conditions.
Government bodies	To check the amounts due for taxation liabilities and to provide data for statistical analysis of the performance of the economy.
Local community	To be assured that the business will continue to provide employment for the local area and to support the local economy.
Environmental bodies	To be assured that activities being carried out by the business are not threatening damage to the environment, wildlife, etc.

Key terms

Profitability ratios: these measure performance, highlighting profit in relation to the resources used in a business.

Liquidity ratios: these measure performance, highlighting a business's ability to pay its day-to-day commitments.

Types of ratio

Ratios can be separated into three categories:

- Profitability ratios: These measure performance, highlighting profit in relation to the resources used in a business, and assess how much profit is made by the business during the current year.
- Liquidity ratios: These measure performance, highlighting a business's ability to pay its day-to-day commitments, and assess the availability of liquid funds in the short term.
- Efficiency ratios: These measure the performance of a business's non-current assets and how efficiently it is managing its current assets, trade receivables, trade payables and inventory.

The examples given here of an income statement and a statement of financial position will be used to analyse the performance of a business in the illustrations that follow.

Assessment Ltd
Income statement for the year ended 31 December 2014

	$	$
Revenue		192 000
Cost of sales		
Opening inventory	11 500	
Purchases	85 500	
Closing inventory	(12 500)	(84 500)
Gross profit		107 500
Less expenses:		
Wages and salaries	12 600	
Administration expenses	1 700	
Selling and distribution costs	1 200	
Directors' remuneration	40 600	
Auditors' fees	2 400	
Depreciation	6 900	
		(65 000)
Operating profit		42 100
Finance costs: debenture interest	2 000	
Preference share dividend paid	800	
		(2 800)
Profit for the year		39 300

Statement of changes in equity for year ended 31 December 2014						
	Total	**Ordinary shares**	**Preference shares**	**Share premium**	**Retained earnings**	**General reserve**
	$	**$**	**$**	**$**	**$**	**$**
Balances at 1 January 2014	102 500	50 000	10 000	14 000	13 500	15 000
Profit for year	39 300				39 300	
Dividends paid	(5 600)				(5 600)	
Transfer of reserves					(5 000)	5 000
	136 200	50 000	10 000	14 000	42 200	20 000

Assessment Ltd Statement of financial position at 31 December 2014			
	$000	**$000**	**$000**
Non-current assets	Cost	Depreciation	Net book value
Premises	153 000	12 000	141 000
Vehicles	32 000	16 000	16 000
	185 000	28 000	157 000
Current assets			
Inventory		12 500	
Trade receivables		16 800	29 300
Total assets			186 300
Equity			
50 000 ordinary shares of $1 each		50 000	
5 000 8% preference shares of $2 each		10 000	
Share premium		14 000	
General reserve		20 000	
Retained earnings		42 200	136 200
Non-current liabilities			
6% debentures (2020–2022)			20 000
Current liabilities			
Trade payables		25 500	
Debenture interest payable		1 900	
Cash and cash equivalents		2 700	30 100
Total equity and liabilities			186 300

Key terms

Profit margin: the amount of profit in cents in relation to each $1 of revenue expressed as a percentage.

Gross profit margin: the percentage of a sale that is profit, namely the amount of gross profit in cents in relation to each $1 of revenue.

Profitability ratios

This table describes the different types of profitability ratio and how they are calculated.

Type of ratio	How to calculate	Description
Profit margin	$\frac{\text{Profit before interest}}{\text{Revenue}} \times 100$	The amount of profit in cents in relation to each $1 of revenue.
Gross profit margin	$\frac{\text{Gross profit}}{\text{Revenue}} \times 100$	The amount of gross profit in cents in relation to each $1 of revenue.

Type of ratio	How to calculate	Description
Mark-up	$\frac{\text{Gross profit}}{\text{Cost of sales}} \times 100$	The percentage added to the cost to calculate the selling price, namely the amount of gross profit in cents added to each $1 of cost of sales.
Expenses/Revenue ratio	$\frac{\text{Expenses}}{\text{Revenue}} \times 100$	The amount of expenses in cents in relation to each $1 of revenue.
Return on capital employed (ROCE)	$\frac{\text{Profit before interest}}{\text{Capital employed}} \times 100$	The amount of profit in cents in relation to each $1 of capital used within the business.

Key terms

Expenses/Revenue ratio: the amount of expenses in cents in relation to each $1 of revenue expressed as a percentage.

Return on capital employed (ROCE): the amount of profit in cents in relation to each $1 of capital used within the business expressed as a percentage.

Illustration 1: Using profitability ratios

Using the information provided for Assessment Ltd, the profitability ratios are as follows:

$$\text{Profit margin} = \frac{42\,100}{192\,000} \times 100 = 21.93\%$$

From each $1 of revenue, $0.2193 is profit.

$$\text{Gross profit margin} = \frac{107\,500}{192\,000} \times 100 = 55.99\%$$

From each $1 of revenue $0.5599 is gross profit.

$$\text{Mark-up} = \frac{107\,500}{84\,500} \times 100 = 127.22\%$$

Each $1 of cost of sales is marked up by 127.22 per cent to achieve gross profit.

$$\text{Expenses/Sales ratio, e.g. wages and salaries} = \frac{12\,600}{192\,000} \times 100 = 6.56\%$$

From each $1 of revenue, 6.56 per cent is used to pay wages and salaries.

$$\text{Return on capital employed} = \frac{42\,100}{(136\,200 + 20\,000)} \times 100 = 26.95\%$$

From every $1 of capital employed (used) within the business $0.2695 is profit.

Key terms

Current ratio: the amount of current assets in dollars to each $1 of current liabilities (sometimes known as the working capital ratio).

Liquid (acid test) ratio: the amount of current assets excluding inventory in dollars to each $1 of current liabilities (sometimes known as the liquid capital ratio).

Liquidity ratios

This table describes the different types of liquidity ratio and how they are calculated.

Type of ratio	How to calculate	Description
Current ratio	Current assets: current liabilities	The amount of current assets in dollars to each dollar of current liabilities.
Liquid (acid test) ratio	Current assets less inventory: current liabilities	The amount of current assets, excluding inventory, in dollars to each dollar of current liabilities.

Illustration 2: Using liquidity ratios

Using the information provided for Assessment Ltd, the liquidity ratios are as follows:

Current ratio = 29 300 : 30 100 = 0.97 : 1

For every $1 that is owed in short-term debt, there are $0.97 of current assets.

Liquid (acid test) ratio = (29 300 – 12 500) : 30 100 = 0.56 : 1

For every $1 that is owed in short-term debt, there are only $0.56 of liquid assets.

Efficiency ratios

This table describes the different types of efficiency ratio and how they are calculated.

Type of ratio	How to calculate	Description
Non-current asset turnover	$\frac{\text{Net revenue}}{\text{Net book value of non-current assets}}$	The amount of sales the business is obtaining from its investment in non-current assets.
Trade receivables turnover (average collection period)	$\frac{\text{Trade receivables}}{\text{Credit revenues}} \times 365$	The average amount of time (in days) it takes for trade receivables (customers) to pay their debts.
Trade payables turnover (average payment period)	$\frac{\text{Trade payables}}{\text{Credit purchases}} \times 365$	The average amount of time (in days) it takes for the business to pay its debts (suppliers).
Rate of inventory turnover (times)	$\frac{\text{Cost of sales}}{\text{Average inventory}}$	The number of times the inventory is sold during a financial period.
Rate of inventory turnover (days)	$\frac{\text{Average inventory}}{\text{Cost of sales}} \times 365$	The number of days it takes for inventory to be sold during a financial period.

Key terms

Non-current asset turnover: the amount of sales the business is obtaining from its investment in non-current assets.

Trade receivables turnover (average collection period): the average amount of time in days it takes for trade receivables (customers) to pay their debts.

Trade payables turnover (average payment period): the average amount of times in days it takes for the business to pay its debts (suppliers).

Rate of inventory turnover (times): the number of times the inventory is sold during a financial period.

Rate of inventory turnover (days): the number of days it takes for inventory to be sold during a financial period.

Getting it right

If the opening and closing inventory is not given, so an average cannot be calculated; then use the closing inventory only.

Illustration 3: Using efficiency ratios

Using the information provided for Assessment Ltd, the efficiency ratios are as follows:

$$\text{Non-current assets turnover} = \frac{192\,000}{157\,000} = 1.22 \text{ times}$$

There are 1.22 times as many dollars of revenue as there are of dollars of non-current assets, or for every $1 of revenue there are $0.82 of non-current assets.

Trade receivables turnover (average turnover collection period) =

$$\frac{16\,800}{192\,000} \times 365 = 31.94 \text{ days} = 32 \text{ days}$$

On average it takes trade receivables 31.94 days to pay their debts to the business.

Getting it right

It is usual to round up to the nearest day for the trade receivables turnover, trade payables turnover and rate of inventory turnover in days. All other ratios should be stated to the nearest two decimal places.

$$\text{Trade payables turnover} = \frac{25\,500}{85\,500} \times 365 = 108.86 \text{ days} = 109 \text{ days}$$

On average it takes the business 108.86 days to pay its debts to credit suppliers (trade payables).

$$\text{Rate of inventory turnover times} = \frac{84\,500}{12\,000} = 7.04 \text{ times} = 7 \text{ times}$$

Inventory was sold on average 7.04 times during the year.

$$\text{Rate of inventory turnover (days)} = \frac{12\,000}{84\,500} \times 365 = 51.83 \text{ days} = 52 \text{ days}$$

Inventory was sold on average every 52 days.

What use are ratios and what can they say about a business?

It is not enough just to calculate ratios. The figures given are absolutes. Ratios are meaningless on their own and have to be analysed and interpreted, which requires skill and judgment, if the owner or manager of a business is to be well informed when making important decisions.

- **Profitability:** Are the owners and managers of a business successful in increasing the business's value over time through trading or providing services?
- **Liquidity:** Are the business's resources well managed so that the business can pay its debts, including running costs, without difficulty from one week to the next, and also provide the owner with a reasonable income?

Businesses can fail if their owners or managers do not give these issues enough attention. There are many cases, for example, of profitable businesses that have not survived because their liquidity has been inadequate.

This table describes the different types of profitability ratio, as well as how to interpret their results and make suggestions about how the figures might be improved upon.

Type of profitability ratio	Possible information re strengths and weaknesses of the business	Possible actions to improve the ratio
Profit margin Gross profit margin Mark-up	In general, an increase in these percentages is likely to be good news, because the business will be making more profit on each item sold. On the other hand, a decrease could be potentially bad news for the business, because less profit would be made on each item sold. Sometimes businesses alter their gross profit margin and mark-up on purpose: perhaps to be more competitive, or to enter a new market. The cost of purchases of inventory may have increased due to limited supply from the supplier. Comparing to other businesses it is possible to comment on whether: – the selling price is out of step with these similar businesses – the business is paying too much or too little for the goods it sells. The profit ratio may change as there is more/less gross profit or costs have been more or less controlled.	Improve sales – Review pricing policy to make the business more competitive. – Consider the quality or range of the products sold. – Review marketing strategies. Control costs – Find a cheaper supplier to improve the gross profit ratio, but ensure that the quality of the product is the same. – Streamline overheads if possible by removing any unnecessary costs and reducing waste to improve profit ratio.

Type of profitability ratio	Possible information re strengths and weaknesses of the business	Possible actions to improve the ratio
Expense/Revenue ratio	An increase in an expense/revenue ratio would normally be bad news for a business because less profit is being made as a proportion of revenue, whereas a decrease in the ratio would mean the reverse.	Control costs. Investigate possible reasons for an increase in costs. However, there may be valid reasons for a change in some expenses: for example, an increase in the wages ratio may be due to an increase in the legal minimum wage.
Return on capital employed (ROCE)	An increase in ROCE is positive because it means that the business is making more profit for every $1 of resources (or capital) employed in the business. A decrease, of course, would mean the reverse. It should be considered how well the owner of the business could do if his capital was invested and earning interest, or if the owner was employed and earning a salary. It is much more risky to own a business than to invest the money in savings etc. Is the return higher than the cost of borrowing the capital if the business has loans? If there is information about other, similar businesses, it is possible to judge whether the resources (capital employed) are being used effectively or not.	Make the best use of resources. For example, decide whether the business has the right assets to achieve the desired level of profit. Work out whether any of the assets are being underused.

This table describes the different types of liquidity ratio, as well as how to interpret their results and make suggestions about how the figures might be improved upon.

Type of liquidity ratio	Possible information re strengths and weaknesses of the business	Possible actions to improve the ratio
Current ratio Liquid (acid test) ratio	An increase in these ratios is usually favourable development for a business because it means that the business will find it easier to find the resources to make payments on time. A decrease would, therefore, be an unfavourable development. Short-term payments could include trade payables, most expenses, loan repayments, owner's drawings, payment of taxes and the purchases of new non-currents assets. The difference between these two ratios is one of timing. The current ratio looks further ahead than the liquid (acid test) ratio. Liquid capital is a more immediate measure of liquidity, hence the term 'liquid (acid test) ratio'. It is possible for a business to have too much working capital and liquid capital. In these situations, the business could have too much money tied up that is not being used effectively – for example too much inventory or too much money sitting in the bank not being used. Levels of liquidity vary considerably depending on the goods or services that the business provides. A local food retailer, where most of the goods will be sold within a short space of time and where cash sales will dominate, will have small liquidity requirements; whereas a furniture store, where much of the inventory is slow moving and where credit sales are far more likely, will have considerable liquidity requirements.	**Increase cash flow** For example, increase sales but also keep control of costs, resulting in increased cash flowing into the business. This may not be immediate, of course, because the business will have to wait for trade receivables to pay. **Reduce drawings** If the owner can take less cash from the business, this will have a positive impact on liquidity. However, the owner's personal commitments may not make this possible. **Increase non-current liability** Arranging a long-term loan would instantly boost liquidity. However, loans have to be repaid and interest charges would be high and would, of course, reduce profits. **Delay expenditure on non-current assets** The owner of the business could delay plans to replace or increase non-current assets. This would mean that cash that would otherwise be spent is retained within the business. However, the delay could have a negative impact on the quality of the business's operations.

This table describes the different types of efficiency ratio, as well as how to interpret their results and make suggestions about how the figures might be improved upon.

Type of efficiency ratio	Possible information regarding strengths and weaknesses of the business	Possible actions to improve the ratio
Non-current asset turnover	This ratio measures the utilisation the business is obtaining from its investment in non-current assets, such as premises and machinery. So if the ratio is low compared to similar businesses, it would indicate that the managers are not using their non-current assets to their full potential.	**Utilise non-current assets** For example, sell any surplus assets or invest in better machinery that, in the long run, would increase turnover.
Trade receivables turnover (average collection period) Trade payables turnover (average payment period)	Many businesses like the trade receivables to pay within 30 days. However, this varies from industry to industry. The more quickly customers pay, the better. It is a particular strength if customers are paying a business more frequently than the business is paying its payables, because the flow of cash through the business will be improved. Generally, the shorter the period, the better for trade receivables turnover. The longer the period, the better for the trade payables turnover (as long as suppliers are not alienated).	**Offer discounts** Discounts can be given to trade receivables who settle their accounts early. **Credit control** Negotiate short credit periods with trade receivables and only allow credit after a period during which the customer has paid in advance before delivery.
Rate of inventory turnover	An increase in the rate of inventory turnover is a strength for the business because it means that inventory is being sold more quickly. Every time an item is sold, some profit will be made. A rapid rate of inventory turnover will release cash and profit more quickly. The more often the business can sell its inventory, the more benefit the business will get. The rate of inventory turnover will depend on the type of product. For example, food produce turns over more quickly than furniture.	**Inventory control** Keeping too much inventory should be avoided. Maybe use a just-in-time inventory system so that inventory levels are kept at a minimum.

Illustration 4: Reporting on a business's performance

Laura Edwards has been looking at her business's end-of-year financial statements for each of the years ended 31 December 2013 and 2014. She has worked out the following accounting ratios based on these statements.

	2013	2014
Gross profit margin	35%	37%
Mark-up	54%	58%

Profit/revenue	18%	16%
Operating expenses/revenue	17%	21%
Return on capital employed	12%	15%
Current ratio	1.6:1	1.4:1
Liquid (acid test) ratio	0.7:1	0.9:1
Rate of inventory turnover	13 times	11 times
Trade receivables turnover	35 days	31 days
Trade payables turnover	27 days	32 days

The following information is available about sales in each of the years ended 31 December.

2013	$440 000
2014	$500 000

Typical liquidity ratios for this type of business are as follows.

Current ratio	1.7:1
Liquid (acid test) ratio	0.9:1

This table shows an analysis of these ratios and suggests areas of strength and weakness for Laura's business.

Category	Strength	Weakness
Profitability	The gross profit margin and mark-up have increased, meaning that the business is making more gross profit per $1 of sales. The return on capital employed has also increased by 3%, meaning that the business is making more profit per $1 of capital invested by the owner.	The profit/sales percentage has fallen and the operating expenses/sales percentage has increased.
Liquidity	The Liquid (acid test) ratio has increased and is now near the average for this type of business. This means that the business will be in a better position to pay its more immediate short-term debts.	The current ratio has decreased and has moved further away from the average for this type of business. This means that the business will have more difficulty paying short-term debts.
Efficiency	The trade receivables turnover has improved meaning that credit customers are paying more quickly than before. This may cut the risk of irrecoverable debts. The trade payables turnover has lengthened, meaning that credit suppliers are being paid more slowly. This will benefit cash flow, particularly as credit customers are paying more quickly than payments are made to trade suppliers.	The rate of inventory turnover has declined. This means that goods are now being sold more slowly than before. As result the business will not receive cash from sales or make profit on sales as quickly as before.

Limitations of accounting information

Accounting information is the starting point for any analysis of a business's performance. However, it should be remembered that there are certain limitations to using accounting information.

- By the time a business has produced its end-of-year financial statements, important events may have occurred that are not reflected in the accounts. Perhaps there has been some difficult economic news affecting the local economy, such as disruption due to severe weather, or bad news affecting the national or international economy, such as a recession or a large increase in the cost of oil.
- The money measurement concept means that financial statements can only include data that has a monetary value. As a result, some important characteristics of a business can be overlooked. It might be important to consider many non-financial factors. Here are some examples of positive and negative factors.
  - The workforce is highly motivated and committed to the success or the business.
  - The business is well located.
  - A new managing director has just been appointed who has a reputation for dramatically improving business performance.
  - Following some recent redundancies, the morale of the workforce has declined sharply.
  - It has been announced that a new road system will be constructed which will divert trade away from the business's premises.
- The valuation of non-current assets can be quite different depending on when the non-current asset was purchased. For example, two businesses could occupy very similar premises, but one business could have been established many years ago when property prices were low, and the other business could have been established more recently when property prices were much higher. As a result, the capital employed by each could be significantly different.
- Inflation is generally ignored when comparing financial statements, but this can distort any analysis. For example, this year's revenue may seem much higher than that of three years ago, but if inflation has been high during the period, the real difference in the business's revenue performance may not be that great.

End-of-chapter questions

1 Calculating income statement ratios

The following extract from the income statement was prepared for the business owned by Jenni Fares.

Jenni Fares Income statement (extract) for the year ended 31 January 2015		
	$	$
Revenue		800 000
Opening inventory	29 000	
Purchases	646 000	
	675 000	
Closing inventory	(35 000)	
Cost of sales		(640 000)
Gross profit		160 000

Calculate the following ratios:

- **a** gross profit margin
- **b** mark-up
- **c** rate of inventory turnover.

In each case, state the formula used.

2 Calculating income statement ratios

The following extract from the income statement was prepared for the business owned by Ismail Cook.

Ismail Cook Income statement (extract) for the year ended 31 October 2014		
	$	$
Revenue		720 000
Opening inventory	32 500	
Purchases	475 000	
	507 500	
Closing inventory	(27 500)	
Cost of sales		(480 000)
Gross profit		240 000

Calculate the following ratios:

- **a** gross profit margin
- **b** mark-up
- **c** rate of inventory turnover.

In each case, state the formula used.

3 Calculating income statement ratios

Misha's income statement was as follows.

His business's revenue for the year ended 31 August 2014 was $320 000.

Misha Income statement (extract) for the year ended 31 August 2014		
	$	$
Gross profit		120 000
Office expenses	6 000	
Rent	24 000	
Salaries	42 000	
		(72 000)
Profit for year		48 000

Calculate the following ratios:

- **a** profit margin
- **b** office expenses as a percentage of revenue
- **c** rent as a percentage of revenue
- **d** salaries as a percentage of revenue.

In each case, state the formula used.

4 Calculating income statement ratios

Georgina's income statement was as follows.

Revenue for the year ended 31 May 2014 totalled $800 000.

Georgina Income statement (extract) for the year ended 31 May 2014		
	$	$
Gross profit		240 000
Insurance	12 000	
Loan interest	9 000	
Wages	56 000	
Depreciation	63 000	
		(140 000)
Profit for year		100 000

Calculate the following ratios:

- **a** profit margin
- **b** wages as a percentage of revenue
- **c** insurance as a percentage of revenue
- **d** loan interest as a percentage of revenue
- **e** depreciation as a percentage of revenue.

In each case, state the formula used.

5 Calculating statement of financial position ratios

The following statement of financial position was prepared for the business owned by Roy Coulins at the end at its financial year. The business had credit sales of $72 000 and credit purchases of $429 000 for the year ended 30 June 2014.

	$	$	$
	Cost	**Depreciation**	**Net book value**
Non-current assets	860 000	215 000	645 000
Current assets			
Inventory		54 000	
Trade receivables		8 000	
Other receivables		2 000	
Cash and cash equivalents		8 000	72 000
Total assets			717 000
Capital			
Opening balance		661 000	
Profit for the year		75 000	
		736 000	
Drawings		59 000	677 000
Current liabilities			
Trade payables		39 000	
Other payables		1 000	40 000
Total capital and liabilities			717 000

Calculate the following ratios:

- **a** current ratio
- **b** liquid (acid test) ratio
- **c** return on capital employed
- **d** trade receivables turnover
- **e** trade payables turnover.

In each case, state the formula used.

6 Calculating statement of financial position ratios

The following statement of financial position was prepared for the business owned by Jack Hall at the end of its financial year. The business had credit sales of $224 000 and credit purchases of $154 000 for the year ended 31 December 2014.

	$	$	$
	Cost	**Depreciation**	**Net book value**
Non-current assets	490 000	196 000	294 000
Current assets			
Inventory		17 000	
Trade receivables		16 000	
Other receivables		1 000	
Cash and cash equivalents		2 000	36 000
Total assets			330 000
Capital			
Opening balance		298 000	
Profit for the year		45 000	
		343 000	
Drawings		(37 000)	306 000
Current liabilities			
Bank loan		7 000	
Trade payables		14 000	
Other payables		3 000	24 000
Total capital and liabilities			330 000

Calculate the following ratios:

- **a** current ratio
- **b** liquid (acid test) ratio
- **c** return on capital employed
- **d** trade receivables turnover
- **e** trade payables turnover.

In each case, state the formula used.

7 Analysing the financial results of a limited company

The financial statements for Over and Out Ltd for the year ended 31 December 2014 were as follows.

Over and Out Ltd Income statement for the year ended 31 December 2014	
	$
Revenue	180 000
Cost of sales	(71 500)
Gross profit	108 500

Other income: rental income	1 500
	110 000
Expenses	(48 900)
Operating profit	61 100
Finance costs: debenture interest	(1 100)
Profit for the year	(60 000)

Additional information:

- Dividends paid during the year: $12 000
- Retained earnings at 1 January 2014: $42 000.

	$000	$000	$000
Non-current assets	Cost	Depreciation	Net book value
Premises	180 000	12 000	168 000
Vehicles	55 000	16 000	39 000
	235 000	28 000	207 000
Current assets			
Inventory		30 200	
Trade and other receivables		22 800	
Cash and cash equivalents		6 300	59 300
Total assets			266 300
Equity			
Issued ordinary share capital			100 000
Share premium			20 000
General reserve			5 000
Retained earnings			90 000
			215 000
Non-current liabilities			
6% debentures (2019–2021)			20 000
Current liabilities			
Trade and other payables			31 300
Total equity and liabilities			266 300

a Use the financial statements for Over and Out Ltd to calculate the following profitability and financial ratios:

i gross profit margin

ii profit margin (using operating profit)

iii return on capital employed

iv current ratio

v liquid (acid test) ratio

vi rate of inventory turnover (using the closing inventory as the average inventory).

b Explain briefly what each of the ratios tells you about the financial results of Over and Out Ltd for the year ended 31 December 2014.

8 Analysing the financial results of a limited company

The financial statements for Falls Ltd for the year ended 31 May 2014 were as follows.

Falls Ltd Income statement for the year ended 31 May 2014	
	$
Revenue	480 000
Cost of sales	(122 500)
Gross profit	257 500
Other income: rental income	12 500
	270 000
Expenses	(188 200)
Operating profit	81 800
Finance costs: debenture interest	(9 800)
Profit for the year	72 000

Additional information:

- Dividends paid during the year: $30 000
- Retained earnings at 1 June 2013: $168 000.

	$000	$000	$000
Non-current assets	Cost	Depreciation	Net book value
Premises	450 000	42 000	408 000
Fixtures and fittings	90 000	26 000	64 000
Vehicles	60 000	20 000	40 000
	600 000	88 000	512 000
Current assets			
Inventory		38 200	
Trade and other receivables		22 300	60 500
Total assets			572 500

Equity			
200 000 ordinary shares of $0.50 each		100 000	
50 000 8% preference shares of $2 each		100 000	
Share premium		40 000	
Retained earnings		210 000	450 000
Non-current liabilities			
6% debentures (2019–2021)			40 000
Current liabilities			
Trade and other payables		20 100	
Debenture interest payable		2 900	
Cash and cash equivalents		59 500	82 500
Total capital and liabilities			572 500

a Use the financial statements for Falls Ltd to calculate the following profitability and financial ratios:

- **i** gross profit margin
- **ii** profit for the year margin
- **iii** return on capital employed
- **iv** current ratio
- **v** liquid (acid test) ratio
- **vi** rate of inventory turnover (using the closing inventory as the average inventory).

b Explain briefly what each of the ratios tells you about the financial results of Falls Ltd for the year ended 31 May 2014.

9 Analysing the financial results of a limited company

Grand Gardening Ltd is a successful garden design company that has been operating for many years.

The ratios for Grand Gardening Ltd and the averages for the industry for the year ended 31 January 2015 were as follows.

	Grand Gardening Ltd	Industry averages
Gross profit percentage	65%	82%
Profit percentage	20%	42%
Current ratio	3.1:1	2.2:1
Liquid (acid test) ratio	2.3:1	1.2:1
Rate of inventory turnover	32 days	24 days
Non-current assets turnover	$30	$40
Return on capital employed	18%	35%

Comment on the results of Grand Gardening Ltd by comparing its ratios with the industry averages.

10 Analysing the financial results of a limited company

The financial statements for Lucky Ltd for the year ended 31 December 2014 were as follows.

Lucky Ltd Income statement for the year ended 31 December 2014	
	$
Revenue	289 500
Cost of sales	(88 000)
Gross profit	201 500
Other income: commission received	10 500
	212 000
Expenses	(148 000)
Operating profit	64 000
Finance costs: debenture interest	(4 000)
Profit for the year	60 000

Additional information:

- Dividends paid during the year: $60 000
- Retained earnings at 1 January 2014: $140 000.

	$000	$000	$000
	Cost	**Depreciation**	**Net book value**
Non-current assets			
Premises			460 000
Delivery vehicles			38 000
			498 000
Current assets			

Inventory		60 000	
Trade and other receivables		44 800	
Cash and cash equivalents		15 200	120 000
Total assets			618 000
Equity			
200 000 ordinary shares of $1 each		200 000	
Share premium		22 000	
General reserve		40 000	
Retained earnings		140 000	402 000
Non-current liabilities			
6% debentures (2019–2021)			120 000
Current liabilities			
Trade payables		92 000	
Debenture interest payable		4 000	96 000
Total equity and liabilities			618 000

The ratio results for last year for Lucky Ltd are shown in the following table.

Gross profit margin	65%
Profit margin	10%
Current ratio	2.1:1
Liquid (acid test) ratio	1.2:1
Return on capital employed	8%

a Calculate the following ratios for Lucky Ltd for the current year:
- **i** gross profit margin
- **ii** profit margin
- **iii** current ratio
- **iv** liquid (acid test) ratio
- **v** return on capital employed.

b Comment on the results and state whether the performance of Lucky Ltd has improved.

11 Reporting on performance

Navin has been looking at his business's end-of-year financial statements for each of the years ended 31 December 2013 and 2014. He has worked out the following accounting ratios based on these statements.

	2013	2014
Gross profit margin	40%	43%
Mark-up	67%	75%
Profit/revenue	8%	7%
Operating expenses/revenue	28%	31%
Return on capital employed	11%	7%
Current ratio	1.2:1	1.3:1
Liquid (acid test) ratio	0·8:1	0.6:1
Rate of inventory turnover	9 times	10 times
Trade receivables turnover	29 days	35 days
Trade payables turnover	36 days	30 days

The following information is available about revenue in each of the years ended 31 December.

2013	$200 000
2014	$180 000

Typical liquidity ratios for this type of business are as follows.

Current ratio	1:3:1
Liquid (acid test) ratio	0.8:1

Prepare a brief report on this business's performance. Make some recommendations on how any weaknesses could be overcome.

12 Commenting on ratios

The following ratios have been calculated as a result of analysing the end-of-year financial statements of Horizon Stores, a business owned by Robin Spencer.

The profitability ratios are as follows.

	For the year ended 31 December		
	2012	2013	2014
Gross profit margin	40%	38%	37%
Mark-up	67%	61%	59%
Profit/revenue	14%	13%	11%
Wages/revenue	8%	9%	10%
Other expenses/revenue	3%	4%	5%
Return on capital employed	12%	11%	10%

Revenue figures for each of these years are as follows.

2012	$600 000
2013	$580 000
2014	$570 000

The liquidity ratios for this business are:

	For the year ended 31 December		
	2012	2013	2014
Current ratio	1.7:1	1.6:1	1.5:1
Liquid (acid test) ratio	0.9:1	0.8:1	0.7:1

The efficiency ratios for this business are:

	For the year ended 31 December		
	2012	2013	2014
Rate of inventory turnover	9 times	10 times	12 times
Trade receivables turnover	26 days	30 days	35 days
Trade payables turnover	32 days	31 days	27 days

The typical efficiency ratios are as follows.

Rate of inventory turnover	12 times
Trade receivables turnover	30 days
Trade payables turnover	30 days

a Comment on the trend in revenue and the business's profitability during the three-year period.

b Comment on the business's liquidity during the three-year period.

c Comment on the business's efficiency ratios during the three-year period.
For each ratio:

- **i** Describe the trend and state whether this is a strength or a weakness or represents a mixed position.
- **ii** Explain what the trend means for the business.

13 Identifying the use of a ratio

What does the ratio of current assets/current liabilities show?

A Asset usage
B Liquidity
C Profitability
D Return on capital employed.

14 Using the inventory turnover ratio

A business turns over its inventory five times a year. Average inventory is $54 000 and revenue is made at a mark-up of one-third.

How much is the revenue?

A $240 000
B $270 000
C $320 000
D $360 000

15 Calculating the liquid (acid test) ratio

A company has the following information in its statement of financial position.

	$000
Trade receivables	150
Bank overdraft	130
Inventory	110
Trade payables	150

What is the liquid (acid test) ratio?

A 0.54:1
B 0.88:1
C 0.93:1
D 1.85:1

16 Explaining changes in profitability ratios

A firm has calculated the following accounting ratios for the year ended 30 June.

Year ended	30 June 2013	30 June 2014
Gross profit on sales	30%	33%
Profit on sales	15%	14%

What could explain the changes in the percentages?

A A fall in interest payments was equal to an increase in administration costs.
B An increase in raw-material costs was covered by an increase in selling price.
C An increase in the advertising budget has allowed the firm to increase the selling price.
D An increase in the advertising budget has led to a rise in sales volume.

17 Explaining changes in the liquid (acid test) ratio

Which actions would increase the liquid (acid test) ratio of a business in the short term?

i Trade receivables paying their debts
ii Paying trade payables
iii Selling a number of surplus non-current assets

iv Selling inventory

- **A** i and ii
- **B** ii and iii
- **C** i and iv
- **D** iii and iv.

18 Calculating the inventory turnover

A company produces the following information concerning inventory turnover.

Year 1 average inventory	$60 000
Inventory turnover	10 times

If the Year 2 average inventory is double Year 1's and the cost of goods sold is increased to $960 000, what will the inventory turnover in Year 2 be?

- **A** 8 times
- **B** 10 times
- **C** 16 times
- **D** 20 times.

19 Calculating the payment period

The following table shows information for a business at the year end.

	$000
Average inventory	25
Credit sales	150
Credit purchases	112
Total purchases	140
Trade payables	28
Trade receivables	39

What is the payment period for trade payables, to the nearest day?

- **A** 68 days
- **B** 73 days
- **C** 92 days
- **D** 95 days.

Topic 1: Financial accounting

Exam-style questions

1 **A purchases ledger control account is to be prepared for the month of January 2015. The following information is available.**

	$
Trade payables at 1 January 2015	7 300
Cash purchases	3 500
Credit purchases	38 600
Contra with sales ledger	1 100
Payments to trade payables	35 800
Returns outwards on credit transactions	2 400

What was the total of trade payables at 31 January 2015?

A $6600
B $7700
C $8800
D $10 100

2 **Recently a business sold some equipment that had cost $8400. The equipment was sold for $1550 at a profit of $600.**
What was the total depreciation of the equipment at the time of the sale?

A $6250
B $6850
C $7450
D $7800

3 **The following information has been extracted from the books of a partnership.**

	$
Non-current assets at cost	84 000
Non-current assets at net book value	63 000
Profit for year	22 400
Revenue for year	165 000

What is the non-current assets turnover ratio?

A 1.96 B 2.62 C 2.81 D 3.75

4 **The following information was extracted from the equity section of a company's statement of financial position at 1 January 2014.**

	$
Issued shares: 400 000 shares of $0.50 each	200 000
Share premium	45 000

On 1 February 2014 the directors of the company made a rights issue of shares which was fully subscribed. The issue was of three shares for every eight shares in issue at this date at a price of $1.20 per share.

What was the balance of the share premium account after the share issue?

A $60 000
B $75 000
C $97 500
D $150 000

5 **Incomplete records and accounting ratios**
Raj owns a business called Gold Medal Sports Supplies which was opened on 1 January 2013. Raj does not keep proper books of account.

The following information is available about the year ended 31 December 2014:

	1 January 2014	31 December 2014
	$	$
Fixtures and fittings at book value	28 400	30 600
Inventory	4 400	4 600
Trade receivables	2 830	1 700
Trade payables	3 490	3 920
Other payables		
electricity charges	780	810
shop rent	440	
Other receivables: shop rent		530

Summary of bank statements for the year ended 31 December 2014:

	Dr	Cr	Balance	
	$	$	$	
Balance			8 200	Dr
Receipts from trade receivables		16 500	8 300	Cr
Cash takings banked		73 900	82 200	
Payments to trade payables	37 600		44 600	Cr
Additional fittings	5 700		38 900	Cr
Shop rent	13 400		25 500	Cr
Electricity charges	4 240		21 260	Cr

Administration expenses	5 730		15 530	Cr
Drawings	18 800		3 270	Dr

Additional information:

- At 31 December 2014 there were unpresented cheques of $1300 for payments made to trade suppliers.
- Raj had taken goods for own use at cost $390 during the year ended 31 December 2014.
- Raj has allowed credit customers cash discounts totalling $540 during the year ended 31 December 2014.
- All cash takings were banked.

a State **two** possible reasons why Raj does not maintain a full accounting system. [2 marks]

b Prepare an income statement for the year ended 31 December 2014. [14 marks]

c Raj's accountant has calculated the following ratios based on the business's performance in the year ended 31 December 2013.

Trade payable turnover	33 days
Trade receivable turnover	29 days
Rate of inventory turnover	11 times

Calculate the following ratios based on the business's income statement for the year ended 31 December 2014. (Give your answers in whole numbers.)

i Trade payable turnover

ii Trade receivable turnover

iii Rate of inventory turnover [6 marks]

d Assess the business's performance with regard to liquidity using the information about three ratios. [8 marks]

[Total: 30 marks]

6 Correction of errors

George prepared a trial balance at the end of his business's financial year on 31 March 2015. However, the totals of the trial balance failed to agree and a suspense account was opened for the difference. George checked the accounting records and discovered the following errors.

- Error 1: The total of the sales journal had been understated by $440.
- Error 2: A payment for carriage inwards $163 had been debited to the carriage outwards account.
- Error 3: The total of the discount received column in the cash book, $378, had been entered on the debit side of the discount received account.
- Error 4: A credit note issued by a supplier, KLZ Ltd, for $239 had been entered in the returns outwards journal as $293.
- Error 5: A credit customer, S. Wilson, had paid $867 by cheque. The entries made for this payment were: debit S. Wilson $876 and credit bank $768.

George is aware that some of these errors did not affect the agreement of the trial balance totals.

a Identify **two** of the errors discovered by George which would not have affected the agreement of the trial balance totals and state the type of error in each case. [2 marks]

b Prepare journal entries to correct the errors. (Narratives are not required.) [8 marks]

c Prepare the suspense account showing the original difference in the trial balance totals.

[5 marks]

[Total: 15 marks]

7 Limited companies: bonus issue and statement of changes in equity

The following is an extract from Zebrex plc's statement of financial position at 1 April 2014.

	$m
Equity	
Authorised ordinary share capital: 1m shares of $0.50 each	15.0
Issued ordinary share capital: fully paid shares of $0.50 each	8.0
Share premium	5.3
Retained earnings	5.6
	18.9

Additional information:

- On 1 June 2014 the directors decided to make a bonus issue of three ordinary shares for every four shares currently issued. The directors wished to maintain reserves in their most flexible form.

- On 30 September 2014 the directors paid a dividend of $0.20 per share on all issued shares at that date.
- On 31 March 2015 the company's income statement showed a profit for the year of $6.7m.

a State one reason why the directors decided to make a bonus issue of ordinary shares. [1 mark]

b Calculate the number of bonus ordinary shares issued on 1 June 2014. [2 marks]

c Explain why a bonus issue may be of limited benefit to a shareholder. [3 marks]

d Calculate the dividend paid to ordinary shareholders on 30 September 2014. [2 marks]

e Prepare a statement of changes in equity at 31 March 2015. [7 marks]

[Total: 15 marks]

8 Partnership profit sharing and admission of a partner

Kelly and Leo have been in partnership for a number of years sharing profits and losses in the ratio of their fixed capitals.

The following balances appeared in the partnership's books at 31 December 2014 after completion of the income statement for the year ended on that date.

	$	
Bank overdraft	2 010	
Fixed capital accounts		
Kelly	116 000	
Leo	58 000	
Current accounts at 1 January 2014		
Kelly	3 200	Dr
Leo	1 800	Cr
Drawings		
Kelly	23 400	
Leo	18 900	
Inventory	22 000	
Non-current assets at book value	165 000	
Profit for year	55 400	
Trade payables	8 490	
Trade receivables	9 200	

The partnership agreement provides that:

- interest should be charged on drawings: Kelly $1300; Leo $900
- interest on capital of 5 per cent per annum should be credited to each partner.

a Give **one** reason why the partners have chosen to have fixed capitals. [1 mark]

b Prepare an appropriation account for the year ended 31 December 2014. [5 marks]

c Prepare Kelly's current account for the year ended 31 December 2014. [5 marks]

On 1 January 2015 the partners agreed to the admission of Martin as a partner. The following terms were agreed.

- Non-current assets should be revalued at $152 000.
- A provision for doubtful debts should be created of 5 per cent of trade receivables.
- Inventory should be revalued as it appears that items valued at $1340 are out of date and should be disposed of. In addition, 50 items which cost $18 are damaged and have a resale value of only $21 after repair costs estimated at $350 has been paid.
- Goodwill is to be valued at $60 000 but will not be recorded in the books of account.
- Martin is to introduce $80 000 as his fixed capital contribution.
- In the new partnership profits will be shared: Kelly 45 per cent, Leo 25 per cent, Martin 30 per cent.
- Partners would continue to use current accounts.
- All adjustments required for the admission of Martin should be made through the partners' capital accounts.

d Prepare the capital accounts of the partners showing the admission of Martin assuming the terms of admission were implemented on 1 January 2015. [10 marks]

Kelly and Leo discussed for some time whether to admit Martin as a partner before finally making a decision. They agreed that Martin's capital contribution would be useful as they intended to expand the business, but were also aware that there could be other benefits and also drawbacks arising from this decision.

e Discuss the potential benefits and drawbacks of admitting Martin as a partner other than the introduction of additional capital. [9 marks]

[Total: 30 marks]

2 Cost and management accounting

Section 2.1: Costing for materials and labour

Key concepts

The techniques used in cost and management accounting are based on all five key concepts:

- true and fair view
- duality
- consistency
- business entity
- money measurement.

Learning objectives

In this chapter you will learn:

- about the purpose of cost accounting
- how costs are classified
- about types of labour cost
- about methods of inventory valuation.

2.1.1: Costing principles

The purpose of cost accounting

Cost accounting enables managers to manage their business effectively and efficiently. Unless managers are fully aware of all of the costs involved in purchasing, or producing, and ultimately selling products, they will not be able to make the correct decisions on which the success of their business is built.

Cost accounting is used by all types of business, both private and publicly owned: manufacturing businesses, service businesses, such as a motor repair garage, retail and wholesale businesses, schools, hospitals, etc. All of these different types of organisation need to know the total costs involved in running the business.

Cost classification

Costs may be classified in one of three ways:

- by element
- by function
- by nature.

Classification by element

In a manufacturing organisation, there are three elements to costs:

- materials – the cost of goods used to manufacture the product
- labour – the wages and salaries costs of employees
- expenses – all other costs including overheads.

Each of these elements may be split into direct or indirect costs.

Direct costs are those costs that can be specifically associated with the manufacture of one unit of production. For example, direct costs include electrical parts in producing a washing machine; wages paid to production line operators or assembly workers; expenses that can be directly associated with the manufacture of a product, such as royalties.

The direct costs of a business form the prime cost of manufacture.

Indirect costs are those parts, generally of lower value, that cannot be specifically associated with the manufacture of one unit of production. For example, indirect costs include nails and screws in the manufacture of furniture; wages and salaries of employees not directly involved in production – such as administrative staff, supervisors; expenses that cannot be directly associated with manufacturing one unit of product, such as rent and rates, light and heat, etc.

The indirect costs of a business form the overheads.

The advantage to management of classifying costs by element is that high-cost elements will be identified and remedial actions taken where possible.

Key terms

Direct costs: costs that can be specifically associated with the manufacture of one unit of production.

Indirect costs: costs that cannot economically be specifically associated with the manufacture of one unit of production.

By element: classifies costs by materials, labour and overheads. Further classifies into direct costs and indirect costs.

Classification by function

Businesses may choose to classify costs by function. For example, a manufacturing business may use the following categories:

- production
- sales and distribution
- administration
- finance.

All costs, both direct and indirect, may be analysed by function.

Non-manufacturing organisations may choose to analyse costs by function and will use headings suitable to their own organisation.

The advantage to management of classifying costs by function is that over-spending or high-cost departments will be identified. Managers may then identify where savings can be made.

Key terms

By function: classifies costs by the functional departments of the business.

By nature: classifies costs by the nature of their behaviour, i.e. fixed, variable, semi-variable, stepped.

Classification by nature

Recognising the nature of costs is essential to the management accountant. Unless it is possible to identify how a cost will behave in the future, accurate budgeting is not possible. By nature, costs will be classified under one of the following headings:

- Fixed
- Variable
- Semi-variable
- Stepped.

Fixed costs

Fixed costs are those costs that do not vary with the levels of business activity. Examples of a fixed cost are rent and rates, administration salaries, insurance, etc. Whatever the level of production or sales (within a relevant range), these costs will remain the same.

Key terms

Fixed costs: costs that do not vary with the level of activity.

Variable costs: costs that change in direct proportion to changes in the level of activity.

Semi-variable costs: costs that have a fixed element as well as a variable element.

Variable costs

Variable costs are those costs that change in direct proportion to changes in the levels of activity. Examples of variable costs are direct materials, sales commissions, piece rate labour costs, etc.

Semi-variable costs

Semi-variable costs are costs that have the characteristics of both a fixed cost and a variable cost. An example of a semi-variable cost may be a telephone bill. The bill may include a rental element that is fixed per month, plus a charge for each call made. If no calls are made, the rental part of the bill still must be paid, but there will be no call charges.

> **Key term**
> **Stepped costs**: costs that remain fixed until a certain level of activity is reached and then rise to a higher fixed level.

Stepped costs

Stepped costs remain fixed until a certain level of activity is reached, at which point they rise to a higher fixed level. The costs will remain at that higher level until the next level of activity requiring a change is reached when they will rise again. An example of a stepped cost is supervisors' salaries. If a supervisor is able to oversee the work of 20 employees, as soon as the 21st employee is taken on, a further supervisor is required.

Labour costs

> **Key terms**
> **Time rate**: employees paid for the agreed time they spend at work.
> **Piece rate**: employees paid at an agreed rate for each unit produced or task completed.
> **Bonus system**: employees offered a bonus payment if output or achievement exceeds a target.

Employee remuneration can be calculated in many different ways. The three main methods are as follows.

Time rate

Employees are paid for the agreed time they spend at work. Any additional hours may be paid at an overtime rate, for example time-and-a-half.

Piece rate

Employees are paid at an agreed rate for each unit of output produced or for each agreed task completed. While it may encourage faster working, management must ensure that quality does not suffer.

Bonus system

Employees are paid their agreed rate, but offered a bonus payment if their output or achievement exceeds their target. The bonus payment may be a percentage figure or a fixed sum per output over target or achievement.

The main purpose of a bonus system is to encourage better efficiency. As is the case with piece rate, the main disadvantage of a bonus system is that greater emphasis must be placed on control procedures to ensure that quality is not suffering at the expense of speed.

Methods of inventory valuation

> **Key terms**
> **FIFO**: assumes that items purchased first are also sold first.
> **AVCO**: calculates the average cost of inventory after each new purchase.
> **LIFO**: assumes that items purchased most recently are sold first.

The valuation of inventory may be difficult because goods are purchased over different time periods and different prices will be paid for the same items. There are three main methods of valuing inventory:

- FIFO (first in, first out)
- AVCO (average cost)
- LIFO (last in, first out).

FIFO

The first in, first out method assumes that the items purchased first were also sold first. The result of this is that any unsold items are considered to be those purchased most recently.

In order to calculate the value of inventory, it is necessary to keep detailed records of the purchase and sale of each item, together with a running total of the balance as follows.

Date	Received			Issued			Inventory valuation			
	Qty	Price	Value	Qty	Price	Value	Qty	Price	Value	Total
		$	$		$	$		$	$	$
May	500	8	4 000				500	8	4 000	4 000
June	1 200	9	10 800				500	8	4 000	
							1 200	9	10 800	14 800
June				500	8	4 000				
				100	9	900	1 100	9	9 900	9 900
July				800	9	7 200	300	9	2 700	2 700
July	1 500	10	15 000				300	9	2 700	
							1 500	10	15 000	17 700
July				200	9	1 800	100	9	900	
							1 500	10	15 000	15 900

Explanation

In June the company purchased a further 1200 items at $9 each and sold 600 items. Using the FIFO method, the 500 items purchased first have now been sold plus 100 of the items costing $9. The closing inventory of 1100 items is therefore all valued at the latest price of $9.

In July the company sold 800 items. These are all taken from the end of June inventory of 1100 items at $9. It then purchased 1500 items at $10. The inventory at the end of July is therefore the remaining 300 items valued at $9 plus the 1500 items now purchased at $10. The company then sold 200 items. On a FIFO basis, these come from the 300 items still in inventory at $9.

As a result of these transactions, the closing inventory at the end of July is represented by 100 items at a cost of $9 plus 1500 items at a cost of $10. A total closing inventory valuation is $15 900.

Advantages of FIFO

The main advantages of adopting the FIFO method of inventory valuation are as follows:

- Closing inventory is based on the most recent prices paid.
- Inventory valuations are based on actual prices paid for items.
- It is logical because it assumes that sales are made from the oldest items of inventory first.

AVCO

The average cost method of inventory valuation involves recalculating the average cost of inventory after each new purchase. Every item is then valued at this average cost.

The average cost is calculated as follows:

$$\frac{\text{Current inventory value + Value of items purchased}}{\text{Number of units in the inventory}}$$

Using exactly the same data as in our FIFO example, the AVCO calculation would be as follows.

Date	Received			Issued	Average cost	Inventory valuation	
	Qty	Price	Value	Qty		Qty	Value
		$	$		$		$
May	500	8	4 000		8.00	500	4 000
June	1 200	9	10 800		8.70	1 700	14 790
June				600	8.70	1 100	7 370
July				800	8.70	300	2 610
July	1 500	10	15 000		9.78	1 800	17 604
July				200	9.78	1 600	15 648

Explanation

In May the company purchased 500 items, paying $8 each, and none were sold.

In June the company purchased a further 1200 items at $9 each. The average cost of the 1700 items in the inventory at this stage is $8.70 ($14 800/1700). The company then sells 600 units. The sale does not affect the average cost and the balance of the inventory is now 1100 items at $8.70.

In July the company sold 800 items. Again, this sale does not affect the average cost, so the balance of the inventory is now 300 items, still at an average cost of $8.70. The company then purchases a further 1500 items at $10. This purchase does affect the average cost, which becomes $9.78 ($2610 + $15 000/1800). Finally, the company sells 200 items, and again this does not affect the average cost. As a result of these transactions, the closing inventory at the end of July is represented by 1600 items at an average cost of $9.78, i.e. a total closing inventory valuation of $15 648.

Advantage of AVCO

The main advantage of adopting the AVCO method of inventory valuation is that identical items in the inventory are given an identical cost.

LIFO

The last in, first out method assumes that the items purchased most recently were sold first. The result of this is that any unsold items are considered to be those purchased earliest.

Detailed calculations of the value of inventory using LIFO are not required.

The effect of inventory valuation on the financial statements

As will be seen from the two examples above, the different methods of valuing inventory produce different results.

The closing inventory valuation is deducted as part of the cost of sales in the income statement. Using the FIFO method, the closing inventory was valued at $15 900. Using the AVCO method, the value of the same inventory was $15 648, a difference of $252. As a result, the cost of sales when using the FIFO method will be lower than when using AVCO and consequently, the profits using FIFO will be higher than when using AVCO.

In the long term, profits using both methods will be exactly the same, as eventually all inventory will be sold. However, in the short term, FIFO will produce higher profits than AVCO.

As FIFO produces a higher inventory valuation, it follows that using this method will also produce higher current assets and net assets on the statement of financial position than AVCO.

End-of-chapter questions

1 **Classify the following costs by nature.**
- Direct materials
- Sales person's commission
- Property rent
- Telephone charges
- Power
- Supervisors' salaries
- Direct labour.

2 A company pays its workers on a time rate basis, but also pays a bonus of $0.50 per unit for production over 500 units per week. Each worker is guaranteed a minimum wage of $320 per week.
Calculate the weekly wage for each of the following workers.

	Hourly rate	Hours worked	Units produced
Worker A	$6.50	45	620
Worker B	$7.20	36	580
Worker C	$7.00	42	718

3 Tariq sells one type of machinery. He provides the following information for the month of March. He had no inventory on hand at 1 March.

Date	Purchases	Sales
1 March	8 @ $1 500	
7 March		4 @ $2 500
9 March	12 @ $1 600	
19 March		6 @ $2 800
25 March	8 @ $1 800	
29 March		12 @ $3 000

a Calculate the value of Tariq's closing inventory at 31 March using the FIFO method.

b Calculate the value of Tariq's closing inventory at 31 March using the AVCO method.

c Which of the above methods of inventory valuation will give the higher profit? Give reasons for your answer.

4 Rupert sells one product. He provides the following information for the month of May. He had no inventory on hand on 1 May.

Date	Purchases	Sales
1 May	12 @ $600	
5 May		6 @ $900
12 May	14 @ $660	
19 May		12 @ $960
24 May	6 @ $670	
29 May		10 @ $990

a Calculate the value of Rupert's closing inventory at 31 May using the FIFO method.

b Calculate the value of Rupert's closing inventory at 31 May using the AVCO method.

Section 2.2: Traditional costing methods

Key concepts

Costing techniques all apply key concepts: **true and fair view; consistency; businesses entity; money measurement**.

It is important to emphasise that the money measurement concept means that costing techniques cannot take account of non-financial factors. This is an important reservation since these techniques are used by owners and managers when making key decisions.

2.2.1: Absorption costing

Absorption costing

The purpose of a cost accounting system is to gather information on all relevant costs to enable decisions to be made. Direct costs, direct materials and direct labour can easily be identified to a particular job or a particular department. Indirect costs such as most overhead costs cause more of a problem.

Absorption costing is a method that absorbs overheads into the total production cost for each cost unit produced. Whereas marginal costing (which we shall consider later) separates variable costs and fixed costs, absorption costing considers all production costs, both fixed and variable.

In absorption costing direct costs are allocated to the relevant cost centre, which is a location such as a production department or service department. Indirect costs such as overheads are apportioned between relevant cost centres.

The process of absorption occurs when all production costs have been allocated and apportioned. The total for each department is then absorbed into a cost unit, such as a product or a service, using an overhead absorption rate (OAR).

The methods of absorption may be:

- the direct labour hour rate
- the direct machine hour rate.

The method selected is based on which factor most influences the overhead. For example, if the production department uses more labour hours than machine hours, it is described as labour intensive and costs would be absorbed using a direct labour hour rate. If the production department uses more machine hours than labour hours, then it is described as machine intensive (or capital intensive) and costs would be absorbed using a direct machine hour rate.

Apportioning overheads

To apportion the overheads, you can either use the elimination (or simplified) method or the continuous allotment (or repeated distribution) method.

The elimination (or simplified) method

The elimination method of apportioning the service departments' overheads is quick, as each service department has its overheads apportioned only once by the other departments.

Learning objectives

In this chapter you will learn:

- what absorption costing is and how to allocate and apportion costs using both the elimination and continuous allotment methods
- how to calculate and apply the overhead absorption rate (OAR)
- how to calculate the full cost using the OAR and a selling price
- the effects of under-absorption and over-absorption
- the benefits and limitations of absorption costing.

Key terms

Cost unit: a unit of production or service that absorbs the cost centre's overheads costs, e.g. a product such as a radio or a service such as a canteen meal.
Allocation: the process of charging costs that derive from a cost centre directly to that particular cost centre.
Production department: where the product is actually made, e.g. the machine department.
Service department: a department that supports the other departments, e.g. technical support or the canteen.
Apportionment: the process of charging overhead costs to a cost centre on a rational basis.
Cost centre: a production or service location whose costs may be attributed to cost units, e.g. a production department.
Overhead absorption rate (OAR): the rate that is used to absorb the overheads into the cost unit. It is usually calculated as either the rate per direct machine hour or the rate per direct labour hour.

Key terms

Labour intensive: the production or service location has more direct labour hours than machine hours.
Machine intensive: the production or service location has more direct machine hours than labour hours.

Illustration 1: Apportioning overheads using the elimination (or simplified) method

Maureen Rose plc manufactures bags. The company has one factory. There are two production departments, cutting and finishing, and two service departments, maintenance and canteen.

The following information is available for Maureen Rose plc for the year ended 31 October 2014.

	$
Overheads:	
Buildings insurance	50 000
Heating and lighting	72 000
Machine insurance	100 000
Rent	120 000
Cutting supervisor	35 800
Finishing supervisors	76 300

Additional information:

	Cutting department	Finishing department	Maintenance	Canteen
Floor area (m^2)	50 000	30 000	15 000	5 000
Machine net book value ($)	150 000	450 000		

The service departments are apportioned to the production departments on the following basis.

	Cutting department	Finishing department	Maintenance	Canteen
Canteen	50%	40%	10%	–
Maintenance	75%	25%	–	–

The overhead apportionment schedule would therefore appear as:

Overhead apportionment schedule for Maureen Rose plc					
Overhead	Basis	Cutting	Finishing	Maintenance	Canteen
		$	$	$	$
Cutting supervisor	Direct	35 800			
Finishing supervisor	Direct		76 300		
Buildings insurance	Floor area	25 000	15 000	7 500	2 500
Heating and lighting	Floor area	36 000	21 600	10 800	3 600

Machine insurance	Machine net book value	25 000	75 000		
Rent	Floor area	60 000	36 000	18 000	6 000
		181 800	223 900	36 300	12 100
Canteen	50 : 40 : 10	6 050	4 840	1 210	(12 100)
Maintenance	75 : 25	28 133	9 377	(35 510)	
		215 983	238 117	0	0

Notes:

1 **Bases of apportionment:** There are several bases used for apportionment. The individual basis to be used for apportioning each overhead is easily identified as it is usually the most realistic one. For example, the most equitable way to apportion the building insurance overhead is by the proportion of floor space held by each department, whereas a better way to apportion the machine insurance is according to the proportion of the total machine net book value. Given the information available, the most realistic basis to be used for the heating and lighting and rent is the proportion of the total floor space in both instances.

2 **Apportionment of the service departments:** The most important thing to recognise is whether there is any interdependency between the service departments. In this case, both service departments support the production departments, but the canteen also supports the maintenance department. Once this has been identified then this service department must be apportioned first to both the production departments and the other service department. In this example, remember to include the 10 per cent of the canteen costs in the apportionment of the total maintenance costs.

Getting it right

When there is interdependency between the service departments, remember to include the first service department apportionment in the second service department apportionment.

The continuous allotment (or repeated distribution) method

If, however, the service department that has any apportionment to the other service department is not apportioned first, the continuous allotment method will result, whereby there is no preferred order to the apportionment and so the apportionment continues until the balance in each service department is zero. Although this method can be more accurate than the simplified method, it is much more time-consuming.

Getting it right

It is recommended that you do not use the continuous allotment (or repeated distribution) method in an examination due to time constraints.

Illustration 2: Apportioning overheads using the continuous allotment (or repeated distribution) method

Using the information from the previous illustration for Maureen Rose plc, the method is the same until the apportionment of the service departments. Starting from this point, the calculation would be as follows.

Getting it right

Make sure that the schedule is clearly laid out, with each part of the process clearly shown.

Also, ensure that the bases used for each overhead are clearly identified.

Overhead	Basis	Cutting	Finishing	Maintenance	Canteen
	%	$	$	$	$
B/d		181 800	223 900	36 300	12 100
Maintenance	75 : 25	27 225	9 075	(36 300)	–
Canteen	50 : 40 : 10	6 050	4 840	1 210	(12 100)
Maintenance	75 : 25	908	302	(1 210)	–
		215 983	238 117	0	0

As can be seen, the same final answer is achieved but the process is longer. This can be a repetitive process if each department apportions their overheads to each other repeatedly.

The overhead absorption rate (OAR)

Calculating the OAR

The stages used to calculate the OAR are as follows.

Step 1: Distinguish between production departments (for example a cutting department) and service departments (for example the canteen).

Step 2: Decide on the correct bases to be used to apportion the overheads between the departments (for example according to the percentage of the total floor space for the cutting department and the proportion of employees working in the department for the canteen).

Step 3: Draw up a schedule to apportion the overheads between all of the departments.

Step 4: Complete the schedule by apportioning the total of the overheads of each service department to each of the production departments.

Step 5: Total up the overheads for each production department.

Step 6: Divide the total for each department by the correct base, for example labour hours or machine hours depending on whether the department is labour intensive or machine intensive, to give the OAR for each production department.

Illustration 3: Calculating the OAR

The directors of Maureen Rose plc absorb their overheads on the following basis:

- The cutting department uses more direct machine hours than direct labour hours. It is, therefore, machine or capital intensive, and overheads are absorbed using direct machine hours.
- The finishing department uses more direct labour hours than direct machine hours. It is, therefore, labour intensive and overheads are absorbed using direct labour hours.

Getting it right

Always state the OAR to two decimal places. So, a calculation of $16.248 would be stated as $16.25.

Always state the base used in the calculation for each production department.

Accuracy is required at this stage as it then enables a more realistic estimation of the full cost of a cost unit to be calculated.

The overheads for the year ended 31 October 2014 were:

- the cutting department: $215 983
- the finishing department: $238 117.

The cutting department has 12 000 machine hours and the finishing department has 14 000 labour hours.

The OAR is the rate at which the overheads are absorbed into the cost unit. It is calculated as:

$$\frac{\text{Department overhead in dollars}}{\text{Department direct machine hours or direct labour hours}}$$

The OAR for the cutting department is, therefore:

$$\frac{\$215\ 983}{12\ 000} = \$18.00 \text{ per machine hour}$$

The OAR for the finishing department is, therefore:

$$\frac{\$238\ 117}{14\ 000} = \$17.00 \text{ per labour hour}$$

Key term

Full cost: the production cost of each cost unit, which includes both direct and indirect costs.

The use of the OAR

Once the OAR has been calculated, it is possible to calculate the full cost of a cost unit.

Illustration 4: Calculating the full cost of a cost unit

Maureen Rose plc has the following information:

- Each bag takes 1.5 hours of machine time in the cutting department and 1 hour and 45 minutes of labour in the finishing department, at $8 per hour, to manufacture.
- Each bag uses 0.5 metres of material at $22 per metre.

The full cost per bag is, therefore:

	$
Materials (0.5 metres × $22 per metre)	11.00
Labour (1.75 hours × $8 per hour)	14.00
Cutting department overheads ($18.00 per machine hour × 1.5 hours)	27.00
Finishing department overheads ($17.00 per labour hour × 1.75 hours)	29.75
Full cost	81.75

The OAR is multiplied by either the machine hours or labour hours for the relevant department (for example the OAR for the cutting department is based on machine hours).

The total production or full cost of producing one bag is, therefore, $81.75. This includes the direct costs and an apportionment of the overheads for each bag.

It is important to appreciate that this method gives only an approximate estimate of what the product actually costs. For example, how realistic is it to absorb a production department's overheads either on machine hours or labour hours, especially if that department is not strongly capital intensive?

Key terms

Under-absorption: this occurs when fewer units are produced than was predicted in the budget and, therefore, not all of the overheads are absorbed into the cost unit.

Over-absorption: this occurs when more units are produced than was predicted and, therefore, more overheads are absorbed into the cost unit.

Under-absorption or over-absorption

Overhead absorption rates are calculated using planned levels of production and budgeted levels of expenditure. As such, this can lead to problems when actual levels of production and/or actual costs are not the same as those budgeted. This will result in an under-absorption or an over-absorption of costs. The resultant difference is recorded as an adjustment within the income statement.

Under-absorption occurs when the actual expenditure is more than budgeted and/or the actual production is less than budgeted.

Over-absorption occurs when the actual expenditure is less than budgeted and/or the actual production is more than budgeted.

Illustration 5: Calculating overhead absorption rates on the basis of direct labour hours

Company A calculated its overhead absorption rates on the basis of direct labour hours for the year ended 31 December 2014 as follows.

	Budgeted	Actual
Production units	60 000	54 000
Direct labour hours	30 000	32 000
Overhead costs	$140 000	$135 000
OAR = $140 000/30 000 = $4.67 per direct labour hour		

	$
Overheads recovered (32 000 × $4.67) =	149 440
Overheads cost	135 000
Over-absorbed overheads	14 440

Illustration 6: Calculating overhead absorption rates on the basis of machine hours

Company B calculated its overhead absorption rates on the basis of machine hours for the year ended 31 December 2014 as follows.

	Budgeted	Actual
Production units	100 000	105 000
Machine hours	40 000	42 000
Overhead costs	$180 000	$205 000
OAR = $180 000/40 000 = $4.50 per machine hour		

	$
Overheads recovered (42 000 × $4.50) =	189 000
Overheads cost	205 000
Under-absorbed overheads	16 000

Benefits and limitations of absorption costing

Benefits

- Absorption costing recognises the fixed costs in the product cost and is therefore suitable for determining the selling price of a product.
- Absorption costing conforms to the accruals/matching concept that requires costs to be matched with revenues for a period.
- Absorption costing avoids the necessity of separating fixed costs from variable costs.
- Absorption costing is the recognised method of inventory valuation.

Limitations

- Absorption costing is not useful for decision-making purposes. In considering fixed costs as part of the product cost, managers will not have a clear understanding of whether accepting a lower price for a product is worthwhile.
- Absorption costing is not useful for responsibility accounting. It would be unfair to hold managers responsible for fixed costs over which they had no control.

End-of-chapter questions

1 Definitions of terms

Explain what the terms 'allocation', 'apportion' and 'absorption' mean.

2 Absorption schedule and OAR

The following information relates to the production departments of Springson Ltd.

	Cutting department	Machining department
Direct machine hours	4 000	33 000
Direct labour hours	30 000	20 000
Cost of machinery	20 000	260 000
Floor area (m^2)	9 000	21 000

The factory overheads for the year ended 31 March 2014 were:

	$
Machinery insurance	28 000
Rent	12 000
Depreciation	56 000
Light and heat	18 000

Required

a Prepare an overhead apportionment schedule apportioning the factory overheads to the appropriate departments.

b Calculate the OARs for each production department. State the bases used and give one reason for your choice.

3 Full cost of a product

A company manufactures several products, one of which is the Danthea. The factory has two production departments (machining and finishing) and one service centre (the canteen). Eighty per cent of the canteen costs are apportioned to the machining department and the rest to the finishing department. The overheads for the year were:

	$
Machining	208 000
Finishing	72 000
Canteen	40 000

The following information is available for one unit of Danthea.

Direct materials	$42
Machining department	5 direct labour hours
Finishing department	2 direct labour hours

Indirect costs are absorbed from the production departments using a direct labour rate.

Direct labour hours for the year were:

- machining department: 120 000 hours
- finishing department: 25 000 hours.

All direct labour is paid at $8.00 an hour.

a Calculate the OAR for each production department.

b Calculate the full cost of one unit of Danthea.

4 Identifying the cause of under-absorption

What will cause under-absorption of fixed production overheads?

A Absorption of overheads is based on actual expenditure and actual activity.

B Actual activity is above budgeted activity.

C Actual activity is below budgeted activity and actual expenditure is as budgeted.

D Actual expenditure of overheads is below budget expenditure.

5 Calculating the OAR

A hospital budgets for overheads totalling $11 500 000 for a financial year. It expects to treat 25 000 patients in the year. Each patient stays an average of ten days and the hospital absorbs overheads on a patient/day basis. Its direct costs for the year are budgeted at $25 000 000.

What is its OAR?

A $46 per patient day

B $100 per patient day

C $146 per patient day

D $460 per patient day.

6 Calculating production units

The following table shows figures for a week's production.

Expected production	10 000 units
Expected production overhead	$50 000
Actual production overhead	$60 000
Under-absorption of overhead	$5 000

What is the actual amount of production in the week?

A 9000 units
B 9167 units
C 11 000 units
D 13 000 units.

7 Using the OAR to calculate the cost of a job
A firm has three jobs performed in separate production departments: A, B, C and D. The overheads of the service departments K, L and M are apportioned to the production departments using the percentages shown in the table below.

	Production departments				Service departments		
	A	**B**	**C**	**D**	**K**	**L**	**M**
Overheads	$6 700	$9 100	$11 600	$3 550	$8 000	$5 000	$6 100
Dept K	25%	30%	20%	10%		15%	
Dept L	60%		30%	10%			
Dept M		30%	50%	20%			

Additional information:

	A	B	C	D
Direct labour hours	2 000	1 200	4 450	1 850
Machine hours	1 900	2 600	2 900	2 400
Direct labour rate	$2.10	$1.70	$2.40	$2.30

Job 315, Dept A	Job 316, Dept B	Job 317, Depts C then D
Direct materials: $190	Direct materials: $1 199	Direct materials: $560 in C Direct materials: $68 in D
56 direct labour hours	178 direct labour hours	160 direct labour hours in C 30 direct labour hours in D
40 machine hours	176 machine hours	150 machine hours in C 20 machine hours in D

Required

a Calculate the OAR for each production department.
b Calculate the cost of each job.

2.2.2: Marginal costing

Learning objectives

In this chapter you will learn:

- the meaning of the terms 'marginal cost', 'variable cost', 'fixed cost', 'semi-variable cost', 'direct cost', 'indirect cost', 'contribution', 'break-even analysis' and 'margin of safety'
- how to calculate the break-even point using the formula and represent the information on a graph
- the limitations of break-even analysis
- to select and apply relevant techniques using marginal costing to aid decision-making for make-or-buy decisions, special orders and limited resources
- the uses, benefits and limitations of marginal costing
- how to reconcile the reported profits using marginal costing and absorption costing.

Key terms

Marginal cost: the cost of producing one extra unit.

Getting it right

Remember that marginal revenues could also be considered, which are those revenues received when one extra unit is sold.

Marginal costing

Marginal costing is a costing method that only considers marginal costs, which are those incurred when one extra unit is produced (for example cost of direct materials, cost of direct labour and any other variable costs that increase as production increases).

The marginal costing method is used when:

- calculating the break-even point for a product
- considering whether to make or buy a product
- calculating the cost of a special order
- a business has a limiting factor that restricts its activities.

Types of marginal cost

Within the marginal costing model it is important to distinguish between the different types of cost, as fixed costs are not considered.

- Variable costs: These vary in direct proportion to the level of production (e.g. direct wages and materials).
- Fixed costs: These do not vary in direct proportion to the level of production (e.g. rent payable, supervisor salaries and insurance).
- Semi-variable costs: These are partly fixed and partly variable (e.g. telephone costs, which have a fixed line rental but a variable call-charge cost).
- Direct cost: This cost is identified with a specific cost unit (e.g. direct labour and direct materials, which are part of the prime cost in a manufacturing account).
- Indirect cost: This cost is not identified with a specific cost unit. Indirect costs are also known as factory overheads in a manufacturing account.

Illustration 1: Applying the correct cost behaviour

Stanley Harold Ltd manufactures golf balls and sells to an international market. The golf balls are sold in box sets of six.

The following information is available for the year ended 31 January 2015.

1. During the year 60 000 sets of golf balls were produced.
2. Materials cost $3 per set of golf balls. The material suppliers allowed a cash discount of 5 per cent if Stanley Harold Ltd paid early. Only 25 per cent of materials were paid for taking advantage of this discount. Material is a variable cost.

Getting it right

Learn the exact definitions of the different types of cost. Give an example where possible as part of your definition.

3 Labour is paid for at a rate of $8 per hour. Unfortunately, orders could not be completed in normal working hours during the year due to staff sickness. The directors of Stanley Harold Ltd agreed to pay overtime to workers so orders could be completed. The overtime was paid on 5000 sets of golf balls at a rate of $14 per hour. Each set of golf balls takes 15 minutes to make. Labour is a variable cost.

4 All other manufacturing costs were fixed and amounted to $298 125. The manufacturing cost for the 60 000 sets of golf balls is therefore:

	$
Material costs:	
with discount 25% × 60 000 × ($4 × 0.95)	57 000
without discount 75% × 60 000 × $4	180 000
Labour costs:	
with overtime 5 000 × ($14 × 0.25)	17 500
without overtime 55 000 × ($8 × 0.25)	110 000
Total variable costs	364 500
Fixed manufacturing costs	298 125
Total costs	662 625

Notes:

- **Layout:** The layout clearly distinguishes between variable and fixed costs. The variable costs are made up of materials and labour.
- **Material costs:** In order to make the calculations easier, the material costs at full price are shown separately to those with a discount. This method is recommended for examination questions.
- **Labour costs:** Once again, in order to make calculations easier, the labour costs are split between those with overtime and those without.

From this illustration, it is possible to further calculate useful costs. For example, the total manufacturing cost per golf ball set is:

$$\frac{662\ 625}{60\ 000} = \$11.04375$$

whereas the variable cost per golf ball can be calculated as:

$$\frac{364\ 500}{60\ 000} = \$6.075$$

The fixed cost per golf ball set can, therefore, be calculated as:

$$\frac{298\ 125}{60\ 000} = \$4.96875$$

Key term

Contribution: the money available to pay fixed costs. Once these are paid, contribution becomes profit.

Contribution

The calculation of contribution is an important part of marginal costing as it identifies the amount made per unit towards covering fixed costs and profit. Once the fixed costs are covered, profit is made. Contribution is calculated as the difference between selling price per unit and variable cost per unit.

Illustration 2: Calculating contribution

Stanley Harold Ltd sells each golf ball set for $18. The variable cost is $6.075 and the fixed costs are $298 125.

The contribution is, therefore:

$18.00 (selling price) less $6.075 (variable cost) = $11.925 (contribution)

If 60 000 golf ball sets are sold a year, a statement can be drawn up to show the total contribution and profit for the year.

Stanley Harold Ltd Statement to show total contribution and profit for the year ended 31 January 2015	
	$
Sales (60 000 × $18)	1 080,000
Variable costs (60 000 × $6.075)	(364 500)
Total contribution	715 500
Fixed costs	(298 125)
Profit for the year	417 375

Note: The calculation for total contribution can be checked as it is the total units sold × contribution per unit.

In this illustration, it would be: 60 000 × $11.925 = $715 500

> **Key terms**
>
> **Break-even point**: the point at which total revenue equals total cost, and so neither profit nor loss is made.
> The formula to find the break-even point in units is:
>
> $$\frac{\text{Total fixed costs}}{\text{Contribution per unit}}$$
>
> The formula to find the break-even point in dollars is:
> Break-even points in units × Selling price
>
> **Contribution-to-sales method**: otherwise known as the profit/volume method, this is an alternative way of finding the break-even point in dollars.
> The formula is:
>
> $$\frac{\text{Total fixed costs}}{\text{Total contribution/Sales}}$$

Break-even analysis

The break-even point

One of the most important marginal costing techniques is break-even analysis, which identifies the level of output necessary to make neither a profit nor a loss. The break-even point is where total revenue equals total costs.

The number of units required to be sold to make the break-even point is calculated as:

$$\frac{\text{Total fixed costs}}{\text{Contribution per unit}}$$

At the break-even point, total revenue equals total cost. There are two methods used to calculate this amount:

- Break-even in units × Selling price
- The contribution-to-sales method: $\frac{\text{Total fixed costs}}{\text{Total contribution/Sales}}$

Getting it right

When asked to provide the formula for break-even, ensure that a complete formula is given including contribution per unit.

Also remember to round up the break-even units to the nearest whole unit as it is not realistically possible to achieve any contribution with only part of a unit.

Getting it right

Take care to ensure that the answer is clearly and correctly expressed in dollars or units.

Key term

Margin of safety: the difference between the number of sales units achieved (or maximum output) and the number of units at the break-even point, where the amount of sales achieved exceeds the break-even point (otherwise a loss is made).

Illustration 3: Applying the formula to find the break-even point

Using information from the previous illustration for Stanley Harold Ltd, we know that:

- the selling price for each golf ball set is \$18
- the variable cost per set is \$6.075
- the fixed costs for the year are \$298 125.

The break-even point is, therefore:

$$\frac{\text{Fixed costs}}{\text{Contribution per unit}} = \frac{\$298\,125}{\$11.925} = 25\,000 \text{ golf ball sets}$$

The revenue at the break-even point is the same as the total cost. From the previous example, this can be calculated as:

Break-even in units × Selling price = 25 000 × \$18 = \$450 000

Alternatively, this can be calculated using the contribution-to-sales method:

$$\frac{\text{Fixed costs}}{\text{Contribution per unit/Selling price per unit}} =$$

$$\frac{\$298\,125}{\$11.925/\$18} = \$450\,000$$

The margin of safety

The margin of safety is the number of units between the number of sales made and the number needed to break even, where the number of sales exceeds the break-even point.

In the previous illustration, Stanley Harold Ltd has a margin of safety of 60 000 – 25 000 = 35 000 golf ball sets. This means that it is making profit on the sales of 35 000 golf ball sets, namely 58.33 per cent of its total sales. The rest is used to cover the fixed costs.

Target profit

The break-even formula can also be amended slightly to find how many units need to be sold in order to achieve a specified target profit, as follows:

$$\frac{\text{Total fixed costs + Target profit}}{\text{Contribution per unit}}$$

Illustration 4: Calculating how many units need to be sold to achieve a target profit

The directors of Stanley Harold Ltd wish to achieve a target profit level of \$35 775.

The golf sets that the business would have to produce and sell would therefore be:

$$\frac{\text{Total fixed costs + Target profit}}{\text{Contribution per unit}} = \frac{\$298\,125 + \$35\,775}{\$11.925}$$

$$= 28\,000 \text{ golf sets}$$

The break-even chart

The following information can all be represented on a break-even chart:

- break-even in units
- break-even in revenue
- margin of safety.

The example here uses figures of 25 000 units (break-even in units), \$450 000 (break-even in revenue) and 35 000 units (margin of safety).

A break-even graph

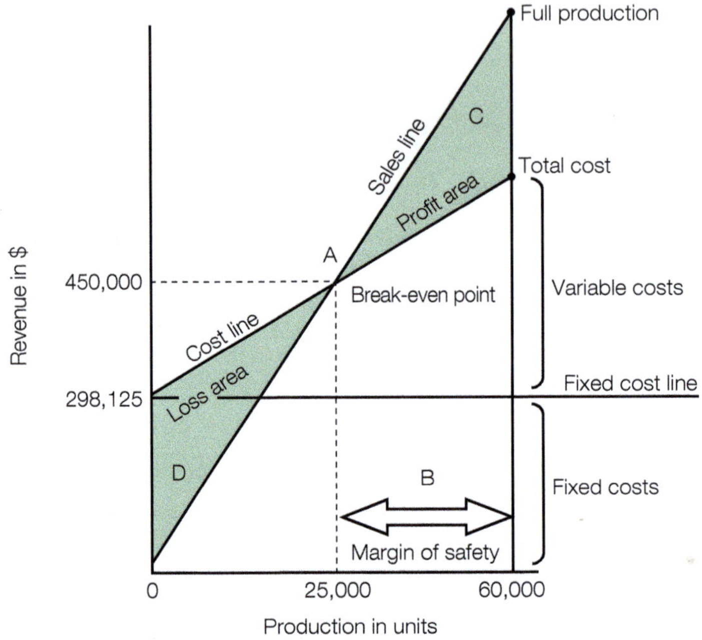

- Point A shows the break-even point where total costs cross total revenues.
- Line B shows the margin of safety as the difference between the breakeven point and the maximum output production level, usually expressed in units.
- C and D show the profit or loss at various production levels as the difference between the total costs and the total revenues lines at different production levels.

The steps for drawing a break-even chart are:

Step 1: Label the axes clearly.

Step 2: Calculate the break-even point using the formula: Fixed costs/ Contribution per unit.

Step 3: Calculate the break-even point in revenue using the formula: Break-even point in units × Selling price per unit.

Getting it right

When preparing the break-even chart, ensure that care is taken to:

- give the chart a title
- clearly label the axes
- identify the break-even point
- draw the lines accurately and label them clearly.

Step 4: Plot the break-even point on the chart (point A). Try to ensure that the break-even sales units and sales revenue are in the middle of the chart.

Step 5: Draw the fixed costs line across the chart as a horizontal line.

Step 6: Draw the sales revenue line starting from (0,0) and going through the break-even point (point A).

Step 7: Draw the cost line starting from the point where the fixed cost line crosses the *y*-axis and going through the break-even point (point A).

Step 8: Complete the chart by identifying the profit and loss areas and the margin of safety (line B).

The limitations of break-even analysis

Break-even analysis has limitations:

- It assumes that there are no changes in the levels of inventory, so that everything produced during the period is assumed to have been sold. This is unrealistic as most businesses have changing levels of inventory throughout the financial year.
- It does not allow product mix and is usually calculated for a single product, which is not realistic.
- Cost behaviour is assumed to be either fixed or variable, so semi-variable costs are not considered. Again, this is unrealistic as many costs have behaviour that is not either perfectly fixed or perfectly variable but a combination of the two.
- Fixed costs are assumed to remain fixed for the whole period of time, so stepped fixed costs are not considered. Stepped fixed costs are costs that remain fixed until a certain level of business activity is reached, when they increase in increments. They will remain fixed at this new increment until the next level of business activity (for example an increase in the storage costs due to an increase in the production level).
- Variable costs are assumed to be perfectly linear with the level of production, so changes in costs are not considered (for example overtime or bulk-buying discounts).
- The selling price is assumed to remain fixed throughout the year, so seasonal sales or discounts are not considered.

Applying marginal costing in decision-making situations

Marginal costing can be used in a variety of business situations:

- when deciding whether to make or buy a product
- when deciding whether or not to accept a special order
- when considering how to maximise profits when there are limited resources available.

Make-or-buy decisions

One of the most common business decisions is whether a business should continue to manufacture a product itself or whether it should buy the product in from a supplier. Often the business is faced with a choice of satisfying customer demand with products bought in as it is unable to produce the goods required itself. On a purely financial basis, the decision whether to make or buy in should be based on whether a positive contribution is made.

Illustration 5: Deciding whether to make or buy a product

Stanley Harold Ltd has six machines that are used in the manufacture of the golf ball sets. One of the machines has broken down and will take four weeks to repair. While the machine is being repaired, the directors could lease a replacement machine at a cost of $3000 per week. The staff would need to be trained to use the machine at a cost of $4000, which would reduce production for one week from 5000 golf ball sets to 4000. Alternatively, the directors can buy the golf ball sets in from a competitor at a cost of $8 per set. The company would be able to buy 5000 a week but would also have to pay a fixed delivery cost of $1275.

The profit under both options for the four weeks would be:

	To manufacture	To buy in
	$	$
Revenue		
To manufacture (4000 × 1 wk + 5000 × 3 wks) × $18	342 000	
To buy in (5000 × 4 wks) × $18		360 000
Costs		
Variable costs to make (4000 × 1 wk + 5000 × 3 wks) × $6.075	(115 425)	
Buy-in cost (5000 × 4) × $8		(160 000)
Lease (4 wks × $3000)	(12 000)	
Delivery costs		(1 275)
Training costs	(4 000)	
Profit	210 575	198 725

You need to identify the behaviour of each cost and revenue. That is, identify whether a cost (a) varies with the level of production and is a variable cost, or (b) does not vary with production and is therefore fixed. In this illustration, the sales, materials and labour and buy-in costs are variable. The lease, training costs and delivery costs are fixed.

This illustration shows that the business makes more profit from manufacturing the golf ball sets itself, despite the extra lease and training costs, as well as the reduction in sales. The recommended action, therefore, would be to continue to manufacture the golf ball sets itself in order to maximise profit.

Special orders

Before accepting a special order, a business must consider both the financial and non-financial factors involved:

- Financial: Does the order provide a positive contribution?
- Non-financial:
  - Will the order lead to further orders and expand market share?
  - Is spare capacity being utilised?
  - Will staff have to be retrained to make the product and will they want to be retrained?
  - Will machinery have to be adapted if the specification of the product has been changed?
  - How reliable is the customer?
  - How much disruption to the normal trading of the business will take place?

Illustration 6: Deciding whether to accept a special order

Stanley Harold Ltd currently manufactures 30 000 golf ball sets a year but has spare capacity. The company receives a new order for 500 golf ball sets at $12 per set. The customer is based overseas in a new market area. There will be extra packaging costs of $512.50 for the order, which is $1.025 per golf set.

Financial factors

The contribution for each golf ball set in the new order is:

	$
Selling price	12.00
Variable manufacturing costs	(6.075)
Extra packaging costs	(1.025)
Contribution	4.90

Although this contribution is lower than the usual contribution of $11.925, the new order does make a positive contribution. The business has already passed the break-even point and is producing more units than are required for the target profit.

The total profit from this order will therefore be: 500 × $4.90 = $2450.

Non-financial factors

The order has been received from a new customer in a new overseas market area, which will expand Stanley Harold Ltd's customer base. However, how reliable is this new customer? Can it be guaranteed that

Getting it right

When making a decision on whether to recommend acceptance of a special order, you should consider both the financial and non-financial factors so that you can give a balanced answer.

the new customer will pay on time? Also, how easy will the distribution of the products to the new customer be?

Once these factors have been considered to the satisfaction of the business managers, then the order should be accepted as it will increase profit because there is a positive contribution.

Limited resources

A business will often manufacture multiple products but have limited resources available to do so (for example limited labour hours or machine hours). In this situation, an optimum production plan has to be devised in order to maximise profit with the resources available.

The process is:

Step 1: Calculate the contribution per unit.

Step 2: Calculate the contribution per limiting factor (for example per labour hour).

Step 3: Rank the products in order of the product with the highest contribution per limiting factor down to the product with the lowest.

Step 4: Devise a production plan to maximise profits using the rank order.

Illustration 7: Devising an optimum production plan

The directors of Stanley Harold Ltd decide to introduce a new product. They intend to manufacture and sell boxes of golf tees.

Information on their two products is as follows.

	A box of golf tees	A set of golf balls
Selling price	$6	$18
Labour	10 minutes at $3.60 per hour	30 minutes at $8 per hour
Materials	$2	$2.075
Expected demand for the following year	24 000 boxes	60 000 boxes

The company only has 32 000 hours available and wishes to maximise profits by devising an optimum production plan.

Step 1: Contribution per unit (Selling price per unit – Variable cost per unit):

Box of golf tees: $6 – $2.60 = $3.40

Set of golf balls: $18– $6.075 = $11.925

Step 2: Contribution per limiting factor (Contribution per unit/ Proportion of labour hours per unit):

Box of golf tees: \$3.40/(1/6) = \$20.40

Set of golf balls: \$11.925/(1/2) = \$23.85

Step 3: The rank order based on the highest contribution per limiting factor is, therefore:

Set of golf balls: 1

Box of golf tees: 2.

Step 4: The optimum production plan to maximise profit is, therefore:

	Hours	Units
Total hours available	32 000	
Set of golf balls (expected demand)	30 000	60 000 sets (30 minutes per set)
Box of golf tees (remaining hours)	2000	12 000 boxes (10 minutes per box)

The number of boxes of golf tees to be produced is based on the remaining hours. There are 2000 hours remaining. Each box takes 10 minutes to produce; there are 60 minutes in an hour, so six boxes can be produced in one hour, making a final calculation of: 2000 hours × 6 = 12 000 boxes.

Comparing marginal and absorption costing

Inventory valuation

The different methods of costing give a different cost per unit, which will give a different valuation of the closing inventory of the finished goods and work in progress. This, in turn, will affect the cost of sales figure and the profit calculation when inventory levels change.

Marginal costing will value inventory at the variable cost, but absorption costing will absorb the fixed costs into the inventory valuation. This will give a higher value of closing inventory, which will be carried forward to the next accounting period as opening inventory, and so fixed costs can be charged to a period other than the one in which they were incurred.

Illustration 8: Inventory valuation and the effect on profit

Maureen Rose plc has the following information for each bag at 31 October 2014.

	$
Selling price per bag	100.50
Materials per bag	11.00
Labour per bag	16.00
Cutting dept overheads	27.00
Finishing dept overheads	29.75

The marginal cost per bag is, therefore, $27.00 ($11.00 + $16.00) and the full absorption cost per bag is $83.75 ($27.00 + $27.00 + $29.75).

During the year ended 31 October 2014, the business produced 8000 bags and sold 7900 bags.

Inventory levels were:

	Number of bags
1 November 2013	800
31 October 2014	900

Fixed costs for the year were $454 000.

The comparative income statements for the year ended 31 October 2014 will appear as follows.

		Marginal costing	Absorption costing
		$	$
Revenue from sales (7 900 × 100.50)		793 950	793 950
Opening inventory	800 × 27 800 × 83.75	(21 600)	(67 000)
Cost of production	8 000 × 27 8 000 × 83.75	(216 000)	(670 000)
Closing inventory	900 × 27 900 × 83.75	24 300	75 375
Contribution		580 650	
Fixed costs		(454 000)	
Profit		126 650	132 325

A reconciliation of the reported profit using marginal costing to the reported profit using absorption costing would be presented as follows.

	$
Marginal costing profit	126 650
Add: fixed costs included in increase in closing inventory (($87.75 – $27.00) × 100 units)	5 675
Absorption costing profit	132 325

Summarised uses, benefits and limitations of marginal costing and absorption costing

	Uses	Benefits	Limitations
Marginal costing	Useful for decision-making as it identifies the extra costs and revenues incurred by the production and sale of an additional unit, for example in relation to make-or-buy decisions, limiting factors.	Easily understood and applied in decision-making, as it is cost effective. Contribution is identified which is useful, for example, in make-or-buy decisions and where there are limiting factors such as limited labour hours.	Indirect and direct costs are both divided into either fixed or variable. Fixed costs are not allocated to cost centres and cost units but are regarded as time based and linked to accounting periods rather than units of output.
Absorption costing	Useful for decision-making as it includes a portion of fixed costs in each cost unit, for example when calculating the selling price using the pricing strategy, full cost plus.	All costs are considered so a total production cost per unit is identified. The effect of an increase in any one cost can be assessed whether direct or indirect.	The final basis used to calculate the OAR may not be relevant for all of the overheads in the production department. New technology has led to a reduction in the use of labour hours as a valid basis. If inventory levels decrease, absorption costing records a lower profit than marginal as costs from previous periods are set against income.

End-of-chapter questions

1 Break-even analysis

Ron owns a business that manufactures kettles at a marginal cost of $18 each.

The selling price is $22.50 per kettle.

The fixed costs are currently $90 000 per annum.

Required

a Explain the term 'marginal cost' and give an example.

b Calculate the total contribution if 25 000 kettles are sold.

c Identify the formula used to calculate the profit margin.

d Calculate the profit to revenue margin if 25 000 kettles are sold.

e Calculate how many kettles will need to be sold to break even if the fixed costs increase next year by 20 per cent.

2 Calculating the selling price based on marginal costs

The managers of Kerry Kent Ltd base their profit margin on the formula: contribution per unit × 50%.

The company has received an order for 20 units of product 104A and wishes to make a profit of $16 per unit.

The expected costs for the total order are:

	$
Direct materials	300
Direct labour	100

Present a detailed calculation of the selling price of each unit of product 104A.

3 Optimum production plan

Donaldson Ltd manufactures only two products, Alto and Bass.

At present, the factory has one machine which is operating at 100 per cent capacity. Only 520 000 labour hours are available in the year.

The cost per unit is:

	Alto	Bass
Direct materials	10 metres at $5 per metre	20 metres at $5 per metre
Direct labour	44 hours at $5 per hour	32 hours at $5 per hour

The selling prices for one unit of Alto and Bass are $390 and $350 respectively.

Maximum sales in units for the year are as follows.

	Alto	Bass
Donaldson's sales (units)	18 000	8000

Required

- **a** Calculate the contribution per unit for each product.
- **b** Calculate the contribution per labour hour per unit for each product.
- **c** State the optimum production plan that Donaldson Ltd could introduce which would maximise profit.

4 Target profits

Sid owns a business in a seaside resort. He sells greeting cards.

On average, each card costs $0.50 to buy and is sold for $1.20.

The annual business fixed costs are $110 000. Sid sets a target profit for the year of $30 000. Unfortunately, Sid's supplier decides to increase the cost of the greeting cards by 30 per cent.

- **a** Calculate the contribution per greeting card before the increase in the cost of the cards.
- **b** Calculate, using this contribution, the number of greeting cards that Sid needs to sell to achieve the target profit of $30 000.
- **c** Calculate the number of extra greetings cards that Sid would need to sell to maintain a target profit of $30 000 following the increase in cost per card.
- **d** Advise Sid of two methods by which the business could maintain profit levels without selling the extra greeting cards.

5 Make-or-buy decision

Cilin Ltd manufactures two products, the Qi and Xi.

The Qi currently has a selling price of $20 per unit and it has a marginal cost of $15.

The Xi is selling well.

The economic climate has led to a decrease in the number of units of Qi sold. The financial manager of Cilin Ltd believes that he must reduce the selling price of the product to $18 to match competitors' prices . He is also considering buying in the product at a cost of $12 each. Each unit would need to be completed at an extra cost of $3. Unfortunately, these products are of lower quality than the ones produced by Cilin Ltd and, if purchased, over 40 per cent of the workforce would need to be made redundant.

Discuss whether Cilin Ltd should make or buy in the product Qi.

6 Calculating variable cost

The cost of producing 2000 units of a product is:

	$
Insurance	2 000
Labour	30 000
Materials	10 000
Rent	6 000
Telephone rental	4 000

What is the variable cost of one unit?

- **A** $20
- **B** $22
- **C** $23
- **D** $24

7 Calculating the contribution per unit

A DVD has a selling price of $10. Associated costs are:

	$
Direct materials	1.20
Direct labour	0.80
Factory overhead (fixed)	1.40
Royalty payment	1.00
Administration overhead (fixed)	0.60

What is the contribution per DVD?

A $5.00
B $6.00
C $7.00
D $8.00

8 Calculating profits using the contribution-to-sales ratio

A company has sales of $192 000, fixed costs of $40 000 and a contribution/sales ratio of one-third.

What are its profits?

A $24 000
B $50 667
C $64 000
D $88 000

9 Calculating the break-even point

A firm sells its product for $10 per unit and has variable costs of $6 per unit. Its fixed costs for the year are:

	$
Factory rent	30 000
Other fixed costs	70 000

What is the break-even point?

A 10 000 units
B 16 667 units
C 17 500 units
D 25 000 units.

10 Calculating the total sales revenue at break-even

A business provides the following information.

	$
Total fixed costs	10 000
Unit selling price	1
Variable unit production costs	0.75

What is the total sales revenue needed to break even?

A $2500
B $7500
C $10 000
D $40 000

11 Calculating changes in break-even points over years

A company manufactures a product.

Information for the last two years is as follows.

	Year 1	Year 2
	$	$
Variable unit costs	6.00	7.00
Fixed overheads per annum	24 000	25 200
Unit sales price	10.00	10.00

In both years, production has been at break-even level.

What is the increase in production in year 2 compared with year 1?

A 2400 units
B 3600 units
C 8000 units
D 8400 units.

12 Inventory valuation and profit

Alpha Ltd manufactures one product. Budgeted production is 8000 units per year. During the year, the budgeted costs are expected to be:

	$
Direct materials	2 000
Direct labour	14 000
Fixed overheads	12 000

The opening inventory was expected to be 200 units and closing inventory 400 units.

Each unit is expected to sell for $4 and 7800 units are expected to be sold.

Prepare expected profit statements for the year using:

a absorption costing absorbing fixed overheads on a per unit basis
b marginal costing.

2.2.3A: Cost–volume–profit analysis

Learning objectives

In this chapter you will learn:

- the advantages and disadvantages of cost–volume–profit analysis
- the limitations of cost–volume–profit analysis
- how to evaluate and interpret cost–volume–profit data.

Cost–volume–profit analysis

Cost–volume–profit analysis (CVP analysis) is an extension of the principles of marginal costing in the previous chapter. CVP analysis looks at the effects of differing levels of activity on the profits of an organisation. Break-even analysis, the management of scarce resources and make-or-buy decisions are all part of CVP analysis.

Key term

Cost–volume–profit analysis (CVP analysis): a technique that looks at the effect of differing levels of activity on profit.

Organisations generally have a prime motive of making profits, but in order to make a profit, the process has to be managed. There is a relationship between the variables in an organisation – selling price; sales volume; variable costs; profit. CVP analysis is an accounting technique that shows the relationship between these variables. It is the analysis of the relationship between cost and volume of activities and the effect of the relationship on profit.

Managers are able to use the concept of CVP analysis to forecast the volume of activity at which the firm will break even or attain a target profit. It enables managers to determine the effect on profit of changes in the selling price, in costs or changes in the level of activity.

Advantages of cost–volume–profit analysis

- Decision-making. CVP analysis is an essential tool used in break-even analysis, scarce resource planning and make-or-buy situations.
- Profit planning. It assists management in determining the most profitable combination of selling price, cost and volume. Managers are able to assess the expected profit at different levels of sales volume.
- Cost control. It assists management in reviewing and controlling costs in order to achieve target profit levels.
- Price setting. It enables managers to determine viable selling prices by concentrating, where necessary, on adjustment to fixed and variable costs in order to meet competitive product pricing.

Disadvantages of cost–volume–profit analysis

- Costs must be accurately analysed into the fixed element and the variable element, but in reality some costs will be semi-variable and fit directly into neither category, for example telephone charges.
- It assumes that fixed costs will remain constant over the relevant range. However, as sales volumes increase, then so some fixed costs may in fact become stepped costs. For example, as more business is undertaken then more supervisors may be required or more storage facilities needed.

Key term

Relevant range: the range of activity over which forecasts and plans apply.

Limitations of cost–volume–profit analysis

While CVP analysis is an invaluable management tool in assessing the effect that changes in variables will have on profit, it has limitations as it is based on a number of assumptions.

- It is only relevant where either a single product is being sold or alternatively there are multiple products that are being sold in a constant mix. Clearly, if the product mix changes, then so, for example, will the break-even point.
- It assumes that all variables other than sales volume remain constant. This is not necessarily true. For example, as volumes increase, the economies of scale may be achieved – bulk buying discounts of direct materials may be introduced, the learning curve may bring about savings in direct labour costs, etc.
- It assumes that the selling price will remain constant, but in reality the selling price may have to fall to achieve the required increase in sales volume.
- As profits are calculated on a marginal cost basis, it is assumed that if absorption costing is used, then production volumes are equal to sales volumes.

Evaluation and interpretation of cost–volume–profit analysis

Evaluation and interpretation of cost–volume–profit information will usually require analysis of break-even data as discussed in the previous chapter, assessing the effect that increases or decreases in variables would have on both break-even and on profit.

Illustration 1: Cost-volume-profit analysis

Storm Ltd is a manufacturer of raincoats which it supplies to many small retail outlets. Recently, sales of the company's raincoats have been failing due to the availability of imported brands which are sold at a slightly lower price.

The directors of Storm Ltd require an annual profit of $130 000, but the last financial year produced a profit of only $80 000 when 60 000 units were made and sold.

		$000
Sales	$20 per unit	1 200
Direct materials	$4 per unit	(240)
Direct labour	$8 per unit	(480)
Fixed costs		(400)
Profit for year		80

The directors are considering the following three options to increase the profitability of the company.

Option 1

Reduce the selling price of the raincoat by 10 per cent. The directors are of the opinion that this price will be less than the imported brands, and that it would result in an increase of 50 per cent in sales units.

		$000
Sales	90 000 units @ $18 per unit	1 620
Direct materials		(360)
Direct labour		(720)
Fixed costs		(400)
		140

Option 2

Invest in more up-to-date machinery at a capital cost of $120 000. This would result in a saving of 25 per cent in labour costs but would increase fixed costs by $35 000 as a result of depreciation and finance costs. Sales volume would remain the same and there would be no change in the selling price.

		$000
Sales	$20 per unit	1 200
Direct materials	$4 per unit	(240)
Direct labour	$6 per unit	(360)
Fixed costs		(435)
		165

Option 3

Invest in an aggressive advertising campaign at a cost of $50 000. At the same time substitute the material used in the production of raincoats with a less-expensive material, reducing material costs by 25 per cent. The directors are of the opinion that the advertising campaign would result in an increase in sales volume of 20 per cent.

		$000
Sales	72 000 units @ $20 per unit	1 440
Direct materials	$3 per unit	(216)
Direct labour	$8 per unit	(576)
Fixed costs		450
		198

Option 3 clearly produces the highest profit and all three options produce a profit in excess of the company's target.

However, more financial analysis should be undertaken before a final decision is made.

Option 1

Contribution is $6 per unit (i.e. Selling price $18 – Variable costs $12).

The sales required to produce the required level of profit of $130 000 would be:

($400 000 + $130 000)/6, i.e. 88 334 units

Option 2

Contribution is $10 per unit.

The sales required to produce the required level of profit of $130 000 would be:

($435 000 + $130 000)/10, i.e. 56 500 units

Option 3

Contribution is $9 per unit

The sales required to produce the required level of profit of $130 000 would be:

($450 000 + $130 000)/9, i.e. 64 445 units

In addition to the financial calculations above, the directors must also consider the potential risks of each option.

Option 1

This requires a sales volume very near the forecast in order to achieve the required level of profit. If the forecast is evenly slightly optimistic the desired level of profit will not be achieved. The directors must consider whether the likelihood that the 50 per cent increase in sales volume will be achieved. On what evidence is this potential increase in sales volume based and how reliable is this evidence?

Option 2

The required sales volume is much lower than the forecast level, so even if the forecast is somewhat optimistic, the required level of profit should still be achieved. However, will the company be able to raise the necessary finance? The directors also need to consider the company's higher risk factor as the gearing ratio will increase. What will be the impact of reduced labour costs and the need for training in the use of new machinery on the workforce?

Option 3

This provides the highest level of profit, but how likely is it that the projected increase in sales volume will materialise? In other words, how certain is it that the advertising campaign will have the desired effect on sales volume. Will the quality of the raincoats decline as a result of using cheaper materials, and if so, will sales volume actually decrease?

Furthermore, the directors may like to consider the possibility of reducing fixed costs by making efficiency savings.

Learning objectives

In this chapter you will learn:

- how to carry out unit costing
- how to prepare job costing statements
- how to prepare batch costing statements.

2.2.3B: Unit, job and batch costing

Unit, job and batch costing

Manufacturing businesses need to account for all of the costs expended on jobs to ensure that the selling price recovers not only the direct costs such as direct materials and direct labour, but also a portion of the business's overheads. We have looked in detail at two major costing methods – marginal costing and absorption costing – and the different ways these methods deal with overheads. This chapter gives an overview of the costing methods employed by different manufacturing processes.

Manufacture may involve producing a single item or alternatively producing a batch of identical items. It may be that the business is manufacturing an item to a customer's specific instructions. Whichever situation is relevant, managers must ensure that all costs relevant to the process are recovered.

Key term

Unit costing: the measure of a company's costs to produce one unit of product.

Unit costing

Unit costing refers to the measure of a company's costs to produce one unit of product. The unit cost of a product is therefore calculated as a total of all relevant variable costs plus relevant fixed costs with the total being divided by the number of units produced.

Illustration 1: Unit costing

Jaime Ltd manufactures one product only. In February, the company produced 2000 units of product and incurred the following costs.

	$
Direct materials	12 200
Direct labour (640 hours @ $6 per hour)	3 840
Variable production overheads	3 200
Fixed production overheads	8 000

The company absorbs all overheads on a per unit basis.

The cost per unit of product is calculated as follows.

	$
Direct materials ($12 200/2 000)	6.10
Direct labour ($3 840/2 000)	1.92
Variable production overheads ($3 200/2 000 units)	1.60
Fixed production overheads ($8 000/2 000 units)	4.00
Total cost per unit	13.62

Calculation of the cost per unit of product enables managers to calculate a selling price to achieve the required profit while ensuring that all relevant costs are accounted for.

Key term

Job costing: the costing of jobs carried out to specific customer requirements.

Job costing

Where a business produces goods or performs services to specific customer requirements and each job is different, job costing is carried out. Each specific order becomes a cost unit and is costed as a separate job. Examples of jobs are:

- repairs to a motor vehicle
- printing 5000 sales leaflets
- building a computer to specific customer requirements.

As each job is individual and unique to the specific customer, the business must look at each job separately and cost each job accordingly. In each of these cases, the business will incur both direct material and labour costs as well as incurring overheads and will calculate a total job cost on which to base the selling price.

Illustration 2: Job costing

Techno Ltd is asked to prepare a quotation to produce a laptop computer for a customer. Techno Ltd adds 30 per cent profit onto the total cost of a job. Overheads are recovered at a rate of 75 per cent of direct labour costs. The quotation is based on the estimated costs as follows.

	$
Direct materials	245.00
Direct labour (15 hours @ $8 per hour)	120.00
Overheads (75% of direct labour costs)	90.00
Total costs	455.00
Add: profit (30% of total costs)	136.50
Amount of quotation	591.50

If the quotation is accepted, on completion of the work the directors of Techno Ltd will compare the actual costs incurred against the quotation and will use the experience for future quotations of a similar nature.

Key term

Batch costing: the costing of a job involving the production of a quantity of identical items.

Batch costing

Batch costing is very similar to job costing, but involves the production of a quantity of identical items, for example 1000 identical wooden boxes.

Illustration 3: Batch costing

Grecko Ltd is asked to prepare a quotation to supply 1000 identical wooden boxes. Grecko Ltd prices all of its quotations to provide a 25 per cent profit margin. Grecko Ltd recovers all overheads on the basis of 125 per cent of direct labour costs. The quotation will be based on the estimated costs as follows.

	$
Direct materials	3 660
Direct labour (100 hours @ $8 per hour)	800
Overheads (125% of direct labour costs)	1 000
Total costs	5 460
Add: profit (25% margin)	1 365
Amount of quotation	6 825

Notes:

- The total profit to provide a 25 per cent margin is calculated as $5460 × 25/75 = $1820
- The cost per wooden box = $5460/1000 = $5.46
- The profit per wooden box = $1820/1000 = $1.82

End-of-chapter questions

1 Explain the difference between job costing and batch costing.

2 Toby owns a small property repair business and has one employee. He has been asked to prepare a quotation to paint a customer's house. Toby adds 25 per cent to the total costs of each job undertaken to provide his own profit.
Toby estimates the total cost of materials will be $450. The job will take 42 hours in total, with the work divided equally between his employee and himself. Toby pays his employee $6 per hour and the overhead recovery rate is $2.50 per labour hour taken on the job.

Required

a Calculate the total costs to complete the job.
b Calculate the final price that Toby should quote the customer to complete the job.

3 PL Printing Ltd has been asked by a customer to prepare a quotation to produce 50 000 printed sales leaflets.
The following information is available for PL Printing Ltd for the current year.

Direct labour rate per hour	$8
Budgeted overheads	$140 400
Budgeted machine hours	31 200

Overheads are recovered on the basis of the number of machine hours. The company's work is charged to customers on the basis of cost plus 40 per cent.

The company estimates that the following costs will be incurred on the batch.

Paper	$360
Ink	$175
Packaging	$62
Machine hours	40
Labour hours	25

Required

a Calculate the total cost of producing the 50 000 leaflets.
b Calculate the total cost per 1000 leaflets.
c Calculate the amount of the quotation to be sent to the customer.

4 Metalco Ltd is asked to prepare a quotation to supply 500 identical parts for an engineering company. The company bases its quotation on the following estimated data.

Direct materials	$3 380
Direct labour/machine hours Machining department Finishing department Assembly department	 320 machine hours 125 labour hours 500 labour hours
Direct labour rates Machining department Finishing department Assembly department	 $6 per hour $6 per hour $5 per hour
Overhead recovery rates Machining department Finishing department Assembly department	 $5 per machine hour $10 per labour hour $2 per labour hour
Profit margin on total quotation	25%

In order to complete the job, Metalco Ltd would have to hire a specialist drill for the minimum hire period of five days at a total cost of $250. The drill would only be required for one day on this job and would not be used for any other jobs that Metalco Ltd is working on.

Required

a Calculate the total costs to complete the job.

b Calculate the cost per part.

c Calculate the final price that Metalco should quote the customer to complete the job.

Section 2.3: The application of accounting to business planning

Key concepts

Business planning can only be effective if the information is based on a **true and fair view** of a business's financial affairs and if techniques are applied in a **consistent** manner. Managers always need to take account of the fact that non-financial factors cannot be reflected in the budgets that have been prepared (the **money measurement** concept).

2.3.1: The application of accounting to business planning

Learning objectives

In this chapter you will learn:

- why businesses need to plan for the future
- what the benefits and limitations of budgetary control are
- the financial and non-financial advantages and disadvantages of budgetary control.

Business planning

All businesses need to plan. In order to develop the business, or indeed in order to even survive, an organisation must actively undertake a process involving not only planning, but also control mechanisms over that planning.

The planning process involves the following steps:

1. **Identify objectives:** These will differ from organisation to organisation at different times. There will be times when the objective is to maximise profitability, there may be other times when the objective is to increase market share.
2. **Identify potential strategies:** In other words, having identified the objectives, the organisation must then identify the different ways in which it may achieve them.
3. **Evaluate the strategies:** Certain potential strategies will usually be discarded as unfeasible, uneconomic or unsuitable for other reasons.
4. **Formulate the long-term plan:** The chosen strategies are incorporated into a long-term plan, usually expressed in financial terms as part of the budgetary process.
5. **Implement the long-term plan:** This involves breaking down the master plan into smaller, more manageable, short-term plans (or budgets).

Always remember, without control, planning is useless. The control process involves the following:

1. **Measure actual results against the plan:** This involves analysing variances and also assessing the continued feasibility of the plan as it stands in the light of up-to-date information.
2. **Respond to divergences from the plan:** Where necessary, the plan should be adjusted, amended or restructured to incorporate the actualities of the situation.

The need for budgets

Key term

Budget: a plan expressed in financial terms.

In any operation, the supply of resources is not infinite. These resources may take many different forms.

- **Financial.** An organisation's activities may be restricted by lack of finance. All products and services must be produced within a clear identified cost.
- **Labour.** An organisation's activities may be restricted by lack of available labour resources.

- **Capacity.** An organisation's activities must be produced within the confines of physical capacity.
- **Timing.** The organisation's products and services must be produced within the time when they are of use to the customer.
- **Quality.** The organisation's products and services must be produced within the tolerance for their own and their customers' quality standards.

Budgets ensure that operations are conducted within these constraints.

Benefits of budget preparation and budgetary control

Budget preparation forces senior managers to look ahead and plan for the future. They set out detailed plans for each department within the organisation, and as such, for each manager too. The result of this is to give the organisation purpose and direction.

The preparation of budgets encourages co-ordination and communication between departments. This in turn ensures that organisational goals are met.

A budget gives a clear indication of managers' areas of responsibility. This in turn provides a framework for responsibility accounting where managers are responsible for the achievement of the corporate targets under their control.

Budgets provide a framework for budgetary control. This enables constant monitoring against targets and enables remedial action to be taken as variances are identified.

Budgets provide the necessary yardstick for senior managers to measure the performance of managers. Variances will be identified as controllable costs or non-controllable costs, with managers only being held responsible for variances on controllable costs.

Budgets motivate employees by providing an achievement target to meet, especially where employees are involved in the budget-setting process.

Budgets enable managers to monitor and manage the allocation of scarce resources.

Key terms

Budgetary control: a system that delegates financial planning to managers and evaluates the performance of managers against targets.

Responsibility accounting: decentralises the business into responsibility centres and holds managers responsible for the performance of that centre.

Controllable costs: costs over which the manager has some control, e.g. the purchase of raw materials.

Non-controllable costs: costs over which the manager has no control, e.g. rent of premises.

Limitations of budget preparation and budgetary control

Budgets are based on estimates and it must always be remembered that forecasting is not an exact science. The strength or weakness of any budgetary control system lies in the accuracy of the forecasts.

A budget that is unrealistic or unachievable is of limited use and may do more harm than good. It could have a negative effect on the workforce, who will feel that they are underperforming, and it may make their productivity decline further.

Budgets can restrict activity so that managers are not innovative and fail to take advantage of unexpected opportunities due to their actions being too strictly controlled.

Through careful control of their budgets, managers may have a surplus available at the end of the year, but rather than save this surplus they will spend it so that their budget for the following year will not be reduced. In this way, budgets may inadvertently encourage the inefficient use of resources.

Budgets must not become too rigid. They must be revised to deal with continuously changing circumstances otherwise they lose all usefulness.

End-of-chapter questions

1 **Which one of the following is *not* a function of a budget?**
   - A Control
   - B Decision-making
   - C Motivating
   - D Planning

2 **Under a system of responsibility accounting, a manager's performance is evaluated on which one of the following matters?**
   - A Directly controlled matters
   - B Directly and indirectly controlled matters
   - C Indirectly controlled matters
   - D Jointly controlled matters with other managers

3 Explain the term 'budgetary control'. Why is it helpful to the management of a business?

4 Explain three limitations of a system of budgets and budgetary control.

5 Explain three benefits of a system of budgets and budgetary control.

Topic 2: Cost and management accounting

Exam-style questions

1 The following information is available for a company.

Budgeted overheads	$180 200
Actual overheads	$196 800
Budgeted machine hours	32 100
Actual machine hours	31 600

What is the overhead absorption rate per machine hour?

A $5.61
B $5.70
C $6.13
D $6.23

2 If the fixed costs of a business increase but all other costs remain the same, what will happen to the break-even point?

A Decrease
B Increase
C Remain the same
D Unable to be calculated

3 The following information is available for a manufacturing business.

Budgeted direct labour hours	6 200	
Actual direct labour hours	5 900	
Budgeted overhead expenses	$68 200	
Under-recovery of overheads		$6 000

What is the amount of the actual overhead expenditure?

A $58 900
B $64 900
C $68 200
D $70 900

4 Which cost will fall as production is reduced?

A Fixed cost per unit
B Variable cost per unit
C Total fixed costs
D Total variable costs

5 Absorption costing

Calvin owns a business manufacturing electrical parts. The business operates two production departments – machining and assembly.

The business also has two service departments – stores and maintenance.

The budgeted overheads for the year ended 31 January 2014 were as follows.

	$
Indirect wages	240 000
Factory rent and rates	42 000
Buildings insurance	30 000
Machinery insurance	40 500
Machinery depreciation	64 800
Lighting and heating	26 000
Power	48 000

The following information is available.

	Machining	Assembly	Stores	Maintenance
Number of indirect employees	6	9	2	3
Floor space (square metres)	15 000	6 000	1 000	3 000
Net book value of machinery ($)	120 000	40 000		20 000
Budgeted machine hours	80 000	40 000		
Budgeted labour hours	18 000	62 000		
Issues from stores	55%	25%		20%
Maintenance hours used	80%	20%		

Required

a Apportion the overhead costs to the four departments and reapportion the service centre costs to the production departments using a suitable basis. [12 marks]

b Calculate an appropriate overhead absorption rate, correct to two decimal places, for each production department. [6 marks]

Additional information:

The actual results for the year ended 31 January 2014 were as follows.

	Machining	Assembly
Factory overheads	$310 150	$188 200
Direct labour hours	18 600	60 350
Machine hours	88 100	41 600

Required

c Calculate the under- or over-absorption of factory overheads for each production department for the year ended 31 January 2014. [6 marks]

d Explain three advantages to a business of using a system of absorption costing. [6 marks]

[Total: 30 marks]

6 **Marginal costing**

Flash Limited manufactures three products, X, Y and Z.

The following budgeted information is available for March 2014.

	Product X $	Product Y $	Product Z $
Selling price per unit	28.00	51.50	69.00
Variable costs per unit			
Direct materials @ $2.20 per kg	4.40	8.80	11.00
Direct labour @ $6 per hour	12.00	21.00	30.00
Variable overheads @ $2.80 per direct labour hour	5.60	9.80	14.00
Maximum demand (units)	1200	1500	300

Fixed overheads are estimated to be $21 000 per month.

Fixed overheads are apportioned pro rata to maximum demand.

Required

a Calculate the contribution per unit for each product. [3 marks]

b Calculate the break-even point in units for each product. [3 marks]

c Calculate the margin of safety in units for each product. [3 marks]

d Calculate the maximum profit that Flash Limited can earn in March 2014. [2 marks]

Due to staff holidays, only 8500 direct labour hours are going to be available in March 2014.

Required

e Calculate the maximum profit for March 2014 taking account of the limited direct labour hours available. [11 marks]

Break-even analysis is a useful tool for management, but it does have limitations.

Required

f State four limitations of break-even analysis. [4 marks]

g Manufacturing companies may sometimes consider selling products at a price below the usual selling price. Identify four circumstances in which a company may consider this to be an acceptable practice. [4 marks]

[Total: 30 marks]

7 **Batch costing**

Novak manufactures garden benches. Each bench passes through two departments, machining and finishing. Budgeted sales for the year ending 31 March 2015 are 5000 benches.

The following information is available.

	Machining	Finishing
Budgeted direct labour hours per bench	1.5	2.5
Budgeted machine hours per bench	3	0.5
Budgeted overheads for the year	$48 000	$30 000
Direct labour rate per hour	$7.00	$8.00

Each bench requires $34 direct material.

Required

a Calculate an appropriate overhead absorption rate for each department. [4 marks]

Novak has been asked by a customer to quote for the supply of 120 benches. He prices all jobs in order to make a gross profit margin of 40 per cent.

Required

b Prepare a detailed quotation to give to the customer. [7 marks]

c Explain the difference between job costing and batch costing. [4 marks]

[Total: 15 marks]

8 Costing and decision-making

Hernandez Limited produces three models of suitcase: Basic, Deluxe and Excel. The company's profit statements for the year ended 31 December 2014 for each model show the following.

	Basic	Deluxe	Excel	Total
Sales (units)	3 200	1 400	800	5 400
Sales (revenue)	96 000	63 000	52 000	211 000
Cost of sales				
Direct materials	38 400	20 200	16 800	75 400
Direct labour	32 800	16 600	7100	56 500
Variable overheads	12 200	8 500	5 500	26 200
Fixed overheads	18 000	10 000	6 000	34 000
Profit/(loss) for the year	(5 400)	7 700	16 600	18 900

Required

a Calculate the contribution per unit for each model of suitcase. [3 marks]

b Calculate the break-even point in units for each model of suitcase. [3 marks]

c Advise the directors whether the company should cease production of the loss-making Basic model of suitcase. Justify your decision. [2 marks]

The directors are considering investing in a large advertising campaign at a cost of $12 000 to promote the Basic model of suitcase. They plan to increase the price of the basic model by 10 per cent and are confident that as a result of the advertising, sales of the Basic will increase by 50 per cent. All other aspects of the business would be budgeted to remain the same as for the year ended 31 December 2014.

Required

d Prepare a marginal cost statement to show the projected profit or loss on the Basic model of suitcase for the year ending 31 December 2015. [5 marks]

e Calculate the revised break-even point in units for the Basic model of suitcase. [2 marks]

[Total: 15 marks]

1 Financial accounting

Section 1.1: Preparation of financial statements

Key concepts

All key concepts (**true and fair view; duality; consistency; business entity; money measurement**) apply to the preparation of financial statements whether it is a manufacturing organisation, a large-scale international limited company or a small not-for-profit organisation. Furthermore, to ensure that a true and fair picture is presented to stakeholders, international accounting standards are now applied in an increasing number of countries worldwide.

1.1.1: Manufacturing businesses

What is a manufacturing account?

A retailer buys and sells completed products whereas a manufacturer makes products to sell. For example, a clothes designer buys material and employs staff in a factory to cut and sew the material into, for example, jackets. The jackets are then sold to a wholesaler who sells them to a fashion boutique in a local shopping centre.

A manufacturing account is therefore prepared to show all the costs associated with the production of these jackets within the factory. A simple manufacturing account is split into two sections:

- The prime cost section: This is where the direct costs are listed and totalled. The direct costs are those costs associated with an individual product. They include the cost of raw materials, the cost of labour employed to make the product and any others direct costs.
- The factory overheads section: This is where all the other costs associated with the production of the products within the factory are identified. These are known as indirect costs and include the factory supervisor's salary, factory rent, machine maintenance and machine depreciation.

Within the manufacturing account, these two sections are combined to calculate the cost of production:

Cost of production = Prime cost + Factory overheads

However, manufacturing is a continuous process and so not all goods are complete or finished at the end of a financial period. These partly finished goods are referred to in the inventory as work in progress. The inventory of work in progress is treated in the same way as any other type of inventory: opening inventory is added to, and closing inventory is subtracted from, the cost of manufacture. Therefore, the movement in work in progress over the financial period is added to the prime cost and factory overheads within the manufacturing account to achieve the cost of productions.

All other non-production costs, such as administration costs, are recorded within the income statement just as they would be for a non-manufacturing business.

Key terms

Cost of production: the total of all the costs of manufacturing products. It is also known as production cost of manufactured goods or production cost of completed goods.
Work in progress: the partly completed or unfinished inventory.

Learning objectives

In this chapter you will learn:

- how to distinguish between, and give examples of, direct and indirect costs
- how to prepare a manufacturing account, identifying the prime cost, work in progress and cost of production
- how to calculate the production cost of an individual manufactured product
- how to explain the need for, and calculate, the unrealised profit
- how to prepare the financial statements of a manufacturer to include entries for both the manufacturing profit and the change in the provision for unrealised profit
- how to prepare the financial statements recording inventory adjusted for the provision for unrealised profit.

Key terms

Manufacturing account: an account prepared at the end of a financial period in order to calculate the production cost of manufactured goods.
Prime cost: the total of all direct costs incurred when producing the products.
Factory overheads: the indirect costs incurred in the production of the products, e.g. depreciation of machinery, factory insurance and factory rent.

Getting it right

Remember that the manufacturing account only includes information about the factory and the actual manufacturing process. All other non-production costs, such as administration, finance and distribution costs, are recorded in the income statement, just as they are for non-manufacturing organisations.

Completing the manufacturing account

Identifying the relevant costs

When completing a manufacturing account from the trial balance, first identify those costs that are part of the production process. These will be the ones needed and all others will be recorded in the income statement. The direct costs are then recorded in the factory overheads section.

It is important to treat the different types of cost correctly, ensuring that only factory costs are within the manufacturing account. These factory costs must then be split between direct costs within the prime cost section and indirect costs within the factory overheads section.

The following table shows an example of how a small manufacturing business's costs might be treated within the financial statements.

	Manufacturing account		**Income statement**
	Prime cost	**Factory overheads**	
Administration expenses			✓
Direct labour	✓		
Direct materials	✓		
Factory insurance		✓	
Factory rent		✓	
Office salaries			✓
Selling and distribution costs			✓

Illustration 1: Completing a simple manufacturing account

On 31 December 2014, an extract of the trial balance of Mahabeer Manufacturing Ltd was as follows (M/I indicates whether the figure should be included in the manufacturing account or the income statement).

Mahabeer Manufacturing Ltd Trial balance (extract) at 31 December 2014			
	Dr ($)	**Cr ($)**	**M/I**
Buildings insurance	56 000		M/I
Carriage inwards on raw materials	2 200		M
Carriage outwards	1 800		I
Depreciation of machinery for the year	11 100		M
Direct wages	54 600		M
Factory rent	16 100		M
Inventory of raw materials at 1 January 2014	17 400		M
Inventory of work in progress	12 500		M
Other factory overheads	14 000		M
Purchases of raw materials	56 800		M

Returns inwards	5 300		I
Returns outwards of raw materials		6 700	M
Revenue		234 000	I

Additional information:

- The business's inventory at 31 December 2014 was: raw materials $19 500 (M); work in progress $14 200 (M).
- The machinery was to be depreciated by $11 100 (M).
- During the year, the company had paid $56 000 for buildings insurance. Of this 75 per cent related to the factory and 25 per cent to the administration buildings.

The business's manufacturing account would therefore be:

Mahabeer Manufacturing Ltd Manufacturing account for the year ended 31 December 2014

	($)	($)	$
Inventory of raw materials at 1 January 2014		17 400	
Purchases of raw materials	56 800		
Carriage inwards	2 200		
	59 000		
Returns outwards	(6 700)		
Net purchases		52 300	
		69 700	
Inventory of raw materials at 31 December 2014		(19 500)	
Cost of raw materials consumed			50 200
Direct wages			54 600
Prime cost			104 800
Buildings insurance		42 000	
Depreciation of machinery		11 100	
Factory rent		16 100	
Other factory overheads		14 000	
			83 200
			188 000
Inventory of work in progress at:			
1 January 2014			12 500
Inventory of work in progress at:			
31 December 2014			(14 200)
Cost of production of manufactured goods			186 300

- The cost of raw materials consumed calculation consists of:

  Opening inventory of raw materials + Net purchases – Closing inventory of raw materials

This is a direct cost and part of the prime cost. It is similar to the calculation of cost of goods sold in the first part of an income statement of a retail business but must not be deducted from revenue. Net purchases are calculated with all the usual adjustments for carriage inwards and returns outwards.

- The insurance will, therefore, be recorded as follows:

Manufacturing account (indirect factory expenses): 56 000 × 75% = 42 000

Income statement (non-production expenses): 56 000 × 25% = 14 000

Getting it right

Remember that the cost of production is a total cost calculated by adding the overheads within the manufacturing account to prime cost. It is a common error for students to deduct, rather than add, the overheads.

It is also important to make sure that the correct labels are used within the manufacturing account, especially 'prime cost' and 'cost of production'.

Bear in mind that the manufacturing account is an ordered record of the production process, starting from raw materials and going through the production process/costs, then work in progress, to achieve the cost of production.

Unit cost

The manufacturing account can be used to calculate the production cost per unit by dividing the production cost by the number of units. This figure can be used by the business to make some important decisions.

The non-production cost (administration costs etc.) per unit can be added to the production cost per unit to achieve the full cost per unit. The business can use this information to calculate the selling price.

Illustration 2: Calculating the production cost per unit

During the year ended 31 December 2014 Mahabeer Manufacturing Ltd produced 3000 tables.

From Illustration 1, the cost of production was $186 300, so the production cost per table is:

$$\frac{\$186\ 300}{3\ 000} = \$62.10$$

The non-production cost (administration costs etc.) per table can be added to the production cost per table to achieve the full cost per unit.

For example, if the non-production cost per table is $27.90, the full cost per table is $62.10 + $27.90 = $90

The business can use this information to calculate the selling price. For example, if the business uses a mark-up of 40 per cent, the selling price will be 1.4 × $90 = $126

The first section of the income statement for a manufacturing business

At the end of the production process, the cost of production is transferred from the manufacturing account to the income statement. The cost of production figure replaces the purchases of goods for resale within the calculation of cost of goods sold.

The completed goods are referred to as finished goods. The first part of the income statement is concerned with comparing the revenue from selling finished goods with the cost of finished goods sold.

Key term

Finished goods: fully completed goods.

Illustration 3: Preparing the first section of the income statement

The inventories of finished goods for Mahabeer Manufacturing Ltd for the year ended 31 December 2014 were:

- at 1 January 2014 $25 100
- at 31 December 2014 $29 400.

When preparing the first section of an income statement, these should be recorded as follows.

Mahabeer Manufacturing Ltd Income statement for the year ended 31 December 2014		
	$	$
Revenue	234 000	
Less returns inwards	(5 300)	
		228 700
Opening inventory of finished goods	25 100	
Cost of production of finished goods	186 300	
	211 400	
Closing inventory of finished goods	(29 400)	
Cost of sales		(182 000)
Gross profit		46 700
Buildings insurance	14 000	
Carriage outwards	1 800	
Other non-production expenses		

Getting it right

The first section of a manufacturer's income statement is similar to that of other business organisations. The key difference is that 'purchases' is replaced by 'cost of production'.

Recording inventory

A retailer will only have one type of inventory: goods for resale. In contrast, there are three types of inventory within a manufacturing business:

- inventory of raw materials
- inventory of work in progress
- inventory of finished goods.

Illustration 4: Showing inventories in the statement of financial position

The statement of financial position for Mahabeer Manufacturing Ltd includes all three types of inventory held at the year end within the current assets and would appear as follows.

Mahabeer Manufacturing Ltd Statement of financial position (extract) at 31 December 2014	
	$
Current assets	
Inventory of raw materials	19 500
Inventory of work in progress	14 200
Inventory of finished goods	29 400
	63 100

Key terms

Transfer price: the production cost of completed goods plus a percentage mark-up.

Factory or manufacturing profit: the difference between the transfer price and the production cost of completed goods.

Manufacturing profit and transfer price

Some manufacturing businesses transfer their products from the factory to the income statement at total production cost plus a notional mark-up percentage. This is referred to as the transfer price. The difference between the production cost of completed goods and the transfer price is called factory profit or manufacturing profit.

The benefits and drawbacks of using a transfer price are detailed in the following table.

Benefits	Drawbacks
This process does not increase the overall profits of the business and merely identifies the profit made by particular cost centres.	The transfer price should be realistic so that direct comparisons with the cost of buying in goods can be made. However, there is a risk of an unrealistic view of the factory profitability being given unless other production prices are researched and used to set the transfer price.
In this way, the profit from manufacturing is separated from the profit made elsewhere within the business. The part that the factory contributed to the overall profitability of the business is recognised.	This technique does not improve the profitability of the business overall, rather it just splits the total profit between different cost centres.
This allows the unit cost of goods manufactured to be compared with the cost of buying in completed goods from an outside source and enables a manager to evaluate a make-or-buy decision.	If a set percentage is used to calculate the transfer price, this may fail to motivate factory managers and other workers, especially if their bonuses are dependent on the amount of factory profit.

Recording manufacturing profit

A manufacturing profit is recorded at the end of the manufacturing account. The transfer price then replaces purchases of goods for resale within the income statement.

Illustration 5: Completing a manufacturing account with a manufacturing profit and a transfer price

Danil Doors Manufacturing Ltd produces wooden doors. All doors are sold to the national market. The company transfers doors from the factory to the income statement at cost plus 20 per cent.

On 31 March 2015 the company's trial balance was as follows.

Information for Danil Doors Manufacturing Ltd for year ended 31 March 2015	
	$
Factory overheads	258 600
Provision for unrealised profit at 1 April 2014	18 000
Purchases of raw materials	220 900

Information for Danil Doors Manufacturing Ltd for year ended 31 March 2015 (cont'd)	
	$
Revenue	1 210 000
Inventory of finished goods at 1 April 2014 (at cost plus 20%)	108 000
Inventory of finished goods at 31 March 2015 (at cost plus 20%)	126 000
Inventory of raw materials at 1 April 2014	63 400
Inventory of raw materials at 31 March 2015	71 200
Inventory of work in progress at 1 April 2014	16 400
Inventory of work in progress at 31 Mar 2015	18 100
Wages	390 000

Additional information:

- Wages owed amounted to $10 000.
- The wages are apportioned 75 per cent to direct labour and the rest is indirect.

The manufacturing account for Danil Doors Manufacturing Ltd for the year ended 31 March 2014 was prepared.

Information for Danil Doors Manufacturing Ltd for year ended 31 March 2014	
	$
Inventory of raw materials at 1 April 2014	63 400
Purchases of raw materials	220 900
Inventory of raw materials at 31 March 2015	(71 200)
Raw materials consumed	213 100
Direct wages	300 000
Prime cost	513 100
Indirect wages	100 000
Factory overheads	258 600
	871 700
Inventory of work in progress at 1 April 2014	16 400
Inventory of work in progress at 31 March 2015	(18 100)
Production cost of manufactured goods	870 000
Factory profit at 20%	174 000
Transfer price	1 044 000

In previous illustrations the manufacturing account finished at production cost of manufactured goods. In this illustration, goods are transferred to income statement at cost plus 20 per cent. Two extra lines are therefore added at the end of the manufacturing account, namely:

- **Factory profit:** The amount of mark-up (in this example, 20 per cent of the production cost).
- **Transfer price:** The production cost of manufactured goods plus the factory profit.

Getting it right

Ensure that the labels 'Factory profit' and 'Transfer price' are clearly shown at the end of the manufacturing account, as often marks will be allocated for the use of these labels.

Key term

Unrealised profit: profit which is not recognised until the inventory is sold and a contract of sale has been negotiated.

Link

There is more about IAS 2 Inventories in A Level Chapter 1.1.4 International accounting standards.

Link

There is more about the realisation and prudence concepts in AS Level Chapter 1.1.5 Accounting concepts and principles.

The provision for unrealised profit

IAS 2 requires that inventory is valued at the lower of cost and net realisable value. In the statement of financial position, inventories of finished goods should be shown at the cost of production: therefore, if a transfer price is used, these inventories will include an element of unrealised profit. Unrealised profits should not be recognised within the statement of financial position as it contravenes both the realisation and prudence concepts.

The realisation concept states that revenue should only be recorded in the business books of account when the goods have been sold for credit or cash, and the prudence concept states that losses should be provided for as soon as they are anticipated, but profits are not recorded until they are realised as it is preferred for profits to be understated rather than overstated.

A provision for unrealised profit is therefore used to:

- remove the unrealised profit from the income statement otherwise profits are overstated by the amount of unrealised profit
- remove the unrealised profit from the inventory of finished goods within the current assets on the statement of financial position so that inventories are not overvalued and are valued at cost and not cost plus a percentage mark-up.

Calculating the provision for unrealised profit

When inventories of finished goods are valued at cost plus a percentage mark-up, the method for calculating the unrealised profit is:

$$\frac{\text{Inventory at cost plus profit percentage}}{100 + \text{Profit percentage}} \times \text{Percentage}$$

Illustration 6: Calculating unrealised profit in finished goods

At 31 March 2015 the inventory of finished goods was valued at $126 000 (cost plus the mark-up of 20 per cent).

The amount of unrealised profit is therefore:

$$\frac{\$126\,000}{100 + 20} \times 20 = \$21\,000$$

This approach should be learned. The percentage added to the denominator is always the same as the percentage by which the calculation is multiplied, namely the mark-up percentage. In this illustration it is 20 per cent.

This approach can also be used to calculate the original cost of the inventory. In the previous illustration, the original cost of the inventory is:

$$\frac{\$126\,000}{120} \times 100 = \$105\,000$$

The difference between the two approaches is only the amount by which the calculation is multiplied, either 20 for the unrealised profit or 100 for the original cost of the inventory.

These answers can be checked:

Cost of inventory + Unrealised profit = Inventory of finished goods at cost plus mark-up percentage

\$105 000 + \$21 000 = \$126 000

Recording the provision for unrealised profit in the statements of financial position

The inventory of finished goods is recorded at the cost price without the unrealised profit.

Illustration 7: Recording the unrealised profit

An extract to show the inventory of finished goods in the statement financial position would be as follows.

Statement of financial position extract for Danil Doors Manufacturing Ltd at 31 March 2015		
	$	$
Current assets		
Inventory of raw materials		71 200
Inventory of work in progress		18 100
Inventory of finished goods	126 000	
Less provision for unrealised profit	(21 000)	
		105 000
		194 300

Whenever completing the current assets, the original cost of inventory of finished goods should always be clearly identified in accordance with IAS 2 Inventories, and prudence and realisation concepts. In this illustration, it is \$105 000.

The provision for unrealised profit is recorded in the income statement as follows:

- first year full amount subtracted from factory profit
- subsequent years: increase in provision subtracted from factory profit, decrease in provision added to factory profit.

Illustration 8: Recording the change in unrealised profit

At 31 March 2015 the closing inventory for Danil Doors Manufacturing Ltd had been valued at $108 000, which included unrealised profit of $18 000.

The change in provision is recorded as follows.

	$
This year's provision for unrealised profit	18 000
Last year's provision for unrealised profit	21 000
Decrease in provision	3 000

This would be recorded in the financial statements as follows.

Income statement for Danil Doors Manufacturing Ltd for the year ended 31 March 2015

	$	$
Revenue		1 210 000
Opening inventory of finished goods	126 000	
Transfer price	1 044 000	
Closing inventory of finished goods	(105 000)	
Cost of goods sold		(1 065 000)
Gross profit		145 000
Factory profit	174 000	
Add increase in provision for unrealised profit	3 000	
		177 000

- Factory profit: this must clearly be identified within the financial statements as otherwise the profit is understated due to the inclusion of the transfer price instead of the production cost of manufactured goods.
- Increase in provision in unrealised profit: the increase in the provision in unrealised profit must also be clearly identified, otherwise the factory profit is overstated. If there is a decrease in the provision then it should be added otherwise the factory profit is understated.

Getting it right

Common errors include either forgetting to bring forward the factory profit or forgetting to show the change in provision in isolation. These two adjustments should be recorded together.

End-of-chapter questions

1 Distinguishing between direct and indirect costs

Identify which of the following costs are direct and which are indirect manufacturing costs.

Cost	Direct	Indirect
Cost of raw materials		
Salary of factory supervisor		
Lease of factory		
Machine depreciation		

2 Distinguishing between direct and indirect costs

Nigel Carr has provided the following information for the year ended 31 January 2015.

	$
Administration costs	56 200
Cost of raw materials	112 600
Factory rent	86 800
Factory heating and lighting	47 000
Manufacturing labour	432 000
Selling and distribution expenses	33 300

Calculate the total direct costs for Nigel Carr for the year ended 31 January 2015.

3 Preparing the prime cost section of a manufacturing account

The following information is available for S. Ramjeet Ltd, a manufacturer of toys, for the year ended 31 March 2015.

	$
Direct wages	33 600
Factory overheads	16 500
Purchases of raw materials	21 000
Other direct costs	1 800
Inventory of raw materials at 1 April 2014	6 200
Inventory of raw materials at 31 March 2015	7 400

Prepare an extract from the manufacturing account to show the prime cost for the year ended 31 March 2015.

4 Preparing a manufacturing account to calculate the cost of production

Kingsdown Doors Ltd has been manufacturing doors for many years. The following information relates to the year ended 30 June 2014.

	$
Inventories at 1 July 2013	
raw materials	26 000
finished goods	35 000
Factory wages	130 500
Factory supervisor's wages	22 500
Purchases of raw materials	132 000
Factory depreciation	12 000
Returns outwards of raw materials	2 300
Carriage inwards on raw materials	1 600
Factory heating and lighting	14 600

Additional information:

Inventories at 30 June 2014 were: raw materials $24 500; finished goods $37 600.

Prepare a manufacturing account for the year ended 30 June 2014 for Kingsdown Doors Ltd, showing clearly:

- the cost of raw materials consumed
- the prime cost
- total factory overheads
- the cost of production.

5 Preparing a manufacturing account to calculate the cost of production

Anderson plc is a manufacturing business. At the end of the accounting year, 31 March 2015, the following information is available.

	$
Factory wages	150 400
Factory power	432 600
Factory salaries	25 700
Factory rent	42 000
Administrative expenses	43 700
Insurance	5 000
Purchases of raw materials	216 500
Revenue	968 900
Returns outwards of raw materials	16 300
Inventories at 1 April 2014	
raw material	27 000
finished goods	61 400

Additional information:

- Inventories at 31 March 2015 were: raw materials $26 600; finished goods $59 400.
- Factory power was due but unpaid at 31 March 2015, $1700.
- Insurance was to be divided 4 : 1 between the factory and administration.

Prepare a manufacturing account for Anderson plc for the year ended 31 March 2015.

6 Calculating the production cost per unit with work in progress

Persad plc is a manufacturing business. The following figures have been extracted from the company's ledgers as at 31 May 2014.

	$
Inventories at 1 June 2013	
raw materials	21 450
work in progress	14 780
finished goods	58 620
Revenue	657 000
Purchases of raw materials	234 090
Direct labour costs	260 000
Indirect labour costs	82 800
Factory overheads (excluding indirect labour costs and depreciation)	138 000
Returns inwards	1 000
Returns outwards of raw materials	980
Carriage inwards on raw materials	750
Carriage outwards	1 340

Additional information:

- At 31 May 2014, inventories were valued as follows: raw materials $22 170; work in progress $13 750; finished goods $60 650.
- At 31 May 2014 factory wages due but unpaid amounted to $8000. One-quarter of this was for indirect labour and the remainder was for direct labour.
- Depreciation of factory machinery for the year ended 31 May 2014 was $25 000.

Required

a Prepare the manufacturing account for the year ended 31 May 2014.

b Explain what is meant by 'work in progress'.

c Calculate the production cost per unit, assuming 35 000 products were made.

7 Preparing the financial statements

Navin plc manufactures cricket bats. The following information is available for the year ended 31 January 2015.

	$000
Carriage inwards on raw materials	15
Carriage outwards	21
Factory wages	460
Heating and lighting	68
Inventories at 1 February 2014	
raw materials	42
work in progress	19
finished goods	132
Machinery at cost	340
Office equipment at cost	90
Office salaries	245
Power	110
Purchase of raw materials	567
Rent and rates	84
Revenue	1 846

Additional information:

- Inventories at 31 January 2015 were (in $000): raw materials $65; work in progress $22; finished goods $146.
- Sixty per cent of the factory wages are direct and the rest are indirect.
- Seventy-five per cent of both the heating and lighting and rent and rates are to be allocated to the factory and the rest to the office.
- Eighty per cent of the power costs are to be allocated to the factory and 20 per cent to the office.
- Depreciation is to be charged on the machinery at 20 per cent per annum using the straight-line method.
- Depreciation is to be charged on the office equipment at 10 per cent per annum using the straight-line method.

Prepare:

a the manufacturing account for the year ended 31 January 2015

b the income statement for the year ended 31 January 2015

c an extract from the statement of financial position as at 31 January 2015 to show the inventories.

8 Unrealised profit

Identify the two concepts that apply to the provision for unrealised profit.

9 Unrealised profit

Nikoloz Ltd manufactures a single product. Its goods are transferred from the factory at cost plus 25 per cent.

The following information is available at 31 October 2014.

	$
Inventory of finished goods at cost plus 25%	42 000
Inventory of raw materials	16 100
Inventory of work in progress	23 800

Prepare a statement of financial position extract to show the inventories held by Nikoloz Ltd at 31 October 2014.

10 Preparing a statement of financial position

Complete the following table.

Inventory at cost ($)	Mark-up ($)	Inventory at transfer price ($)
12 000	20	?
26 000	40	?
?	25	50 000
?	10	33 000

11 Calculating the provision for unrealised profit

Tabco Products is a manufacturing business. It transfers all goods manufactured to the income statement at production cost plus 20 per cent.

The following figures relate to inventories held by the business.

	As at 1 December 2013	As at 30 November 2014
Inventories of		
raw materials	27 000	28 000
work in progress	9 000	8 500
finished goods	22 200	23 400
Provision for unrealised profit	3 700	3 900

Required

a Calculate the amount of provision for unrealised profit to be entered in the income statement for the year ended 30 November 2014. What effect will the change have on the gross profit?

b Show in detail how the information relating to all inventories should be shown on the statement of financial position as at 30 November 2014.

c Explain why it is necessary for Tabco Products to provide for unrealised profit.

12 Financial statements including transfer price

Marco plc manufactures garden chairs. The following information is available for the year ended 31 January 2015.

	$000
Carriage inwards on raw materials	12
Carriage outwards	24
Factory wages	527
Heating and lighting	70
Inventories at 1 February 2014	
raw materials	40
work in progress	20
finished goods at transfer price	132
Machinery at cost	440
Office equipment at cost	110
Office salaries	190
Factory power	105
Purchase of raw materials	568
Rent and rates	80
Revenue	1 920

Additional information:

- Inventories at 31 January 2015 (in $000): raw materials $42; work in progress $18; finished goods at transfer price $150.
- Depreciation is to be charged on the machinery at 20 per cent per annum using the straight-line method.
- Depreciation is to be charged on the office equipment at 10 per cent per annum using the straight-line method.
- The company transfers goods manufactured to the income statement at cost plus 20 per cent.
- The following expenses should be divided between the factory (4/5) and the office (1/5): heating and lighting; rent and rates.

Required

Prepare:

a the manufacturing account for the year ended 31 January 2015

b the income statement for the year ended 31 January 2015

c an extract from the statement of financial position as at 31 January 2015 to show the inventories.

1.1.2: Not-for-profit organisations

Learning objectives

In this chapter you will learn:

- about the main features of a not-for-profit organisation
- how to prepare a receipts and payments account and the difference between capital and revenue expenditure
- how to prepare an income account and a trading account
- how to prepare an income and expenditure account, including the results of the income and trading accounts
- how to prepare a statement of financial position for a not-for-profit organisation.

What is a not-for-profit organisation?

Although a not-for-profit organisation will have objectives that are quite different to a business, it is essential that members are given a true and fair view of the organisation's affairs.

Most business organisations have the same objective and that is to maximise profit. However, not-for-profit organisations, such as clubs and societies, are there to provide a service. For example, a cricket club is run so that its members have somewhere to meet and play cricket, and a charity is there to provide relief to those in need.

Neither of these organisations' main objective is to trade or to make profit. The financial statements produced by organisations like this are, therefore, different from those produced for trading organisations. For example, as they do not trade to make a profit, there is no need for an income statement.

The following table gives examples of organisations whose objective is either profit maximisation or to provide a service.

Organisation	Profit maximisation	Providing a service
Bakery	✓	
Taxi driver	✓	
Local conservation society		✓
Local sports club		✓
Dentist surgery	✓	
Sports and social club		✓

A not-for-profit organisation may have a section that hopes to make a profit, but the main aim of the organisation as a whole is to provide a service. For example, a sports and social club may sell refreshments at a profit. However, the aim of the club is to provide social and sporting events to its members without making an overall profit.

Receipts and payments accounts

Key term

Receipts and payments account: an account used by not-for-profit organisations to record a summary of cash receipts and payments.

As not-for-profit organisations do not trade for a profit, many operate on a cash basis. Their only written financial record is a cash book. The first and most simple financial statement is, therefore, a receipts and payments account, which is a summary of this cash book for a period of time. For cash-based organisations that bank all of their cash receipts, the receipts and payments account is just another name for the cash account.

Link

There is more about revenue and capital expenditure in AS Level Chapter 1.1.4 Capital and revenue expenditure.

The receipts and payments account summarises all of the money received for a period and all of the payments, whether these are revenue or capital expenditure. Revenue expenditure is expenditure on the day-to-day running costs of an organisation whereas capital expenditure is expenditure on non-current assets, such as purchasing a non-current asset. For a profit-making organisation, revenue expenditure is recorded in the income statement whereas capital expenditure is recorded in the statement of financial position. However, there is no such distinction in a receipts and payments account, which records all expenditure.

Illustration 1: Preparing a simple receipts and payments account

Just as in a cash book, the receipts are recorded on the debit side and the payments are recorded on the credit side of the receipts and payments account.

On 31 December 2014, the receipts and payments account of the Runners-Up Sports Club was, therefore, as follows.

Runners-Up Sports Club
Receipts and payments account for the year ended 31 December 2014

	$		$
Balance b/d at 1 January 2014	123	Clubhouse repairs	2 210
Subscriptions received	16 420	Administration	455
Competition ticket sales	234	Sports equipment	3 100
Social evening ticket sales	4 828	Club staff wages	10 000
Refreshment takings	8 160	Ground maintenance	600
Balance c/d at 31 December 2014	163	Competition prize	242
		Social evening costs	3 611
		Staff costs	1 010
		Refreshment purchases	3 150
		Refreshments staff	4 100
		Secretary's expenses	1 450
	29 928		29 928
		Balance b/d at 1 January 2015	163

Income and expenditure accounts

The main features

Key term

Income and expenditure account: an account that records the income and expenditure for a period of time, adjusted for non-cash items as well as prepayments and accruals and showing either a surplus or a deficit.

When a club does not operate on a cash basis, but also has assets and liabilities, an income and expenditure account is used. An income and expenditure account is very similar to an income statement, in that capital expenditure is not included and there are adjustments for non-cash items such as depreciation, as well prepayments and accruals.

The following table shows the difference between the two types of account.

Details	Receipts and payments account	Income and expenditure account
Subscriptions and other income	Cash received only	Cash received in year, less income received in advance for next year, plus income owing for next year
Club expenses	Cash paid only	Cash paid in year, less expenses paid in advance for next year, plus expenses owing for next year
Depreciation of non-current assets	Not included	Recorded as an expense
Capital expenditure	Recorded as a payment	Not included

Illustration 2: Preparing a simple income and expenditure account

In addition to Illustration 1 the following information is available about the Runners-Up Sports Club for the year ended 31 December 2014:

- The cost of the club's sports equipment at 1 January 2014 was $14 200. At that date, the provision for depreciation was $2000. Depreciation is provided at 10 per cent per year using the straight-line method.
- At 1 January 2014, $800 was owing for staff wages for the previous year. At 31 December 2014, there was $500 owing for staff wages for the current year.
- The annual subscription is $40 per member. At 1 January 2014 subscriptions due amounted to $240. At 31 December 2014 three members had paid their subscriptions for the next year's membership but four members still owed the current year's subscriptions.

The income and expenditure account of the Runners-Up Sports Club was, therefore, as follows.

Runners-Up Sports Club Income and expenditure account for the year ended 31 December 2014		
	$	**$**
Income		
Subscriptions (see below)	16 220	
Social evening ticket sales	4 828	
Competition ticket sales	234	
Refreshments takings	8 160	
		29 442
Expenditure		
Clubhouse repairs	2 210	
Administration	455	
Wages ($10 000 less opening balance due $800 plus closing balance due $500)	9 700	
Competition prizes	242	
Social evening costs	3 611	

> **Key term**
>
> **Surplus (or deficit) of income over expenditure**: in the case of a not-for-profit organisation 'surplus' replaces the term 'profit' as used in an income statement, and 'deficit' replaces the term 'loss'.

Staff costs for social evenings	1 010	
Refreshments purchases	3 150	
Refreshments staff	4 100	
Secretary's expenses	1 450	
Ground maintenance	600	
Sports equipment depreciation (original $14 200 + new $3 100) × 10%	1 730	
		(28 258)
Surplus of income over expenditure		1 184

The amount within the income and expenditure account for subscriptions could be calculated using a subscriptions account. In this example, this would appear as follows.

Subscriptions account

	$		$
Balance b/d at 1 January 2014	240	Cash received during the year	16 420
Income and expenditure account	16 220	Balance c/d at 31 December 2014	160
Balance c/d at 31 December 2014	120		
	16 580		16 580
Balance b/d at 1 January 2015	160	Balance b/d at 1 January 2015	120

Alternatively. It is possible to calculate the year's income from subscriptions by taking the following steps:

Step 1: Start with the amount received ($16 420)

Step 2: Add any adjustment that *is* about subscriptions for the year under review (the end-of-year subscriptions due: $160)

Step 3: Deduct any adjustment that *is* about subscriptions for any other year (the opening amount due: $240 – which relates to last year – and the end-of-year amount received in advance $120 – which relates to next year).

Step 4: Calculate the subscription income

$16 420 + $160 – $240 – $120 = $16 220

> **Getting it right**
>
> The income and expenditure account is not a cash book or receipts and payments account, so opening and closing cash balances are not included. Only revenue expenditure is included, so the purchase of non-current assets is excluded.

Profit-making activities

Occasionally a not-for-profit organisation will have an activity on which a profit or loss can be made. For example, a golf club may hold a social evening for its members where there is a competition and where refreshments are provided. It is possible to make a profit on all of these activities. An income account is, therefore, drawn up for each activity, with the profit or loss being transferred to the income and expenditure account. A profit is transferred to the income section and a loss is transferred to the expenditure section.

Illustration 3: Preparing an income account

(Referring again to the Runners-Up Sports Club and using some of the information shown in Illustrations 1 and 2)

Once a year, the Runners-Up Sports Club holds a social evening to raise funds for the club. During the evening, there is a competition.

The following information taken from the receipts and payments account relates to the evening.

	$
Evening ticket sales	4 828
Competition fees	234
Competition prizes	242
Social evening costs	3 611
Evening staff cost	1 010

There are two income accounts, one for the evening tickets and one for the quiz.

Evening tickets account

	$	$
Ticket sales		4 828
Evening costs	3 611	
Staff cost	1 010	
		(4 621)
Profit for the evening		207

Competition account

	$
Ticket sales	234
Prizes	(242)
Loss on the competition	(8)

The loss on the competition would be listed among the expenses within the income and expenditure account and the profit on the evening would be listed among the income items. This form of presenting information about the social evening and competition is more useful to members as it clearly identifies how successful, or not, these activities have been.

From the club's point of view, this clearly shows that the total profit for the evening was only $199. If it wanted to hold future events, the club would have to decrease the cost of the competition prizes or, alternatively, sell more tickets.

Trading accounts

If the club had a café in the clubhouse selling refreshments, then there would also be a small-scale trading account. The profit on refreshments should be recorded in the income section within the income and expenditure account.

Illustration 4: Preparing a trading account

Referring again to the information given in Illustrations 1 and 2, the Runners-Up Sports Club has a café in the clubhouse that sells refreshments to its members The information relating to this café for the year ended 31 December 2014 was as follows.

	$
Refreshments takings	8 160
Refreshments purchases	3 150
Refreshments inventory at 1 January 2014	1 240
Refreshments inventory at 31 December 2014	2 130
Refreshments staff wages	4 100

Here is the café's trading account.

Runners-Up Sports Club
Refreshments trading account for the year ended 31 December 2014

	$	$
Takings		8 160
Opening inventory	1 240	
Purchases	3 150	
	4 390	
Closing inventory	(2 130)	
		(2 260)
Gross profit		5 900
Staff wages		(4 100)
Profit		1 800

The refreshments profit of $1800 should be shown in the income section within the income and expenditure account.

The income and expenditure account is very useful to club members. In just one account it is possible to establish what costs the club is incurring and how those costs are being covered by various sources of income. To illustrate this point, if members take a real interest in the club's finances, from looking at this account they will be in good position to judge whether an increase in their subscription is justified or not.

Incorporating the results of the income and trading accounts

The results of the income and trading accounts should be recorded in the income and expenditure account.

Illustration 5: Preparing an income and expenditure account that includes the results from income and trading accounts

Taking into account the information from Illustrations 3 and 4, the revised income and expenditure account for the Runners-Up Sports Club would be as follows.

Runners-Up Sports Club
Income and expenditure account for the year ended 31 December 2014

	$	$
Income		
Subscriptions	16 220	
Social evening profit	207	
Refreshments profit	1 800	
		18 227
Expenditure		
Clubhouse repairs	2 210	
Administration	455	
Wages	9 700	
Secretary's expenses	1 450	
Ground maintenance	600	
Competition loss	8	
Sports equipment depreciation	1 730	
		(16 153)
Surplus of income over expenditure		2 074

Getting it right

Remember to show all your workings especially for the calculation of any profit or loss on an activity, and for adjustments to expenses, income from members' subscriptions, etc.

Key terms

Accumulated fund: this amount is all assets, less all liabilities, and replaces capital in the statement of financial position of a not-for-profit organisation.

Statement of affairs: a basic statement of financial position, which lists all assets, less all liabilities, in order to calculate the accumulated fund/capital.

The statement of financial position

The statement of financial position of a not-for-profit organisation is very similar to that of a profit-making organisation. The main difference is that capital is replaced with an accumulated fund:

Accumulated fund = Assets – Liabilities

This is often calculated using a statement of affairs, which is a summary statement of all the assets and liabilities on a certain day.

Illustration 6: Preparing the statement of financial position

Based on the previous illustrations, the statement of financial position for the Runners-Up Sports Club is as follows.

Runners-Up Sports Club Statement of financial position for the year ended 31 December 2014			
	$	$	$
Non-current assets			
Equipment (original $14 200 + new $3 100)		17 300	
Provision for depreciation (original $2 000 + new $1 730)		(3 730)	
			13 570
Current assets			
Refreshments inventory		2 130	
Other receivables: subscriptions due		160	2 290
			15 860
Financed by:			
Accumulated fund (see details below)		13 003	
Surplus of income over expenditure		2 074	
			15 077
Current liabilities			
Other payables:			
Wages owing		500	
Subscriptions received in advance		120	
Bank overdraft		163	783
			15 860

The subscriptions due is income receivable and is therefore other receivables as money is owed to the club. They are listed among the current assets.

The subscriptions received in advance are the equivalent of money owed back to members at this date and are treated as other payables.

The calculation of the opening balance of the accumulated fund is found by listing and totalling assets at the beginning of the year and subtracting any liabilities In other words, the opening balance is found by compiling a statement of affairs.

Statement of affairs at 1 January 2014	
	$
Equipment ($14 200 – $2 000)	12 200
Refreshments inventory	1 240
Bank	123
Subscriptions due	240
	13 803
Less wages owing	(800)
Accumulated fund at 1 January 2014	13 003

An accumulated fund is increased by adding any surplus of income over expenditure or reduced by subtracting any deficit of income over expenditure.

Donations

Occasionally a not-for-profit organisation may receive gifts or donations. It is normal practice to include these as income in the year in which they are received, and this is the right treatment to adopt unless there are clear instructions to the contrary. Just occasionally a donation may be very substantial. The organisation's committee might take the view that to show so large a donation in the income and expenditure account would give rather a distorted view of the annual surplus of income over expenditure. The committee may ask the treasurer to record this exceptional donation as a separate item on the statement of financial position. Where this recommendation is made the donation should appear as a separate item alongside the accumulated fund.

Life membership schemes

Some not-for-profit organisations offer members the opportunity to pay a one-off subscription which will entitle the members to use the facilities indefinitely. Life membership schemes, as they are called, usually require the member to pay a much larger sum than for an annual subscription. From the accounting point of view, the question arises as to how to treat these particular subscriptions. Ideally the income from a life membership subscription should be spread over the years the member uses the organisation's facilities. However, this is obviously impossible to judge accurately. It is usual, therefore, for the committee to ask the treasurer to spread the income from life membership schemes over a set number of years (say six years).

Illustration 7: Accounting for life membership schemes

The Stadium Athletics Club offers its members life membership on payment of $600. The following information is available about the life membership scheme for the year ended 31 March 2015.

	$
Balance of life membership fund, 1 April 2014	8 300
Receipts from new life members during the year ended 31 March 2015 (7 × $600)	4 200

The club's policy is to treat 15 per cent of the membership fund as income in any particular year.

Based on this information the following records should be prepared by the club's treasurer.

Life membership fund			
Dr			**Cr**
	$		**$**
Transfer to income and expenditure account (15% of fund)*	1 875	Balance at 1 April 2014 b/f	8 300
Balance at 31 March 2015 c/d	10 625	Bank: receipts during year	4 200
	12 500		12 500
		Balance b/d, 1 April 2015	10 625
*i.e. 15% of the opening balance plus any receipts for the year			

Income and expenditure account for the year ended 31 March 2015 (extract)	
	$
Income	
Life membership fund	1 875

Statement of financial position at 31 March 2015 (extract)	
	$
Non-current liabilities	
Life membership fund	10 625

End-of-chapter questions

1 Recording items in the correct financial statement

Identify in which financial statement(s) each of the following items should be recorded.

Item	Receipts and payments account	Income and expenditure account	Statement of financial position at year end
Payment for refreshment supplies			
Closing bank balance			
Subscriptions due at year end			
Loan received from member			

2 Preparing the receipts and payments account

The following information is available for Sports First, a local community sports club, for the year ended 31 March 2015.

	$
Subscriptions received	18 620
Refreshments takings	9 460
Refreshments purchases	6 510
Administration	735
Additional sports equipment	5 950
Club staff wages	7 050
Ground maintenance	805
Refreshments staff wages	6 460
Secretary's expenses	450

The cash balance at 1 April 2014 was $450.

Prepare a receipts and payments account for Sports First for the year ended 31 March 2015.

3 Preparing a receipts and payments account to discover missing cash

The following information is available for Charlie's Chess Club, a chess club run from a local village hall by a retired teacher, for the year ended 31 October 2014.

	$
Membership subscriptions for the year	2 400
Hall hire	685
Tournament fees paid	810
Tournament costs	680
Refreshments	300

The cash balance at 1 November 2013 was $450.

Unfortunately, Charlie has been ill and so the records have not been maintained properly. The cash balance at 31 October 2015 was $305.

Charlie does not believe that all the money received has been banked.

Prepare the receipts and payments account for the year ended 31 October 2014 to calculate the amount of unbanked cash.

4 Preparing an income and expenditure account

Kingsly Theatre Club is an amateur dramatic club that has existed for many years. The club rents a local theatre with a café and the members regularly give performances to the town's residents. The treasurer has provided the following information for the year ended 30 June 2014.

	$
Refreshments inventory at 1 July 2013	2 600
Refreshments inventory at 30 June 2014	3 500
Refreshments staff wages	13 500
Refreshments takings	42 500
Refreshments purchases	22 000
Production expenses	10 400
Rent	16 500
Membership subscriptions	8 300
Performance ticket sales	12 600
Theatre costs: for example heating	1 700

Additional information at 30 June 2014:

- There were 14 members who had not paid their annual membership fees of $25 each.
- An invoice for refreshments purchases of $300 had not been recorded.

- It was discovered that some of the refreshments inventory, cost $50, had passed its sell-by date and had to be thrown away.

Required

a Prepare the refreshments trading account for the year ended 30 June 2014, showing the profit or loss made on the refreshments.

b Prepare an income and expenditure account for Kingsly Theatre Club for the year ended 30 June 2014.

5 Preparing an income and expenditure account

Walking Fit, a club for walkers over the age of 50, has the following information available for the year ended 31 March 2015.

Receipts and payments account			
	$		$
Balance b/d at 1 April 2014	123	Barbecue evening costs	31
Members' subscriptions	1 420	Administration	55
Competition ticket sales	234	Hiking equipment	1 410
Social evening ticket sales	828	Advertising costs	180
Barbecue evening sales	52	Maps	70
		Competition prizes	142
		Social evening costs	461
		Balance c/d at 31 March 2015	308
	2 657		2 657

Additional information:

	1 Apr 2014	31 Mar 2015
	$	$
Member subscriptions in arrears	70	92
Member subscriptions in advance	32	12
Social evening expenses owing	–	981
Valuation of hiking equipment	7 000	?

- The cost of maps should be regarded as revenue expenditure.
- Depreciation for the year on hiking equipment is $220.

a Prepare the subscriptions account for the year ended 31 March 2015.

b Prepare the income and expenditure account for the year ended 31 March 2015.

6 Calculating the accumulated fund for the statement of financial position

The following information is available for a sailing club.

	$
Cash in hand at 1 January 2015	20
Sailing equipment valuation	12 600
Prepaid subscriptions at 1 January 2015	400
Subscriptions due at 1 January 2015	250
Bank overdraft at 1 January 2015	650
Amount owing for equipment at 1 January 2015	1 100

What is the value of the club's accumulated fund at 1 January 2015?

7 Preparing an income and expenditure account and statement of financial position

Cuppa and Cake is a charity that runs a small café to raise money for local children. The following information has been prepared by the treasurer for the year ended 31 December 2014.

Receipts and payments account			
	$		$
Balance b/d at 1 January 2014	23	Purchase of refreshments	2 931
Refreshments sales	3 620	Administration	60
Second-hand book sales	101	Rental of premises	210
Greeting card sales	49	Advertising costs	80
Donations	152	Cleaning expenses	142
		Donations to children's charities	484
		Purchase of greeting cards	21
		Balance c/d at 31 December 2014	17
	3 945		3 945

Additional information:

	1 Jan 2014	31 Dec 2014
	$	$
Refreshments inventories	270	292
Payables (amounts due for refreshments)	132	112
Advertising costs owing	38	–
Rental of premises paid in advance	70	62

Prepare:

a a statement of affairs to show the charity's accumulated fund at 1 January 2014

b the charity's refreshment account for the year ended 31 December 2014

c the charity's income and expenditure account for the year ended 31 December 2014

d the charity's statement of financial position at 31 December 2014.

8 Preparing the income and expenditure account and statement of financial position

Hole in One is a golf club. The following information has been prepared by the treasurer for the year ended 31 December 2014.

Receipts and payments account

	$		$
Balance b/d at 1 January 2014	1 420	Refreshments purchases	22 800
Refreshments sales	33 620	Administration	260
Subscriptions	52 100	Golf course maintenance	8 610
		Advertising costs	1 680
		Cleaning expenses	2 842
		Refreshments staff wages	10 400
		Purchase of golf equipment	12 500
		Golf professional's salary	18 000
		Greenkeeper's wages	5 300
Balance c/d at 31 December 2014	1 602	Clubhouse expenses	6 350
	88 742		88 742

Additional information:

	1 Jan 2014	31 Dec 2014
	$	$
Refreshments inventory	3 270	4 292
Amounts owing to suppliers of refreshments inventory	1 430	1 110
Refreshments staff wages owing	380	240
Subscriptions received in advance	1 700	1 640
Subscriptions due and unpaid	400	900
Clubhouse valuation	120 000	114 000
Golf equipment valuation	42 300	44 600

Prepare:

a a statement of affairs to show the club's accumulated fund as at 1 January 2014

b the subscriptions account for the year ended 31 December 2014

c the refreshments trading account for the year ended 31 December 2014

d the club's income and expenditure account for the year ended 31 December 2014

e the club's statement of financial position at 31 December 2014.

9 Preparing an income and expenditure account and statement of financial position

Sing to the Sky is a club that promotes choral singing among teenagers. Every year an outdoor concert with an evening barbecue is given at the clubhouse to raise funds for the club. The following information has been prepared by the treasurer for the year ended 31 December 2014.

Receipts and payments account

	$		$
Balance b/d at 1 January 2014	230	Purchase of concert refreshments	930
Refreshments sales at concert	2 120	Administration expenses	50
Concert entrance fees	1 600	Concert costs	1 050
Concert barbecue sales	250	Concert advertising	180
		Clubhouse expenses	1 090
		Singing teacher's fees	600
		Club brochures	120
		Concert barbecue costs	140
		Balance c/d at 31 December 2014	40
	4 200		4 200

Additional information:

	1 Jan 2014	31 Dec 2014
	$	$
Inventory (concert refreshments)	170	190
Payables (concert refreshments)	230	210
Advertising costs owing	30	–
Brochure costs prepaid	85	65
Singing teacher's fees owing	50	150
Clubhouse at valuation	52 000	50 000

Prepare:

a a statement of affairs to show the club's accumulated fund as at 1 January 2014

b the concert account for the year ending 31 December 2014 to find the profit or loss made on the annual concert and barbecue

c the club's income and expenditure account for the year ended 31 December 2014

d the club's statement of financial position at 31 December 2014.

10 Preparing an income and expenditure account and statement of financial position

Support Our Town (S.O.T.) is a charity that runs a small town's annual fundraising carnival.

The following information has been prepared by the treasurer of the charity for the year ended 31 January 2015.

Receipts and payments account

	$		$
Balance b/d at 1 February 2014	670	Refreshment purchases	22 400
Refreshment sales	34 910	Administration	100
Donations for carnival floats	22 600	Carnival floats decoration costs	4 610
		Advertising costs	680
		Rubbish removal and clear-up costs	2 100
		Charity donations	25 500
		Event insurance	950
		Town community charges	1 200
		Petrol costs	260
		Balance c/d at 31 January 2015	380
	58 180		58 180

Additional information:

	1 Feb 2014	31 Jan 2015
	$	$
Refreshments inventory	370	492
Trade payables for refreshments	1 920	1 870
Carnival floats at valuation	1 200	1 140
Event insurance prepaid	150	100
Town community charges owing	200	250

Prepare:

a a statement of affairs to show the charity's accumulated fund at 1 February 2014

b the refreshments trading account for the year ended 31 January 2015

c the charity's income and expenditure account for the year ended 31 January 2015

d the charity's statement of financial position at 31 January 2015.

11 Preparing end-of-year financial statements including life membership

The Curtain-up Drama Club was formed several years ago. The club operates a life membership scheme. The club's treasurer is able to supply the following information about the year ended 31 December 2014.

At 1 January the club had the following assets and liabilities.

	$
Costumes and stage sets at valuation	11 900
Rent prepaid	270
Subscriptions due from members	90
Cash at bank	3 150
Administration expenses due	140
Subscriptions received in advance	320
Life membership fund	5 600

Receipts and payments account for the year ended 31 December 2014

Receipts	$	Payments	$
Balance at bank 1 January 2014	3 150	Rent of premises	1 740
Members' subscriptions	3 200	Purchase of new costumes and stage sets	8 800
Life membership subscriptions	1 300	Production costs	2 300
Special donation	6 000	Administration expenses	490
Ticket sales for productions	4 480	Competition prizes	380
Competition receipts	630	Balance at bank 31 December 2014	5 050
	18 760		18 760

It is the treasurer's policy to regard 10 per cent of the life membership fund as income for the year. The club committee has decided that the special donation should not be regarded as income for the year under review.

On 31 December:

- members' subscriptions due were $220
- members' subscriptions received in advance were $110
- $180 was owing for rent of premises
- some administration expenses were prepaid $50
- costumes and stage sets were valued at $17 500.

Prepare:

a a calculation of the club's accumulated fund at 1 January 2014

b a subscriptions account for the year ended 31 December 2014

c an income and expenditure account for the year ended 31 December 2014

d a statement of financial position at 31 December 2014.

12 Preparing end-of-year financial statements including life membership

The treasurer of the Glades Social Club is able to provide the following information about the club's most recent financial year which ended on 30 June 2014.

Assets and liabilities at 1 July 2013

	$
Cash at bank	3 840
Club buildings cost	
Cost	280 000
Provision for depreciation	21 000
Club furniture and equipment at valuation	17 500
Inventory: refreshments	870
Subscriptions due	650
Subscriptions received in advance	210
General expenses due	380
Life membership fund	14 500

Receipts and payments account for the year ended 30 June 2014

Receipts	$	Payments	$
Balance at bank 1 July 2013	3 840	Purchase of refreshments	1 750
Members' subscriptions	6 750	General expenses	4 440
Life membership subscriptions	2 250	Purchase of furniture and equipment	6 750
Loans from members	600	Balance at bank 30 June 2014	3 290
Donations	320		
Sales of refreshments	2 470		
	16 230		16 230

Additional information:

- The loans from members are interest free, but are to be repaid in January 2015.
- Suppliers of refreshments were owed $310 on 30 June 2014.
- General expenses were prepaid $60 on 30 June 2014.
- There was a refreshments inventory valued at $380 on 30 June 2014.
- Members' subscriptions $480 were due on 30 June 2014.
- Members' subscriptions $710 had been received in advance for the year ended ending 30 June 2015.
- The club buildings should be depreciated by 2.5 per cent on cost.
- The treasurer valued the furniture and equipment at $20 500 on 30 June 2014.
- The club's policy is to regard 10 per cent of the life membership fund as income for the year under review.

Prepare:

a a calculation of the club's accumulated fund at 1 July 2013

b a subscriptions account for the year ended 30 June 2014

c a refreshments trading account for the year ended 30 June 2014

d an income and expenditure account for the year ended 30 June 2014

e a statement of financial position at 30 June 2014.

1.1.3: Limited liability companies

Learning objectives

In this chapter you will learn:

- about statutory requirements in regard to financial statements
- how to prepare a statement of cash flows
- how to interpret a statement of cash flows
- how to analyse statements of cash flows using ratios.

Statutory financial statements

All limited companies must publish their financial statements. This is a legal obligation for all limited companies whether they are private limited companies (Ltd) or public limited companies (plc). The financial statements are available so that the shareholders can review the performance of the company in which they have made an investment.

Each limited company must file a full set of statutory accounts with the registrar of companies comprising:

- the income statement
- the statement of financial position
- the statement of changes in equity
- the statement of cash flows
- notes to the accounts
- the directors' report
- the auditors' report.

Link

There is more about published income statements, the statement of financial position and the requirements of IAS 1 in A Level Chapter 1.1.4 International accounting standards.

There is more about the statement of changes in equity in AS Level Chapter 1.4.4B Limited companies: financial statements. The directors' report and the auditors' report are covered in A Level Chapter 1.1.5 Auditing and stewardship of limited companies.

This list of requirements is more extensive than that required by one of the international accounting standards (IAS 1 Presentation of financial statements). This is because the statutory requirement includes the directors' report and auditors' report, but the international standard does not mention these reports. (International accounting standards set out the rules and guidelines for the preparation of accounting statements.)

All of these documents must be sent to each shareholder of the company in advance of the company's annual general meeting (AGM). The directors then have the responsibility to submit copies of the documents to be filed with the registrar of companies. These documents are available for inspection by all members of the general public.

The Companies Act 2006, which superseded the Companies Act 1985, details the rules that regulate all limited companies. The basic rule that must be remembered is that the financial statements must give a true and fair view of the financial position of the company.

Link

There is more about true and fair view in A Level Chapter 1.1.5 Auditing and stewardship of limited companies.

Directors must not attempt to window dress the company's accounts. Window dressing involves trying to make the financial statements look better that they really are, for example by:

- including recognised, but unrealised, profits in the business
- drawing cheques on the last day of the financial year, but not sending them immediately to suppliers in order to artificially reduce liabilities
- capitalising some expenses that should have been transferred to the income statement.

Notes to the accounts

Financial statements are followed by notes that give more details about information which is usually shown in a summarised form within the financial statements. For example, the statement of financial position will be followed by a note giving much more detailed information about:

- non-current assets including information about additions during the current financial year, disposals, depreciation charges, revaluations, etc.
- directors' remuneration
- average number of employees and their costs to the company (i.e. wages, pensions, etc.)

Notes are also used to give additional explanations that should help users understand the contents of the financial statements, and the bases (for example depreciation methods) used.

Link

There is more about schedules of non-current assets in A Level Chapter 1.1.4 International accounting standards.

What is a statement of cash flows?

The statement of cash flows must be produced by limited companies as part of their financial statements. The income statement shows the profitability of an organisation; the statement of financial position shows the financial position of the company at a given date; the statement of cash flow shows the inflows and outflows of cash and cash equivalents over the course of the financial year.

It is important to remember that profit does not necessarily mean cash, and as such, the statement of cash flows is an important measure of the health of an organisation. The statement of cash flows details actual physical movements of cash – whether cash in the business increases or decreases.

Key terms

Statement of cash flows: a statement showing how cash inflows have been generated and how these have been spent (cash outflows).

Cash and cash equivalents: cash on hand and cash at the bank, together with short-term liquid investments that can easily be converted into cash.

Long-term investments: investments of over 12 months.

Long-term borrowings: borrowings due for repayment after more than 12 months.

Format

IAS 7 Statement of cash flows gives the guidelines for the presentation of the statement of cash flows. The statement is divided into three separate sections.

- **Operating activities:** The revenue-producing items, movements in inventory, trade receivables and trade payables, and payments for taxation and interest.
- **Investing activities:** The purchase and sale of non-current assets and other long-term investments.
- **Financing activities:** Movements on long-term borrowings and changes in share capital.

The final part of the statement shows the net increase or decrease in cash and cash equivalents for the year that is added to or deducted from the balance of cash and cash equivalents at the start of the year to produce the closing balance of cash and cash equivalents.

Layout

The following shows the layout of a statement of cash flows. The final figure at the end (cash and cash equivalents at the end of the year) can be checked back to the statement of financial position to confirm that no errors have been made (usually cash, plus bank, minus bank overdraft).

Key term

Operating activities: cash generated from operating activities, including changes in working capital items.

	$	$
Operating activities		
Profit from operations (before tax and interest)		XXX
Add: depreciation		XXX
Add: loss on sale of non-current assets		XXX
Deduct: profit on sale of non-current assets		(XXX)
Add: decrease (or deduct increase) in inventories		(XXX) or XXX
Add: decrease (or deduct increase) in trade receivables		(XXX) or XXX
Add: increase (or deduct decrease) in trade payables		(XXX) or XXX
Subtotal = cash from/(used in) operations		XXX
Deduct: taxation paid in the period		(XXX)
Deduct: interest paid in the period		(XXX)
Total = net cash from/(used in) operating activities		XXX
Investing activities		
Add: sale proceeds from sale of non-current assets	XXX	
Deduct: purchase of non-current assets	(XXX)	
Add: interest received	XXX	
Add: dividends received	XXX	
Subtotal = cash from/(used in) investing activities		XXX
Financing activities		
Add: receipts from issue of share capital	XXX	
Add: receipts from loans taken out	XXX	
Deduct: repayment of share capital	(XXX)	
Deduct: repayment of loans	(XXX)	
Deduct: dividends paid	(XXX)	
Subtotal = cash from/(used in) financing activities		XXX
Subtotal = net increase/(decrease) in cash and cash equivalents		XXX
Cash and cash equivalents at the start of the year		XXX
Cash and cash equivalents at the end of the year		XXX

Key terms

Investing activities: cash generated or spent on the sale and purchase of non-current assets, dividends received and interest received.

Financing activities: the issue or repayment of share capital, long-term borrowings and the payment of dividends.

Profit from operations (before tax and interest): Take straight from the income statement.

Depreciation: Take straight from the income statement. This is added back to the profit from operations because it does not involve the movement of cash, it is a bookkeeping entry.

Loss on sale of non-current assets/Profit on sale of non-current assets: Take straight from the income statement. As is the case with depreciation, these items do not involve the movement of cash. The proceeds of sale are the movement of cash.

Increase/decrease in inventories, trade receivables and trade payables: These involve the movement of cash:

- An increase in inventories will result in a cash outflow to pay for the additional items; a decrease in inventory will result in a cash inflow.
- An increase in trade receivables will result in a cash outflow as more customers have not yet paid; a decrease in trade receivables will result in a cash inflow.
- An increase in trade payables will result in a cash inflow as less money has been paid to suppliers; a decrease in trade payables will result in a cash outflow.

Taxation paid in the period: The amount of taxation actually paid in the period. It will not necessarily be the same as the figure on the income statement.

Interest paid in the period: The amount of interest actually paid in the period. It will not necessarily be the same as the figure on the income statement.

Sale proceeds from the disposal of non-current assets: The actual proceeds from the sale of non-current assets.

Purchase cost of non-current assets: The actual amount of money paid for non-current assets. This figure will often have to be calculated from the net book value (NBV) of all non-current assets.

Interest received: The actual amount of interest received in the period.

Dividends received: The actual amount of dividends received in the period.

Receipts from issue of share capital: The actual amount of money received from the issue of share capital in the period which may include a share premium.

Receipts from loans taken out: The actual money received from loans taken out in the period.

Repayment of share capital: The actual amount of money repaid to shareholders in respect of a share repayment in the period.

Repayment of loans: The actual amount of money repaid off loans in the period.

Dividends paid: The actual amount of dividends paid to shareholders in the period.

Illustration 1: Preparing a statement of cash flows

The following information is available for PH Reg Ltd for the years ended 31 March 2014 and 31 March 2015.

Statement of financial position at 31 March 2015

	2015		2014	
	$000	$000	$000	$000
Non-current assets				
Plant and machinery		126		102
Current assets				
Inventory	113		80	
Trade receivables	98		76	
Cash and cash equivalents	27	238	6	162
Total assets		364		264
Equity				
Ordinary share capital	120		100	
Share premium	15		10	
Retained earnings	123	258	96	206
Current liabilities				
Trade payables	69		54	
Cash and cash equivalents	35		–	
Taxation	2	106	4	58
Total equity and liabilities		364		264

Income statement extract for the year ended 31 March 2015

	2015 ($)	2014 ($)
Profit from operations	45	26
Interest paid	(5)	(3)
Profit before taxation	40	23
Taxation	(2)	(4)
Profit for the year after taxation	38	19

Additional information:

During the year ended 31 March 2015, non-current assets with a net book value of $25 000 were sold for $22 000.

Dividends paid during the year ended 31 March 2015 were $11 000.

Depreciation charge for the year ended 31 March 2015 was $18 000.

Required

Prepare a statement of cash flows for PH Reg Ltd for the year ended 31 March 2015.

	Note	$000	$000
Profit from operation	1		45
Add: depreciation	2		18
Add: loss on sale of non-current assets	3		3
Deduct: increase in inventories	4		(33)
Deduct: increase in trade receivables	5		(22)
Add: increase in trade payables	6		15
Cash from operating activities			26
Deduct: interest paid	7		(5)
Deduct: taxation paid	8		(4)
Net cash from operating activities			17
Investing activities			
Add: proceeds from sale of non-current assets	9	22	
Deduct: purchase cost of non-current assets	10	(67)	
Net cash used in investing activities			(45)
Financing activities			
Add: receipts from issue of share capital	11	25	
Deduct: dividends paid	12	(11)	
Net cash from financing activities			14
Net decrease in cash and cash equivalents			(14)
Cash and cash equivalents at start of the year	13		6
Cash and cash equivalents at end of the year	14		(8)

Notes:

1. The profit from operations taken straight from the income statement.
2. Depreciation taken straight from additional information.
3. NBV of sales $25 less proceeds on sale $22 = $3.
4. Inventories have increased from $80 to $113 = $33.
5. Trade receivables have increased from $76 to $98 = $22.
6. Trade payables have increased from $54 to $69 = $15.
7. Interest paid taken straight from the income statement.
8. As taxation is due for payment nine months after the year end, the amount from the statement of financial position will be the amount paid in this period.
9. Proceeds from the sale of non-current assets taken straight from the additional information.

Getting it right

Learn this formula – it will often be required.

10 To calculate the purchase cost of non-current assets:

Opening NBV

Less: depreciation charge for the year

Less: NBV of assets sold

Less: closing NBV

Equals: additions to non-current assets at cost

($102 – $18 – $25 – $126 = $67)

11 Receipts from issue of share capital = increase in ordinary share capital plus increase in share premium account ($10 + $5).

12 Dividends paid taken straight from the additional information.

13 Cash and cash equivalents at the start of the year taken straight from the 2014 statement of financial position.

14 The cash and cash equivalents at the end of the year can be checked to ensure that no errors have been made. The final figure of ($8) is represented by the cash and cash equivalents of $27 less the bank overdraft of $35.

Interpreting a statement of cash flows

The importance of the statement of cash flows should not be underestimated. While the income statement informs the reader of the financial statements about the profitability of the organisation, profits alone do not ensure the success of the business. Cash flow is essential to the continued success of any business: without cash, the business will not survive.

The statement of cash flows is a better indication of the liquidity of an organisation than any other part of the financial statements. It details the inflows and outflows of cash, showing the reader which areas of the business are expanding or contracting.

It is important to remember that making profits does not necessarily mean that the company will have cash in the bank, for a variety of reasons.

A company will often invest in non-current assets to ensure the future profitability of the business, but it takes time for the profits from these investments to filter through the business. An investment in non-current assets will often be matched with an increase in long-term borrowings to finance the investment.

Changes in the working capital items of inventories, trade receivables and trade payables will have an impact on the cash position of the business. An increase in inventories or trade receivables will result in a cash outflow – cash is tied up in the inventory or cash is owed by trade receivables. Similarly, a decrease in trade payables will also result in a cash outflow – more trade payables have been paid what is owed.

Much information can be seen from an examination of the statement of cash flows. The statement links to the income statement, showing the amount of profit made with how much of that profit has generated cash and what has happened to that cash. Remember, without profits the business will not generate cash, but without cash the business will not be able to pay amounts due and will not survive.

Analysing the statement of cash flows is useful because it:

- details how the business has generated cash inflows
- shows how the business has used those cash inflows during the year
- draws attention to current and future liquidity problems, enabling corrective action to be taken
- highlights whether the company has increased its loans and whether those loans were taken to finance non-current asset purchase for the future or whether they were to finance day-to-day running costs (a danger sign)
- highlights changes in the share capital structure of the business
- highlights how well the business is managing its cash resources
- enables potential investors to compare the cash position of the business with other investment opportunities.

End-of-chapter questions

1 Statutory financial statements

Identify the financial statements that must be included in a company's published accounts in accordance with the requirements of the Companies Act 2006.

2 Window dressing

Explain the term 'window dressing'. Illustrate your answer with an example.

3 Preparing the reconciliation of profit from operations

You are provided with the following information for a business with a year end of 31 December.

	2014 ($)	2013 ($)
Operating profit for the year	82 310	67 550
Depreciation charge for the year	10 420	8 300
Loss on sale of non-current assets	800	–
Inventories	42 100	38 300
Trade receivables	26 240	28 180
Trade payables	19 640	17 110

Required

Prepare a reconciliation of profit from operations to the cash from operating activities for the year ended 31 December 2014.

4 Preparing the reconciliation of profit from operations

	2015 ($)	2014 ($)
Operating profit for the year	95 242	98 514
Depreciation charge for the year	13 420	15 370
Profit on sale of non-current assets	915	–
Loss on sale of non-current assets	–	1 500
Inventories	38 520	40 100
Trade receivables	32 718	31 940
Trade payables	22 357	24 875
Taxation paid	12 200	14 130
Interest paid	8 640	10 270

Required

Prepare a reconciliation of profit from operations to the net cash from operating activities for the year ended 31 March 2015.

5 Preparing a statement of cash flows

The last two years' statements of financial position of TFR Ltd at 31 March are as follows.

Statement of financial position at 31 March 2015				
	2015		2014	
	$000	$000	$000	$000
Non-current assets		156		138
Current assets				
Inventory	83		81	
Trade receivables	101		96	
Cash and cash equivalents	15	199	–	177
Total assets		355		315
Equity				
Ordinary share capital	145		120	
Share premium	27		22	
Retained earnings	44	216	30	172
Non-current liabilities				
Bank loan (repayable 2019)		34		18
Current liabilities				
Trade payables	87		92	
Cash and cash equivalents	–		11	
Taxation	18	105	22	125
Total equity and liabilities		355		315

Additional information:

- The operating profit for the year ended 31 March 2015 was $60 000 (2014: $62 000).
- There were no sales of non-current assets in the year.
- The depreciation charge for the year was $12 000 (2014: $16 000).
- Interest paid for the year was $9000 (2014: $6000).
- Equity dividends paid during the year were $19 000.

Required

Prepare a statement of cash flows for TFR Ltd for the year ended 31 March 2015.

6 Preparing a statement of cash flows

The last two years' statements of financial position of STB Ltd at 31 March are as follows.

Statement of financial position at 31 March 2015				
	2015		2014	
	$000	$000	$000	$000
Non-current assets		259		224
Current assets				
Inventory	128		102	
Trade receivables	132		118	
Cash and cash equivalents	–	260	14	234
Total assets		519		458
Equity				
Ordinary share capital	210		180	
Share premium	15		–	
Retained earnings	107	332	131	311
Non-current liabilities				
Bank loan (repayable 2019)		42		20
Current liabilities				
Trade payables	102		109	
Cash and cash equivalents	23		–	
Taxation	20	145	18	127
Total equity and liabilities		519		458

Additional information:

- The operating profit for the year ended 31 March 2015 was $30 000 (2014: $85 000).
- Non-current assets with a cost of $24 000 and accumulated depreciation of $19 000 were sold during the year for $8000.
- The depreciation charge for the year was $12 000 (2014: $16 000).
- Interest paid for the year was $9000 (2014: $6000).
- Equity dividends paid during the year were $25 000.

Required

Prepare a statement of cash flows for STB Ltd for the year ended 31 March 2015.

7 Preparing statement of cash flows from full set of financial statements

Seddel Ltd's financial statements prepared on 30 June 2014 are shown below.

SEDDEL Ltd Income statement for the year ended 30 June 2014	
	$000
Revenue	17 848
Cost of sales	(11 935)
Gross profit	5 913
Distribution costs	(596)
Administration expenses	(723)
Operating profit	4 594
Finance costs	(535)
Profit before tax	4 059
Tax	(648)
Profit after tax	3 411

Statement of changes in equity for the year ended 30 June 2014 (extract) retained earnings	
	$000
Balance 1 July 2013	494
Profit for the year	3 411
	3 905
Dividends paid	(1 830)
Balance 30 June 2014	2 075

Statement of financial position at 30 June						
	2014			2013		
	$000	$000	$000	$000	$000	$000
	Cost	Accumulated depreciation	Net	Cost	Accumulated depreciation	Net
Non-current assets	19 900	5 052	14 848	*16 448*	*4 882*	*11 566*
Current assets						
Inventories		362			*381*	
Trade and other receivables		133			*109*	
Cash and cash equivalents		52			*41*	
			547			*531*
Total assets			15 395			*12 097*
Equity						
Issued share capital						
4.8m ordinary shares of $1 each			4 800			*4 000*
Capital reserves						
Share premium			1 200			*800*
Revenue reserve						
Retained earnings			2 075			*494*
			8 075			*5 294*

Non-current liabilities						
8% debentures (2024)			6 600			*6 200*
Current liabilities						
Trade and other payables		72			*102*	
Tax liabilities		648			*501*	
			720			*603*
Total equity and liabilities			15 395			*12 097*

Note 1
Non-current assets

		$000
Cost		
At 1 July 2013		16 448
Additions		4 500
Disposals		(1 048)
At 30 June 2014		19 900
Depreciation		
At 1 July 2013		4 882
Charge for the year		1 012
Disposals		(842)
At 30 June 2014		5 052
Net book value		
At 30 June 2014		14 848
At 1 July 2013		11 566

Additional information:

The proceeds from the sale of non-current assets in the year ended 30 June 2014 was $88 000.

Required

Prepare a statement of cash flows for the year ended 30 June 2014.

8 **Preparing statement of cash flows including bonus issue of shares**

Vortex plc's statements of financial position at 31 December 2013 and 2014 are shown below.

VORTEX plc
Statements of financial position at 31 December

	2014			2013		
	$m	$m	$m	*$m*	*$m*	*$m*
	Cost	Accumulated depreciation	Net	*Cost*	*Accumulated depreciation*	*Net*
Non-current assets						
Property plant and equipment						
Land and buildings	135.0	0.7	134.3	*118.5*	*4.7*	*113.8*
Machinery	212.0	85.0	127.0	*192.0*	*74.0*	*118.0*
Fixtures and fittings	62.0	27.0	35.0	*68.0*	*26.0*	*42.0*
	409.0	112.7	296.3	*378.5*	*104.7*	*273.8*
Current assets						
Inventories		72.4			*84.7*	
Trade and other receivables		100.3			*93.2*	
Cash and cash equivalents		11.1				
			183.8			*177.9*
Total assets			480.1			*451.7*
Equity						
400m ordinary shares of 50¢ each			200.0			*140.0*
Share premium						*21.0*
Retained earnings			60.4			*41.6*
			260.4			*202.6*
Non-current liabilities						
6% debentures (2025)			48.0			*61.0*
Current liabilities						
Trade and other payables		68.6			*59.8*	
Tax liabilities		103.1			*121.4*	
Cash and cash equivalents					*6.9*	
			171.7			*188.1*
Total equity and liabilities			480.1			*451.7*

Additional information:

- There were no disposals of machinery during the year ended 31 December 2014.
- There were no purchases of fixtures and fittings during the year ended 31 December 2014.
- Fixtures and fittings were disposed of during the year ended 31 December 2014. Depreciation of $5.3m had been charged on these assets; proceeds from the disposal amounted to $0.9m.
- The land and buildings were revalued on 31 March 2014.
- On 30 June 2014 the company made a bonus issue of three shares for every seven shares currently held. The bonus issue was financed in such a way as to maintain maximum dividend flexibility.
- Interest charges for the year ended 31 December 2014 totalled $3.9m.
- Dividends paid during the year ended 31 December 2014 totalled $28m.

Required

a Prepare a journal entry to record the bonus issue of shares. (A narrative is not required.)
b Calculate the profit before tax and interest for the year ended 31 December 2014.
c Prepare a statement of cash flows for the year ended 31 December 2014.

Learning objectives

In this chapter you will learn the disclosure requirements of:

- IAS 1 Presentation of financial statements
- IAS 2 Inventories
- IAS 7 Statement of cash flows
- IAS 8 Accounting policies
- IAS 10 Events after the reporting period
- IAS 16 Property, plant and equipment
- IAS 36 Impairment of assets
- IAS 37 Provisions, contingent liabilities and contingent assets
- IAS 38 Intangible assets.

1.1.4: International accounting standards

Introduction

The accounting standards are designed to ensure the implementation of the five fundamental accounting concepts: true and fair view; duality (double entry); consistency; business entity; money measurement.

Recently considerable progress has been made to ensure that financial statements are prepared using the same rules and guidelines internationally. A team of leading accountants from many countries has the task of preparing and updating these international accounting standards.

The standards are designed to protect those who use financial statements and to prevent these stakeholders being misled. They are designed to ensure:

- **Comparability:** so that stakeholders can rely on information in the statements being comparable from one year to the next and from one business to another; this provides a foundation for confident assessment of business's financial performance.
- **Relevance:** so that stakeholders can be assured that the information provided has been designed to meet their needs.
- **Reliability:** so that stakeholders can be confident that the information provided would have been the same whoever had produced the statements. In other words the information will be objective (factual rather than opinion) and present a true and fair view of the business.
- **Understandability:** so that the content of financial statements should be accessible and comprehensible by those with reasonable familiarity with financial terminology and techniques.

The rules, which are sometimes referred to as IASs (International Accounting Standards) or IFRSs (International Financial Reporting Standards), are now in force in many countries worldwide.

The standards have been designed to ensure that those responsible for preparing a company's financial statements (the directors) are required to follow strict rules regarding their preparation and presentation. The standards are focused on where, in often very complex organisations, there is potential uncertainty or potential disagreement about how financial information should be treated.

IAS 1 Presentation of financial statements

The standard requires directors to prepare:

- a statement of profit or loss and other comprehensive income for the period

- a statement of changes in equity for the period
- a statement of cash flows for the period (see IAS 7)
- a statement of financial position at the end of the period
- accounting policies and explanatory notes (this also has its own specific IAS).

The standard makes specific mention of the following accounting concepts that must be applied:

- going concern
- accrual basis of accounting
- consistency
- materiality.

Link

See AS Level Chapter 1.1.5 Accounting concepts and principles for more information about these concepts.

The standard requires the inclusion of figures from the previous years in order that users can make relevant comparisons. It should be noted that the standard does not usually permit the offsetting of information as this could obscure important facts about the company (e.g. a bank overdraft offset against a positive bank balance).

In addition, the standard requires notes to be published providing an explanation of the company's accounting policies, i.e. the bases used in the treatment of items in the statements – for example depreciation methods – and where appropriate, notes providing more detail about items shown within the statements.

Statement of comprehensive income (formerly the income statement)

The statement must show:

- revenue
- finance costs
- the charge for taxation.

Expenses may be analysed to provide information that is relevant and reliable:

- for a manufacturing organisation in such a way as to identify raw materials, depreciation, etc.
- for a non-manufacturing organisation in such a way as to identify cost of sales, administration expenses, distribution expenses, etc.

Illustration 1: IAS 1 and the statement of comprehensive income

The following information is available for the financial year ended 31 March 2015 for GXQ Ltd, and the preceding year ended 31 March 2014.

	Year ended 31 March 2015	Year ended 31 March 2014
	$m	$m
Administration expenses	4.9	4.7
Cost of sales	48.7	42.3
Distribution expenses	14.8	14.2
Finance charges	3.1	2.7
Other income	0.8	1.1
Revenue	83.9	76.1
Tax	1.6	1.9

The company's statement of comprehensive income is as follows.

GXQ Ltd		
Statement of comprehensive income for the year ended 31 March 2015		
	Year ended 31 March 2015	*Year ended 31 March 2014*
	$m	*$m*
Revenue	83.9	*76.1*
Cost of sales	(48.7)	*(42.3)*
Gross profit	35.2	*33.8*
Other income	0.8	*1.1*
Distribution expenses	(14.8)	*(14.2)*
Administration expenses	(4.9)	*(4.7)*
Operating profit	16.3	*16.0*
Finance charges	(3.1)	*(2.7)*
Profit before tax	13.2	*13.3*
Tax	(1.6)	*(1.9)*
Profit for the year	11.6	*11.4*

Notes:

- The illustration demonstrates how comparative figures (for the previous year) are shown and that much of the information is in summarised form.
- Distribution expenses will include, for example, the cost of transporting goods to customers, depreciation of motor vehicles.
- Administration expenses will include the cost of all office functions.

- The statement will be followed by notes which disclose material (i.e. significant) items such as the profit/loss on the disposal of non-current assets.
- The statement could be continued to show other non-routine items, for example gains or losses from currency conversions for international operations, to give a final total for 'total comprehensive income for the year'.

Link

There is more about statements of changes in equity in AS Level Chapter 1.4.4B Limited companies: financial statements.

Link

There is more about statements of cash flow in A Level Chapter 1.1.3 Limited liability companies.

Statement of changes in equity

This statement is designed to inform users of changes in share capital and reserves during the financial year. It is a requirement that it shows realised and unrealised gains. An example of an unrealised gain would be an upward revaluation of property.

The statement of changes in equity shows dividends paid during the year only. A note in the published accounts will detail proposed dividends.

Statement of cash flows

This statement provides users with a focus on a company's liquidity. It shows the key decisions and events which have generated cash and how that cash has been used.

Statement of financial position

The standard requires that the minimum information to be disclosed in a statement of financial position is as follows:

Non-current assets

  Property, plant and equipment

  Intangible assets

  Financial assets (such as shares in another company)

Current assets

  Inventories

  Trade and other receivables

  Cash and cash equivalents

Issued share capital and reserves

Non-current liabilities

Current liabilities

  Trade and other payables

  Provisions (such as a possible liability arising from a legal case)

  Tax liabilities

To avoid over-detailed statements, the standard permits the use of notes to set out more information about these categories.

The standard does not specify any particular layout for the statement of financial position. So, for example, it is permissible to present a statement of financial position where current liabilities are deducted from current assets to show a figure for net current assets (or liabilities), i.e. the working capital of the company.

Illustration 2: IAS 1 and the statement of financial position

Jassar plc is a company that supplies sports equipment in the Middle East. The following information is available at 31 January 2015.

	At 31 January 2015	At 31 January 2014
	$m	$m
Cash and cash equivalents	2.4	1.2
Debentures 7%	13.0	14.0
Goodwill	10.5	11.0
Inventories	17.2	16.4
Investment property	4.5	2.8
Issued share capital	80.0	80.0
Property, plant and equipment	73.5	67.8
Provisions	0.5	0.7
Retained earnings	13.9	3.5
Tax liability	2.1	3.2
Trade and other payables	4.8	3.7
Trade and other receivables	6.2	5.9

The company's statement of financial position is as follows.

Jassar plc		
Statement of financial position at 31 January 2015		
	31 January 2015	***31 January 2014***
	$m	***$m***
Non-current assets		
Goodwill	10.5	*11.0*
Property, plant and equipment	73.5	*67.8*
Investment property	4.5	*2.8*
	88.5	*81.6*
Current assets		
Inventories	17.2	*16.4*

	31 January 2015	31 January 2014
	$m	$m
Trade and other receivables	6.2	5.9
Cash and cash equivalents	2.4	1.2
	25.8	23.5
Total assets	114.3	105.1
Equity and reserves		
Share capital	80.0	80.0
Retained earnings	13.9	3.5
	93.9	83.5
Non-current liabilities		
Debentures	13.0	14.0
Current liabilities		
Trade and other payables	4.8	3.7
Tax liability	2.1	3.2
Provisions	0.5	0.7
	7.4	7.6
Total equity and liabilities	114.3	105.1

Notes:

The statement will be accompanied by notes providing explanatory information about items shown on the statement of financial position, for example detailed information about share capital, a further breakdown of property, plant and equipment. The notes must provide sufficient details to enable users to understand the contents.

IAS 2 Inventories

Inventories may take the form of:

- raw materials
- work in progress
- finished goods manufactured by the business
- products purchased with the intention of resale
- items purchased for internal use (e.g. stationery supplies).

The standard requires that inventories are to be valued at the lower of cost and net realisable value.

Cost means the purchase price plus any additional costs incurred in order to put the goods into a saleable condition (e.g. carriage charges).

Key term

Net realisable value: sale price less any costs necessary in order to make a sale.

Link

FIFO and AVCO methods of valuation are covered in AS Level Chapter 2.1.1 Costing principles.
See A Level Chapter 2.3.1 Standard costing for information about standard costs.

Net realisable value is the sale value less any estimated costs that will be required in order to put inventories into a saleable condition (e.g. repairs to damaged items).

The standard accepts valuations based on the FIFO and AVCO methods, but does not permit the use of the LIFO method. It is also possible to use standard cost when this is close to actual prices paid for inventories.

Illustration 3: Applying IAS 2 Inventories

At 31 December 2014 the inventory lists of AutoTech Ltd included 30 items, each of which cost $70. This product is normally sold at $100 each. All of these items have been damaged in the storeroom. Twenty-five items with only minor damage can be sold for $79 each. The other items will have to be repaired at an estimated cost of $11 per item and then be sold for $78 each.

In accordance with IAS 2 these damaged items will be valued as follows.

At cost	25 × $70	Cost ($70) is lower than realisable value $79 each	*i.e. $1 750*
At net realisable	5 × ($78 – $11) i.e. $67	Net realisable value ($67) is lower than cost ($70)	*i.e. $335*
		Total	*$2 085*

Illustration 4: Valuing a manufacturer's finished goods and work in progress

Nimesh Ltd make 'teqs'. During the year ended 31 December 2014 the company made and sold 5000 teqs, and at 31 December 2014 it had in addition 500 finished teqs awaiting delivery to customers and 400 items that were assessed at one-quarter finished.

The costs incurred in producing these teqs were as follows.

	$
Direct materials	39 000
Direct labour	33 000
Production overheads	12 000
Total production costs	84 000

Number of teqs produced was as follows.

Finished products sold	5 000
Finished products in store	500
Work in progress	
(400 items × ¼ finished)	100
Total units	5 600

So each unit will be valued at cost $84 000/5600 = $15 per unit

Work in progress	400 × ¼ × $15	$1 500
Finished goods	500 × $15	$7 500

IAS 7 Statement of cash flows

The main requirements of IAS 7 are covered in A Level Chapter 1.1.3 Limited liability companies.

IAS 8 Accounting policies

In full the title of this standard is Accounting policies, changes in accounting estimates and errors.

IAS 8 provides a definition of accounting policies:

The specific principles, bases, conventions, rules and practices applied by an entity in preparing and presenting financial statements.

'Bases' means accounting methods used to implement policies: for example the choice of FIFO for inventory valuation; the choice of the straight-line method of depreciation.

The standard stipulates:

- All accounting policies specifically detailed in any of the international standards must be implemented.
- Where the standards do not cover particular situations, the directors must make their own decision as to the appropriate policy to be applied.
- Directors should base their judgment on the overriding requirement to provide a true and fair view of the company's affairs, by ensuring users are given reliable, relevant and understandable information.
- Directors must ensure that their policies are applied consistently to similar situations.

In regard to errors, the standard requires any material errors in financial statements to be corrected when discovered. Comparative figures would also need to be amended if they are affected by the error.

IAS 10 Events after the reporting period

This standard covers the treatment of events that occur after the date of the statement of financial position but before the statement is authorised by the directors. The standard described two types of event after the reporting period.

Adjusting events

These are events after the reporting period which provides further evidence of conditions that existed at the end of the reporting period.

Where such an event would have a material effect on the financial statements, they must be changed before they are authorised by the directors.

Non-adjusting events

These are events that have arisen after the end of the reporting period. There is, therefore, no adjustment necessary to the financial statements. However, where the event is material, then the matter should be disclosed in notes to the accounts.

Proposed dividends are regarded as non-adjusting events and are, therefore, not shown in a statement of financial position. Information about proposed dividends is shown by way of a note to the accounts.

Illustration 5: Distinguishing between adjusting and non-adjusting events

The directors of MaxiForm Ltd prepared financial statements for the year ended 30 September 2014. The directors were due to authorise the publication of these financial statements on 31 December 2014.

The following events have come to the attention of the directors. The company's accountant has indicated whether the event is an adjusting or a non-adjusting event.

Event	Type
Fraud has been discovered which shows that the value of certain items in the financial statements is incorrect.	Adjusting
A major credit customer was declared bankrupt in November 2014 and will not make payment for goods sold in August 2014.	Adjusting
A warehouse was flooded in December 2014 resulting in significant damage to some of the company's products.	Non-adjusting
In December 2014 the directors announced the decision to open a new store in July 2015.	Non-adjusting
Some vehicles were in the process of being sold in September 2014. The actual selling price was agreed in October 2014.	Adjusting

IAS 16 Property, plant and equipment

This standard prescribes the required treatment of tangible non-current assets, i.e. they have a physical presence. Non-current assets should be recognised in the accounts when the cost of the asset can be measured reliably and when it is probable that future economic benefits will flow to the entity.

Non-current assets should be recorded at cost, which could include not just the purchase price but also other costs incurred in order to prepare the asset for use: delivery charges, installation costs, import duties, etc. In the case of property, additional costs might include legal fees and architect's fees.

> **Key term**
>
> **Carrying amount**: the net book value of a tangible non-current asset based on cost less accumulated depreciation to date.

Non-current assets may be included in the financial statements using the cost model or the revaluation model.

- The cost model: the asset is recorded at its historical cost, less any accumulated depreciation to produce a figure that is called the carrying amount, i.e. the net book value.
- The revaluation model: the asset is recorded at its fair value which in most cases will be the market value if the asset were to be sold. In the case of land and buildings, however, the standard requires a professional revaluation to be carried out. The standard also requires that all of a category of non-current asset must be revalued. For example, it would not be permissible to revalue part of a company's property; all of the land and buildings would have to be revalued.

The standard clarifies that day-to-day servicing costs and repairs should be treated as revenue expenditure to be charged to the income statement. Regular replacement of a non-current asset, on the other hand, can be treated as part of the carrying amount.

Tangible non-current assets, with the exception of land, are subject to depreciation. The standard requires that the cost of an asset is systematically spread over its useful life using either the straight-line or reducing-balance method.

The useful life of an asset must be determined by considering the following:

- expected usage of the asset
- expected physical wear and tear
- obsolescence
- legal limits imposed on the use of the asset.

The standard uses the term 'derecognition' to cover the situation where an asset is sold or is no longer providing any economic benefit to the company. The profit or loss on the disposal of any non-current asset is shown in the income statement.

The standard requires published accounts to include a schedule of non-current assets. A schedule of non-current assets includes the following information:

- opening and closing costs
- additions at cost
- disposals at cost
- revaluation adjustments
- opening and closing accumulated depreciation
- adjustments to depreciation arising from disposals
- depreciation of the year
- the net book value of the non-current assets at the beginning and end of the year.

Illustration 6: A schedule of non-current assets

Here is an example of a schedule of non-current assets.

Salz Ltd				
Schedule of non-current assets at 31 March 2015				
	Premises	Plant and machinery	Equipment	Total
	$000	$000	$000	$000
Cost				
At 1 April 2014	1 400	450	110	1 960
Revaluation	600	–	–	600
Additions	–	80	30	110
Disposals	–	–	(20)	(20)
At 31 March 2015	2 000	530	120	2 650
Depreciation				
At 1 April 2014	70	225	32	327
Revaluation	(70)	–	–	(70)
Provided in year	–	53	18	71
Disposals	–	–	(16)	(16)
At 31 March 2015	–	278	34	312
Net book value				
At 31 March 2015	2 000	252	86	2 338
At 1 April 2014	1 330	225	78	1 633

Key terms

Recoverable amount: the higher of an asset's fair value and its value in use.

Fair value: the amount for which an asset could be sold net of any selling costs.

Value in use: the estimated value of future cash flows.

Impairment loss: the loss arising when an asset's value has decreased so that its recoverable amount is less than its carrying amount.

IAS 36 Impairment of assets

The purpose of this standard is to ensure that non-current assets are not shown in financial statements at a value higher than what is called the recoverable amount. This term is used to mean the higher of an asset's fair value (the amount for which the asset could be sold less any selling costs) or value in use (the total of estimated future cash flows). An impairment loss arises where the recoverable amount is lower than the carrying amount. The standard requires any such loss to be recorded in the income statement.

The standard requires all non-current assets to be reviewed at the date of each statement of financial position in order to establish whether any impairment has occurred. This requirement includes goodwill.

Illustration 7: Calculating an impairment loss

At 31 December 2014 the following information was available about a company's motor vehicles.

Valuations	Definition	Amount
Carrying amount	Net book value	$146 000
Fair value	Value if sold less any selling costs	$139 000
Value in use	Estimated future cash flows	$135 000
Recoverable amount	Higher of fair value and value in use	$139 000

The recoverable amount for the motor vehicles at 31 December 2014 is less than the carrying amount by $7000 (i.e. $146 000 less $139 000). Therefore, there is an impairment loss of $7000 to be recorded in the company's income statement for the year ended 31 December 2014.

There are a number of signs that the impairment of a non-current asset may have occurred. For example, the asset:

- is no longer in use
- has been damaged
- has become obsolete
- has suffered a decline in its market value.

IAS 37 Provisions, contingent liabilities and contingent assets

The purpose of the standard is to provide guidelines for ensuring that users of published financial statements are properly informed of the details concerning liabilities, contingent liabilities, provisions and contingent assets.

The standard provides a detailed definition of the familiar accounting term 'liabilities' and emphasises that a liability:

- arises from past events
- is a current obligation of the company
- is expected to result in an outflow of resources (i.e. payment) on settlement.

So the purchase of goods on credit from a supplier will give rise to a liability of a known value (i.e. the amount stated on the invoice) and is shown on the statement of financial position.

Provisions are defined as a liability of uncertain timing or amount. In other words, it is known that an obligation exists but the amount can only be estimated.

The standard requires that provisions must be shown as a liability in the financial statements where:

Key terms

Provision: a liability of uncertain timing or amount.
Liability: a present obligation arising from past events which will lead to a payment being made.

Key terms

Contingent liability: a possible obligation arising from past events that depends on some future uncertain event outside the business's control.

Contingent asset: a possible asset arising from past events that depends on some future uncertain event outside the business's control.

- the obligation arises from past events
- the amount of the obligation can be reliably estimated
- payment is probable (a higher than 50 per cent chance).

A contingent liability arises from past events when:

- the obligation is possible (less than 50 per cent chance)
- the amount of the obligation cannot be reliably estimated
- the obligation is dependent on uncertain future events.

In all cases a contingent liability is a possible obligation. The standard requires contingent liabilities to be disclosed in a note to the accounts. If the likelihood of a liability arising is regarded as remote then no disclosure is required.

A contingent asset is a possible asset that will arise from past events but only when certain future events occur which are not in the control of the business. Probable contingent assets must be disclosed as a note to the financial statements, but possible or remote contingent assets are not disclosed. As an example, a contingent asset would arise if a company was suing another business or individual and where, if the case was successful, the company would receive damages.

Illustration 8: Provisions, contingent liabilities and contingent assets

TXQ Wholesale Chemicals Ltd's financial year ended on 31 December 2014. In September 2014 an accident occurred involving some of the company's products and as a result the company was sued by a number of individuals.

Case 1: was decided in early December and the court requires the company to pay $18 000 in damages.

Case 2: had not been decided by 31 December 2014, but the company has been advised that it is probable the company will lose the case and be required to pay damages estimated at $15 000.

Case 3: will be brought before the courts in March 2015. The company has been advised that there is 25 per chance of the company losing the case and being required to pay damages estimated at $25 000.

The treatment of each of these situations in the financial statements at 31 December 2014 will be as follows.

Case	Treatment in the financial statements	Reason
1	Liability in statement of financial position	Current obligation which must be paid
2	Provision in statement of financial position	Probable liability; reliable estimate of amount
3	Contingent liability	Possible obligation (less than 50 per cent certainty) dependent on outcome of court case

Key terms

Intangible asset: an identifiable non-monetary asset without physical substance.

IAS 38 Intangible assets

An intangible asset is defined as an identifiable non-monetary asset without physical substance.

An intangible asset must have the following characteristics:

- It must be identifiable.
- It must be controlled by the entity.
- The entity must be able to obtain future economic benefits from the asset.

Intangible assets may be purchased from an external source or might be self-generated.

Intangible assets include the following:

- patented technology, e.g. computer software
- trademarks
- customer lists
- marketing rights
- franchise agreements.

An intangible asset can be recognised when:

- it is probable that the future economic benefits attributable to the asset will flow to the entity, and
- the cost of the asset can be reliably measured.

Where these criteria cannot be met then expenditure must treated as an expense in the income statement.

Research and development costs

Research expenditure arises from investigations that are conducted with the intention of gaining new scientific knowledge of a general nature. Research expenditure is regarded as an expense to be shown in the income statement on the grounds that it would be impossible to know whether any economic benefit will arise.

Development expenditure arises where knowledge is applied to the production of new or improved products. The treatment of development expenditure is based on the possibility that future economic benefit could arise for the business. Where this is the case development expenditure can be treated as an intangible asset (i.e. the expenditure can be capitalised) as long as:

- the project is capable of completion
- the business intends to complete the project leading to use or sale
- the business can demonstrate how the project will generate economic benefit.

The standard stipulates that the following cannot be regarded as intangible assets and that expenditure must be charged to the income statement:

- internally generated brands, customer lists, etc.
- internally generated goodwill
- start-up costs
- training costs
- advertising and promotional costs
- relocation costs.

Intangible assets must be valued at either cost or at valuation:

- **Cost:** the asset is shown in the statement of financial position at cost less accumulated amortisation (i.e. depreciation) and impairment losses.
- **Revaluation:** the asset is shown in the statement of financial position at a revalued amount based on its fair value less accumulated amortisation and impairment losses.

End-of-chapter questions

1 Identifying the correct standard

In each of the following situations identify the number of the standard which should be applied and the title of that standard.

	Situation	IAS number	IAS title
a	Accruals, going concern, consistency and materiality concepts must be applied		
b	A company has paid a significant amount to acquire some valuable technology patents		
c	The lower of cost and net realisable value must be used		
d	Financial statements must include comparative figures		
e	The useful life of an asset should take account of wear and tear		
f	A loss has occurred because the recoverable amount for some equipment is less than its carrying amount		
g	A statement of changes in equity must be published		
h	Machinery repair costs should be treated as an expense in the income statement		
i	The directors have chosen to use the reducing-balance method of depreciation		
j	Some research expenditure has been charged to a company's income statement		
k	A schedule of non-current assets must be included in the published accounts		

	Situation	IAS number	IAS title
l	Internally generated goodwill has been written off in the income statement		
m	The AVCO method may be used		
n	It is possible that a company may lose a court case in progress at the end of the financial year and be required to pay damages		
o	At the end of a financial year a company's premises were damaged by a flood. The insurance company valued the extent of the damage shortly after the preparation of the financial statements.		

2 Purpose of international accounting standards

Explain why international accounting standards are important to a shareholder in a limited company. Illustrate your answer by referring to IAS 1 Presentation of financial statements.

3 Applying international accounting standards

The following situations have arisen affecting the financial affairs of Hexamon Ltd. The company's year end was 28 February 2015.

- **a** The company owns some machinery that has been under-used during the financial year ended on 28 February 2015 because of a fall in demand. The machinery has a net book value of $32 000. The financial director assessed the machinery's value in use to be $20 000; it appears the machinery could be sold for $23 000 but the company would have to pay selling expenses of $4000.
- **b** The company is being sued by a customer, MRB Ltd, for $25 000. The court case began in early January 2015 but no judgment had been made at the time of preparing the financial statements. The company's legal adviser has said that it is possible MRB Ltd will win its case and receive the amount mentioned.
- **c** On 28 February 2015 the directors agreed to propose a dividend of $0.05 per share on the company's 1 million ordinary shares of $1 each on the profits for the year ended 28 February 2015.

For each situation:

- **i** state the international accounting standard that should be applied (number and name)
- **ii** explain the main requirements of the accounting standard which apply to situation
- **iii** state how the situation should be treated in the published financial statements of the company for the year ended 28 February 2015.

4 Applying international accounting standards

The following situations have arisen affecting the financial affairs of MQP Ltd. The company's year end was 31 December 2014. The company's financial statements were authorised by the directors for publication on 31 March 2015.

- **a** The company's inventory at 31 December 2014 included 420 items that cost $12 per item which would normally sell at $20 each. It has been noticed that 46 items have been damaged. Fourteen items have relatively little damage and could be sold for $14 each. The other damaged items, however, will require some expenditure in order to put them in a saleable condition. It is estimated that a total of $128 will need to be spent before these items can also be sold for $14 each.
- **b** The company's statement of financial position at 31 December 2014 included a trade receivable who owed the company $7200. On 24 February 2014 the company was notified that the trade receivable had been declared bankrupt and would not be able to pay any of the amount due.
- **c** In November 2014 the company was sued by a customer. The court case has yet to be decided, but the company's legal adviser has warned that it is probable that the company will lose the case and damages are reliably estimated to amount to $14 800.

For each situation:

- **i** state the international accounting standard that should be applied (number and name)
- **ii** explain the main requirements of the accounting standard which apply to situation
- **iii** state how the situation should be treated in the published accounts of the company for the year ended 31 December 2014.

Learning objectives

In this chapter you will learn:

- about the role of the auditor
- about the role of directors and their responsibilities to shareholders
- about the term 'stewardship'
- about the importance of 'true and fair view' in the preparation of financial statements.

1.1.5: Auditing and stewardship of limited companies

Introduction

An important feature of larger limited companies is the fact that the owners (the shareholders) do not take part in the day-to-day running of the business. Instead shareholders appoint directors to manage the company's affairs on their behalf. This separation of ownership and control leads to the idea of stewardship and the idea that directors have a duty to manage the business's resources to the best of their ability on behalf of the shareholders. It also leads to some important legal requirements to ensure that the interests of shareholders are safeguarded.

The role of auditors

The law requires that limited companies have their accounts audited annually. (It should be noted that usually smaller companies are exempt from this requirement.) It is the shareholders who appoint the auditors, not the directors; it is to the shareholders that the auditors report every year. This legal requirement is designed to ensure that shareholders can have confidence that the stewards of the company (the directors) are giving them a true and fair view of the company's affairs, so that they are in a good position to make valid decisions about their investment.

The law requires auditors to do the following:

- Provide an independent check of the company's accounting records. In order for this to happen, it is important that auditors are not influenced in any way by the directors of the company.
- Carry out their duties objectively, so that their opinions and judgments are based on evidence that they have been able to verify during the course of their work.
- Ensure that the accounts comply with current accounting standards and the requirements of the Companies Acts.
- Ensure that the accounts provide shareholders with a true and fair view of the company's financial position.
- Ensure that the accounts are free from significant errors.

In order to carry out their responsibilities, the law requires auditors to be suitably qualified and to be given reasonable access to the company's accounting records and to have questions answered within a reasonable time.

Internal and external audits

The independent audit described above is sometimes referred to as an *external audit*. It is also usual for large-scale organisations to carry out *internal audits*. Internal audits are conducted by the organisation's own

Getting it right

It is a common error to think that auditors actually prepare the financial statements. This is the responsibility of the directors, not the auditors.

staff whose main responsibility is to report on whether the company's own financial regulations have been followed. Internal auditors report to the management of the organisation for which they work.

The cost of an external audit, which can be considerable in the case of a large public company, is charged to the company's income statement along with other expenses.

True and fair

At the core of the responsibilities of auditors and directors is the duty to ensure that shareholders are given a true and fair view of the company's financial position. This is known as the true and fair concept.

The law requires auditors to confirm whether or not the financial statements represent a true and fair view of the company's affairs. This is normally taken to mean that the financial statements:

- agree with the company's records
- are free from bias
- include information about all of the company's assets and all of the liabilities
- include assets that are valued in accordance with international accounting standards and that the values arise from the application of relevant accounting concepts
- include an income statement which reports a profit or loss that follows legal requirements and that is in accordance with international accounting standards
- include a fair assessment of the company's cash flows in accordance with international accounting standards
- are prepared so that there is consistency from one year to the next.

The assumption is that if financial statements are comparable, reliable, relevant and understandable, they will present a true and fair picture of the company's financial affairs.

It is sometimes thought that auditors should be able to confirm that no fraud has taken place. Checking for fraud is not the duty of auditors. However, should the audit process reveal anything suspicious (e.g. alterations to source documents) the auditors must, of course, bring this to the attention of the shareholders.

Key term

Annual report: a document summarising a limited company's activities which must be sent to shareholders each year. It is often referred to as the 'annual report and accounts'.

The auditors' report

A company's annual report must contain a report from the auditors. Usually this is quite a short statement. The most important part of the report is the auditors' opinion that the financial statements:

- give a true and fair view of the company's affairs
- have been properly prepared in accordance with international accounting standards

Key terms

Unqualified auditors' report: where the auditors are of the opinion that the financial statements give a true and fair view.

Qualified auditors' report: where the auditors express some reservations which mean that they have concluded that the financial statements do not give a true and fair view.

- comply with the requirements of the Companies Acts.

A statement like this, where there are no reservations, is called an unqualified report.

The report will also include the following:

- a note that clarifies the roles of the auditors and directors
- a statement about the scope of the audit which explains how it was conducted and confirming that the audit provides a sound basis for the auditors' opinion.

Where applicable the report will include any reservations the auditors may have, for example:

- if there are significant inconsistencies and/or errors in the financial statements
- if the financial statements are misleading in any way
- if the directors' report contains statements which are inconsistent with the auditors' view of the company's affairs.

Where a report contains reservations, it is referred to as a qualified report.

The role of the directors

Directors are appointed by the shareholders. Their main responsibilities to shareholders include the following:

- The maintenance of proper accounting records which enable financial statements to be prepared in accordance with the requirements of the Companies Acts and international accounting standards.
- Preparing annual financial statements, i.e.:
  - income statement
  - statement of changes in equity
  - statement of financial position
  - statement of cash flows.
- Taking care of the company's resources.
- Deciding the company's accounting policies.
- Implementing suitable accounting controls.
- Confirming that accounting standards have been followed.
- Supporting the work of auditors by providing reasonable access to accounting records and responding to questions raised.
- Preparing an annual report to shareholders on the way in which they have managed the company, i.e. how they have discharged their stewardship role (the directors' report).

The directors' report

The Companies Act 2006 requires that the directors of the company prepare a report at the end of the financial year for submission to the shareholders. The main contents of the directors' report are as follows:

- A statement of the affairs of the company, which may include non-monetary issues not highlighted by the financial statements.
- The principal activities of the company and any significant changes made during the year.
- Details of significant events that have occurred since the financial year end.
- Details of significant future events.
- A statement of employees' involvement in:
  - information
  - consultation
  - common awareness.
- Details of own shares purchased or charged.
- Non-current assets:
  - significant changes
  - any difference between book value and market value of land.
- Proposed dividends.
- Transfers to reserves.
- A statement of policy on:
  - the health and safety of employees
  - disabled persons.
- Details of political and charitable donations.
- Details of any directors serving during the year, including:
  - name
  - interests in the shares of the company
  - share options granted or exercised during the year.
- Details of the company's policy on the payment of suppliers.
- Information on research and development being carried out.

The role and duties of shareholders

Shareholders delegate the responsibility for running a company to the directors. It follows that the main duty of a shareholder is to elect directors. Through their voting powers shareholders can re-elect directors or remove them when not satisfied. In some situations shareholders may be asked at the annual general meeting to give consent to directors' actions (e.g. changing the name of the company).

It is important to note that shareholders do not normally have the right to interfere in the day-to-day management of the company, or have access to the company's accounting records (other than the annual report).

Shareholders are also required by law to appoint auditors except where the law gives exemption to small companies.

It is important to remember that directors may also be shareholders in a company.

End-of-chapter questions

1 True or false?

Indicate whether each of the following statements is true or false by placing a tick (✓) in the appropriate column.

		True	False
a	Auditors are appointed by directors.		
b	Auditors report to the shareholders.		
c	If auditors provide a qualified report it means they do not believe the accounts show a true and fair view of the company's financial affairs.		
d	Shareholders elect directors.		
e	Auditors must ensure that the company's accounts are free from fraud.		
f	Directors must include a report on their management of the company as part of the annual report.		
g	Auditors prepare the financial statements.		
h	Shareholders have the right to look at the day-to-day accounting records of the company in which they have invested.		
i	Auditors must act independently.		

2 The importance of auditors

Explain why it is a legal requirement that shareholders appoint auditors.

3 The role of auditors and directors

At a recent annual general meeting of the Yushui Company Ltd, the shareholders reappointed the directors of the company and the firm of Kashchei & Co was appointed as auditors for the next financial year.

In regard to the financial records of the company, explain the responsibilities to the shareholders of:

a the directors

b the auditors.

4 **Meaning of stewardship**
Explain what is meant by the term 'stewardship' in respect of a company's financial affairs.

5 **Meaning of true and fair**
Describe three aspects of a company's financial statements which would confirm that they represent a true and fair view of the company's financial affairs.

6 **Reservations in an auditors' report**
Give two reasons why auditors might express reservations in their report to shareholders.

7 **Directors and auditors**
In what ways are directors required to help auditors in their role?

8 **The auditors' report**
- a Explain the distinction between a qualified and unqualified auditors' report.
- b Describe three important elements of an unqualified auditors' report.

Section 1.2: Business purchase and merger

Key concepts

When preparing the accounting records for a business purchase or merger, it is particularly important to apply the **business entity** concept as transactions will need to be recorded in the accounting systems of each business entity involved in the purchase or merger. In other words, the records required must be produced from the perspective of each organisation involved in the situation. All of the other key concepts will apply to the detailed records of each purchase or merger: **duality, consistency, true and fair view, money measurement**.

1.2.1: Business purchase and merger

Learning objectives

In this chapter you will learn:

- how to record the purchase of a sole trader by a limited company
- how to calculate any positive or negative goodwill arising on the purchase of a business
- how to record the purchase of a business by using cash; issuing shares; or issuing shares, issuing debentures and using cash.
- how to record the purchase of a partnership by a limited company
- how to record a merger by means of combining or purchasing assets and liabilities of unincorporated businesses to form a partnership or limited company
- how to calculate the return on an investment and evaluate a business before acquiring it.

A limited company purchasing another business

A business can be sold as a going concern to another business, which will continue to trade. The one remaining business is, therefore, made up of the combined assets of both businesses. This can be done using a variety of methods.

Purchase consideration

If a company purchases a going concern, the purchase price for the business can consist of:

- cash
- issuing shares in the purchasing company to the original owners
- issuing debentures in the purchasing company to the original owners
- any combination of the above.

The general principles are:

1. The assets bought are often not stated at the same value in the purchasing limited company's books as they were stated in the selling business's books. This is because the assets have been revalued to arrive at an agreed current valuation between the parties. This is often referred to as their fair value. A fair value reflects the assets' condition at the date.
2. The price paid for a business is called the purchase consideration. If there is difference between the net assets purchased and the purchase consideration, it is recorded in the books of the purchasing company. If purchase consideration is greater than the value of the net assets, this is referred to as positive goodwill. If, on the other hand, purchase consideration is less than the value of the net assets, this is referred to as negative goodwill.

Key terms

Purchase consideration: the price paid for a business.

Positive goodwill: the difference between the value of the net assets and the price paid for the business, when the latter is greater.

Goodwill

When a business is bought as a going concern, the purchasing business will often pay more for the business than the value of the net assets taken over. This is called positive goodwill and is recorded as an intangible non-current asset.

Goodwill could arise because:

- a large number of customers will continue to trade with the new owner
- the business has a good reputation
- the business workforce is experienced, efficient and reliable
- the business is situated in a good location
- the business has long-term, good relationships with its suppliers.

Goodwill does not necessarily exist within a business. If a business has a bad reputation, with an inefficient workforce, then the owner will not be likely to achieve the value of the net assets when the business is sold. If the purchase consideration is less than the value of the net assets, then negative goodwill arises and is often recorded as a capital reserve.

A limited company purchasing a sole trader

Different ways of purchasing a sole trader

This is the simplest form of business purchase and can be completed by one of the following methods:

- **Paying cash for the net assets:** The amount of cash can exceed the value of the net assets, which will then be recorded as goodwill within the statement of financial position. This is shown in Illustration 1.
- **Issuing shares or debentures for the value of the net assets:** If the value of the shares or debentures exceeds the value of the net assets, then once again goodwill has arisen and should be recorded as an intangible non-current asset. This is shown in Illustration 2.
- **A combination of the above:** This is shown in Illustration 3.

Illustration 1: Purchasing a sole trader using cash

The directors of Everyday Ltd decide to purchase the business of M Hardy on 1 May 2014.

The statements of financial position of the two businesses before the purchase are as follows.

	M Hardy ($)	Everyday Ltd ($)
Machinery	17 000	110 000
Inventory	13 000	50 000
Cash and cash equivalents		90 000
	30 000	250 000
Capital/share capital	30 000	200 000
Retained earnings		50 000
	30 000	250 000

The purchase consideration has been agreed as $60 000 cash.

The agreed values of the assets taken over are:

Inventory $10 000

Machinery $30 000

The goodwill is, therefore, calculated as

$60 000 – ($10 000 + $30 000) = $20 000

The new statement of financial position for Everyday Ltd after the purchase will now be:

	Everyday Ltd ($)
Goodwill	20 000
Machinery ($110 000 + $30 000)	140 000
Inventory ($50 000 + $10 000)	60 000
Cash and cash equivalents ($90 000 – $60 000)	30 000
	250 000
Share capital	200 000
Retained earnings	50 000
	250 000

You will notice that in this instance the total of the statement remains the same as there has only been a movement in assets.

Getting it right

Be careful and remember to calculate the goodwill on the revalued amounts for the net assets and not on the net asset values within the last statement of financial position.

Illustration 2: Purchasing a sole trader by issuing shares

If the purchase had been made by issuing 50 000 shares at $1 each at a premium of 50 per cent, then the total purchase consideration would have been $75 000. If the assets are valued at $40 000, this leaves goodwill at $35 000. An increase in both share capital of $50 000 and share premium of $25 000 will arise.

The statement of financial position should then be:

	Everyday Ltd ($)
Goodwill	35 000
Machinery ($110 000 + $30 000)	140 000
Inventory ($50 000 + $10 000)	60 000
Cash and cash equivalents	90 000
	325 000
Share capital (200 000 + 50 000 × $1)	250 000
Share premium (50 000 × 0.05)	25 000
Retained earnings	50 000
	325 000

In this instance the total of the statement has increased by $75 000 because of the issue of shares.

Illustration 3: Purchasing a sole trader by issuing shares, issuing debentures and using cash

If the purchase consideration had been the issue of 10 000 shares of $1 each at a premium of 40 per cent, $30 000 of 7 per cent debentures and $40 000 in cash, then the goodwill would have been $14 000 (share capital) + $30 000 (debentures) + $40 000 (cash) = $84 000 – $40 000 = $44 000

The statement of financial position should, therefore, be as follows.

	Everyday Ltd ($)
Goodwill	44 000
Machinery ($110 000 + $30 000)	140 000
Inventory ($50 000 + $10 000)	60 000
Cash and cash equivalents ($90 000 – $40 000)	50 000
	294 000
Share capital (200 000 + 10 000 × $1)	210 000
Share premium (10 000 × 0.04)	4 000
Retained earnings	50 000
	264 000
7% debentures	30 000
	294 000

In this instance, the total of the statement has increased by $14 000 because of the issue of shares.

Use of temporary accounts

In all of the previous illustrations it has been assumed that all of the transactions happen at the same time. However, a temporary account can be opened and then closed once the purchase consideration has been completed. This account shows the transactions with the sole trader. In Illustration 3, the temporary account will be as follows.

M Hardy			
	$		$
Purchase consideration		Assets taken over	
Share capital	10 000	Machinery	30 000
Share premium	4 000	Inventory	10 000
Debentures	30 000	Goodwill	44 000
Cash	40 000		
	84 000		84 000

This personal account is sometimes replaced by a business purchase account.

Taking over liabilities as well as assets

Sometimes a company taking over a sole trader business not only pays for the assets but also assumes responsibility for paying the trade payables.

Illustration 4: Taking over responsibility for the trade payables

The following information is available for a sole trader before the business is purchased by a limited company:

- premises valued at $500 000
- inventory valued at $40 000
- trade payables $30 000.

The purchase consideration is $560 000 cash and the company has also agreed to pay off the trade payables in full.

The total cash paid for business is, in effect, $560 000 + $30 000 = $590 000

The goodwill is, therefore, $590 000 – ($500 000 + $40 000) = $50 000

A limited company purchasing a partnership

Link

There is more about realisation accounts in AS Level Chapter 1.4.3B Dissolution of partnerships.

The entries to record the purchase of a partnership are very similar to those of a sole trader, with the exception of a personal account for each partner.

In the partnership's books the process is:

- The partnership is dissolved by using a realisation account.
- The total purchase consideration is credited to the realisation account and debited to a personal account in the name of the company.

In the company's books the process is:

- The new company's records are drawn up after the purchase, including details of goodwill, if any, and the payments made to each partner.

Illustration 5: The purchase of a partnership by a limited company

Bob and Clark are in partnership, sharing profits and losses equally. They decide to sell the partnership to Dodger Ltd for $120 000. The purchase consideration is $20 000 in cash, $60 000 in debentures and 10 000 in $1 ordinary shares.

The statement of financial position for Dodger Ltd before the purchase was as follows.

	Dodger Ltd
	($)
Net assets	765 000
500 000 $1 ordinary shares	500 000
Share premium	50 000
Revaluation reserve	100 000
Retained earnings	115 000
	765 000

The statement of financial position for Bob and Clark Partnership before the purchase was as follows.

	Bob and Clark partnership $
Net assets	95 000
Capital accounts:	
Bob	55 000
Clark	40 000
	95 000

The company's statement of financial position after the purchase of Bob and Clark partnership would be as follows.

	Dodger Ltd
	($)
Net assets ($765 000 – $20 000 + $120 000)	865 000
	865 000
510 000 $1 ordinary shares (500 000 + 10 000)	510 000
Share premium ($50 000 + $30 000)	80 000
Revaluation reserve	100 000
Retained earnings	115 000
	805 000
Debentures	60 000
	865 000

The 10 000 shares are worth the difference between the purchase consideration and the value of the cash + debentures:

$$120\,000 - (20\,000 + 60\,000) = 40\,000$$

Each share is, therefore, worth $\frac{40\,000}{10\,000}$ = $4 each

This is made up of $1 nominal value and $3 share premium.

Partnership's books of account

The realisation account used to calculate any profit or loss on the dissolution of the partnership is as follows.

Realisation account			
	$		$
Net assets	95 000	Purchase consideration	120 000
Profit on dissolution: Bob 50%	12 500		
Profit on dissolution: Clark 50%	12 500		
	120 000		120 000

The capital accounts recording the dissolution of the partnership are as follows.

Capital accounts					
	Bob	Clark		Bob	Clark
	$	$		$	$
Shares 50:50	20 000	20 000	Balance b/d	55 000	40 000
Debentures	30 000	30 000	Profit on realisation	12 500	12 500
Cash	17 500	2 500			
	67 500	52 500		67 500	52 500

The amount owed by the company to the partnership and the settlement is shown as follows.

Dodger Ltd			
	$		$
Realisation account	120 000	Bank	20 000
		Debentures	60 000
		Shares (10 000 shares)	40 000
	120 000		120 000

The final cash payments to the partners are recorded as follows.

Cash and cash equivalents			
	$		$
Dodger Ltd	20 000	Capital account: Bob	17 500
		Capital account: Clark	2 500
	20 000		20 000

Illustration 6: A more complex example

Rachel and Peter are in partnership, sharing profits and losses equally. R & P Ltd is a company formed to take over the partnership business on 1 November 2014.

The terms of the sale of the partnership business to R & P Ltd are as follows.

1 All the assets and liabilities of the partnership are to be taken over by the company except for the loan from Peter. Goodwill will be shown in the company's books of account. The following asset revaluations will be made.

	$
Non-current assets	85 000
Inventory	31 000
Trade receivables	21 650

2 The purchase consideration has been agreed at $170 000. This will be settled as follows: $20 000 8 per cent debenture stock and 100 000 ordinary shares of $1 each issued as fully paid. Both the debenture stock and the shares will be issued to Rachel and Peter in proportion to the balances on their capitals at 31 October 2014.

3 The net amount due to, or due from, each partner will be settled between the partners privately.

4 After purchasing the partnership business, the company will issue for cash 20 000 ordinary shares of $1 each to their friend, Dillon, on the same terms as those issued to Rachel and Peter.

The statement of financial position before the acquisition of the partnership by the newly formed company R & P Ltd is as follows.

Rachel and Peter
Statement of financial position at 31 October 2014

	$	$
Non-current assets at net book value		60 000
Current assets		
Inventory	43 000	
Trade receivables	22 000	
Bank	19 650	
		84 650
		144 650
Financed by		
Capital accounts		
Rachel	60 000	
Peter	40 000	
		100 000

Current accounts		
Rachel	4 000	
Peter	(650)	
		3 350
Non-current liabilities		
Loan from Peter		20 000
Current liabilities		
Trade payables		21 300
		144 650

Partnership books of account

The following accounts record the dissolution of the partnership.

Realisation			
Dr			Cr
	$		$
Net assets ($144 650 – $21 300)	123 350	Purchase consideration	170 000
Profit on realisation	46 650		
	170 000		170 000

Capitals					
	Rachel $	Peter $		Rachel $	Peter $
Current account		650	Balances b/f	60 000	40 000
Debentures (3:2)	12 000	8 000	Current account	4 000	–
Shares*	90 000	60 000	Loan account	–	20 000
Final settlement in cash**	–	14 675	Profit on realisation	23 325	23 325
			Final settlement in cash**	14 675	–
	102 000	83 325		102 000	83 325

* 100 000 shares of $1 each are issued as part of the settlement of the purchase consideration. The amount to be settled in shares is purchase price $170 000 less debenture stock $20 000. Therefore, the value of the shares is $150 000, i.e. the shares are issued at a premium of $0.50.

** The capital accounts close as each partner makes a final settlement privately. In this case Rachel pays Peter $14 675.

R & P Ltd			
Dr			**Cr**
	$		**$**
Realisation: purchase consideration	170 000	Capitals: debenture stock	20 000
		Capitals: shares	150 000
	170 000		170 000

Limited company's books of account

The company's statement of position after the completion of all the transactions will be as follows.

Notes:

Goodwill is calculated as follows: Purchase consideration less net current assets taken over at valuation, i.e.:

	$	$	$
Purchase consideration			170 000
Net current assets	85 000		
Inventory	31 000		
Trade receivables	21 650		
Bank	19 650		
		157 300	
Less trade payables		(21 300)	
			(136 000)
Goodwill			34 000

R & P Ltd Statement of financial position at 1 November 2014		
	$	**$**
Non-current assets		
Intangibles: goodwill		34 000
Tangibles at valuation		85 000
		119 000
Current assets		
Inventory	31 000	
Trade receivables	21 650	
Cash and cash equivalents ($19 650 + cash from Dillon $30 000)	49 650	
		102 300
		221 300

Financed by		
Share capital: 120 000 shares of $1 each		
(100 000 shares to Rachel and Peter; 20 000 shares to Dillon)		120 000
Share premium (120 000 × $0.50 premium)		60 000
		180 000
Non-current liabilities		
Debentures		20 000
Current liabilities		
Trade payables		21 300
		221 300

Getting it right

Remember always to state the number, nominal value and type of shares issued within the statement of financial position.

The merger of businesses

A merger is the creation of a new business by combining two businesses. Risks and benefits are shared within the new business and no one business is dominant. All profits from the new business are shared.

Illustration 7: The merger of two sole traders to form a partnership

Two sole traders, J Smith and B Brown, decide to merge and form a partnership. Their capital contribution is agreed at the value of their net assets.

Their statement of financial position before the merger was:

	J Smith	**B Brown**
	$	**$**
Machinery	47 000	190 000
Motor vehicle	0	20 000
Inventory	23 000	40 000
Bank	0	90 000
	70 000	340 000
Capital	50 000	240 000
Profit and loss	5 000	50 000
	55 000	290 000
Loan	10 000	50 000
Bank overdraft	5 000	–
	70 000	340 000

Assets are revalued:

	J Smith $	B Brown $
Machinery	55 000	240 000
Inventory	21 000	34 000

B Brown takes the motor vehicle for his own use at the book value of $20 000. Each partner will take responsibility for his own loans and these are not to be brought into the partnership.

The statement of financial position of the partnership after the merger is as follows.

	Smith and Brown $
Machinery ($240 000 + $55 000)	295 000
Inventory ($21 000 + $34 000)	55 000
Bank ($90 000 – $5 000)	85 000
	435 000
Capital: Smith ($55 000 + $21 000 – $5 000)	71 000
Capital: Brown ($240 000 + $34 000 + $90 000)	364 000
	435 000

Getting it right

Workings can be shown within the answer as in the illustration. It is recommended that they are shown in brackets to distinguish them from the final answers.

Illustration 8: The merger of two sole traders to form a limited company

Smith and Brown, from the previous illustration, decide to merge to form Smown Ltd instead of a partnership. Each of them will receive two ordinary shares for each $1 of capital invested.

The statement of financial position for the new limited company would, therefore, be:

	Smown Ltd $
Machinery	295 000
Inventory	55 000
Cash and cash equivalents	85 000
	435 000
870 000 ordinary shares of $0.50 each	435 000

Smith would receive 71 000 × 2 = 142 000 shares

Brown would receive 364 000 × 2 = 728 000 shares

Link

There is more about the treatment of goodwill in partnership accounts in AS Level Chapter 1.4.3A Partnerships: preparation of accounts.

Illustration 9: The merger of a partnership business and a sole trader business

Samad and Tariq are in partnership sharing profits and losses: Samad 70 per cent and Tariq 30 per cent.

On 1 March 2015 they merged their business with the business owned by Kaylee, who is a sole trader.

It was agreed that in the new business profits and losses would be shared: Samad 50 per cent, Tariq 25 per cent and Kaylee 25 per cent.

The statements of financial position for each business immediately prior to the merger were as follows.

Statements of financial position at 28 February 2015

	Samad and Tariq	Kaylee
	$	$
Non-current assets at net book value	180 000	90 000
Current assets		
Inventory	27 000	16 000
Trade receivables	17 000	9 000
Cash at bank		1 000
Total assets	224 000	116 000
Capital accounts		
Samad	140 000	
Tariq	70 000	
Kaylee		110 000
Current liabilities		
Trade payables	11 000	6 000
Bank overdraft	3 000	
Total capital and liabilities	224 000	116 000

The terms of the merger were as follows.

1 The goodwill of each business was agreed as: Samad and Tariq $42 000; Kaylee $28 000. No goodwill account is maintained in the books of the new business.

2 It was agreed to take over all of Kaylee's assets, but that non-current assets were revalued at $105 000 and inventory at $13 000. Kaylee agreed to settle her business's trade payables from her private resources.

3 The following revaluations were agreed for the assets of the business owned by Samad and Tariq: non-current assets $220 000, inventory $20 000.

4 It was agreed that the total of the partners' capitals should be $400 000 in the new business and that the balances of the partners' capital accounts should be in the same ratio as the profit and loss sharing ratio. It was agreed that this would be put into effect by each partner transferring funds to the business from his or her private resources or by withdrawing funds from the business's bank account.

5 It was agreed that the books of the partnership would continue and that the new business would be called STK.

The following need to be prepared:

- the capital accounts of the partners in the new business at 1 March 2015
- the statement of financial position of the new business at 1 March 2015.

These are prepared using the following steps.

Step 1: Review what will be transferred from the sole trader business to the merged business.

Kaylee will be transferring the following to the new business.

	$
Goodwill	28 000
Non-current assets at valuation	105 000
Inventory	13 000
Trade receivables	9 000
Cash at bank	1 000
Kaylee's capital (before writing off goodwill)	156 000

Alternatively, it is possible to work out the capital (before writing off goodwill) that Kaylee will transfer to the new business as follows.

	$
Capital before merger	110 000
Increase in value of non-current assets	15 000
Decrease in value of inventory	(3 000)
Goodwill	28 000
Trade payables settled privately by Kaylee	6 000
Kaylee's capital (before writing off goodwill)	156 000

Note: The fact that Kaylee pays off her business's trade payables is the equivalent of her introducing additional capital into the business.

Step 2: Before the merger of the partnership of Samad and Tariq with the business owned by Kaylee, calculate the effect of the revaluations (but before writing off goodwill).

	$
Goodwill	42 000
Increase in value of non-current assets	40 000
Decrease in value of inventory	(7 000)
Revaluation surplus (before writing off goodwill)	75 000

The revaluation surplus is shared between the partners in their profit and loss sharing ratio: 70 per cent for Tariq (70/100 × $75 000, i.e. $52 500); 30 per cent for Tariq (30/100 × $75 000, i.e. $22 500).

Step 3: Use the existing capital accounts of Samad and Tariq to prepare the capital accounts in the books of STK (as the books of the partnership will be used by the new business). It will be necessary to:

- add a column for the capital of Kaylee
- record the revaluation surplus in the capitals of Samad and Tariq
- write off the total goodwill of the new business as no goodwill account is to be shown in the books of account; the goodwill will be written off using the new profit and loss sharing ratio of the enlarged partnership (see W1 below)
- ensure that the closing balances of the capital accounts total $400 000 and are in the same ratio as the profit and loss sharing agreement (see W2)
- make entries for the withdrawal of funds from the bank account where a partner needs to reduce the balance on his or her capital account to meet the required value of the closing balance; or make entries to introduce additional capital where a partner needs to increase the balance in his or her capital account to meet the required value of the closing balance.

Dr		Capital accounts					Cr
	Samad	Tariq	Kaylee		Samad	Tariq	Kaylee
Goodwill written off (see W1)	35 000	17 500	17 500	Opening balance	140 000	70 000	
Bank			38 500	Capital introduced			156 000
Balances c/d	200 000	100 000	100 000	Revaluation surplus	52 500	22 500	
(see W2)				Bank	42 500	25 000	
	235 000	117 500	156 000		235 000	117 500	156 000
				Balances b/d	200 000	100 000	100 000

Notes:

W1: The total goodwill of the new business is $70 000 (i.e. $42 000 original partnership of Samad and Tariq + $28 000 sole trader business owned by Kaylee). The total goodwill is written off in the new profit and loss sharing ratio, i.e. Samad 50 per cent ($35 000), Tariq 25 per cent ($17 500) and Kaylee 25 per cent ($17 500).

W2: The closing balances of the capital accounts must total $400 000 and be in the new profit and loss sharing ratio, i.e. Samad 50 per cent ($200 000), Tariq 25 per cent ($100 000) and Kaylee 25 per cent ($100 000).

Step 4: Prepare the new business's statement of financial position immediately after the merger on 1 March 2015. This requires:

- combining the revaluation figures for the non-current assets and inventories
- combining the figures for trade receivables
- calculating a new bank balance based on the combined balances of the original businesses and the amounts paid in or withdrawn by the partners to achieve the required capital account balances
- including the trade payables from the original partnership business.

STK
Statement of financial position at 1 March 2015

	$	$
Non-current assets		325 000
Current assets		
Inventories	33 000	
Trade receivables	26 000	
Cash at bank (W3)	27 000	
		86 000
		411 000
Capital accounts		
Samad	200 000	
Tariq	100 000	
Kaylee	100 000	
		400 000
Current liabilities		
Trade payables		11 000
		411 000

W3: The updated balance of cash at bank is calculated as follows.

	$
Bank balance from original partnership	(3 000)
Bank balance from sole trader business	1 000
Additional capital introduced by Samad	42 500
Additional capital introduced by Tariq	25 000
Capital withdrawn by Kaylee	(38 500)
	27 000

Key term

Return on investment ratio: this measures the return on the funds invested by the owners.

Link

Other evaluation ratios are discussed in AS Level Chapter 1.5.1 Analysis and communication of accounting information to stakeholders and A Level Chapter 1.5.1 Further interpretation and analysis ratios

Using the return on investment ratio to evaluate a business before purchase

Various ratios can be used to evaluate a business before purchase. Obviously it is important to assess the profitability and liquidity of a business before going ahead with a purchase, but there is one ratio that is used solely by investors to calculate the return on their investment: the return on investment ratio (ROI). This is calculated as:

$$\frac{\text{Profit before interest and taxation}}{\text{Owner's investment}} \times 100$$

or alternatively:

$$\frac{\text{Operating profit less preference share dividends}}{\text{Owner's investment}} \times 100$$

This ratio can be used for owners within all types of business, such as sole traders, partnerships and limited companies.

Benefits and drawbacks of a potential merger

Businesses merge when there is agreement that they will be more successful as one entity rather than operating separately. In other words, mergers occur to gain economic advantages.

Mergers often occur where the strengths of one business overcome the weaknesses in the other business involved in the merger. This idea that the new organisation is stronger, i.e. greater than the 'sum of its parts', because the different parties complement each other is often referred to as 'synergy'. For example, one business may have a strong market base in one part of the country, but be less significant in another region, whereas the reverse is true of the second business. The merged businesses will have a strong market base in a wider geographical area. Merged businesses are likely to be perceived as more important and enjoy greater status and have greater market presence. Merged businesses gain the following advantages:

- **Economies of scale:** the merged businesses can operate more efficiently acting as one entity, saving on many running costs, particularly labour and accommodation costs. In the case of service departments, for example, it will be possible to have just one department for such services as finance, HR, marketing, technical support and maintenance. The savings in labour costs are likely to occur throughout the entire combined organisation. For example, a combined finance department needs just one finance director, as well as fewer accounting clerks arising from the elimination of inefficiencies and any duplication of activities. Economies of scale also apply to the production element of the two businesses, as any duplication of production activities can be eliminated. An important saving can occur in the cost of materials, as the enlarged business is likely to be able to negotiate larger discounts because it is possible to buy materials in greater bulk.
- **Research and development:** in some businesses much effort is put into the discovery of new products or technology. As a result of merger, businesses can pool the experience of their highly skilled research staff and potentially greatly improve the chances of successful outcomes to research.
- **Diversification:** as a result of a merger, it may be possible to offer a broader range of products or services which will result in an increased market share.
- **Vertical integration:** some businesses merge to ensure that there is control of both the production and sale of a product. For example, a manufacturing company could merge with its main distributor. As a result, the distributor's profit margin is eliminated and so costs are reduced.

There are, however, potential drawbacks when businesses merge that affect the businesses themselves, their staff and their customers.

- **Costs:** the costs of merging businesses can be high and may escalate during the negotiations prior to the merger taking place.
- **Higher prices:** these can arise because the merged business enjoys some degree of monopoly having reduced competition. This, of course, is a disadvantage for consumers.

- **Job losses:** mergers frequently result in staff cutbacks. This may not just be a major disadvantage for the employees affected, but may cost the merged business a considerable amount in redundancy payments and result in anxiety and a loss of morale among remaining staff.
- **Reduced staff motivation:** this can arise not just because the process of merger may be unsettling with some individuals losing their jobs, but also because larger organisations can find it more difficult to encourage and motivate employees who may feel somewhat alienated by the sheer scale of the new organisation.

End-of-chapter questions

1 **Preparing entries to close a partnership and sell to a limited company**
Marion and Nigel are in partnership, sharing profits and losses in the ratio 4 : 1, respectively. They sell the partnership assets to Opus Ltd for $210 000.
The purchase consideration is made up of $30 000 cash and 60 000 ordinary shares of $1 each. Shares in Opus Ltd are to be shared according to the profit-sharing ratio.

Prior to the sale of the partnership, the net assets were $100 000. The balances on the capital accounts were $60 000 (Marion) and $40 000 (Nigel).

Prepare ledger entries to close the partnership books of account.

2 **Preparing entries to close a partnership and sell to a limited company**
Xavier and Zeb are in partnership, sharing profits and losses in the ratio 3 : 1, respectively. They have agreed to sell their business to Young Ltd. The purchase consideration is $400 000, comprising $40 000 in cash, $120 000 in 8 per cent debentures and 80 000 ordinary shares of $0.20 each. The debentures are to be shared equally and the shares according to the profit-sharing ratio.

The statement of financial position prior to the purchase was:

	$
Net assets	280 000
Capital:	
Xavier	200 000
Zeb	80 000
	280 000

Prepare ledger entries to close the partnership books of account.

3 **Preparing entries to close a partnership and sell to a limited company**
Tom, Dick and Harry were in partnership, sharing profits and losses in the ratio 3 : 2 : 1, respectively. Business profits have been falling consistently over the past few years and the partners have decided to dissolve the partnership with effect from 31 December 2014.

The business was sold to Sally plc. The purchase consideration was $210 000, consisting of 100 000 ordinary shares of $0.50 each and $30 000 in 7 per cent debentures. The shares were divided in the profit-sharing ratio and the debentures were shared equally between the partners. The company took over the partnership's net assets with the exception of the bank account.

The statement of financial position of the partnership at 31 December 2014 was as follows.

	$	$
Non-current assets		
Premises at cost	70 000	
Machinery at cost	50 000	
Vehicles at cost	40 000	
		160 000
Current assets		
Inventory	8 000	
Trade receivables	10 000	
Bank	5 000	
		23 000
		183 000
Capital accounts		
Tom		110 000
Dick		50 000
Harry		21 000
		181 000
Current liabilities		
Trade payables		2 000
		183 000

Additional information at 31 December 2014:

- Dissolution expenses amounted to $1000.
- All cash transactions were processed through the business bank account.

Required

Prepare the following to show the closing entries in the partnership books of account:

a a realisation account to dissolve the partnership
b the partners' capital accounts
c a bank account
d the account of Sally plc.

4 Recording the dissolution of a partnership and preparing the statement of position of the new limited company

Ali, Broc and Cheema have been in partnership trading as Abche. They share profits and losses in the ratio 3 : 2 : 1. Gavin and Hanuko have been in partnership trading as Gavu. They share profits and losses equally.

At 31 March 2015 the summarised statement of financial position of both businesses was as follows.

	Abche	Gavu
	$	$
Premises	100 000	70 000
Machinery	35 000	13 000
Vehicles	78 000	–
Investments at cost	12 000	–
Inventory	10 000	5 000
Trade receivables	14 000	9 000
Balance at bank	8 500	4 000
	257 500	101 000
Less trade payables	7 500	6 000
	250 000	95 000
Less 8% loan from Cheema	30 000	
	220 000	
Capital accounts:		
Ali	100 000	
Broc	70 000	
Cheema	50 000	
Gavin	–	50 000
Hanuko	–	45 000
	220 000	95 000

The partners agreed to form a limited company, ABCOGH Ltd, to take over both businesses.

All Abche's assets were transferred to ABCOGH Ltd with the exception of three vehicles, investments, trade receivables and balance at bank.

All Gavu's assets were transferred to ABCOGH with the exception of trade receivables and balance at bank.

The agreed values of assets taken over by the company are:

	Abche	Gavu
	$	$
Premises	170 000	100 000
Machinery	30 000	10 000
The remaining vehicles	40 000	–
Inventory	9 000	5 000

The purchase consideration for Abche was $240 000 as follows:

- 57 000 7 per cent preference shares of $1 each to be distributed in profit-sharing ratios
- sufficient 6 per cent debenture stock to give Cheema the same return as he had received on his loan to the partnership
- the balance as ordinary shares of $1 at a premium of $0.30 per share distributed to the partners in proportion to their capital account balances at 31 March 2015.

Abche collected $12 900 cash from trade receivables. Trade payables accepted $7100 in full settlement of amounts due to them.

The three vehicles that have been used by the partners were taken over by them as follows.

Partner-agreed takeover price	
	$
Ali	10 000
Broc	7 500
Cheema	7 800

The investments at cost were purchased by Broc at an agreed value of $13 400.

The purchase consideration for Gavu was $134 000 as follows:

- 43 000 7 per cent preference shares of $1 each to be distributed equally.
- The balance as ordinary shares to be shared equally.

Costs involved in dissolving the Abche partnership amounted to $6400; costs to dissolve the Gavu partnership were $3100.

Gavu collected $7000 cash from trade receivables. Trade payables were paid the amounts due to them.

Required

a Prepare partnership capital accounts at 31 March 2015 for both businesses to show the closing entries in both sets of partnership books of account.

It was agreed that the issued ordinary share capital would be held as follows: Ali 30 per cent; Broc 10 per cent; Cheema 20 per cent; Gavin 20 per cent; Hanuko 20 per cent.

It was further agreed that the transfer price of any ordinary shares would be at $1.30 per share.

Required

b Calculate the number of ordinary shares received by each partner.

c Calculate the amounts of cash payable or receivable by each shareholder to achieve the required shareholding.

d Prepare a statement of financial position for ABCOGH Ltd at 31 March 2015 immediately after incorporation.

e Explain briefly one possible reason why the partners decided to change their business into a limited company.

Section 1.3: Consignment and joint venture accounts

Key concepts

The **business entity** concept is important in both consignment accounts and joint ventures as it is necessary to make entries in separate books of account and to see transactions from different points of view: consignor and consignee; each participant in the joint venture.

The other key concepts also apply: **true and fair view; duality (double entry)**; **consistency** and **money measurement**.

1.3.1: Consignment and joint venture accounts

Consignment accounts

Selling goods through an agent

Many businesses trading overseas choose to sell goods through an agent. The business selling goods in this way is referred to as the consignor. The agent receiving the goods is referred to as the consignee. In these situations the consignor can take advantage of the consignee's local knowledge and contacts, without the expense of establishing a separate branch.

The main features of consignment accounting are:

1 The consignor retains possession of the goods until they are sold by the consignee. This has important implications for the way consignment transactions are recorded.

2 It is usual for the consignor to send the consignee a pro-forma invoice. This document provides the consignee with detailed information about the goods in the consignment. Unlike an ordinary invoice it does not notify the consignee that any payment is due.

3 When the consignee sells goods an account sales is sent to the consignor. This document informs the consignor of the amount due from the consignee based on the sales proceeds less the consignee's expenses.

4 The consignee's reward for acting as an agent for the consignor is a commission based on the sale proceeds.

5 In some cases, the consignee agrees to take responsibility for any irrecoverable debts that may arise from the sale of goods. Where this arrangement is made, the consignee receives an additional reward called a del credere commission. Any irrecoverable debts that arise in these circumstances are a loss to the consignee and do not reduce the amount owed by the consignee to the consignor.

Consignor's accounting records

The consignor will use the following accounts to record transactions relating to a consignment:

- **Consignment outwards account:** to record the value of any goods sent to a consignee.
- **Consignment to (name of consignee) account:** to record all income and expenses relating to the consignment. The balance of this account represents the profit or loss on the consignment.
- **Consignee account:** the purpose of this personal account is to record the amount due from the consignee and settlements made by the consignee.

Learning objectives

In this chapter you will learn:

- about the main features of consignment accounts
- how to prepare the accounting records for consignments in the books of the seller and of the agent receiving the goods
- how to calculate the value of unsold goods held by the consignee
- about the main features of joint ventures
- how to record joint venture transactions in ledger accounts
- how to calculate the profit or loss for joint ventures.

Key terms

Consignor: the business selling goods through an agent.
Consignee: the agent receiving goods from the consignor.
Pro-forma invoice: document recording details of goods sent as a consignment. This document does not charge the consignee for the goods.
Account sales: document sent by the consignee to the consignor detailing sales proceeds and expenses incurred by the consignee.
Del credere commission: a commission charge by a consignee in return for taking responsibility for any irrecoverable debts arising from the sale of goods on consignment.

Illustration 1: The consignor's accounting records

Brackham Ltd recently sent a consignment of goods for sale to its agent, Krugel & Co in Durban, South Africa. The following details are available:

A 400 crates of goods at $80 per crate were sent to consignee.

B Brackham Ltd paid shipping costs $1700 and export duties $920 by cheque.

C Brackham Ltd received an account sales from Krugel & Co. The consignee reported that two cases of goods had been damaged in transit. However, all remaining cases were sold for $48 000; landing charges paid by consignee were $2450. The consignee had charged commission of 5 per cent and a del credere commission of 2 per cent.

D Brackham Ltd received the amount due from Krugel & Co.

BOOKS OF BRACKHAM LTD

Dr	Consignment outwards account				Cr
			A	Krugel & Co	32 000

Dr	Consignment to Krugel & Co, Durban				Cr
A	Consignment outwards	32 000	C	Krugel & Co:	
B	Bank:			Sale proceeds	48 000
	Shipping costs	1 700			
	Export duties	920			
C	Krugel & Co:				
	Landing charges	2 450			
	Commission (5%)	2 400			
	Del credere commission (2%)	960			
E	Income statement (profit)	7 570			
		48 000			48 000

Dr	Krugel & Co, Durban				Cr
C	Consignment, sales proceeds	48 000	C	Consignment expenses	
				Landing charges	2 450
				Commission	2 400
				Del credere commission	960
			D	Bank, net proceeds	42 190
		48 000			48 000

Getting it right

To avoid making incorrect entries in the ledger accounts, keep in mind the purpose of each account. For example, the 'consignment to *** account' is there to establish the profit or loss on the consignment, so it needs to include the income from the sale of goods and all the expenses relating to the consignment, whoever paid for them.

Notes:

1 The balance of the consignment account (E) represents a profit (or loss) on the consignment and is transferred to the consignor's income statement.

2 At the end of the consignor's financial year, the consignment outwards account is closed by transfer to the credit of the purchases account. This transfer ensures the consignor's income statement records the gross profit on goods sold other than on consignment as a separate record of profits on these goods appears in the consignor's books (the consignment account).

3 Any loss in the value of inventory is not recorded in the accounts. Any loss of inventory or damage to inventory will affect the profit on the consignment as the sales figure will be less than it would otherwise have been.

Consignee's accounting records

The consignee never owns the goods received on consignment, so the only accounting records required are as follows:

- **Personal account for consignor** to record the amount owing to the consignor
- **Commission account(s)** to record the income from the consignment.

Illustration 2: The consignee's accounting records

Based on the information in Illustration 1, the consignee's accounting records will be:

BOOKS OF KRUGEL & CO, DURBAN

Dr	Brackham Ltd				Cr
C	Bank, landing charges	2 450	C	Bank, gross proceeds	48 000
C	Commission	2 400			
C	Del credere commission	960			
D	Bank, net proceeds	42 190			
		48 000			48 000

Dr	Commission				Cr
			C	Brackham Ltd	2 400

Dr	Del credere commission				Cr
			C	Brackham Ltd	960

Note: The commission accounts will be closed at the end of the consignee's accounting year by transfer to the income statement.

Unsold inventory

It is highly likely that some part of a consignment will be unsold at the end of the consignor's financial year. This inventory is valued in strict accordance with accounting concepts. As a result, it is necessary to ensure that the value of the inventory takes account of not just the cost of the goods but also any expenses incurred that relate to those goods.

Illustration 3: Valuing unsold goods

Watson Doyle Ltd sent goods on consignment to Andrass & Co in Copenhagen, Denmark on 1 November 2014. The following details are available:

- The consignment consisted of 15 containers each costing $3600.
- Watson Doyle Ltd paid expenses of $5800 on the consignment.
- Andrass & Co paid customs charges $2400 and storage expenses of $1500 on the consignment.
- By 31 December 2014, Andrass & Co had sold 12 containers for $52 000 and charged commission of 5 per cent, i.e. $2600.

To calculate the cost of the unsold inventory it is necessary to take account of the cost of the unsold containers and an appropriate proportion of the expenses relating to the consignment. It is important to note that only those expenses relating to the whole consignment should be considered. This means that the commission of $2600 is not included in the calculation as it does not relate to the unsold items.

Calculation:

	$	$
Unsold containers (3 × $3 600)		10 800
Portion (1/5) of expenses which relate to the whole consignment		
Paid by Watson Doyle Ltd	5 800	
Paid by Andrass & Co		
Customs charges	2 400	
Storage expenses	1 500	
(i.e. 1/5 of total of these expenses)	9 700	1 940
Closing inventory valuation		12 740

Notes:

1 The process for calculating closing inventory demonstrates an application of the accruals concept, as it ensure that costs are matched to income for each accounting period.

2 In the consignor's accounts the closing inventory is recorded in the consignment account to ensure that the profit on the consignment for each financial period takes account of unsold inventory.

Illustration 4: Consignment account showing closing inventory

Dr	Consignment to Krugel & Co, Durban				Cr
	Consignment outwards	32 000		Andrass & Co	
	Bank:			Sale proceeds	52 000
	Expenses	5 800		(12 containers sold)	
	Andrass & Co			Balance c/d	
	Customs duties	2 400		(3 unsold containers)	12 740
	Storage charges	1 500			
	Commission	2 600			
	Income statement (profit)	20 440			
		64 740			64 740
	Balance b/d	12 740			

Notes:

The closing inventory appears as a debit balance brought down in the consignment account. The inventory will be shown on the consignor's statement of financial position at 31 December 2014.

No entries are required in the consignee's books for unsold inventory as the consignee does not own the goods.

Getting it right

Make sure any unsold inventory is valued to include an appropriate proportion of expenses paid on the unsold goods. Exclude commission from this calculation.

Joint ventures

What is a joint venture?

A joint venture arises when two or more businesses decide that it is in their interests to work together on a specific project or series of projects. Each project will be of a temporary nature.

A joint venture is, in effect, a partnership for one transaction.

Here are some examples of where a joint venture may be appropriate:

- opportunity to purchase goods at a favourable price, e.g. where a business is closing down and selling off its inventory cheaply
- buying shares when a government privatises a public utility, in the hope of making a substantial gain from any increase in the value of the shares

Key term

Joint venture: a short-lived arrangement by two or more participants to act together in the hope of making a profit on a project.

- where an individual has invented a new product but needs to work with others to cover the cost of developing and marketing the product.

Main features of joint venture accounting

- The participants will agree on a profit- or loss-sharing ratio for the joint venture.
- Assuming the joint venture is relatively small in scale, it is usual for each participant to keep its own records of its involvement in the joint venture. This requires some special accounting records which are illustrated below.
- In the case of large-scale joint ventures, usually it is worthwhile setting up a completely separate accounting system, a separate bank account, etc. In these situations the accounting requirements follow normal procedures.

The accounting records for a small-scale joint venture

Each participant will need to set up a joint venture account which is part of that business's double-entry system.

The joint venture account will record all transactions which have involved that participant, i.e. any proceeds from sales and amounts paid out for expenses.

The joint venture account will also record payments received from, or paid to, other participants.

At the end of the project, the profit or loss on the joint venture will also be recorded in the joint venture account.

Key term

Memorandum account: any account that is not part of the double-entry record but is used to record additional information and calculate important financial details.

The profit or loss on the joint venture is calculated in a separate account. This account is not part of the double-entry system, so it is an example of a memorandum account; it is called a memorandum joint venture account. It will include all the income and all the expenses of the joint venture irrespective of who received the proceeds or paid the expenses.

Illustration 5: Accounting records of a joint venture

Ryoma and Yasmin have agreed to form a joint venture sharing profits and losses in the ratio: Ryoma three-fifths, Yasmin two-fifths. They planned to purchase an empty property, make improvements to modernise the facilities, and sell the property at a profit.

The details are as follows:

A Ryoma and Yasmin purchased the property at auction for $72 000. They paid equal amounts in cash.

B Ryoma purchased materials and new fittings for $14 700.

C Yasmin paid builders $9300.

D Ryoma undertook to redecorate the property and was to be given an allowance of $2700 for his work.

E Yasmin undertook to sell the property paying advertising costs of $1800.

F The property was sold and Yasmin received $118 000.

G The profit on the joint venture was divided according to the agreement.

H Yasmin settled the amount due to Ryoma.

The accounting records are as follows.

BOOKS OF RYOMA

Joint venture with Yasmin

Dr					Cr
	Bank:		H	Bank:	
A	Property	36 000		Receipt from Yasmin	63 900
B	Materials and fittings	14 700			
D	Allowance, decorating work	2 700			
G	Profit on joint venture	10 500			
		63 900			63 900

BOOKS OF YASMIN

Joint venture with Ryoma

Dr					Cr
	Bank:		F	Bank:	
A	Property	36 000		Proceeds from sale	118 000
C	Builders	9 300			
E	Advertising	1 800			
G	Profit on joint venture	7 000			
H	Bank, Payment to Ryoma	63 900			
		118 000			118 000

MEMORANDUM RECORDS

Ryoma and Yasmin

Dr	Memorandum joint venture				Cr
	Property	72 000		Sale of property	118 000
	Materials and fittings	14 700			
	Allowance, decorating work	2 700			
	Builders	9 300			

Getting it right

The final settlement between the participants in a joint venture should result in the closure of the joint ventures account in each set of books. If this does not happen, it will be necessary to check the entries for errors.

	Advertising	1 800			
	Profit on joint venture				
	Ryoma 3/5	10 500			
	Yasmin 2/5	7 000			
		118 000			118 000

Notes:

1 Where a participant is to receive an allowance or some benefit from the joint venture, the amount is recorded as a debit entry in the relevant joint venture account. The debit entry has the effect of increasing the amount due to the participant.

2 In each participant's books of account the profit on the joint venture will be posted to the business's income statement.

End-of-chapter questions

1 **Recording a consignment in the accounts of the consignor and the consignee**

Hamish Powertools Ltd sells goods on consignment to its agent in Hong Kong, Kai Inc. The following transactions occurred.

2015		
Jan	5	Hamish Powertools Ltd sent 16 containers to Kai Inc. The pro-forma invoice showed the goods cost $1 300 per container.
	5	Hamish Powertools Ltd paid shipping charges $200 per container, insurance $3 400 and customs duties $1 750 by cheque.
Feb	11	Kai Inc sent Hamish Powertools Ltd an account sales that showed all the goods on consignment had been sold for $44 000. Kai Inc had paid landing fees of $1 900 and storage costs of $2 100. Kai Inc charged commission of 6% and del credere commission of 2% on gross sales proceeds.
Feb	13	Hamish Powertools Ltd received the amount due from Kai Inc.

Prepare the ledger accounts required to record these transactions in the books of:

Hamish Powertools Ltd; and Kai Inc, Hong Kong.

2 **Recording a consignment in the accounts of the consignor and the consignee**

Carlos Rodriguez of Venezuela sells goods on consignment to BQT Inc of New York. The following details are available concerning a recent consignment.

2014		
Sept	23	A pro-forma invoice showed that goods with a value of $15 400 had been sent by Carlos Rodriguez to BQT Inc.
	26	Carlos Rodriguez paid air freight charges of $3 400 and customs duties $750 by cheque.
Dec	19	The consignee had paid storage charges of $820. Some of the goods had been damaged in transit and could not be sold; the value of these goods was $850. The loss on these goods was not covered by insurance. The remainder of the consignment had been sold on credit for $29 700. The consignee had managed to collect all the amounts due from trade receivables with the exception of $400; this amount had been written off as an irrecoverable debt by the consignee. The account sales recorded that commission had been charged by the consignee of 5% and a del credere commission of 3%.
Dec	24	The consignor received the amount due from the consignee.

Prepare the following ledger accounts to record these transactions:

- in the books of the consignor: the consignment account to show the profit or loss on the consignment
- in the books of the consignee: the consignment from Carlos Rodriquez account; total trade receivables account.

Calculate the net income made on this consignment by the consignee.

3 **Calculating the value of unsold inventory**

Recently Harry Clarke sent goods on consignment to his agent in Kenya. Harry sent 320 crates of goods at $60 per crate. Harry paid carriage and insurance totalling $4200 on these goods. At the end of Harry's financial year, the consignee sent an account sales which showed the following details.

	$
Sale proceeds: crates sold at $80 each	19 200
Less: storage and import duties on whole consignment	(2 100)
Less: commission 5%	(960)
Net proceeds	16 140

a Calculate the value of the closing inventory of unsold goods.

b State the double entry required to record the value of unsold inventory in Harry Clarke's books of account.

4 **Recording a consignment in the accounts of the consignor and the consignee including unsold inventory**

Julia Harper sells goods through her agent Xera Retail in Quebec, Canada.

2014		
May	4	Julia Harper sent goods to Xera Retail valued at cost $23 400.
	4	Julia Harper paid transport costs of $4 350 and insurance $720.
June	7	Julia Harper was notified that goods with a value of $470 had been damaged in transit and could not be sold. The insurance company agreed to pay her $390 in compensation.
July	11	Xera Retail sent an account sales to Julia Harper which recorded the sale of goods valued at cost $15 600 for $28 300. Xera Retail had paid storage expenses of $2 190 on the original consignment. The consignee also deducted commission of 5% on the sales proceeds.
Aug	4	Julia Harper received the amount due for the net proceeds of part of the consignment.
Aug	31	Julia Harper prepared end-of-year financial statements.
Oct	11	Xera Retail sent an account sales recording the sale of the unsold inventory for $14 900. The amount due was settled less commission of 5%.

Prepare the following ledger accounts.

a In the books of Julia Harper the consignment to Xera Retail account to record the information given above. The account should show the profit transferred to income statement at 31 August 2014 and the profit on the sale of the remaining goods at 11 October 2014.

b In the books of Xera Retail, the account of Julia Harper closed at 11 October 2014.

5 **Recording joint venture accounting records**

Dwight and Zamran formed a joint venture, sharing profits and losses equally. They agreed to purchase a quantity of electrical goods from a wholesale business that was closing down. The following transactions occurred.

2015		
Feb	1	Dwight paid $12 400 for some of the electrical goods; Zamran paid $7 200 for the remaining items. Payments were made by cheque.
	3	Dwight paid by cheque for the goods to be taken to a storage unit, $750.
	4	Zamran paid $560 for rent of the storage unit by cheque.
	9	Zamran received $10 800 for sales of goods.
	15	Dwight paid advertising costs of $280 by cheque.
	23	Dwight received $14 230 for sales of goods.

	27	Zamran agreed to take over the unsold inventory for $2 900.
	28	A joint venture memorandum account was prepared. The participants settled the amounts due from or to each other.

Prepare joint venture accounts in the books of:

a Dwight

b Zamran; and

c the memorandum joint venture account.

6 Recording joint venture accounting records

Helen, Ian and Jane have formed a joint venture to grow and sell vegetables. The vegetables will be grown on land owned by Helen. Ian will help with the cultivation and harvesting of the vegetables. Jane has agreed to be responsible for selling the produce at local markets. It was agreed that profits and losses on the joint venture should be shared equally.

The following details are available.

2014		
Feb	1	It was agreed that Helen should be entitled to rent of $500 for the use of her land.
	3	Helen paid $150 for seeds and plants.
May	31	It was agreed that Helen should be entitled to a wage of $400 and Ian $900 for their work in growing the vegetables.
June	15	Jane purchased a second-hand van for $5 200 to help transport the vegetables to markets.
	30	Jane received $2 400 for sales of vegetables and paid one-third of this amount to Helen and one-third to Ian.
July	31	Jane banked a further $5 200 from the sale of vegetables.
Aug	3	Ian agreed to take the remaining vegetables for personal use for an agreed amount of $200.
	14	It was agreed that Jane should receive a 5% commission on all sales proceeds.
	28	The second-hand vehicle was sold by Ian and he received a cheque for $4 500.
	31	Helen, Ian and Jane settled the amounts owed or owing to each other by cheque.

Prepare joint venture accounts in the books of:

a Helen

b Ian

c Jane; and

d the memorandum joint venture account.

Section 1.4: Computerised accounting systems

Key concepts

Computerised accounting systems have now largely replaced manual methods. Computer software packages are designed to implement the fundamental accounting concepts: **true and fair view; duality; consistency; business entity; money measurement**.

Learning objectives:

In this chapter you will learn:

- about the advantages and disadvantages of introducing a computerised accounting system
- about the process of computerising a business's accounts
- about methods for ensuring the security of computerised accounting data.

1.4.1: Computerised accounting systems

Introduction

These days it is becoming increasingly unusual to find anyone keeping accounting systems manually. Computer technology and the development of specialised accounting software packages have completely changed the way most businesses keep their financial records. For smaller businesses software packages are available which are reasonably inexpensive; for larger businesses it is now entirely usual for systems to be specially designed to meet the needs of the organisation. Even in the most basic situations, it has now become standard practice for someone to use computer spreadsheets to aid the recording of financial information.

Accounting software

There are many different accounting software packages, but they all have certain key features in common.

- **Automatic processing:** source documents are the starting point for all accounting systems whether manual or computerised. However, once the computer operator has selected the appropriate information from a source document and has input the data into the software program, the other accounting processes become automatic, so that ledger accounts are instantly updated. Trial balances, income statements, statements of financial position, etc. can be produced whenever they are required. Accounting software systems closely follow the accounting cycle for the recording of everyday transactions.
- **Integration of functions:** most software packages will not only automatically produce all the accounting records with which you are familiar from the simple act of inputting the right data, they will go further by producing important records that are not normally part of any manual system. The most obvious example is the updating of inventory records after every purchase and sale. Software programs often include a facility to provide payroll records and produce documents such as invoices and credit notes.
- **Management information:** software packages are capable of providing the owner or manager of a business with much information which can help with the running of the business in an effective way. This information can be provided almost instantaneously and with virtually no effort. A good example would be what is called an 'aged trade receivable analysis'. This means that, whenever required, a software program can provide a list of every trade receivable, how much is owed, how long the amount has been owed for, listed in such a way as to clearly show late payers.
  In a manual system, keeping track of outstanding debts can be such a time-consuming process that it does not get done often enough. As a result, a business using a software package has the opportunity to maintain much tighter control of its trade receivables.

Key term

Audit trail: a step-by-step record of the entries made for a transaction extending back to the original source of information or evidence for the transaction.

There are many other software applications that can provide information for managers to assist with decision-making. For example, there are programs to help with:

- audit trails (reports that track the origins of figures in the accounting system, from the original source document through to figures in the end-of-year financial statements)
- ratio and performance analysis
- break-even analysis
- the application of costing systems
- the production of budgets, making flexible budgeting much more straightforward
- capital investment decisions.

Main benefits of computerised accounting processes

- **Greater accuracy:** because computer processes are automatic they are error free. Of course, human error can still occur at the critical stage when data is input into the system or when formulae are used in a spreadsheet. It should be noted that faults in software are not uncommon and could lead to serious problems if undetected.
- **Greater speed:** because record updating, calculations, etc. occur virtually instantaneously.
- **Simultaneous updating:** all relevant records are updated from just one entry.
- **Improved accessibility:** it is usually far easier to track down particular details in a computerised accounting system.
- **More information available:** reports on a wide range of matters can be produced with ease, so those making decisions are much better informed. However, it is important to note that sometimes managers can be overwhelmed by the information that is available unless someone takes responsibility for carefully selecting the reports that are to be produced.
- **Possibility of a reduction in staffing costs:** because so much of the work done in keeping the accounting system is automatic, computerisation can mean there is a reduction in staff required to keep the books of account. This, in turn, can lead to a saving in wages.

Potential disadvantages of computerised accounting systems

- **Capital expenditure:** installing a computerised accounting system can be expensive. The cost of the equipment and the software can be high. It is also quite likely that the hardware and the software will have to be upgraded regularly. However, costs have fallen markedly in recent times.

- **Training costs:** when introducing a computerised accounting system, it is almost inevitable that staff will need training. From time to time staff will need training updates, which will add to the costs.
- **Risk of data loss:** computer systems can 'crash' or suffer from viruses, and there can be difficulties keeping data secure.
- **Maintenance and support costs:** computer systems are rarely trouble free and it is likely that businesses will experience an increase in maintenance costs and have to pay for technical support.
- **Period of transition:** businesses often find that it is necessary to run the old manual system alongside the new computerised system for at least a few months to ensure that all goes well during the period of transition. This can place an additional strain on staff and on the business's resources.

From the employee's point of view

Introducing a computerised accounting system can bring many benefits to a business, but how would employees feel about this important change?

For some staff, the opportunity to learn new skills and receive free training will be exciting. Some individuals will realise that their own career and salary prospects are being developed because there is often a demand for more highly skilled staff. Other staff may feel threatened by these changes. They may feel that they will not be able to cope with learning new skills, and that they risk losing their jobs, especially if the introduction of the new systems is likely to lead to less work being available. Staff may be anxious about the health and safety issues that can arise when working with computers: eye strain and RSI (repetitive strain injury) are possible examples.

Special features of computerised accounting systems

> **Key term**
>
> **Inventory control**: the automatic updating of inventory records which can help to identify missing items when compared to physical records, and help to identify shortages of products in time for new supplies to be ordered.

- Inventory control**:** every purchase, sale and return transaction can also be used to automatically update records of inventories of every product. When inventories are checked physically the computerised records can provide an important basis for comparison. Do the physical and computerised records agree? Is there evidence that inventories are missing? Inventory control has been a significant development since it enables shortages in particular products to be identified in time for new supplies to be ordered. Large supermarket chains, for example, have seen this as fundamental to their success.
- **Credit control:** as well as producing reports on how long every trade receivable is taking to pay, a computerised system can produce reports on when each trade payable should be paid. This could be important if valuable cash discounts are not to be missed.
- **Payroll:** computer software programs can produce all of the detailed information about wage and salary calculations, payslips, payroll registers, etc.

Other aspects of computerisation

Once a business has computerised systems, it will have access to some useful facilities:

- **Spreadsheets:** a program that uses a template formed of columns and rows on which it is possible to organise numerical information, make calculations and try out various scenarios with changes made automatically. Spreadsheets have become an invaluable tool for accountants, particularly those who are concerned with preparing budgets and forecasts.
- **Databases:** a program that stores data under various headings decided by the user. Databases can hold vast amounts of information and produce comprehensive reports on various aspects of a business's finances, e.g. sales performance.
- **Internet:** can provide an extensive range of online facilities that can support the accounts and other important departments of a business, e.g. online buying, selling and banking.

Introducing a computerised accounting system

The introduction of a computerised accounting system requires careful planning. Managers need to consider whether to:

- buy a standard software package, most of which are designed to meet the needs of smaller businesses
- make use of a standard software package but with adaptations designed to meet specific requirements
- have a computerised accounting system that has been designed especially for the business (because of the high cost this is usually only possible for a large business).

Choosing the right option is by no means easy as it requires managers to have a really clear idea of what they want to achieve for the business both immediately and for some time into the future.

It is usually considered desirable to run any existing accounting system alongside the new system for a period of time. This is done to avoid the risk of data loss or disruption through faults in the new system. Managers need to consider that this will place an additional strain on staff and on the business's resources.

Managers must also give data security a high priority, particularly with regard to **backing-up data**. Every organisation needs to introduce back-up procedures to protect itself from accidental or malicious data loss. This means that where data is lost it can be quickly restored with only the most recent inputs having to be repeated. Data loss can occur because of:

- hardware or software faults
- virus infection or hacking

Key term

Backing-up data: ensuring that data is copied frequently in case the original data is lost or corrupted. The back-up copy can be used to restore the original data.

- power failure
- accidental or malicious deletion of files.

Managers need to consider the frequency with which back-ups occur, the extent of the back-up, and the format to be used for the back-up. The frequency of back-ups will determine just how much data input has to be repeated. Back-ups can be made on a networked or removable hard drive or on CDs. Back-up procedures can be automated.

Other security considerations

- **Access:** managers need to consider who has access to the accounting system. For example, they may need to consider who has access to the rooms where computers are in use, and how to protect data when external technical support is needed to look at computer faults.
- **Passwords:** the use of passwords for computer operators is commonplace to ensure that employees can only access appropriate elements of the whole accounting system.
- **Encryption:** this process uses technology to encode sensitive data to ensure confidentiality.
- **Protection against viruses:** computer systems require the installation of programs and upgrades to protect against viruses.
- **Extranet:** this is a private network using internet technology which can be accessed only by selected individuals and groups. This means that organisations can restrict access to sensitive information to key groups such as shareholders, suppliers, customers, employees, etc.
- **Compliance with data protection requirements:** there are legal requirements concerning the personal data that can be stored on computer systems and how this data can be used.

Key term

Encryption: the process of coding data so that only those who have been authorised can access and read the data.

End-of-chapter questions

1 Identifying benefits and disadvantages of computerising accounting records

Here is a list of possible benefits and disadvantages of computerising accounting records. The items are in random order. In each case decide whether the item should be considered an advantage (mark it with an 'A') or a disadvantage (mark it with a 'D') from the business's viewpoint.

	Item	A or D
1	Cost of training	D
2	Improved accuracy	A
3	Aged receivables analysis	A
4	Automatic processing and updating	A
5	Computer virus	D
6	Technical support	D
7	Management reports	A
8	Increased speed of processing	A
9	Reduced workload for staff	A
10	Cost of computer installation	D
11	Security breach ('hacking')	D
12	Frequency of software upgrades	D

2 Organising information about technology

Prepare a table based on the following example in which the benefits and disadvantages of installing a computerised accounting system are summarised. The points made should be from the viewpoint of the owner of the business. Each point made should be briefly described.

	Advantage	Disadvantage
Cost		
Staffing		
Information		

3 Organising information about technology

Prepare a table based on the following example in which the benefits and disadvantages of installing a computerised accounting system are summarised. The points made should be from the viewpoint of the staff. Each point made should be briefly described.

	Advantage	Disadvantage
Workload		
Career prospects		

4 Management information

Computerised accounting systems are used to record the day-to-day financial transactions of a business. They can also provide managers with information to assist with decision-making. Describe in detail two ways in which management can be assisted by a computerised accounting system.

5 Introducing a computerised accounting system

Describe five key issues to be considered by the manager of a medium-sized business which is considering the introduction of a computerised accounting system.

6 Security of computerised accounting information

What steps would you introduce to ensure that a business's computerised accounting information was secure?

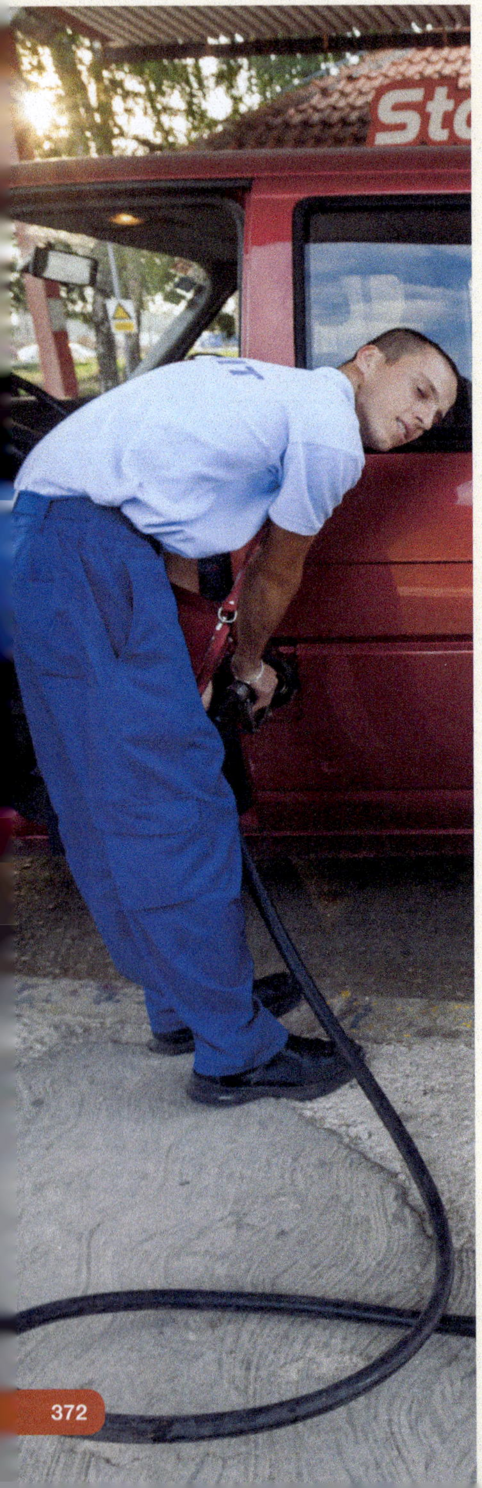

Section 1.5: Analysis and communication of accounting information

Key concepts

It is important to remember that stakeholders are likely to make important decisions as a result of assessing a business's performance: whether to invest, whether to sell an existing investment, whether to supply goods on credit to a business, whether to provide finance, etc. Stakeholders rely on financial statements to present a **true and fair view** of a business's affairs, and to be prepared on a **consistent** basis, so that they can make a valid assessment of a business's performance. Stakeholders also need to be aware that financial statements are based on the **money measurement concept**, and so do not show other significant aspects of a business's performance (for example the impact that a business's operations have on the environment). These non-financial factors may be significant when making a final judgment on a business's performance.

Learning objectives

In this chapter you will learn:

- how to identify a range of gearing, investment (stock exchange) and further liquidity ratios
- the formulae to be used when calculating each ratio
- how to calculate each ratio on data given
- what each ratio can tell you about the financial structure and performance of a business.

1.5.1: Further interpretation and analysis ratios

Ratio analysis and interpretation

Before beginning this chapter, it is recommended that you review AS Level Chapter 1.5.1 Analysis and communication of accounting information to stakeholders. Remember that the best ratio analysis requires a review of a trend of ratios over several years. One year in isolation does not identify whether the business is improving performance or whether it is declining. Once again, the following financial statements will be used to analyse the performance of the business.

Assessment Ltd Income statement for the year ended 31 December 2014		
	$	$
Revenue		192 000
Cost of sales		
Opening inventory	11 500	
Purchases	85 500	
Closing inventory	(12 500)	(84 500)
Gross profit		107 500
Less expenses:		
Wages and salaries	12 600	
Administration expenses	1 700	
Selling and distribution costs	1 200	
Directors' remuneration	40 600	
Auditors' fees	2 400	
Depreciation	6 900	
		(65 400)
Operating profit		42 100
Finance costs:		
Debenture interest		(2 000)
Preference dividends		(800)
Profit before taxation		39 300
Taxation		(5 000)
Profit after taxation		34 300

Statement of changes in equity (extract) for year ended 31 December 2014		
	$	$
Retained earnings 1 Jan 2014		13 500
Add profit for year		34 300
Less dividends paid		(5 600)
		42 200

Assessment Ltd Statement of financial position at 31 December 2014			
	$000	$000	$000
	Cost	depreciation	Net book value
Non-current assets			
Premises	153 000	12 000	141 000
Vehicles	32 000	16 000	16 000
	185 000	28 000	157 000
Current assets			
Inventory		12 500	
Trade and other receivables		16 800	29 300
Total assets			186 300
Capital and reserves			
50 000 ordinary shares of $1 each		50 000	
5 000 8% preference shares of $2 each		10 000	
Share premium		14 000	
General reserve		20 000	
Retained earnings		42 200	136 200
Non-current liabilities			
10% debentures (2020–2022)			20 000
Current liabilities			
Trade and other payables		27 400	
Cash and cash equivalents		2 700	30 100
Total capital and liabilities			186 300

Ratios are used to analyse and interpret financial data for the interested stakeholders. One of the most important groups of stakeholders for a limited company is the equity shareholders, who are particularly interested in the gearing, the general solvency of their business, and the investment ratios. Equity shareholders are interested in the return on their investment which is variable and dependent on: the business's performance; whether the business has enough cash to survive everyday trading; plus the market value of the shares and the degree of risk within the business.

Key term

Gearing: this ratio is the relationship between fixed cost capital and total capital.

Gearing

Gearing ratio

Gearing is the relationship between fixed cost capital and total capital. Fixed cost capital is made up of debentures and preference shares. Debenture holders receive a fixed rate of interest however profitable a business is, and preference shareholders receive a fixed rate of dividends if there are sufficient profits available.

Available cash funds are first used to pay both the debenture interest and the preference dividends, with equity shareholders' dividends being dependent on the remaining levels of profit and the availability of cash funds. Gearing is, therefore, important to an equity shareholder as it measures the level of risk.

Gearing is calculated as:

$$\frac{\text{Fixed cost capital}}{\text{Total capital}} \times 100$$

Alternatively it can be expanded to:

$$\frac{\text{Non-current liabilities + Preference share capital}}{\text{Issued ordinary share capital + All reserves + Non-current liabilities + Preference shares}} \times 100$$

Using the information provided for Assessment Ltd, the gearing ratio is:

$$\frac{20\,000 + 10\,000}{136\,200 + 20\,000} \times 100 = 19.2\%$$

When the ratio is less than 50 per cent, the business has low gearing. This means that it has low borrowing or low fixed cost capital as a proportion of its total capital and long-term finance.

> **Key term**
>
> **Low gearing**: this is when a business has low borrowing as a proportion of its total capital and long-term finance.

- 19.2 per cent of its total capital is provided by people other than ordinary equity shareholders
- 80.8 per cent of capital employed is provided by ordinary equity shareholders.

An equity shareholder is paid after both debenture interest and preference dividends have been paid. The higher the proportion of total capital that comprises these, the lower the amount of profit available for equity shareholders.

Therefore, it is not in the interest of equity shareholders to invest in a low-geared business, especially when profits are low. However, in times of high profits the amount paid to debenture holders and preference shareholders remains fixed, so ordinary shareholders will receive a greater return.

Investment in a low-geared business has less risk than that in a high-geared business. If a business is high-geared and becomes unable to pay its long-term debts, it is likely to be forced into liquidation by those long-term capital providers.

Also, a high-geared business may find it difficult to borrow further funds because of this risk. Banks may also be reluctant to lend further to such a business as they may feel that finance should be provided by the ordinary shareholders themselves.

Plus, the higher the gearing, the greater the likelihood of high interest payments, which will further reduce the profit available to be used for dividend payments to the ordinary shareholders.

Gearing ratio	Description	Borrowing	Debt	Risk
Greater than 50%	High gearing	High borrowing	High debt	High risk
Less than 50%	Low gearing	Low borrowing	Low debt	Low risk
50%	Neutral	Medium	Medium	Medium

To reduce gearing, a business can:

- issue new ordinary shares
- redeem debentures
- retain profits.

To increase gearing, a business can:

- issue debentures
- buy back ordinary shares in issue
- issue new preference shares.

Key term

Income gearing: this ratio measures the amount of profit that is used up to pay interest.

Income gearing ratio

Income gearing measures the amount of profit that is used up to pay interest.

The calculation is:

$$\frac{\text{Interest expense}}{\text{Profit before interest and tax}} \times 100$$

For Assessment Ltd, the ratio will be:

$$\frac{2000}{42\,100} \times 100 = 4.75\%$$

This means that 4.75 per cent of operating profit is used to pay interest. A high-geared business often has high interest payments due to the high level of borrowing and debentures. It follows that income gearing will also be high.

However, this is not always the case as the business may be highly geared due to a high proportion of preference shares rather than high levels of debentures.

Investment ratios

There are various ratios, particularly used by equity shareholders, which indicate how well a business is doing in relation to its shares.

Key term

Earnings per share (EPS): this ratio indicates how much of the company's profit can be attributed to each issued equity share.

Earnings per share ratio

This is the most frequently used investment ratio as it generally gives the best view of performance. Earnings per share (EPS) indicates how much of the company's profit can be attributed to each issued equity share.

It is used to compare:

- the results of one particular company over a number of years
- the performance of one company's equity shares against the performance of another company's equity shares

Getting it right

It is important to remember that the earnings are stated in cents and not dollars. Also, a common error made is to not adjust when the shares are not $1 each. It is the number of shares that is required not the nominal value.

For example, if Assessment Ltd had $0.50 shares instead of $1 shares, then the number of shares would have been 100 000 (50 0000/0.50).

- the earnings against a return available from alternative investments.

Earnings are calculated as the profit after tax and after the deduction of preference share dividends. That is the earnings relevant to equity shareholders.

The ratio is calculated as:

$$\frac{\text{Profit after tax and preference dividends in cents}}{\text{Number of ordinary shares}}$$

From the results for Assessment Ltd:

$$\frac{3\,430\,000¢}{50\,000} = 68.\,6¢ \text{ (i.e. \$0.686)}$$

This means that each equity share earns 68.6¢ during the year. This does not represent actual cash in the form of dividends but the profit attributable to equity shareholders.

Price/earnings (P/E) ratio

The price earnings (P/E) ratio compares the market price of the shares to the earnings per share. It puts price into context as a multiple of earnings. It represents the number of years' earnings that investors are prepared to pay to purchase one of the company's shares.

Key term

Price earnings (P/E): this ratio compares the market price of the shares to the earnings per share.

The higher the ratio, the greater the demand for shares and so the greater the confidence investors have in the future of the business. A low P/E means that there is little demand for the shares. The ratio enables potential investors to assess whether the expected future earnings make the share a worthwhile investment.

The ratio is calculated as:

$$\frac{\text{Market price per ordinary share in cents}}{\text{Earnings per share in cents}}$$

For Assessment Ltd, if the market price of one equity share is $3.43, then the P/E ratio is:

$$\frac{343}{68.6} = 5$$

This means that it takes five years to recover the market price of the shares with earnings. Buyers are paying five times the earnings to acquire shares in Assessment Ltd.

Any increase in the market price of an equity share will increase the ratio. Usually, an increase in the market price of shares is in response to an increase in the demand for the shares. Demand increases as confidence increases:

- a high P/E ratio indicates expected growth in the future
- a low P/E ratio indicates expected poor performance in the future.

Dividend yield ratio

Shareholders invest in businesses for two reasons:

- to gain an annual return on their investment in the form of dividends
- to make a capital gain when selling the shares with an increase in their market value.

Key term

Dividend yield: this ratio measures the real rate of return of an ordinary share by comparing the dividend paid to the market price of a share.

Dividend yield measures the real rate of return of an ordinary share by comparing the dividend paid to the market price of a share. It shows the actual percentage return an investor can expect based on the current market price and so expresses the actual dividend as a percentage of the current market price of the share.

The ratio is calculated as:

$$\frac{\text{Total ordinary dividend paid}}{\text{Market price of all equity shares}} \times 100$$

For Assessment Ltd the market price was \$3.43 per equity share. There are 50 000 shares, so the market price of all equity shares is:

$3.43 \times 50\,000 = \$171\,500$

The ratio is, therefore: $\frac{\$5600}{\$171\,500} \times 100 = 3.27\%$

This yield is low, especially given the high earnings per share. It appears that the earnings are not being passed on to the equity shareholders.

Another approach to calculate this ratio is:

$$\frac{\text{Declared rate of dividend} \times \text{Nominal value of equity shares}}{\text{Market price of ordinary shares}}$$

The dividend per share is $\frac{\$5600}{50\,000} = 0.112¢$

$0.112 \times (1/3.43) \times 100 = 3.27\%$

Dividend cover ratio

Key term

Dividend cover: this ratio compares the amount of profit earned by an ordinary share with the amount of dividend paid.

As ordinary dividends vary with the level of profit, an investor is often concerned as to whether a company will be able to continue to pay its current rate of ordinary share dividend in the future. Dividend cover gives this indication by comparing the amount of profit earned by an ordinary share with the amount of dividend paid, thereby giving the shareholder some idea as to the proportion that the ordinary dividends bear compared to the amount available for distribution to ordinary shareholders.

The ratio is calculated as:

$$\frac{\text{Profits available for ordinary dividends}}{\text{Ordinary dividend paid}}$$

For Assessment Ltd, the ratio will be: $\frac{34\,300}{5600} = 6.125$ times

This is quite high. A high figure is favourable as it suggests that the company will be able to continue to pay the current level of ordinary dividends even if profits fall. This may also be an indication that the directors operate a conservative approach to dividend payment as much of the profits are being reinvested back into the company.

This further confirms the results from the dividend yield, which showed that despite a high earnings per share, the dividend yield was low and, therefore, the earnings were not being passed on to the ordinary shareholder.

If the ratio had been low, this may be due to a more reckless dividend policy. A small reduction in company profits may then have an adverse effect on dividends in the future.

Key term

Dividend per share: this ratio indicates how much each ordinary share actually received as a dividend.

Dividend per share ratio

The dividend per share ratio indicates how much each ordinary share actually received as a dividend.

It is calculated as:

$$\frac{\text{Ordinary dividend paid}}{\text{Number of issued ordinary shares}}$$

For Assessment Ltd, the ratio will be: $\frac{5600}{50\,000} = 11.2¢$

Each ordinary shareholder, therefore, received 11.2¢ per share held. This should be compared to previous years to see if there was an improvement or decline in the rate paid out per share.

Key terms

Solvency: the ability to pay all outstanding debts when they fall due, as shown by an excess of assets over liabilities.

Working capital cycle: this ratio shows the length of time taken between making a payment for goods taken into inventory and the receipt of cash from the sale of inventory to the customers.

Further liquidity ratios

Long-term investors are interested in the solvency of a business: does the business have enough assets to cover its debts? Solvency is an excess of assets over the amount of liabilities. However, some assets are difficult to dispose of and so many investors prefer to assess the liquidity of a business by examining the working capital.

Working capital cycle ratio

The working capital cycle shows the length of time taken between making a payment for goods taken into inventory and the receipt of cash from the sale of inventory to the customers. Obviously the shorter the time the better! If there is a long delay between buying the inventory and then selling the goods and receiving the money from the customers, this can cause cash flow problems both within and outside the working capital.

There would be a lack of cash available to pay for everyday trading within the working capital (for example the purchase of inventory from suppliers) but also outside working capital (for example the purchase of non-current assets, the repayment of a loan, the payment of tax and, significantly to an investor, the payment of dividends).

If the cycle is short, then the value of working capital to be financed from other sources will be lower.

The cycle can be shortened by the business:

- reducing inventory levels held
- speeding up trade receivables collection period
- delaying payment to trade payables.

The main reason that the cycle gets longer is that there is a quicker payment of trade payables.

The working capital cycle (in days) is calculated as either:

Trade receivables turnover (in days) + Inventory turnover (in days) – Trade payables turnover (in days)

or:

Average collection period + Inventory turnover (in days) – Average payment period

For Assessment Ltd, these individual ratios were calculated in AS Level Chapter 1.5.1 Analysis and communication of accounting information to stakeholders:

- Trade receivables in days = 32 days
- Trade payables in days = 109 days
- Inventory turnover in days = 52 days

The working capital cycle is, therefore:

$$32 + 52 - 109 = -25 \text{ days}$$

This means that the business is selling its inventory and collecting its money in from the trade receivables within 84 days but then delays payment to trade payables by a further 25 days.

> **Key term**
>
> **Net working assets/revenue**: this ratio calculates the percentage of revenue that is net working assets.

The net working assets/revenue ratio

The net working assets/revenue ratio calculates the percentage of revenue that is net working assets, where net working assets are inventories + trade receivables – trade payables.

The ratio is calculated as:

$$\frac{\text{Net working assets}}{\text{Revenue}} \times 100$$

For Assessment Ltd, the ratio would be:

$$\frac{12\,500 + 16\,800 - 25\,500}{192\,000} \times 100 = 1.98\%$$

This shows that for every dollar of revenue, there are nearly two cents of net working assets, which appears to be low. In other words, the value of net assets is 1.98 per cent of each $1 of revenue. This could be improved upon.

> **Getting it right**
>
> It is important to remember to calculate ratios to the number of decimal places required by the question in the examination. It is also important to round correctly.
>
> A good approach would be to state the answer in full and then to state the rounded amount – for example whole days.

Preparing financial statements from ratios

It is possible to construct financial statements from ratios as shown in the following illustration.

Illustration 1: Constructing an income statement and statement of changes in equity from ratios

The following information is available concerning the financial affairs of YQX Ltd for the year ended 31 December 2014.

Administration expenses	?
Cost of sales	?
Distribution expenses	One-third of administrative expenses
Dividends paid	$0.05 per share
Finance charges	?
Gross profit margin	45%
Income gearing	20%
Inventory at 1 January 2014	25 750
Inventory at 31 December 2014	29 250
Operating profit	?
Profit margin (operating profit margin)	12.5%
Rate of inventory turnover	14 times
Retained earnings at 1 January 2014	$82 000
Revenue	?
Share capital	800 000 ordinary shares of $1 each

Step 1: Prepare a template for the income statement and enter any known figures. Alongside the template make notes using the information given and also add any implications arising from the information (here shown in bold).

YQX Ltd			***Notes***
Income statement for year ended 31 December 2014			
	$	**$**	
Revenue			
Less: opening inventory	25 750		*Rate of inventory turnover is 14,*
purchases			***so cost of sales must be 14 × average inventory***
closing inventory	(29 250)		
Cost of sales			***Cost of sales must be 55% of revenue***
Gross profit			*Gross profit is 45% of revenue*
Less: administrative expenses			

distribution expenses			*one-third of administrative expenses*
Operating profit			*12.5% × Revenue*
Less finance charges			*Income gearing is 20%,*
Profit for year			***so finance charges are 20% of operating profit***

Step 2: Prepare workings to show how missing figures are calculated.

Workings:

Finding cost of sales:

Average inventory is ($25 750 + $29 250)/2 i.e. $27 500

Cost of sales is 14 × $27 500 = **$385 000**

Finding revenue:

Cost of sales is 55 per cent of revenue (because gross profit is 45 per cent of revenue)

i.e. Revenue is $385 000/55 × 100 = **$700 000**

Finding gross profit:

Gross profit is revenue less cost of sales, i.e. $315 000.

Finding operating profit:

Operating profit is 12.5% × Revenue, i.e.12.5% × $700 000 i.e. **$87 500.**

Finding total expenses:

Total expenses are gross profit less operating profit, $315 000 – $87 500 = $227 500

Finding administrative and distribution expenses:

Distribution expenses are one-third of administrative expenses and both expenses combined are $227 500.

So distribution expenses are one-quarter of total expenses (i.e. **$56 875**), and administrative expenses are three-quarters of total expenses (i.e. **$170 625**).

Finding finance charges:

The income gearing ratio is 20 per cent, so finance charges are 20 per cent of operating profit, i.e. **$17 000.**

Profit for the year:

Operating profit less finance charges.

Dividends paid:

Dividends paid are 800 000 × $0.05, i.e. $40 000.

Step 3: Set out completed statements

YQX Ltd Income statement for year ended 31 December 2014		
	$	$
Revenue		700 000
Less: opening inventory	25 750	
purchases	414 250	
closing inventory	(29 250)	
Cost of sales		(385 000)
Gross profit		315 000
Less: administrative expenses	170 625	
distribution expenses	56 875	
		(227 500)
Operating profit		87 500
Less finance charges		(17 500)
Profit for year		70 000

Statement of changes in equity (extract) for the year ended 31 December 2014	
	$
Retained earnings at 1 January 2014	82 000
Add profit for year	70 000
	152 000
Less dividends paid	(40 000)
Retained earnings at 31 December 2014	112 000

End-of-chapter questions

1 **Investment ratios**

A company has capital of one million ordinary shares of $1 each. The company pays a dividend of 6 per cent. The profits for the year after tax were $480 000. The sales revenue for the year was $4 million. The market price of a share is $1.40.

a What is the dividend yield?
b What are the earnings per share?
c What is the price/earnings per share?

2 **Investment ratios**

The following information is available for two companies for the year ended 28 February 2015.

	Bailey Ltd	Malib Ltd
	$	$
Operating profit	260 000	330 000
Debenture interest	0	63 000
Taxation	57 000	71 000
Preference dividend	16 000	32 000
Ordinary dividends	38 000	42 000
Retained profit for the year	149 000	122 000

Information at 28 February 2015:		
Ordinary shares of $1 each	195 000	
Ordinary shares of 25¢ each		200 000
8% preference shares	200 000	400 000
Share premium	50 000	130 000
Revaluation reserve	100 000	60 000
Retained earnings	425 000	550 000
7% debentures	0	900 000
Market price per ordinary share	4.20	1.40

a Calculate the following investment ratios for the two companies:
   i gearing ratio
   ii dividend cover
   iii earnings per share
   iv dividend paid per share
   v dividend yield
   vi price earnings ratio.

b Comment on the information gained from each of the ratio calculations.

3 Investment ratios

The following information is provided for Ace Ltd at 31 March 2015.

Ordinary shares of $1 each	$3 486 000
6% preference shares of $10 each	$1 400 000
7% debenture stock 2025/2026	$1 000 000
Reserves	$2 114 000
Operating profit	$1 250 000
Taxation	$380 000
Dividend cover	6 times
Market price per ordinary share	$5.50

Complete the following table.

	Formula	31 March 2013	31 March 2014	31 March 2015
Interest cover		16.4 times	17.1 times	
EPS		17.8¢	18.74¢	
Ordinary dividend paid per share		3.1¢	3.3¢	
P/E ratio		24.5	25.7	
Dividend yield		0.6%	0.6%	
Gearing		23%	18.62%	

Comment on the trends shown over the three years.

4 Investment ratios

The following information is available for two companies for the year ended 31 October 2014.

	Gilchrist Ltd	Burrell Ltd
	$	$
Operating profit	2 458 000	1 276 000
Debenture interest	0	300 000
Taxation	983 000	382 000
Preference dividend	240 000	60 000
Ordinary dividends	393 000	320 000
Retained profit for the year	842 000	214 000
Ordinary shares of 50¢ each	3 960 000	0
Ordinary shares of $1 each	0	3 500 000
6% preference shares	4 000 000	1 000 000
Share premium	1 320 000	1 980 000
Revaluation reserve	500 000	0
Retained earnings	1 840 000	638 000
10% debentures	0	3 000 000
Market price per ordinary share	1.10	2.10

a Calculate the following investment ratios for the two companies:
   i gearing ratio
   ii dividend cover
   iii earnings per share
   iv dividend paid per share
   v dividend yield
   vi price earnings ratio.

b Comment on the information gained from each of the ratio calculations.

5 Preparing financial statements from accounts ratios and an extract from a statement of changes in equity for the year ended 31 March 2015

The following information relates to the business of Lozon Ltd for the year ended 31 March 2015.

Rate of inventory turnover (calculated using average inventory)	8 times
Gross margin	35%
Profit margin	12%
Income gearing	40%
Administrative expenses	2 × distribution costs
Dividends paid	$0.05 per share
Issued share capital	250 000 ordinary shares of $0.50 each
Inventory at 1 April 2014	$28 000
Inventory at 31 March 2015	$34 000
Retained earnings at 1 April 2014	$39 000

Required

a Working to the nearest dollar, prepare an income statement for the year ended 31 March 2015 in as much detail as possible and an extract from a statement of changes in equity at 31 March 2015.

The directors of Lozon Ltd have decided to invest in Zeng Ltd. The following information relates to Zeng Ltd for the year ended 31 March 2015.

	$
Profit from operations	100 000
Finance charges	(40 000)
Preference dividend	(8 000)
Ordinary dividend	(20 000)
Retained profit for the year	32 000
Non-current assets	850 000
Current assets	80 000
2020 8% debentures	500 000
Ordinary shares of $1	100 000
8% $1 preference shares	100 000
Retained profit	230 000
Market value of one ordinary share at 31 March 2015	$2.50

Required

b Calculate the following ratios for Zeng Ltd, giving your answer to two decimal places.

Dividend yield	?
Dividend cover	?
Dividend per share	?
Earnings per share (EPS)	?
Price earnings ratio	?
Gearing ratio	?

Required

c Based on these calculations, were the directors of Lozon Ltd correct to invest in Zeng Ltd?

Explain your answer.

6 Investment ratios

The following information is available about Gamble plc:

- In 2001 it issued at $0.75 a number of ordinary shares with a nominal value of $0.50 each.
- During 2007 Gamble Ltd issued $200 000 6 per cent debentures repayable in 2018.
- On 1 January 2014 retained earnings were $62 000.
- On 31 December 2014 the non-current assets had a value of $610 000.

Further information relating to 2014 is as follows:

- Income gearing was 6.25 per cent.
- The tax charge for the year was calculated as 20 per cent of profit before tax.
- The ordinary dividends paid during the year were $54 000.
- Earnings per share were $0.22.
- Dividends per share were $0.09.
- The directors decided to create a general reserve of $30 000.
- The market value of the ordinary shares was $2.50.

Required

a Starting with profit from operations, prepare a statement to calculate the retained profit for the year ended 31 December 2014.

b Giving as much detail as possible, prepare the statement of financial position at 31 December 2014.

c Calculate:

i the dividend cover

ii the price earnings ratio

iii the dividend yield

iv the gearing ratio

v the return on capital employed.

Vox plc is a company in the same line of business as Gamble plc and is in a similar location.

The following ratios have been calculated for Vox plc.

Gearing ratio	63.8%
Return on capital employed	22.1%
Dividend cover	1.8 times

Required

d Compare and comment on the performance of Gamble plc and Vox plc in the light of these ratios.

7 Investment ratios

The following information is available for Kanka Trading Ltd for the year ended 31 October 2014.

Kanka Trading Ltd
Statement of financial position

	At 31 October 2014	*At 31 October 2013*
	$	*$*
Non-current assets	18 000 000	*16 500 00*
Current assets		
Inventory	706 000	*680 000*
Trade receivables	4 800 000	*3 800 000*
Cash and cash equivalents	81 000	*1 050 000*
Total assets	23 587 000	*22 030 000*
Net assets	15 887 000	*14 630 000*
Equity		
Issued share capital:		
16 000 000 ordinary shares of 50¢ each	8 000 000	*8 000 000*
Share premium	110 000	*110 000*
Revaluation reserve	950 000	*550 000*
General reserve	900 000	*900 000*
Retained earnings	5 927 000	*5 070 000*
Total equity and liabilities	15 887 000	*14 630 000*
Non-current liabilities		
Debentures	1 100 000	*1 000 000*
Current liabilities		
Trade payables	6 600 000	*6 400 000*
	23 587 000	*22 030 000*
Market price per ordinary share	$1.10	*$0.90*

Extract from the income statement

	For year ended 31 Oct 2014	*For year ended 31 Oct 2013*
	$	*$*
Operating profit	2 845	*3 000*
Interest payable	(88)	*(80)*
Profit before taxation	2 757	*2 920*
Taxation	(850)	*(900)*
Profit after taxation	1 907	*2 020*
Ordinary dividends	650	*790*
Retained profit for the year	1 257	*1 230*

Calculate for both years:

a the dividend cover
b earnings per share
c the price earnings ratio
d the dividend yield
e the gearing ratio.

Exam-style questions

1 **Not-for-profit organisation financial statements**

The treasurer of the Grandford Sports Club provided the following information at the end of the club's most recently completed financial year ended 31 March 2015.

At 1 April 2014 the club's assets and liabilities included the following.

	$
Clubhouse and sports ground at book value	90 000
Sports equipment at book value	17 400
Inventory: café refreshments	680
Members' subscriptions	
due	450
received in advance	150
Amount due to suppliers of refreshments	80
Life membership fund	12 800
Interest-free loans from members	4 000

Receipts and payments account for the year ended 31 March 2015

	$	$
Balance at bank 1 April 2014		2 280
Receipts		
Life membership fund	4 400	
Members' subscriptions	7 550	
Disposal of sports equipment	240	
Café takings	2 970	
Sports competition ticket sales	2 590	
		17 750
		20 030
Payments		
Secretary's honorarium	820	
Suppliers of refreshments for café	2 240	
Repayment of interest-free members' loans	2 200	
Additional sports equipment	7 900	
Sports competition expenses	1 330	
Sports club repairs	5 330	
Travel expenses	950	
		(20 770)
Balance at bank 31 March 2015 overdrawn		740

Additional information:

- The annual member's subscription is $50. Subscriptions have been at this level for some years. At 31 March 2015, 14 members had not paid their subscription for the year ended on that date; four members had paid their subscription in advance for the year ended 31 March 2016. The treasurer had not been able to collect subscriptions due for the year ended 31 March 2014 from two members and it had been decided to write these amounts off.
- The club's policy is to treat 12.5 per cent of the life membership fund as income for the year.
- At 31 March 2015 suppliers of café refreshments were owed $480 and secretary's honorarium $120 was due but unpaid.
- Some sports equipment with a book value of $800 had been sold during the year. At 31 March 2015 the treasurer valued sports equipment at $22 900.
- Property is to be depreciated by 2 per cent per annum using the reducing-balance method.
- Café refreshments are always sold with a mark-up of 20 per cent. At 31 March 2015 café refreshments inventory was valued at $720. It is believed that some cash takings may have been stolen from the café during the year resulting in an uninsured loss.

a Prepare a subscriptions account showing the income from members' annual subscriptions for the year ended 31 March 2015. [5 marks]

b Prepare a café refreshments account for the year ended 31 March 2015. State the amount of cash takings stolen. [5 marks]

c Prepare an income and expenditure account for the year ended 31 March 2015. [8 marks]

The club committee recently reviewed the receipts and payments account and income and expenditure account for the year ended 31 March 2015. One committee member expressed concern and suggested immediate action should be taken to increase the club's income, including an increase in the annual membership subscription. Another committee member, however, was of the opinion that there was no need for any concern.

d Discuss whether there is any need for immediate action to increase the club's income. Take account of the information shown in the receipts and payments account and income and expenditure account for the year ended 31 March 2015. [7 marks]

[Total: 25 marks]

2 Manufacturer's financial statements; finished goods valued at transfer price

Osomo Ltd is a manufacturing organisation. On 31 December 2014 the following information was extracted from the company's books.

	$000
Administration expenses	36
Carriage inwards (raw materials)	6
Debentures 8% (2024)	150
Debenture interest	12
Direct wages	474
Factory utility charges	43
Indirect factory wages and salaries	47
Insurance	32

Inventories at 1 January 2014	
Raw materials	38
Work in progress	29
Finished goods at transfer price	92
Inventories at 31 December 2014	
Raw materials	49
Work in progress	33
Finished goods at transfer price	138
Maintenance of factory plant and machinery	27
Plant and machinery	
at cost	280
provision for depreciation at 1 January 2014	70
Provision for unrealised profit at 1 January 2014	12
Purchases of raw materials	482
Rent paid	139
Returns outwards (raw materials)	4
Revenue	1 471
Selling and distribution expenses	72

Additional information:

- The company transfers goods from the manufacturing account at a transfer price of cost plus 15 per cent.
- Rent $9000 had been paid for the three months to 28 February 2015.
- Rent and insurance should be allocated: factory 75 per cent, office 25 per cent.
- Direct wages $11 000 were due but unpaid at 31 December 2014.
- Depreciation should be provided on plant and machinery at 30 per cent per annum using the reducing-balance method. (Depreciation on office non-current assets has already been included in the administration and selling and distribution expenses.)
- Tax on profits for the year ended 31 December 2014 has been estimated at $32 000.

a Suggest **one** reason why the company transfers goods from the manufacturing account at a transfer price. [1 mark]

b Prepare a manufacturing account for the year ended 31 December 2014. [10 marks]

c Prepare an income statement for the year ended 31 December 2014. [7 marks]

d Prepare the provision for unrealised account for the year ended 31 December 2014. [3 marks]

e Explain the accounting treatment for the finished goods valued at transfer price. [4 marks]

[Total: 25 marks]

3 Purchase of a sole trader business by a limited company

The directors of Esplan Ltd have agreed to take over the business owned by Rakesh on 1 March 2015. Rakesh plans to retire. Both businesses operate as retailers of electrical goods.

The summarised statements of financial position of both businesses on 28 February 2015, immediately before the acquisition, are shown below.

Rakesh Statement of financial position at 28 February 2015	
	$
Non-current assets at book value	138 000
Inventories	14 400
Trade receivables	8 900
Cash at bank	2 300
	163 600
Capital	152 000
Trade payables	11 600
	163 600

Esplan Ltd Statement of financial position at 28 February 2015	
	$
Non-current assets	282 000
Inventories	27 900
Trade receivables	18 500
Cash and cash equivalents	11 700
	340 100
Issued shares: 250 000 of $1 each	250 000
Retained earnings	37 600
Debentures 7%	40 000
Trade payables	12 500
	340 100

It was agreed that the company would take over all the assets and liabilities except the bank balance. The assets taken over were revalued as follows.

	$
Non-current assets	125 000
Inventories	11 000
Trade receivables	8 500

The purchase consideration of $180 000 was to be settled as follows:

- the issue of 90 000 ordinary shares of $1 each
- the issue of 7 per cent debentures, $30 000
- a cash payment of $15 000.

All transactions relating to the takeover were completed on 1 March 2015.

a State **four** potential benefits of the company taking over the business owned by Rakesh. [4 marks]

b Calculate the profit made by Rakesh on the takeover of his business by Esplan Ltd. [4 marks]

c Prepare a summarised statement of financial position of Esplan Ltd on 1 March 2015 immediately after the takeover of Rakesh's business had taken place. [11 marks]

In recent years Rakesh had achieved a return on capital employed of 12 per cent per annum. He hopes to be able to invest all the cash available after the takeover in an investment earning interest of 5 per cent per annum. Rakesh is aware that Esplan Ltd has maintained a dividend of policy of $0.20 per share for the last few years. Rakesh believes he will be better off financially after the takeover.

d Do you agree that Rakesh will be better off financially after the takeover? Provide detailed financial information to support your answer. [6 marks]

[Total: 25 marks]

4 Statement of cash flows; value of a cash flow statement to a shareholder

The published accounts of Kranak plc included the following information.

Statements of financial position at 31 March		
	2015	***2014***
Non-current assets	2 915	2 593
Current assets		
Inventories	324	395
Trade and other receivables	75	59
Cash and cash equivalents	9	–
	408	*454*
Total assets	3 323	*3 047*
Equity and reserves		
Share capital	2 100	*2 100*
Revaluation reserve	120	–
Retained earnings	640	*463*
	2 860	*2 563*
Non-current liabilities		
Debentures 10%	300	*300*
Current liabilities		
Trade and other payables	52	*44*
Tax	111	*129*
Cash and cash equivalents	–	*11*
	163	*184*
Total equity and liabilities	3 323	*3 047*

Notes to the accounts:

1 Schedule of non-current assets at 31 March 2015

	Premises	Plant and machinery	Equipment	Total
	$000	$000	$000	$000
Cost				
At 1 April 2014	1 900	670	260	2 830
Revaluation	120	–	–	120
Additions	–	295	52	347
Disposal	–	–	(30)	(30)
At 31 March 2015	2 020	965	282	3 267
Depreciation				
At 1 April 2014	80	120	37	237
Revaluation	(80)	–	–	(80)
Provided in year	–	165	49	214
Disposals	–	–	(19)	(19)
At 31 March 2015	–	285	67	352
Net book value				
At 31 March 2015	2 020	680	215	2 915
At April 2014	1 820	550	223	2 593

Proceeds from the sale of equipment amounted to $6000.

2 Dividends paid

Dividend payments totalled $315 000 during the year ended 31 March 2015.

A shareholder is not clear why a cash flow statement is included in the published accounts, and is not sure what value it has when assessing the company's performance.

a State **one** reason why the cash flow statement has been included in the company's published accounts. [1 mark]

b Prepare a statement to show the reconciliation of profit from operations to net cash flow from operating activities for the year ended 31 March 2015. [14 marks]

c Prepare an extract from the statement of cash flows for the year ended 31 March 2015 showing details of investing activities. [3 marks]

d Discuss the value of a statement of cash flows to the shareholder. [7 marks]

[Total: 25 marks]

2 Cost and management accounting

Section 2.1: Activity-based costing (ABC)

Key concepts

The **consistency** concept is applicable in the use of costing techniques and the valuation of inventories of finished goods.

2.1.1: Activity-based costing (ABC)

Introduction

The fundamental difficulty in costing is trying to establish an accurate total cost for a product. Knowing the cost of making a product is critical to the success of a manufacturing organisation because:

- it forms the basis for deciding the selling price of the product
- it helps managers know whether the business is truly competitive and whether they need to focus on reducing costs
- it helps managers know whether part of the business's output is no longer economic and should be abandoned.

It follows that if a business fails to accurately assess the cost of its products, either the business will make insufficient profits by charging too little for its products, or alternatively it will face a fall in demand because its prices have been set too high in what may be a very competitive market.

There is normally no difficulty concerning the allocation of direct costs of materials and labour to a unit of production. The problem that every costing technique attempts to address is how to ensure the absorption of overheads. Traditional methods use what may be called a simplistic approach by dividing overheads by the number of machine hours or labour hours to determine an absorption rate. These methods can provide rather poor-quality information for managers, particularly as has been seen in times when overheads have increasingly formed a higher proportion of total costs.

Activity-based costing (often called ABC) approaches the problem of overhead absorption with far greater precision, enabling a more accurate determination of the cost of making a product, leading to managers having the opportunity of setting a selling price which can produce the desired level of profits while also being competitive. ABC is useful in service industries as well as manufacturing organisations.

The concept of activity-based costing (ABC)

ABC is a relatively new technique that attempts to establish exactly what causes overheads to arise, i.e. what activities during the production process create overhead costs. The technique then apportions these overheads to products but in proportion to the activities caused by the manufacture of each product: the more a particular product causes an overhead, the higher the amount of the overhead that will be allocated.

First activities are organised into groups of costs, referred to as cost pools. In other words a cost pool includes all the costs which are incurred when certain operations are performed with an organisation. Cost pools often coincide with departments or services centres. The

Learning objectives

In this chapter you will learn:

- how to apportion overheads
- how to calculate the total cost of a unit
- how to value inventory
- about the effect of different methods of overhead absorption on profit
- how to apply activity-based costing techniques to make decisions.

Link

See AS Level Chapter 2.2.1 Absorption costing for more about absorption rates.

Key term

Cost pools: the location of a group of costs.

intention is usually to ensure each cost pool deals with a specific activity as this improves the outcome in terms of accuracy of costing a product.

Key term

Cost driver: a factor that causes a change in the cost of an activity.

The technique establishes what are called cost drivers, i.e. activities that cause costs to arise (drive costs) within each cost pool.

Here are some examples of cost pools and cost drivers:

Cost pool	Cost driver
Machine set-ups	Numbers of times a set-up is required for particular products
Quality checks	Number of quality checks required for particular products
Raw material supply	Number of transfers required from stores for particular products
Transfer of partly finished goods	Number of transfers from one machine to another required by particular products

Illustration 1: Using ABC to apportion overheads

Metrex Ltd manufactures a product called 'twex'. The product comes in two forms: basic and deluxe.

The company has the following cost pools and has established that the cost drivers within each cost pool are as shown.

Cost pool	Cost driver	Overhead cost per month	Information about each product
Machine set-ups	Numbers of times a set-up is required for particular products	$21 000	Basic: 2 set-ups per unit Deluxe: 4 set-ups per unit
Quality checks	Number of quality checks required for particular products	$4 250	Basic: 1 quality check per unit Deluxe: 3 quality checks per unit
Transfer of partly finished goods	Number of transfers from one machine to another required by particular products	$22 500	Basic: 3 transfers per unit Deluxe: 7 transfers per unit
Total overheads		$47 750	

During January 2015 the company's production was:

	Number of units
Basic	8 000
Deluxe	3 000

Here is how the overheads for each cost pool will be allocated using ABC.

Workings

	Cost drivers	Totals	Overhead allocation rate
Machine set-ups	Basic: 2 × 8 000, i.e. 16 000	28 000	$21 000/28 000 i.e. **$0.75 per set-ups**
	Deluxe: 4 × 3 000 i.e. 12 000		
Quality checks	Basic: 1 × 8 000, i.e. 8 000	17 000	$4 250/17 000 i.e. **$0.25 per check**
	Deluxe: 3 × 3 000, i.e. 9 000		
Transfer of partly finished goods	Basic: 3 × 8 000, i.e. 24 000	45 000	$22 500/45 000 i.e. **$0.50 per transfer**
	Deluxe: 7 × 3 000, i.e. 21 000		

Overhead allocation

	Basic		Deluxe	
		$		$
Set-ups	16 000 × $0.75	12 000	12 000 × $0.75	9 000
Quality checks	8 000 × $0.25	2 000	9 000 × $0.25	2 250
Transfers	24 000 × $0.50	12 000	21 000 × $0.50	10 500
Totals		26 000		21 750

Notes:

The table shows a refined allocation of overheads based on activities that cause overheads. Using traditional costing techniques the total overheads of $47 750 would have been allocated in a more arbitrary way (machine hours or labour hours).

Getting it right

It is always worthwhile to check that the total of overheads allocated to each product equals the overall total of overheads (here $26 000 + $21 750 does equal total overheads of $47 750).

Calculating the total cost of one unit

In order to calculate the cost of one unit it is necessary to add together the direct cost of production and the overheads allocated using the technique illustrated above.

Illustration 2: Calculating the cost of one unit of production

Referring to the manufacture of twexes (see Illustration 1), the direct costs of production are as follows.

	Basic	Deluxe
	$	$
Direct materials per unit	2.50	3.40
Direct labour per unit	3.80	4.90

For the month of January 2015 the total costs of producing each product are:

	Basic		Deluxe	
		$		$
Direct materials	8 000 × $2.50	20 000	3 000 × $3.40	10 200
Direct labour	8 000 × $3.80	30 400	3 000 × $4.90	14 700
Total overheads (see Illustration 1)		26 000		21 750
Total cost of production		76 400		46 650

The cost of producing one unit of each product is therefore as follows.

	Total cost of production/ number of units	Cost per unit $
Basic	$76 400/8 000	9.55
Deluxe	$46 650/3 000	15.55

Valuing closing inventories

In accordance the requirements of IAS 2 Inventories, the cost of unsold units would form the basis of valuation. Cost would take account of direct costs and factory overheads (as established in Illustration 2).

The effect of different methods of overhead absorption on profit

When ABC is used, the profit profile for a product is likely to be different to the profile produced if traditional methods are used. This is because ABC produces a more refined allocation of overheads, whereas traditional methods might be considered arbitrary.

Illustration 3: The effect of different methods on profit

Oretex Ltd manufactures high-quality garden seats. The company's total overheads for a year are \$800 000. The company has available a total of 10 000 labour hours per year. The labour rate is \$15 per hour. The company makes garden seats to order for a number of well-known distributors. The profit margin used by the company is 20 per cent on cost.

Recently the company received an order for 150 garden seats of a particular design from Abadi Ltd. It is expected that the order will require five labour hours per unit. The materials will cost \$60 per unit.

It has been established that the company has the following cost pools and cost drivers.

Cost pool	Cost driver	Overhead cost per year	Forecast annual total	Order from Abadi Ltd
Machine set-ups	Numbers of times a set-up is required for particular products	\$400 000	1 600 set-ups	200 set-ups
Inspections	Time take to carry out inspections	\$240 000	4 000 hours	75 hours
Packaging and despatch	Number of units	\$160 000	3 200 units	150 units
Total overheads		\$800 000		

Using traditional costs methods

Using traditional methods the project would be costed using an absorption rate based on labour hours.

The absorption rate is

$$\frac{\text{Total overheads}}{\text{Total labour hour}} \text{ i.e. } = \frac{\$800\,000}{10\,000} \text{ i.e. \$80 per labour hour}$$

		$
Direct materials	150 × $60	9 000
Direct labour	150 × 5 labour hours × $15 per hour (i.e. 750 × $15)	11 250
Overheads	750 × $80 OAR per labour hour	60 000
Total cost		**80 250**

Using traditional methods the profit made would be:

	$
Total cost	80 250
Profit margin (20% × cost)	**16 050**
Selling price	96 300

Using ABC

Overheads would be allocated as follows.

Workings to find the overhead allocation rate for each cost driver

Cost pool	Cost driver	Overhead cost per year	Forecast annual total	Overhead allocation rate
Machine set-ups	Number of times a set-up is required for particular products	$400 000	1 600 set-ups	40 000/1 600 set-ups i.e. $250 per set-up
Inspections	Time taken to carry out inspections	$240 000	4 000 hours	240 000/4 000 hours i.e. $60 per inspection hour
Packaging and despatch	Number of units	$160 000	2 000 units	$80 per unit
Total overheads		$800 000		

So for the order from Abadi Ltd:

		$
Direct materials	150 × $60	9 000
Direct labour	150 × 5 labour hours × $15 per hour (i.e. 750 × $15)	11 250
Overhead: machine set-ups	200 set-ups × $250 per set-up	50 000
Overhead: inspections	75 hours × $60 per inspection hour	4 500
Overhead: packaging and despatch	150 units × $80 per unit	12 000
Total cost		**86 750**

Using ABC the profit made would be:

	$
Total cost	86 750
Profit margin (20% × cost)	**17 350**
Selling price	104 100

Comparison of profits using different costing techniques

	$
Traditional costing	16 050
ABC	17 350
Extra profit from ABC	**1 350**

Notes:

By using the ABC technique Oretex Ltd ensures that overheads are more precisely allocated to the project.

As a result the company will make a higher profit ($1350) because the project absorbs a more appropriate (and higher) amount of the company's annual overheads.

The traditional method results in an under-absorption of overheads and reduces the amount of profit to be made.

Advantages and disadvantages of activity-based costing (ABC)

The main advantages of ABC are:

- It provides more reliable information for decision-making.
- It is possible to set selling prices that will achieve the desired level of profit, because the cost of a unit of product is established with greater precision.
- Managers will become more aware of aspects of the production process that are closely scrutinised using this technique. This may lead to closer attention being paid to looking for situations where costs can be reduced by being more efficient. This idea is sometimes called activity-based management.
- Managers will become aware of products that are no longer economic and should be abandoned.

The main disadvantages are:

- It is expensive to develop, implement and maintain a system of ABC. This is because each aspect of the production process requires a detailed study to establish cost drivers. In the case of each product it will be necessary to determine the extent to which each cost driver affects production.
- ABC may require an extensive programme of training.
- It is often the case that specialist consultants are required to set up the system.
- Operating the system is likely to be time consuming.

End-of-chapter questions

1 Calculating the allocation of overheads

Morad Industries Ltd manufactures two products: breves and minims.

The company has the following cost pools and has established that the cost drivers within each cost pool are as shown.

Cost pool	Cost driver	Overhead cost per month	Information about each product
Machine set-ups	Numbers of times a set-up is required for particular products	$59 500	Breve: 4 set-ups per unit Minim: 3 set-ups per unit
Issues from stores	Number of times raw materials are transferred from the stores for particular products	$33 250	Breve: 2 issues per unit Minim: 5 issues per unit
Total overheads		$92 750	

During November 2014 the company's production was:

	Number of units
Breve	14 000
Minim	21 000

Calculate the total overheads that should be allocated to breves and to minims.

2 Calculating the allocation of overheads

Thespa plc manufactures two products: matons and cratons.

The company has the following cost pools and has established that the cost drivers within each cost pool are as shown.

Cost pool	Cost driver	Overhead cost per month	Information about each product
Transfers of partly finished goods	Number of transfers from one machine to another required by particular products	$34 000	Matons: 3 transfers per unit Cratons: 2 transfers per unit
Quality checks	Number of quality checks required for particular products	$17 800	Matons: 4 transfers per unit Cratons: 6 transfers per unit
Total overheads		$51 800	

During November 2014 the company's production was:

	Number of units
Matons	40 000
Cratons	25 000

Calculate the total overheads which should be allocated to cratons and matons.

3 Calculating a selling price using activity-based costing

Using the information given in Question 1, calculate the selling price of a breve and a minim. The directors of Morad Industries Ltd wish to achieve a profit margin of 20 per cent on cost.

It should be noted that the direct costs for each product are as follows.

	Direct materials	Direct labour
Breves	5 kg @ $2.20 per kg	3 hrs @ $7 per hour
Minims	4 kg @ $2 per kg	2.4 hrs @ $8 per hour

Calculate the selling price per unit of a breve and of a minim.

4 Calculating a selling price using activity-based costing

Using the information given in Question 2, calculate the selling price of a maton and a craton. The directors of Thespa plc wish to achieve a profit margin of 50 per cent on cost.

It should be noted that the direct costs for each product are as follows.

	Direct materials	Direct labour
Matons	0.5 kg @ $4.20 per kg	1.5 hrs @ $6.40 per hour
Cratons	0.75 kg @ $6.40 per kg	0.8 hrs @ $9 per hour

Calculate the selling price per unit of a maton and of a craton.

5 Calculating closing inventory values

Referring to information in Questions 1 and 3, calculate the total value of Morad Ltd's closing inventory assuming that:

- 10 per cent of the annual production of breves remains unsold
- 5 per cent of the annual production of minims remains unsold.

6 **Calculating closing inventory values**
Referring to information in Questions 2 and 4, calculate the total value of Thespa plc's closing inventory assuming that:

- 4 per cent of the annual production of matons remains unsold
- 6 per cent of the production of cratons remains unsold.

7 **Evaluating activity-based costing**
RVL Ltd is a large manufacturing organisation producing a range of kitchen appliances. Currently the company uses traditional methods to establish the cost of each product, and operates with a profit margin of 25 per cent on cost. The company has introduced more automated manufacturing processes in the last few years. As a result direct costs have fallen considerably, but factory overheads now occupy a far greater proportion of total costs. The company's finance director has recommended that the company should switch to using activity-based costing.

Discuss the finance director's recommendation.

8 **Decision-making using activity-based costing**
Fratelli Ltd manufactures two products: hexo and zaco.

The following information is available about production costs.

- The direct costs of product are as follows.

	Hexo	Zaco
	$	$
Direct materials per unit	14.00	19.00
Direct labour per unit	11.00	12.00

- The company total factory overheads are $50 000. (Other overhead costs can be ignored.)
- Annual production is:

Hexo	500 units
Zaco	1 500 units

- It has been established that the company has the following cost pools and cost drivers.

Cost pool	Cost driver	Overhead cost per month	Information about each product
Machine set-ups	Numbers of times a set-up is required for particular products	$36 000	Hexo: 3 set-ups per unit Zaco: 2 set-ups per unit
Quality checks	Number of quality checks required for particular products	$14 000	Hexo: 4 quality checks per unit Zaco 1 quality checks per unit

Currently both products sell at $53 per unit. The company operates in a very competitive market and pricing was based on a survey of the prices charged by rival companies. However, the directors are not convinced that the company should continue to produce both products, although all production is currently being sold.

a Prepare a calculation of the cost of making a hexo unit and a zaco unit.

b What advice would you give the directors regarding the production and pricing of both products?

Section 2.2: Budgeting and budgetary control

Key concepts

Business planning can only be effective if information is based on a **true and fair view** of a business's financial affairs and if techniques are applied in a **consistent** manner. Managers always need to take account of the fact that non-financial factors cannot be reflected in the budgets or in standard costing techniques (the consequence of the **money measurement** concept).

2.2.1: Budgeting and budgetary control

What is budgetary control?

A budget is a short-term financial plan of standard costs and revenues prepared for the future to control resources so that the business objectives can be achieved. All functional budgets are used to prepare the master budget, which is a forecast income statement and forecast statement of financial position.

Budgeting is the preparation of the budgets for each budget centre, and budgetary control refers to the responsibility that each budget centre manager has to:

- justify the use of resources
- control costs
- achieve the activities set by the budget in accordance with the business's objectives.

Each manager's performance is then evaluated by comparing actual results against the targets set for the budget centre, so that any underachievement can be analysed and any remedial action can be taken.

The benefits

The benefits of using budgetary control are as follows:

- **Control:** A budget is a formal authorisation to a budget centre manager of a specified amount to be allocated to specified activities, thereby ensuring that resources such as cash and labour hours are controlled.
- **Planning:** By using a budget, the use of resources (e.g. cash, materials and labour hours) is planned in order to achieve the objectives of the business.
- **Communication and co-ordination:** Budgets communicate plans to managers responsible for carrying them out. They also ensure co-ordination between managers of sub-units, so that each is aware of the others' requirements (for example between the stores, production and sales departments).
- **Motivation:** Budgets are often intended to motivate managers to perform in line with organisational objectives. This applies especially if the managers have been included in the drawing up of the budgets, which will then be realistic and achievable, and if there are rewards for achievement of the budget targets.
- **Performance evaluation and monitoring:** The performance of managers is often evaluated by reference to budgetary standards. Any variance between the budget and actual results will then be assessed and corrective action taken.

Learning objectives

In this chapter you will learn:

- what the benefits and limitations of budgetary control are
- how to prepare a range of budgets
- how to prepare a set of forecast financial statements
- how to evaluate the performance of a business based on budgeted information
- to make recommendations as to how the performance of a business, as revealed by a budget, could be improved.

Key terms

Master budget: this budget is taken from the functional budgets and consists of a budgeted income statement and budgeted statement of financial position.

Budgeting: the preparation of the budgets.

Budget centre: a department or area for which a budget has been set up.

- **Aid to decision-making**: If all managers base their decision-making around their budgets, then all departmental decisions will relate to the corporate plan and business objectives.

The limitations

The limitations of using budgetary control are as follows:

- A budget must be produced within the limiting factors that surround the business, for example:
  - the amount of market demand for its product
  - the number of skilled employees available
  - the availability of material supplies
  - the space available either as a working area or for storage
  - the amount of cash or credit facilities available to finance the business.
- A budget that is unrealistic or unachievable is of limited use and may do more harm than good. It could have a negative effect on the workforce, who will feel that they are under performing and it may make their productivity decline further.
- A budget must not be set too low as this is also demotivational. This can happen when there is no goal congruence, or agreement, between the objectives of the manager and the objectives of the business. Some managers may feel that the budget is to be used to evaluate and judge their performance, and so may endeavour to set the budget to an easily achievable target, which at the same time may not motivate their teams.
- Budgets can restrict activity so that managers are not innovative and fail to take advantage of unexpected opportunities as their actions are too strictly controlled.
- Through careful control of their budgets, managers may have a surplus available at the end of the year, but rather than save this surplus they will spend it so that their budget for the following year will not be reduced. In this way, budgets may inadvertently encourage the inefficient use of resources.

Therefore, a budget is only as useful as the standards used to set it. If set too high, it is unachievable and demotivates the workforce; if set too low, it fails to motivate and can lead to inefficiencies and an unproductive workforce.

The effect of budgeting on a business's employees is sometimes referred to as behavioural aspects. Reference has already been made to how budgets can motive or demotivate staff depending on whether targets derived from budgets are too easily achievable, just achievable, or not achievable. Studies have shown that where a manager's overall performance is evaluated by reference to their success in meeting departmental budgets, managers can suffer from the pressure this

Getting it right

Benefits and limitations must be applied to the scenario of the question, with careful note taken as to whether the business provides a service or produces a product.

involves while also possibly receiving rewards in the form of bonuses where things go well. Pressure on managers can, of course, lead to stress and occasionally to poor working relationships with colleagues.

Types of functional budget

The following are types of functional budget:

- the sales budget
- the production budget
- the labour budget
- the purchases budget
- the trade receivables budget
- the trade payables budget
- the cash budget.

Key term

Functional budget: a budget relating to a particular business function (area).

Getting it right

All budgets usually have a vertical breakdown of data for each period or month.

The sales budget

The sales budget records the number of units expected to be sold as well as the expected sales value per period.

Key term

Sales budget: a summary of the expected sales units and sales value for the future.

Illustration 1: The sales budget

Rowan Hall owns a business that manufactures a single product, the Connie. The business operates over 13 periods a year. Each period consists of four weeks with five working days in each week. Last year Rowan Hall had a fixed production of 6000 units per period regardless of the level of sales, but this year he wants to introduce a system of budgetary control.

The following information is available for Rowan Hall for the first four periods of the new year.

	Period 1	Period 2	Period 3	Period 4
Expected sales (units)	1 200	1 400	1 500	1 400

Each unit of Connie sells for $100.

Sales budget for Rowan Hall for the first four periods				
	Period 1	**Period 2**	**Period 3**	**Period 4**
Sales units	1 200	1 400	1 500	1 400
Sales value	$120 000	$140 000	$150 000	$140 000

This is a forecast predicting what the sales will be in the future, perhaps based on the previous periods' sales or on market research.

Key term

Production budget: the calculation of expected production in units, based on the information from the sales budget and accounting for movements in inventory of finished goods.

The production budget

The production budget is the key budget as all production costs will be based on the quantities stated within it.

Illustration 2: The production budget

Rowan Hall maintains closing inventory at a level sufficient to cover eight days of sales for the next period. However, storage constraints restrict inventory to a maximum of 580 units. It is assumed that sales accrue evenly within each period. At the start of period 1, there are expected to be 480 units in inventory.

Production budget for Rowan Hall for the first three periods (units)

	Period 1	Period 2	Period 3
Sales	1 200	1 400	1 500
Opening inventory	(480)	(560)	(580)
Closing inventory: restricted	560	580	560
Production	1 280	1 420	1 480

This budget is in units only and is co-ordinated with the information from the sales budget.

The closing inventory is equivalent to eight days of the next period's sales. There are 20 days in a period (13 periods a year, each period has four weeks with five days in a week). Closing inventory is, therefore, calculated as 8/20 × next period's sales (e.g. closing inventory for period 1 is calculated as 8/20 × 1400 = 560).

Due to storage restrictions, the amount in closing inventory is limited to a maximum of 580 units. The business can therefore be seen in period 2 to be working to maximum capacity.

The closing inventory of one month becomes the opening inventory of the next month.

The units of production are calculated in units as:

Sales – Opening inventory + Closing inventory units.

Getting it right

Remember that this budget is in units only. A common mistake is to try to calculate the cost of production or to give inventory values.

Labour budgets

Labour budgets help managers plan the use of the labour hours available. These budgets are used to plan the efficient use of the workforce's time and to show the resulting labour costs.

Illustration 3: Preparing a labour budget

The production manager of Wow Ltd is planning the use of labour required for one of its products, 'zwelps'. Each zwelp takes six hours to complete in the machining department. Planned production for each of the three months ending 31 October 2015 is as follows.

	August	September	October
Units	800	900	700

The labour rate in the machining department is $8 per hour; there are 5000 labour hours available in each of the months in the budget.

Here is the labour budget.

Labour budget for each of the three months ending 31 October 2015 (machining department)			
	August	September	October
Production	800 units	900 units	700 units
Labour required	4 800 hours	5 400 hours	4 200 hours
Labour cost	$38 400	$43 200	$33 600
Surplus hours	200		800
Shortfall hours		400	

The production manager will now be aware that:

- there will be unused labour hours in August and October which could be used for production of another product
- additional labour will be required in September, which may mean reducing production of this product (or another product) or employing casual labour.

Key term

Purchases budget: a calculation of the expected value of purchases of materials based on the production levels as shown by the production budget.

The purchases budget

The purchases budget provides information on the cost of materials.

Illustration 4: The purchases budget

Each Connie consists of two metres of material which costs $15 per metre. The material cost per unit is therefore $30.

Purchases budget for Rowan Hall for the first three periods			
	Period 1	Period 2	Period 3
Production units	1 280	1 420	1 480
Material cost ($30 × units)	$38 400	$42 600	$44 400

Rowan Hall can see from this budget that the cost of purchases is increasing in line with the level of production. Perhaps he should negotiate a bulk-buying discount with the suppliers.

Key term

Trade receivables budget: a summary of the expected movement in money owed by the customers to the business.

The trade receivables budget

The trade receivables budget identifies the amount of money expected to be owed by customers each period.

Illustration 5: The trade receivables budget

Rowan Hall expects 20 per cent of each period's sales to be paid in cash. Therefore, 80 per cent of each period's sales will be on credit terms: half of the credit sales will pay after one period and the other half will pay after two periods. At the start of period 1 there are trade receivables of

$80 000 of which half will pay during the first period and the other half will pay in the second period. There was also a debt from two periods before of $45 000, which is expected to be paid in period 1. Of this debt, $10 000 is expected to be an irrecoverable debt.

Trade receivables budget for Rowan Hall for the first three periods

	Period 1 ($)	Period 2 ($)	Period 3 ($)
Balance b/d	125 000	136 000	160 000
Credit sales	96 000	112 000	120 000
Receipts:			
Credit sales from previous period	(40 000)	(48 000)	(56 000)
Credit sales from two periods before	(35 000)	(40 000)	(48 000)
Irrecoverable debt	(10 000)	–	–
Balance c/d	136 000	160 000	176 000

- This budget is co-ordinated with the sales budget.
- Credit sales: These are calculated as total sales less 20 per cent (cash receipts). For example, in period 1 the total sales are $120 000 less the cash receipts of $24 000 = $96 000 credit sales.
- Receipts: Half of the credit sales are received after one month and the other half two months later. For example, in period 1 the credit sales are $96 000 of which half will pay in period 2 and the other half in period 3.
- In period 1 the receipts from credit sales are from trade receivables from the previous year which are one period old and, therefore, half ($40 000) will be received in period 1 and the other half in period 2.
- In period 1 there are also receipts from credit sales, which are from trade receivables from the previous year. These are two periods old and, therefore, all will be received in period 1. However, an adjustment must be made for $10 000 of this debt which is bad and will not be recovered. The irrecoverable debt is recorded separately.
- Balance c/d: The balance c/d is the amount of trade receivables outstanding for the period and is carried forward to the next period and recorded as balance b/d.
- The closing balance is made up of $120 000 credit sales from period 3 and $56 000 being 50 per cent of the credit sales from period 2.
- It can clearly be seen that the amount of trade receivables is increasing, therefore so is the risk of further irrecoverable debts. Rowan Hall should try to encourage more cash sales, perhaps by increasing the amount of cash discount.

The trade payables budget

The trade payables budget identifies the amount of money owed to suppliers at the end of each period.

Key term

Trade payables budget: a summary of the expected movement in money owed by the business to the suppliers.

Illustration 6: The trade payables budget

Rowan Hall pays for 25 per cent of his purchases in cash. Therefore, 75 per cent of each period's purchases are on credit terms: 80 per cent of the credit purchases are paid after one period and 20 per cent will be paid after two periods. At the start of period 1 there are $22 500 of trade payables, of which $18 000 will be paid in the first period and the rest in the second period. There is also an amount owing from two periods before of $4000, which is expected to be paid in period 1.

Trade payables budget for Rowan Hall for the first three periods

	Period 1 ($)	Period 2 ($)	Period 3 ($)
Balance b/d	22 500	29 300	37 710
Credit purchases	28 800	31 950	33 300
Payments:			
Credit purchases from previous period	(18 000)	(23 040)	(25 560)
Credit purchases from two periods before	(4 000)	(4 500)	(5 760)
Balance c/d	29 300	37 710	39 690

- This budget is co-ordinated with the purchases budget.
- Credit purchases: These are calculated as total purchases less 25 per cent (cash payments). For example, in period 1 the total purchases are $38 400 less the cash payments of $9600 = $28 800 credit purchases.
- Payments: 80 per cent of the credit purchases are paid after one month and 20 per cent are paid two months later. For example, in period 1 the credit purchases are $28 800 of which 80 per cent ($23 040) will be paid in period 2 and 20 per cent ($5760) in period 3.
- In period 1 the payments to trade payables are for 80 per cent of purchases for the previous period, and 20 per cent of purchases for the period before that.
- In period 1 there are also payments to credit purchases which are to trade payables from the previous year. These are two periods old and, therefore, all will be paid in period 1.
- Balance c/d: The balance c/d is the amount of trade payables outstanding for the period. It is carried forward to the next period and recorded as balance b/d.
- The closing balance is made up of $33 300 credit purchases for period 3 and $6390 being 20 per cent of the credit purchases from period 2.
- It can clearly be seen that Rowan Hall owes an increasing amount to his trade payables.

Key term

Cast budget: a financial plan for the future cash inflows and outflows for period of time which is used to control the use of cash resources so that the business objectives can be achieved.

The cash budget

A cash budget is a financial plan of future cash income (inflows) and cash expenditure (outflows) for both revenue and capital items for a period of time. It is drawn up to help managers become aware of any potential shortage or surplus of cash resources. This means that, in the case of a shortage, funds can be sourced from elsewhere or an overdraft arrangement can be made with the bank and in the case of a surplus,

Getting it right

A common error is to include non-cash items within a cash budget. The most common examples include depreciation and irrecoverable debts.

funds can be invested so that greater returns can be made on the money. A cash budget considers all cash income and expenditure but ignores non-cash items such as depreciation.

Benefits:

- All cash resources are controlled to avoid overdrafts or surplus cash being held.
- All cash expenditure can be planned (for example a wage rise or purchase of a new expensive machine).
- Co-ordination and communication is ensured between all departments (for example, the production department does not plan to over-produce products without arranging for there to be enough purchases of materials for production, and the purchasing department cannot plan to purchase material unless there is enough cash available to for it).
- Performance can be monitored, so overdrafts and their interest charges can be avoided, plus enough cash resources are available for any planned expenditure. This means that activities are not restricted through a lack of funds, or that the purchase of a non-current asset can be delayed until funds are available.
- Cash targets are achieved and staff are motivated.

Limitations:

- Restrictions are placed on expenditure. This could lead to a lack of funds available for an unexpected opportunity, which if not undertaken could mean profits are lost.
- If the targets are set too high and cash restrictions are too tight, then staff may become demotivated.
- If the targets are set too low and there are few restrictions on cash resources, then staff may overspend and cash is wasted.

Preparing a cash budget

There are various possible layouts for a cash budget but the most common one is shown below.

Illustration 7: The cash budget

Robert Ray runs a small shop selling books. His shop is open six days a week, for six hours a day.

His expected sales and purchases for the next three months are:

	Month 1	Month 2	Month 3
Book sales	$900	$650	$600
Purchases of inventory	$200	$300	$400

His customers all pay in cash.

Robert buys 20 per cent of his inventory from one supplier paying in cash and receiving a 5 per cent discount. All the rest of the inventory is bought on one month's credit. He owes $180 at the start of month 1 for credit purchases from the previous month.

Robert employs one part-time assistant for three hours a week and pays her $5 an hour.

His rent is $200 a quarter payable in months 1, 4, 7 and 10.

His other overheads are $120 a month.

He also intends to take out a small loan in month 1 of $400. This will be paid back at $50 a month starting in month 2.

Robert pays himself $300 a month and does not like to go overdrawn. He also would like to go holiday in month 6 but this will cost $700.

At the start of month 1, his bank balance was $280.

Prepare a cash budget for Robert Ray for the next three months and state whether he can save for the holiday.

	Cash budget for Robert Ray for months 1–3			
		Month 1	Month 2	Month 3
		$	$	$
	Receipts			
	Book sates	900	650	600
	Loan	400		
A	**Total receipts**	1300	650	600
	Payments			
W1	Purchases: cash	38	57	76
W2	Purchases: credit	180	160	240
W3	Assistant's wages	60	60	60
	Rent	200		
	Overheads	120	120	120
	Loan repayment		50	50
	Drawings	300	300	300
B	**Total payments**	898	747	846
A–B	**Net cash flow**	402	(97)	(246)
	Balance brought forward	280	682	585
	Balance carried forward	682	585	339

W1: The cash purchases are calculated as 20% × month's purchases × 0.95.

W2: The credit purchases are calculated as 80% × previous month's purchases.

W3: Wages are $5 × 3 hours × 4 weeks = $60 per month

As can be seen from the cash budget. Robert has avoided going overdrawn by taking out a loan in month 1. However, his bank balance is still declining despite the loan and he will need to think of a way of improving his cash flow to avoid an overdraft in the future. He is certainly in no position to save for a holiday costing $700 unless he can increase his revenue or decrease his cash payments.

Getting it right

It is important to identity clearly which items are income (inflows) and which as expenditure (outflows). This can be done with the use of subheadings or brackets. Columns of figures mean very little and do not constitute a budget.

The master budget

Information is taken from all of the functional budgets and a set of forecast financial statements is produced. This is known as the master budget.

Key term

Forecast financial statements: the forecast income statement and statement of financial position based on the functional budgets contained within the master budget.

Link

There is more about standard costs in A Level Chapter 2.3.1 Standard costing.

Illustration 8: Preparing the master budget

Rowan Hall wishes to produce a set of forecast final accounts from his functional budgets as a means of evaluating his expected profitability.

- The standard cost per unit is:

	$
Direct materials	30
Direct labour (24 + 30)	54
	84

- Inventory will be valued on the basis of the standard cost per unit.
- Overheads for the period are expected to be $45 600, including depreciation of $8500.
- It is assumed that there is no opening or closing inventory of raw materials or work in progress.

Forecast income statement for Rowan Hall for periods 1–3

	$	$
Revenue (1 200 + 1 400 + 1 500 units) × $100 (note 1)		410 000
Opening inventory (480 units × $84) (note 2)	40 320	
Cost of production (1 280 + 1420 + 1 480) × $84 (note 3)	351 120	
Closing inventory (560 units × $84) (note 4)	(47 040)	
Cost of sales		(344 400)
Gross profit		65 600
Irrecoverable debt	10 000	
Depreciation	8 500	
Overheads	37 100	
		(55 600)
Profit for the year		10 000

Note 1: This is calculated using the information from the sales budget. Each period's sales units are added together and then multiplied by the selling price.

Note 2: This is calculated using the opening units from period 1 in the production budget which is then multiplied by the standard cost per unit.

Note 3: This is calculated using the information from the production budget. Each period's production units are added together and then multiplied by the standard cost.

Alternatively the cost of production can be calculated as:

Materials from the purchases budget

$38 400 + $42 600 + $44 400 = $125 400

Plus labour from the labour budget

$69 120 + $76 680 + $79 920 = $225 720

Note 4: This is calculated using the closing inventory of units from period 3 in the production budget, which is then multiplied by the standard cost per unit.

Additional information:

- Non-current assets are expected to have a book value of $161 500.
- The balance at the bank is expected to be $18 200 overdrawn.
- The amount owing on a long-term loan is expected to be $10 000.
- The capital b/d is expected to be $312 310.
- The drawings for the period are expected to be $5660.

Forecast statement of financial position for Rowan Hall at end of period 3

	$	$
Non-current assets		161 500
Current assets		
Inventory	47 040	
Trade receivables	176 000	
		223 040
		384 540
Equity		
Capital b/d		312 310
Profit for the year		10 000
Drawings		(5 660)
Total equity		316 650
Non-current liabilities		
Long-term loan		(10 000)
Current liabilities		
Bank overdraft	(18 200)	
Trade payables	(39 690)	
Working capital		47 890
		384 540

The closing inventory is the amount in the income statement which is calculated by multiplying the closing inventory in period 3 in the production budget by the standard cost.

The amount of trade receivables is calculated from the trade receivables budgets.

The amount of trade payables is calculated from the trade payables budget.

Rowan Hall can see from the forecast financial statements that he does expect to make a profit albeit a small one. He is expected to have a positive working capital but also an overdraft in the bank (which would be ascertained from a cash budget). He has a considerable amount of trade receivables, which needs careful monitoring otherwise he will open himself up to the possibility of irrecoverable debts. So, it is recommended that he looks into reducing the level of trade receivables to improve his liquidity and cash position.

Getting it right

Previously, questions have been set on preparing the forecast financial statements, as this tests both budgeting and the layout of the income statement and statement of financial position. You also have to know about acceptable methods of inventory valuation to complete the income statement.

You may come across any of these budgets, which means that you must know all of them!

Limiting factors

A business's activities are inevitably subject to restrictions for a number of possible reasons, known as limiting or key factors. Here are some examples:

- demand for the product
- shortage of materials used in production
- shortage of labour
- lack of available machine hours
- lack of storage facilities.

Knowledge of a particular limiting factor will help decide which functional budget should take priority in the budgeting sequence. For example, if there is a forecast shortage of materials then the purchase budget will be prepared first.

Flexing the budget

Businesses often review a budget after a period of time. The aim of standard costing is to highlight areas of good practice and also areas where problems have arisen. Comparisons can then be made between the standard (budgeted) costs and the actual costs. This has little validity unless comparing like with like. For example, comparing material costs for actual production of 200 units with budgeted costs for 120 units is of very little use.

Key term

Flexing the budget: adjusting the standard costs within a budget for actual levels of activity.

It is, therefore, necessary to adjust each budget, as cost patterns vary according to the various levels of activity; this process is called flexing the budget. It is an important aspect of budgetary control because it can help managers:

- avoid making invalid decisions based on misleading information
- identify favourable and adverse variances when the flexed budget is compared to actual performance.

Illustration 9: Preparing a flexed budget

The following information is available about the business owned by Vikash for the month of December 2014.

	Budget	Actual
Production (units)	10 000	9 000
Direct materials	20 000	17 800
Direct labour	45 000	42 300
Variable overheads	16 000	14 100
Fixed overheads	28 000	29 400

Using knowledge of cost behaviour, the budget for 10 000 units can be flexed (i.e. varied) to show the budget (or standard) costs for 9000 units. It is then possible to calculate variances.

Here is the information again showing a flexed budget and variances.

	Budget	Flexed	Actual	Variances
Production (units)	10 000	9 000	9 000	
Direct materials	20 000	18 000	17 800	$200 favourable
Direct labour	45 000	40 500	42 300	$1 800 adverse
Variable overheads	16 000	14 400	14 100	$300 favourable
Fixed overheads	28 000	28 000	29 400	$1 400 adverse

Notes:

1 Using only the original data, managers could suppose that there was a favourable variance on materials (i.e. actual was $2200 less than the budget), but of course this is incorrect. Production was less than the budget so, of course, materials actually used should have been less.

2 All variances should be investigated. The causes of favourable variances should be looked into as it is possible they could be continued and even applied to other aspects of the business. The causes of adverse variances will need to be discovered so that managers take appropriate action to ensure that where possible they are addressed.

Link

The causes of variances are looked at in more detail in A Level Chapter 2.3.1 Standard costing.

End-of-chapter questions

1 **Budgetary control**
Explain the term 'budgetary control'. Why is it helpful to the management of a business?

2 **Uses of a budget**
Identify a budget which is not useful to each of the following businesses and give a reason why:

- a a school
- b a firm of accountants
- c a leisure complex
- d a high street butcher.

3 **Limitations and benefits of a budget**
'Departmental managers should be left to their own devices and not restricted by budgets as then they are free to act in an unrestricted manner and so innovation will be achieved.' Discuss.

4 **Uses of a budget**
Identify two uses for each of the following budgets:

- a a cash budget
- b a production budget
- c a trade receivables budget.

5 **Preparing a production budget**
Jameson Ltd operates over 13 periods a year. Each period consists of four weeks with five working days in each week.

The sales for the next four periods are expected to be as follows:

	Period 1	Period 2	Period 3	Period 4
Sales (units)	9 200	9 800	10 400	9 600

Assume that sales accrue evenly within each period.

The inventory at the start of period 1 was 3680 units.

It is the company's policy to maintain the closing inventory of units at a level that is sufficient to cover eight days of sales for the next period. However, storage constraints restrict inventory to a maximum of 4000 units.

Prepare the production budget in units for each period for periods 1–3.

6 **Uses of a budget**
Identify two uses for each of the following budgets:

- a a labour budget
- b a trade payables budget
- c a master budget.

7 Preparing a labour budget

Romets Ltd manufactures a range of car accessories, one of which is called a 'grix'. Grix take 3.5 labour hours to assemble and the labour rate for assembly staff if $7.20 per hour.

The following is the budgeted production for the first months of 2016.

	January	February	March
Units	420	390	440

The number of labour hours available in the assembly department in each of these months is 1450.

a Prepare a labour budget for each of the three months ending 31 March 2016.

b What advice would you give the production manager concerning any shortfall in, or surplus of, labour hours in February 2016?

8 Preparing functional budgets and the master budget

Katerina plans to manufacture glassware, starting on 1 October 2016.

The following information is available for the four months ending 31 January 2017:

- Each piece of glassware will be sold for $8, which is a mark-up of 300 per cent on material costs.
- Closing inventory is to be maintained at 20 per cent of next month's sales.
- In October, 250 pieces of glassware are expected to be sold. This is to increase by 20 per cent in November and by a further 30 per cent in December. However, in January and February sales are expected to drop to 180 pieces for each month.
- Each month Katerina expects that 50 per cent of sales will pay in cash and will receive a cash discount of 5 per cent. Of the remaining 50 per cent, only 60 per cent will pay the following month and the remainder will pay the month after that.
- Katerina will pay for all of her purchases a month in arrears, except to one supplier who wants immediate payment and will give a 2 per cent discount to Katerina if she pays in the month of purchase. This supplier will amount to 25 per cent of her purchases.
- Katerina will invest $2000 into the business, which will be placed in the bank on 1 October 2016. Her monthly overheads are expected to be $520 per month and she will pay herself 50 per cent of the closing bank balance (before the deduction of drawings) each month as wages.

For each of the four months ending 31 January 2017 prepare:

a a sales budget

b a production budget

c a material purchases budget

d a trade receivables budget

e a trade payables budget

f a cash budget

g a master budget.

9 Preparing a trade receivables budget

Ali Khan has a business selling computer games. All games are sold on credit to high street retailers.

His predicted sales for the next three months are:

Month 1	2 030 games
Month 2	2 240 games
Month 3	2 160 games

Each game is sold for $20 each. Ali expects 60 per cent of each month's sales to be paid for one month after sale. The rest will pay two months after the sale. At the start of month 1, Ali is owed $58 000: $42 000 from the previous month and $16 000 from two months earlier.

He has heard a rumour that Jermaine, one of his major customers, is having financial problems and may stop trading during month 1. Jermaine owes $15 400 from two months ago. Ali is concerned that he does not have good credit control management and believes that there are measures he could take to stop this level of debt arising with one customer.

a Prepare a trade receivables budget for the period month 1 to month 3.

b Explain one approach Ali could take to improve his credit control management and explain the effect it would have on the trade receivables budget for months 1–3.

10 Preparing a trade payables budget

TickTock Ltd is a small company that sells antique clocks. The following budgeted information is available for the five months ending 31 October.

	June	July	August	September	October
Expected purchases of clocks	60	80	120	100	80

Each clock costs $12.50. Each month 25 per cent of the purchases are expected to be on a cash basis. A total of 60 per cent of the amount owed to the trade payables is expected to be paid after one month. The remainder is expected to be paid after two months.

Prepare a trade payables budget for TickTock Ltd for each of the three months ending 31 October.

11 The benefits and limitations of using a cash budget

Explain two benefits and two limitations of using a cash budget.

12 Preparing a cash budget

Alexon Ltd is a company selling bicycles. The directions have an overdraft facility of $30 000, but are concerned about liquidity and wish to prepare a cash budget for the three months ending 30 June 2016.

The directors provide the following information.

Sales	
Month	**$**
March	12,000
April	15,000
May	24,000
June	30,000

Additional information:

Thirty per cent of all sales are on a cash basis with payment received immediately. The remaining 70 per cent of sales are on one-month credit terms. The company offers 5 per cent discount to credit customers and expects all amounts to be received on time.

- Purchases represent 40 per cent of the sales price and suppliers are paid one month in arrears. Purchases are made in the same month in which they are sold.
- Operating expenses are expected to be $2500 per month (including depreciation of $400) and are paid in the month incurred.
- Directors' salaries total $6000 per month.
- In May, the company must pay a tax bill of $12 000 and has agreed to purchase non-current assets at a price of $8000.
- On 1 June the directors plan to issue 10 000 ordinary shares of $1 each at a premium of 50¢. This will increase the issued share capital to $50 000. The directors expect the share issue to be fully subscribed.
- The directors propose to pay an interim dividend of 15¢ per share on 30 June to all shareholders of ordinary shares on that date.
- The balance on the company's bank account at 1 April is expected to be $18 700 overdrawn.

Required

a. Prepare a cash budget for each of the three months ending 30 June 2016.
b. Advise the directors what steps could be taken to improve the company's liquidity.

13 Preparing a cash budget

David Ltd is a small business that manufactures teddy bears.

The following information is available for the next four months:

	January	February	March	April
Expected	2 000	2 200	2 300	2 200
Production and sales (teddy bears)				

Additional information:

- Each teddy bear sells for $15.
- Each month 20 per cent of the sales are expected to be on a cash basis and customers will receive a 5 per cent cash discount for prompt payment.
- Fifty per cent of trade receivables are expected to pay after one month. The remainder are expected to pay after two months.
- Trade receivables on 1 January are expected to be: $21 600 from December sales (of which $10 800 will be paid in January and the balance in February) and $7200 from November sales (which will be paid in January).
- Overheads are $8200 per month.

- Each teddy bear costs $8 to make ($3 for material costs and $5 for labour). The materials are paid for one month after purchase and the labour costs are paid in the month of employment. On 1 January there is $5700 owing for materials purchased in December.
- Teddy bears are produced in the same month in which they are sold.
- There is $2100 in the bank on 1 January.

Required

Prepare a cash budget for David Ltd for each of the four months January to April.

14 Preparing a cash budget

- Shafiq hopes to start a new business on 1 March selling surfboards.
- His balance at bank on that day will be $3200.
- He intends to sell each surfboard for $160. On 1 June, the price will increase to $190 per surfboard.
- The variable cost per surfboard is expected to be $85.
- In preparation for the summer season, Shafiq intends his inventory level to be 60 surfboards by 1 June.
- Shafiq intends to employ his brother, Massod, to help out in the workshop for three months from 1 March. Massod will be paid $40 per day for five days a week.
- With Massod's help, Shafiq hopes to make up to a maximum of ten surfboards a week, whereas he can only make up to six surfboards alone.
- The inventory on 31 July is expected to be 28 surfboards. His fixed overheads, excluding depreciation, are expected to be $500 per month.
- Any bank suplus over $1000 at the end of each month will be taken as Shafiq's personal drawings.
- All transactions will be on a cash basis.

Expected sales are:

1 March to 30 April	May	1 June onwards
4 surfboards a week	7 surfboards a week	10 surfboards a week

Note: Assume that each month consists of four weeks.

Required

a Prepare a production budget for each of the five months ending 31 July, assuming Massod is employed.

b Prepare a cash budget for each of the five months ending 31 July. Include the maximum amount that Shafiq can withdraw for personal use.

15 Consider limiting factors within budgets

The table shows the budgeted resources required for production and sales, and the available resources.

Market research shows sales demand for 120 000 units.

	Resources required per unit	Resources available
Material	4.0 kg	460 000 kg
Direct labour hours	3.0	400 000 hours
Machine hours	0.5	70 000 hours

Identify the principal limiting factor in this case.

16 Preparing a production budget and budgeted income statements

Peishan owns a business manufacturing drinking mugs. The business operates over 13 four-week periods with five working days in each week.

Previously, Peishan had fixed production at 18 000 mugs per period, regardless of the level of sales. This year Peishan has decided to introduce a system of budgetary control.

The sales for the first four periods of this year are expected to be as follows.

	Period 1	Period 2	Period 3	Period 4
Mugs (units)	14 500	15 200	16 100	17 400

Sales are expected to occur evenly throughout each period.

Inventory at the start of period 1 is 2900 mugs.

Inventory is now to be maintained at a level sufficient to cover four days of the next period's expected sales.

Each mug costs $0.60 to make and is sold for $1.45.

a Prepare the production budget in units for each of the periods 1–3.

b Prepare comparative budgeted trading sections of the income statement for Peishan for periods 1–3, using:
  i the production budget prepared in answer to **a**.
  ii a fixed production level of 18 000 mugs per period

Assume that inventory is valued at cost.

c Explain two benefits for Peishan's business of introducing a production budget.

17 Preparing a flexed budget

Carmon plc manufactures mountain bikes. The following information is available about productions costs budgeted for March 2017 and actual costs for that month.

	Budget	Actual
Production (units)	1 200	1 320
Direct materials	26 400	29 700
Direct labour	32 400	33 500
Variable overheads	19 500	22 340
Fixed overheads	27 200	26 100

Required

a Prepare a flexed budget for March 2017.

b Calculate variances for each cost.

c Explain the importance of preparing flexed budgets.

Section 2.3: Standard costing

Key concepts

Standard costing is an important technique that is used by managers to compare actual costs and revenues with expected costs and revenues. Managers investigate any variances (differences between actual figures and expected figures) and make important decisions based on these investigations. It is important, therefore, that methods are applied **consistently** and that managers are aware of non-financial factors (a consequence of the **money measurement** concept).

2.3.1: Standard costing

Learning objectives

In this chapter you will learn:

- what standard costing is and what its purposes are
- about the different types of standard and how standards are set
- how standard unit costs are set
- what the advantages and disadvantages of standard costing are
- about the uses of a standard hour
- how to calculate material, labour and sales variances
- how to reconcile budgeted costs with actual costs
- how to reconcile budgeted profit with actual profit
- about possible reasons for variances.

Key term

Standard costing: a technique that determines what a resource should cost or how long a process should take and compares this to what actually happened.

Standard costing and its purposes

Standard costing is a technique that determines what a resource should cost or how long a process should take and then compares this standard with what actually happened. In this way, organisations are able to see how efficiently they are working by comparing what should have been achieved with what actually was achieved by calculating a variance.

Standards will be set for material costs and the amount of material that should be used, together with labour costs and the amount of time that a process should take.

Standard costing may be used in a variety of different businesses, but it is most commonly found in a manufacturing business. The most important uses of standard costing include:

- acting as a control device so that managers can compare the standard with what actually happened and take corrective action where necessary
- assisting in the budget-setting process
- providing information when quoting for a job
- providing targets and motivation for employees
- assisting in decision-making for the future
- providing costs for inventory.

Types of standard

There are three different types of standard:

- **Ideal standard:** This assumes that there will be no breakdown of machinery, that all employees will work at 100 per cent efficiency and that there will be no idle time, there will be no wastage and that the ideal price will always be paid for both materials and labour. Standards set on this basis are usually unrealistic.
- **Attainable standard:** This recognises that ideal conditions will not always exist, that there will be wastage of materials, employees will not be 100 per cent productive and machines may break down. As a result, realistic consideration is given to these facts in setting the standards.
- **Basic standard:** This refers to a standard set and never reviewed. Standards should be constantly reviewed and amended when circumstances dictate.

Calculating standard unit cost

Setting standards involves setting both technical standards (how much material should be used, how much time should be taken) and cost standards (the price of materials and the labour rate).

> **Key term**
>
> **Standard cost card**: a summary of the standard material usage, the standard time taken and the basis of overhead recovery for each product.

A standard cost card will normally be produced for each product. This will include:

- the quantity and price of each material to be used
- the time and rate of each grade of direct labour to be used
- the basis and amount of overhead recovery.

Setting the standards for the standard cost card can be undertaken in a variety of ways depending on the nature of the organisation.

Setting direct material standards

The standard for the amount of direct material used is set by:

- referring to the product specification
- observing the manufacturing process
- reviewing past data for the amount of wastage
- assessing the quality of material to be used
- assessing the quality of direct labour to be used.

The standard for the cost of direct material is set by:

- reviewing supplier price lists
- assessing the amounts of discount available
- reviewing any price increases already notified
- assessing if prices will change due to seasonality
- reviewing predicted inflation rates and exchange rates.

Setting direct labour standards

The standard for the amount of direct labour used is set by:

- observing the manufacturing process
- assessing any changes in the manufacturing process
- reviewing past efficiency levels
- assessing the quality of direct labour to be used

The standard for the cost of direct labour is set by:

- referring to the current payroll records
- assessing the need for overtime rates to be paid
- reviewing any agreed future wage increases
- reviewing the grade of direct labour to be used.

The advantages and disadvantages of standard costing

Advantages

- By comparing standard costs with actual costs, managers are able to control the business more effectively.

- Productivity should improve as a result of the increased motivation of staff having realistic and achievable targets.
- Budgets and forecasts can be prepared more easily due to the standard data having been prepared.

Disadvantages

- Standards must be reviewed regularly and amended if they are to be of use.
- Collecting the necessary information and maintaining the system can be a time-consuming and costly process.
- Standard costs are most suitable for businesses with established repetitive processes.

Standard hours

Key term

Standard hour: a measure of a quantity of work undertaken under ideal conditions in one hour.

If an organisation is producing one product only, the principles outlined above will enable accurate monitoring and control of the operation. However, in an organisation producing more than one product using different resources, the task becomes more difficult.

A standard hour is a measure of a quantity of work undertaken, not a measure of time. For example, if 50 units of a product should be produced under ideal conditions in one hour, the standard hour is 50 units.

The principle use of the standard hour is when an organisation produces more than one product. Under these circumstances, it is possible to calculate the total standard hours of production.

Illustration 1: Calculating standard hours

A department produces three different products, each taking a variable amount of time. In order to monitor and control the output of the department, production can be expressed as standard hours of production.

50 units of product A taking 1 hour each	50 standard hours
30 units of product B taking 30 minutes each	15 standard hours
180 units of product C taking 20 minutes each	60 standard hours
Total standard hours of production	125 standard hours

In this way, the total output of the department can be expressed as 125 standards hours, regardless of the products being produced.

Getting it right

Remember that a standard hour is a measure of a quantity of work undertaken, not a measure of time.

Variance analysis

Key term

Variance: a difference between the standard and what actually happened.

One of the main uses of standard costing is to enable variances to be calculated. A variance is the difference between a standard cost and the actual cost.

Key terms

Favourable variance: when the actual cost is less than the standard cost or when the actual revenue is more than the standard revenue.

Adverse variance: when the actual cost is more than the standard cost or when the actual revenue is less than the standard revenue.

Variances may be favourable or adverse. A favourable variance is when the actual cost is less than the standard cost, which has a positive effect on profit. An adverse variance is when the actual cost is more than the standard cost, which has a negative effect on profit.

It is important to remember that managers should investigate both favourable and adverse variances as they both indicate a deviation from the plan and require explanation.

The key to successful variance analysis is to remember that you must always compare like with like. For this reason, the budgeted production or the budgeted usage must always be flexed to what the actual production or usage was.

For example, if the budgeted production was 800 units but the actual production was only 700 units, then clearly a lesser amount of direct material or direct labour should have been used. For this reason, we always compare the actual amount of direct material or direct labour that should have been used for the actual production with the amount that was actually used.

Direct material cost variances

Key terms

Direct material total variance: the difference between what the direct material for the actual output should have cost and what it actually cost.

Direct material price variance: the difference between the standard cost and the actual cost of the actual amount of direct material used.

Direct material usage variance: the difference between the standard usage of material and the actual usage of material for the actual production, valued at the standard cost.

The direct material total variance is the difference between what the direct material for the actual output should have cost, less what it actually cost. A total variance may have been caused due to more or less material being used for the output or by a higher or lower price being paid for the quantity of material used. As a result, this total variance can then be subdivided into a price variance and a usage variance.

- The direct material price variance is the difference between the standard cost and the actual cost of the actual quantity of material used.
- The direct material usage variance is the difference between the standard quantity of material that should have been used for the actual number of units of product actually produced and the actual quantity used, valued at the standard cost.

Illustration 2: Calculating direct material variances

Product A has a standard direct material cost as follows:

5 kilos of material X at $2 per kilo = $10 per unit.

During January 2015, 100 units of product A were produced using 520 kilos of material X, which cost $1092 ($2.10 per kilo).

		$
Total variance	100 units should cost ($10)	1 000
	100 units actually cost	1 092
	Total variance	$92 adverse

Price variance	520 kilos should cost ($2)	1 040
	520 kilos actually cost	1 092
	Price variance	$52 adverse
Usage variance	100 units should use (5 kilos)	500 kilos
	100 units actually used	520 kilos
		20 kilos adverse
	× standard price per kilo	× $2
	Usage variance	$40 adverse

As a check for your workings, the total variance should always equal the price variance plus or minus the usage variance. In this instance, $52 adverse plus $40 adverse equals $92 adverse.

Getting it right

It is important to remember that the material usage variance is first calculated in units of material used and must then be multiplied by the standard price per unit of material to find the usage variance in monetary terms.

Calculating direct material variances using formulae

The direct material cost variances may be calculated using formulae. Using the same data as in the previous example, the variances would be calculated as follows.

Material price variance

Actual quantity of material (AQ) × (Actual price paid per kilo (AP) – Standard price per kilo (SP))

The formula is AQ(AP – SP)

The variance is, therefore, calculated as 520($2.10 – $2.00) = $52 adverse.

Material usage variance

Standard price (SP) × (Actual quantity of material used (AQ) – Standard quantity of material (SQ))

The formula is SP(AQ – SQ)

The variance is, therefore, calculated as $2(520 – 500) = $40 adverse.

Direct labour cost variances

The direct labour total variance is the difference between what the direct labour for the actual output should have cost, less what it actually cost. A total variance may have been caused due to more or less labour being used for the output or by a higher or lower price being paid for the hours of labour used. As a result, this total variance can then be subdivided into a rate variance and an efficiency variance.

- The direct labour rate variance is the difference between the standard cost and the actual cost of the actual amount of time taken.

Key terms

Direct labour total variance: the difference between what the direct labour for the actual output should have cost and what it actually cost.

Direct labour rate variance: the difference between the standard cost and the actual cost of the amount of direct labour used.

Key term

Direct labour efficiency variance: the difference between the standard usage of labour and the actual usage of labour for the actual production, valued at the standard cost.

▶ The direct labour efficiency variance is the difference between the hours that should have been worked to produce the number of units actually produced and the actual hours worked, valued at the standard cost per hour.

Illustration 3: Calculating direct labour variances

Product B has a standard direct labour cost as follows:

4 hours of grade P labour at \$3 per hour = \$12 per unit.

During February 2015, 200 units of product B were produced and the direct labour cost of grade P labour was \$2418 for 780 hours of work (\$3.10 per hour).

		$
Total variance	200 units should cost (\$12)	2 400
	200 units actually cost	2 418
	Total variance	\$18 adverse
Rate variance	780 hours should cost (\$3)	2 340
	780 hours actually cost	2 418
		\$78 adverse
Efficiency variance	200 units should take (4 hours)	800 hrs
	200 units actually took	780 hrs
	Efficiency variance	20 hrs favourable
	× standard price per hour	× \$3
	Efficiency variance	\$60 favourable

As a check for your workings, the total variance should always equal the rate variance plus or minus the efficiency variance. In this instance, \$78 adverse less \$60 favourable equals \$18 adverse.

Getting it right

It is important to remember that the labour efficiency variance is first calculated in time taken and must then be multiplied by the standard price per unit of time to find the efficiency variance in monetary terms.

Calculating direct labour variances using formulae

The direct labour cost variances may be calculated using formulae. Using the same data as in the previous example, the variances would be calculated as follows.

Labour rate variance

Actual hours (AH) × (Actual labour rate paid AR – Standard labour rate (SR))

The formula is AH(AR – SR)

The variance is, therefore, calculated as 780(\$3.10 – \$3.00) = \$78 adverse.

Labour efficiency variance

Standard labour rate (SR) × (Actual hours worked (AH) – Standard hours (SH))

The formula is SR(AH – SH)

The variance is, therefore, calculated as \$3(780 – 800) = \$60 favourable.

Flexing the budget

It will often be necessary to flex budgeted information, because actual production will be more or less than had been expected. This will ensure that variances are based on truly comparative data.

Illustration 4: Calculating variances using a flexed budget

Quelto plc manufactures office desks of one particular design. The following budgeted information is available for November 2014.

Production (units)	2 500
Direct materials	17 500 kg at \$2.30 per kg
Direct labour	10 000 hrs at \$6.80 per labour hour

These budget figures are only valid for that level of production.

Actual data for November 2014 was as follows.

Production (units)	2 250
Direct materials	16 400 kg at \$2.20 per kg
Direct labour	8 800 hrs at \$7.00 per labour hour

Before calculating any variances the budgeted information must be flexed to reflect the fact that production was less than had been planned. In fact production was 250 units less than planned (i.e. one-tenth less than expected).

So the flexed budget will show quantities of materials and the number of standard hours reduced by one-tenth. Here is the information required for the variance analysis set out side by side.

	Flexed budget	Actual
Production (units)	2 250	2 250
Direct materials	15 750 kg at \$2.30 per kg	16 400 kg at \$2.20 per kg
Direct labour	9 000 hrs at \$6.80 per labour hour	8 800 hrs at \$7.00 per labour hour

The direct materials and direct labour variances can now be calculated as follows.

Direct materials: ***total*** *variance*

Standard (15 750 × $2.30)	$36 225
Actual (16 400 × $2.20)	$36 080
Total variance	$145 favourable

Direct materials: ***price*** *variance*

Price difference ($2.30 – $2.20) actual quantity 16 400 kg =	$1 640 favourable

Direct materials: ***usage*** *variance*

Quantity difference (16 400 – 15 750 kg) × standard price $2.30 =	$1 495 adverse

Direct labour: ***total*** *variance*

Standard (9 000 × $6.80)	$61 200
Actual (8 800 × $7.00)	$61 600
Total variance	$400 adverse

Direct labour: ***rate*** *variance*

Rate difference ($6.80 – $7.00) actual hours 8 800 =	$1 760 adverse

Direct labour: ***efficiency*** *variance*

Quantity difference (9 000 – 8 800 hrs) × standard rate $6.80 =	$1 360 favourable

Sales variances

The sales total variance is the difference between the standard (expected) revenue and the actual revenue. This total variance may have been caused by more or less units of the product being sold or it may have been caused by the sales price being more or less than the standard selling price. As a result, the total variance can be split into a volume variance and a price variance.

- The sales volume variance is the difference between the standard quantity of sales and the actual quantity of sales valued at the standard selling price per unit.
- The sales price variance is the difference between actual quantity of sales at the standard price and the actual quantity of sales at the actual price.

Key terms

Sales total variance: the difference between the standard (expected) revenue and the actual revenue.
Sales volume variance: the difference between the standard quantity of sales and the actual quantity of sales valued at the standard selling price.
Sales price variance: the difference between the actual quantity of sales at the standard price and the actual quantity of sales at the actual price.

Illustration 5: Calculating sales variances

In March 2015, the budgeted sales volume of product C was 5000 units at a selling price of $40 each. The actual sales volume was 4800 units at a selling price of $39.

		$
Total variance	Budgeted sales (5 000 × $40)	200 000
	Actual sales (4 800 × 39)	187 200
	Total variance	$12 800 adverse
Volume variance	Standard quantity of sales	5 000 units
	Actual quantity of sales	4 800 units
		200 units adverse
	× standard selling price per unit	× $40
		$8 000 adverse
Price variance	Actual sales at standard price	192 000
	Actual sales at actual price	187 200
		$4 800 adverse

Calculating sales variances using formulae

The sales variances may be calculated using formulae. Using the same data as in the previous example, the variances would be calculated as follows.

Sales volume variance

Standard selling price (SSP) × (Actual sales units (AS) – Standard sales units (SS))

The formula is SSP(AS – SS)

The variance is, therefore, calculated as $40(4800 – 5000) = $8000 adverse.

Sales price variance

Actual units sold (AS) × (Actual selling price (ASS) – Standard selling price (SSP))

The formula is AS(ASS – SSP)

The variance is, therefore, calculated as 4800($39 – $40) = $4800 adverse.

Getting it right

When calculating variances, it is essential that you state whether they are adverse or favourable.

Fixed overhead variances

It is assumed, of course, that fixed overheads will remain the same whatever the level of production within the capacity of the existing plant. As you know, traditional costing attempts to ensure that fixed overheads are absorbed into the cost of making each unit by using an overhead absorption rate based on machine hours or labour hours.

Absorption rates are based on standard labour hours or standard machine hours. A standard hour is a measure of how many units of a product are expected to be made in an hour (so it is a measure of quantity rather than time). For example, a standard hour could be six units, meaning that six units should be made in an hour based on direct labour working efficiently, or using a machine efficiently.

These variances are linked as follows.

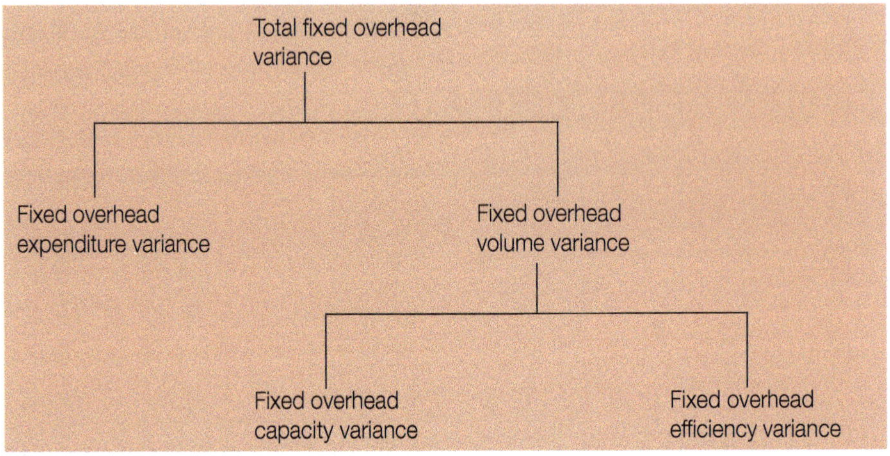

Illustration 6: Calculating fixed overhead variances

Cutfed Ltd produces 'prets'. The following information is available about fixed overheads.

	Budget	Actual
Fixed overheads	$50 000	$54 000
Direct labour hours	10 000	11 000
Direct standard hours	10 000	10 300

Before calculating the variances, it is easy to see that:

- fixed overheads were higher than standard (i.e. adverse variance)
- standard hours were higher than in the budget, so actual production was higher meaning that more overheads would be absorbed (i.e. favourable variance)
- the fixed overhead absorption rate is $5 per hour (i.e. budget fixed overheads of $50 000/10 000 hours).

Variance calculations are as follows.

Fixed overhead TOTAL variance

Actual fixed overhead	–	Actual standard hours × the fixed overhead absorption rate, i.e. 10 300 × $5	
$54 000	–	$51 500	$2 500 adverse

Note: This variance shows that at the level of actual production fixed overheads were $2500 more than the standard.

This variance is then broken down into two sub-variances (for expenditure and volume):

Fixed overhead EXPENDITURE variance

Actual expenditure	–	Budget expenditure	
$54 000	–	$50 000	$4 000 adverse

Note: This variance identifies the portion of the total variance which was due to actual expenditure on fixed overheads being more than the standard.

Fixed overhead VOLUME variance

Actual production less budgeted production	×	Standard fixed overhead rate	
10 300 – 10 000, i.e. 300	–	$5	$1 500 favourable

Note: This means that an additional $1500 of standard fixed overhead will be recovered because more units were produced.

The volume variance can now be investigated further by calculating an efficiency variance and a capacity variance.

Fixed overhead EFFICIENCY variance

Standard hours of output – actual hours of output	×	Standard fixed overhead rate	
11 000 – 10 300 = 700	–	$5	$3 500 adverse

Note: The business lost 700 standard hours of output × $5.

Fixed overhead CAPACITY variance

Actual hours of production – standard hours of production	×	Standard fixed overhead rate	
11 000 – 10 000 = 1000	–	$5	$5 000 favourable

Note: The business gained 1000 units of production, perhaps because there was an unexpected increase in demand for the project.

Reconciling the budgeted costs with the actual costs

If the calculated variances are summarised, you will be able to reconcile the budgeted costs to the actual costs. Adverse variances are added to the budgeted costs as they have cost more than budget; favourable variances are deducted from the budgeted costs as they represent a saving on budget.

Illustration 7: Reconciling budgeted costs with actual costs

The total budgeted direct costs for a business were $87 220. The actual cost of direct material was $51 310 and the actual cost of direct labour was $36 230, which gives total actual costs of $87 540.

The following variances have been calculated.

Direct material price variance	$410 adverse
Direct material usage variance	$240 favourable
Direct labour rate variance	$330 adverse
Direct labour efficiency variance	$180 favourable

The reconciliation will appear as follows.

	$
Total budgeted direct costs	87 220
Direct material price variance	410 adverse
Direct material usage variance	240 favourable
Direct labour rate variance	330 adverse
Direct labour efficiency variance	180 favourable
Total actual direct costs	87 540

Reconciling the budgeted profit with the actual profit

In exactly the same way as shown above, by including the sales variances in the reconciliation, the budgeted profit can be reconciled with the actual profit. A favourable sales variance will be added to the budgeted profit, while an adverse sales variance will be deducted from the budgeted profit.

Illustration 8: Reconciling budgeted profit with actual profit

A business's budgeted profit was $42 400.

The following variances have been calculated.

Direct material price variance	$1 200 favourable
Direct material usage variance	$1 850 adverse
Direct labour rate variance	$1 620 adverse
Direct labour efficiency variance	$1 020 adverse
Sales volume variance	$3 480 favourable
Sales price variance	$1 330 adverse

The reconciliation will appear as follows.

	$
Budgeted profit for the period	42 400
Direct material price variance	1 200 favourable
Direct material usage variance	1 850 adverse
Direct labour rate variance	1 620 adverse
Direct labour efficiency variance	1 020 adverse
Sales volume variance	3 480 favourable
Sales price variance	1 330 adverse
Actual profit for the period	41 260

Investigating the reasons for variances

When variances have been calculated, managers will want to know why their budgeted figures are different to what actually happened. Variances on their own do not explain any differences, they only highlight areas that require further investigation by managers to enable corrective actions to be taken.

There are many possible causes for variances to arise and some of these are listed below.

Variance	Direction	Possible cause
Material price	Adverse	Higher prices charged by suppliers Unexpected delivery costs Better-quality materials No bulk discounts Scarcity of materials
	Favourable	Lower prices charged by suppliers Lower-quality materials Unexpected discounts
Material usage	Adverse	Lower-quality material Theft, deterioration, obsolescence Lower-skilled workforce
	Favourable	More skilled, efficient workforce Efficient production processes Higher-quality material
Labour rate	Adverse	Unexpected overtime Productivity bonuses Higher-skilled workforce Pay increases
	Favourable	Lower-grade workforce No overtime or bonuses paid
Labour efficiency	Adverse	Lower-quality material Lower-skilled workforce Lack of training or supervision Machine breakdowns Bad working conditions

	Favourable	More skilled workforce Better-quality materials Better training/supervision Advances in machine technology
Sales price	Adverse	Respond to increased competition Respond to changes in fashion Respond to lack of demand
	Favourable	Lack of competition Better-quality product so higher demand Market leader
Sales volume	Adverse	Changes in trends/fashion Loss of market share Low quality resulting in lack of demand
	Favourable	Changes in trends/fashion Higher quality increasing demand Lack of supply by competitors

End-of-chapter questions

1 Calculating direct material price and usage variances

Peter Ltd produces one product, the Baz. The standard direct material cost of each unit was as follows:

2.5 kilos of material at $4.80 per kilo = $12 per unit.

During February 2015, the company budgeted to produce 4500 units of Baz but actual production was 5200 units, using 12 480 kilos of direct material, which cost $59 280.

Required

Calculate the direct material price variance and the direct material usage variance for February 2015.

2 Calculating direct labour rate and efficiency variances

Paul Ltd produces one product, the Pax. The standard direct labour cost of each unit was as follows:

4.25 hours of direct labour at $6.20 = $26.35 per unit.

During March 2015, the company budgeted to produce 6000 units of Pax, but actual production was 5800 units using 25 520 hours of direct labour which cost $160 776.

Required

Calculate the direct labour rate variance and the direct labour efficiency variance for March 2015.

3 Calculating sales volume and price variances

Mary Ltd produces one product, the Marl. The budgeted sales for April 2014 were 13 000 units at a selling price of $1.90 per unit. The actual sales during April 2014 were 12 200 units at a selling price of $1.94.

Required

Calculate the sales volume variance and the sales price variance for April 2014.

4 Calculating direct material and direct labour variances

Colin Ltd produces one product, the Col. The standard direct costs for each unit of Col are as follows:

7 metres of material at $5.75 per metre.

1.5 hours of direct labour at $5.60 per hour.

During January 2015, Colin Ltd budgeted to produce 4400 units of Col but actually produced 5200 units. Production used 6.5 metres of material for each unit at a cost of $5.85 per metre. The total cost for direct labour was $44 330, paid at a rate of $5.50 per hour.

Required

Calculate the following variances for Colin Ltd for January 2015:

a direct material price variance
b direct material usage variance

c direct labour rate variance
d direct labour efficiency variance.

5 Calculating direct material and direct labour variances

Patrick Ltd produces one product, the Rick. The standard direct costs for each unit of Rick are as follows:

4 kilos of material at $42.50 per kilo.

30 minutes of direct labour at $7.40 per hour.

During February 2015, Patrick Ltd produced 2900 units of Rick, which was 350 units more than budget. Production costs were as follows:

Direct material: 11 020 kilos at $44.20 per kilo.

Direct labour: 1425 hours at $7.60 per hour.

Required

Calculate the following variances for Patrick Ltd for February 2015:

a direct material price variance
b direct material usage variance
c direct labour rate variance
d direct labour efficiency variance.

6 Calculating direct material, direct labour and sales variances

Deborah Ltd produces one product, the Deb. The budgeted sales for each unit of Deb in March 2015 were 1500 units at a price of $32 per unit. The actual sales were 1750 units at a price of $34.50. The standard direct costs for each unit of Deb were as follows:

8.5 kilos of material at $1.80 per kilo.

45 minutes of direct labour at $8 per hour.

During March 2015, Deborah Ltd produced 1860 units of Deb, which was 60 units more than budget. Production costs were as follows:

Direct material: 14 880 kilos costing a total of $26 040.

Direct labour: 1420 hours costing a total of $11 644.

Required

Calculate the following variances for Deborah Ltd for March 2015:

a direct material price variance
b direct material usage variance
c direct labour rate variance
d direct labour efficiency variance
e sales volume variance
f sales price variance.

7 Calculating direct material, direct labour and sales variances

Kathryn Ltd produces one product, the Kath. The budgeted sales for each unit of Kath in April 2014 were 4200 units at a price of $26. The actual sales were 4280 units at a price of $25.50. The standard direct costs for each unit of Kath were as follows:

2.5 metres of material at $3.90 per metre.

1.5 hours of direct labour at $6.50 per hour.

During April 2014, Kathryn Ltd produced 4400 units of Kath, the budgeted production was 4200 units. Production costs were as follows:

Direct material: 11 660 metres at 3.85 per metre.

Direct labour: 7700 hours at $6.35 per hour.

Required

Calculate the following variances for Kathryn Ltd for April 2014:

a direct material price variance
b direct material usage variance
c direct labour rate variance
d direct labour efficiency variance
e sales volume variance
f sales price variance.

8 Calculating actual direct costs from variances

Jemima Ltd produces one product, the Jem. The total budgeted direct costs for the business for January 2015 were $84 550. The following variances have been calculated.

	$
Direct material price variance	2 140 adverse
Direct material usage variance	1 280 favourable
Direct labour rate variance	2 205 favourable
Direct labour efficiency variance	4 655 adverse

Required

Calculate the actual direct costs for Jemima Ltd for January 2015.

9 Calculating actual profit from variances

Mandy Ltd produces one product, the Mand. The total budgeted profit for the business for February 2015 was $38 400. The following variances have been calculated.

	$
Direct material price variance	2 995 adverse
Direct material usage variance	3 120 favourable
Direct labour rate variance	1 940 favourable
Direct labour efficiency variance	5 820 adverse

Required

Calculate the actual profit for Mandy Ltd for February 2015.

10 Calculating fixed overhead variances

Carsley plc manufactures 'grats'. The following information is available concerning fixed overhead expenditure for the year ended 31 March 2015.

	Budgeted	Actual
Fixed overheads	84 000	81 300
Direct labour hours	12 000	11 000
Standard labour hours	12 000	11 200

Calculate fixed overhead variances for the production of grats.

11 Reconciling budget and actual profit

Orpen Ltd had budgeted to make a profit of $72 500 for the year ended 31 December 2014. However, actual profit was less than expected and an investigation has shown the following variances occurred.

Variance	$
Direct labour efficiency	450 favourable
Direct labour rate	220 adverse
Direct materials price	990 adverse
Direct materials usage	140 favourable
Fixed overhead	3 600 adverse

Prepare a statement reconciling the budgeted profit with the actual profit for the year ended 31 December 2014.

Section 2.4: Investment appraisal

Key concepts

All management techniques are designed to aid decision-making. In the case of capital investment appraisal, owners and managers are likely to be responsible for deciding on expenditure that is likely to be in many thousands, if not many millions, of dollars. The importance of having **true and fair** information that has been prepared in a **consistent** manner is, therefore, paramount. As always, owners and managers need to be aware of non-financial factors that could influence their decisions.

2.4.1: Investment appraisal and sensitivity analysis

What is meant by capital investment appraisal?

Capital investment appraisal is the process of calculating the future cash flows of a capital project (for example the purchase of a new machine or capital investment in the development of a new product) in order to make a decision as to whether the capital project should be undertaken.

There are four methods of capital investment to be considered:

- payback
- accounting rate of return (ARR)
- net present value (NPV)
- internal rate of return (IRR).

Payback

Payback is the time it takes for the cash inflow generated by a capital project to equal the cash outflow. Put more simply, it is the length of time that is required for the net cash inflows to cover the cost of investment: the shorter the payback period, the better. This is especially important if the business has cash flow problems or will have to borrow the money for the capital project, as the inflows can first be used to reduce the loan and then can be used for other potential income-earning purposes.

Learning objectives

In this chapter you will learn:

- what capital investment is
- what payback is, how to calculate it, and what the advantages and disadvantages of this method of capital investment appraisal are
- what the accounting rate of return (ARR) is, how to calculate it, what its advantages and disadvantages as a method of appraisal are
- what the net present value (NVP) is, how to calculate it, what its advantages and disadvantages are
- what the discounted payback method is and how to use it
- what the internal rate of return (IRR) is, how to calculate it, what its advantages and disadvantages are
- what sensitivity analysis is.

Key term

Capital investment appraisal: the process of using cash flows to decide whether a capital project should be undertaken.
Payback: a calculation of how long it takes to generate enough cash inflows to cover the initial cost of a capital project.
Cash inflow: monies received by a business (e.g. by the sale of goods).
Cash outflow: monies paid out by a business (e.g. on production costs).

Illustration 1: Calculating payback

Jacklyn Ltd has manufactured a single product for many years. One of the production machines needs replacing at a cost of $80 000.

The machine is expected to last four years. The financial director of Jacklyn Ltd has calculated the expected cash flows for the new machine as follows.

	Inflows $	Outflows $
Year 1	50 000	15 000
Year 2	70 000	35 000
Year 3	80 000	40 000
Year 4	90 000	40 000

The cash inflows are from the sale of the manufactured goods, whereas the cash outflows are all the production costs excluding depreciation as this does not involve the movement of cash.

	Net cash inflows	Cumulative net cash inflows
Year 1	$35 000	$35 000
Year 2 **A**	$35 000	$70 000
Year 3	**C** $40 000	**B** $110 000
Year 4	$50 000	$160 000

At the end of year 2 the cumulative net cash flow was $70 000. Only another $10 000 is needed to cover the cost of the replaced production machine. The payback period is therefore somewhere between the end of year 2 and the end of year 3.

Payback is calculated as:

$$A + \frac{(\text{Cost of investment} - B)}{C} \times 365\ \text{days}/52\ \text{weeks}/12\ \text{months}$$

where

- A is the year with the cumulative net cash flow nearest the cost of investment
- B is the cumulative net cash flow of the nearest year
- C is the net cash flow of the next year.

If the payback for this machine is calculated in years and months, it works out as:

$$2\ \text{years and}\ \frac{(80\,000 - 70\,000) \times 12}{40\,000}\ \text{months}$$

$$= 2\ \text{years and}\ 3\ \text{months}$$

It therefore takes 2 years and 3 months to make enough net cash flows to cover the initial cost of the investment of $80 000. Once this period has passed, the business has covered its capital costs.

The answer can also be written in years and days, or years and weeks. For this illustration, it would be 2 years and 91.25 days or 2 years and 13 weeks.

It is important to show the workings for all stages in case of addition errors. Cumulative net cash inflows are the net cash inflow of one year added to the cumulative net cash inflow at the previous year. They need only be calculated up to the year nearest the cost of investment. In this illustration this is year 2.

Getting it right

Be careful when rounding the payback amount. The usual practice is to round up to two decimal places. Also, make sure that you know what form the answer should take, for example stating the payback in years and days.

Beware of depreciation. A common error is to include depreciation as a cash outflow. This is incorrect, as depreciation does not involve the movement of cash.

The advantages and disadvantages of payback

Advantages

- It is easy to calculate, simple to understand and widely used.
- It is used by many businesses as the need for quick cash flow has grown in importance in recent years. It should be remembered that a small manufacturer is unlikely to want to wait long for payback, whereas a large organisation can perhaps wait a little longer as it may have better access to cash flow or more reasonable rates of borrowing.
- It recognises that cash received earlier is preferable to cash received later in a project's life, as this reduces the risk involved in the project.
- It recognises the project that most benefits a business's liquidity.

Disadvantages

> **Key term**
>
> **Time value of money**: a concept stating that money received or paid out in the future does not have the same value as money today.

- It ignores the time value of money (e.g. $3000 received today does not have the same purchasing value as $3000 received in three years' time).
- It ignores the money made after the payback date (e.g. very little money might be made after the payback date or, alternatively, considerable money might be made after payback, but neither of these possibilities is considered).
- It ignores the fact that different projects have different patterns of cash flows. Some projects take longer to get off the ground yet generate more net cash flows over a longer period.
- It ignores the whole life of the capital project. The project may last a long time after the payback date, during which time large cash inflows are received and/or large outflows are paid out (for example expensive repairs for updating the capital project). These net cash inflows are ignored so that a capital project which makes significant net cash inflows over the long term is rejected in favour of a capital project with a quicker payback but which only makes smaller total net cash inflows.

Accounting rate of return (ARR)

> **Key term**
>
> **Accounting rate of return (ARR)**: the return on the investment into the project expressed as a percentage of the average investment over the period.

The accounting rate of return (ARR) shows the return on the investment into the project expressed as a percentage of the average investment over the period. Here, return means profit not net cash flows.

The formula to be used is:

$$\frac{\text{Average annual profit}}{\text{Average investment}} \times 100$$

When the straight-line method of depreciation is used, the easiest way to calculate average investment is:

$$\frac{\text{Initial investment} + \text{Scrap value}}{2}$$

Illustration 2: Calculating the ARR

The machine that Jacklyn is intending to purchase costs $80 000 and is expected to last four years. It is to be depreciated using the straight-line method and at the end of four years is expected to have a scrap value of $10 000.

	Cash inflows	Cash outflows	Annual depreciation	Annual profit
	$	$	$	$
Year 1	50 000	15 000	17 500	17 500
Year 2	70 000	35 000	17 500	17 500
Year 3	80 000	40 000	17 500	22 500
Year 4	90 000	40 000	17 500	32 500

Average annual profit is $\frac{17\,500 + 17\,500 + 22\,500 + 32\,500}{4} = \$22\,500$

Average investment is $\frac{80\,000 + 10\,000}{2} = \$45\,000$

Therefore, ARR is $\frac{22\,500}{45\,000} \times 100 = 50\%$

The advantages and disadvantages of the ARR

Advantages

- It is fairly easy to calculate.
- The results can be compared with the present profitability.
- It considers the aggregate earnings of the project.

Disadvantages

- Like the payback method, it does not consider the time value of money.
- Again like the payback method, it does not recognise the timing of the cash flows.

Net present value (NPV)

In order to make a meaningful comparison between today's original cost of a capital project and its future net cash flows, it is necessary to use a discount factor to discount the value of future cash flows back to the present, so that they are equivalent in value to a cash flow now. This enables a like-with-like comparison to be made.

Using the net present value (NPV) method, the discount factor is called the cost of capital and is usually based on the weighted average cost of capital available to the business; that is, the average cost that is needed to raise the required amount of capital to fund the project.

Key terms

Discount factors: the rate used to calculate the value of future cash flows in terms of their value if they were received today.

Net present value (NPV): this method uses the present value of net cash flows to ascertain whether the capital project should be undertaken on financial grounds.

Cost of capital: the discount factor used in capital investment appraisal to discount future cash flows so that they are equivalent in value to cash now.

Illustration 3: Calculating the cost of capital

This illustration explains how a business establishes its cost of capital. Jacklyn Ltd has the following capital structure.

	$	Rate of return	Cost of capital
Ordinary shares (currently paying a dividend of 12%)	500 000	12%	$60 000
5% preference shares	200 000	5%	$10 000
	700 000		$70 000

The average cost of capital is, therefore

$$\frac{\text{Cost of capital per annum}}{\text{The value of capital}} = \frac{\$70\,000}{\$700\,000} = 10\%$$

The NPV is the sum of the net cash flows (future cash inflows less future cash outflows after each has been discounted back to the present) less the initial cost of the investment.

Illustration 4: Calculating the NPV

In the illustration on Jacklyn Ltd, the net cash inflows have been calculated as follows.

	$
Year 1	35 000
Year 2	35 000
Year 3	40 000
Year 4	50 000

The new machine will cost $80 000.

There is a cost of capital of 10 per cent, which means that it will cost Jacklyn Ltd $8000 (10 per cent of the $80 000) to raise the capital to fund the new machine.

The discount factors are:

Year 1	0.909
Year 2	0.826
Year 3	0.751
Year 4	0.683

Here is a statement to calculate the NPV of the machine.

Year	Net cash flow $	×	Discount factor	=	Present value $
0	(80 000)		1.000		(80 000)
1	35 000		0.909		31 815
2	35 000		0.826		28 910
3	40 000		0.751		30 040
4	50 000		0.683		34 150
				NPV	44 915

In year 0 the discount factor is 1 as there has been no passage of time, so there is no change in the value of money.

In year 1 the discount factor is 0.909 as a year has passed. The net cash flow of $35 000 is multiplied by 0.909 to give a present value of $31 815.

This process continues throughout the life of the machine, with the discount factor reducing as time passes.

At the end of the life of the machine, the total of net cash inflow of $80 000 has a total positive NPV of $44 915. The positive NPV means that, from a financial point of view, the machine should be purchased because the discounted present value of the net cash inflows exceeds the initial cost of the machine. (The minimum acceptable solution is a zero NPV as this means there is a balance with the cost of funds.)

If there is a choice of capital projects then the one with the highest positive NPV should be considered on financial grounds.

A negative NPV should be rejected on financial grounds as it means that the sum of future net cash inflows does not cover the initial cost of the investment.

Getting it right

Before a decision can be made as to whether to undertake an investment, both financial and non-financial aspects need to be considered. For example, a capital project may yield a high positive net value, but because it creates excessive pollution, which would create bad publicity for the business and adversely affect sales, the decision may be made to invest in the capital project with the lower NPV because it does not create excessive pollution.

The advantages and disadvantages of NPV

Advantages

- It considers the time value of money by using discount factors.
- It includes all of the net cash flows from the whole life of the capital project.
- Greater importance is given to earlier cash flows.

Disadvantages

- It is more complex to calculate than the payback and ARR methods.
- The life of the project is difficult to predict.
- Inflows and outflows are difficult to predict.
- The current cost of capital may change over the life of the project.
- It is based around selecting the relevant cost of capital, which may be difficult to determine with any reliability: the higher the cost of capital, the lower the NPV.

- It should not be considered on its own, for the project may still not be worth investing in due to the social non-financial factors and a slow payback, which could outweigh the benefit of the positive NPV.

Discounted payback

A common criticism of the payback method is that it does not consider the time value of money. To overcome this, many businesses discount the cash flows using a relevant cost of capital as per the NPV calculations and then calculate the payback period.

Illustration 5: Calculating discounted payback

The net cash flows for Jacklyn Ltd have been calculated as:

	$
Year 1	35 000
Year 2	35 000
Year 3	40 000
Year 4	50 000

The cost of capital is 10 per cent and so the discounted cash flows have been calculated as:

Year	Net cash flow $	×	Discount factor	=	Present value $
1	35 000		0.909		31 815
2	35 000		0.826		28 910
3	40 000		0.751		30 040
4	50 000		0.683		34 150

The cost of the investment was $80 000, so the discounted payback can be calculated as:

$$2 \text{ years and } \left(\frac{19\,275}{30\,040} \times 365\right) \text{ days} = 2 \text{ years and } 234.2 \text{ days}$$

This method is particularly useful when a business is facing liquidity problems and needs a quick repayment on a capital investment. Although the discounted payback period is longer than the non-discounted payback it does give a truer picture as the value of future net cash flows is considered.

Internal rate of return (IRR)

The internal rate of return (IRR) is an alternative method that also considers the time value of money. It measures the rate of interest that discounts the net cash flows back to the initial cost of the project. This rate will give an NPV of zero.

The calculation involves an element of trial and error.

Key term

Internal rate of return (IRR): this method measures the rate of interest that discounts the net cash flows back to the initial cost of the project.

The process is:

1 Use two discount rates; one to give a negative NPV and another to give a positive NPV.

2 Calculate the NPVs using these rates.

3 Apply this formula:

$$\frac{\text{Lower rate} + (\text{\% difference between rates} \times \text{NPV using lower \% rate})}{\text{Total difference between the two NPVs}}$$

Illustration 6: Calculating the IRR

Jacklyn Ltd has a positive NPV of $44 915 with a 10 per cent discount factor and a negative NPV of $4820 with a 36 per cent discount factor.

The IRR is therefore

$$10\% + 26\% \times \frac{44\,915}{49\,735} = 33.48\%$$

Once calculated, the IRR is compared to the cost of capital.

- If the cost of capital is higher than the IRR, then the project should not be taken up.
- If the cost at capital is lower than the IRR, then the project should be taken up.

In this illustration, the cost of capital is 10 per cent, which is lower than the IRR, so the project should be taken up.

Getting it right

If two alternative projects are being compared, then the one with the higher IRR should be selected, as long as it is higher than the cost of capital.

The advantages and disadvantages of the IRR

Advantages

- It considers the time value of money by using discount factors.
- It includes all the net cash flows from the whole life of the capital project.
- Greater importance is given to earlier cash flows.

Disadvantages

- It is more complex to calculate than the payback and ARR methods.
- The life of the project is difficult to predict.
- Inflows and outflows are difficult to predict.
- The current cost of capital may change over the life of the project.
- The calculation requires an element of trial and error to find a positive NPV and a negative NPV.
- It is not 100 per cent accurate.

Key term

Sensitivity analysis: this tries to determine how susceptible the outcome of a project is to changes in future costs and revenues.

Sensitivity analysis

Sensitivity analysis is an assessment of what could go wrong with a project. It measures the effect on one variable element in an appraisal if there is a change in another. For example, what would happen to cash inflows if a key customer pulled out? With capital investment appraisal, sensitivity analysis measures the effect on the decision to invest if there are changes to the cash inflows or outflows. Many capital investments involve large amounts of money and long periods of time. Forecasting for the life of the investment can, therefore, be difficult and potentially unreliable. Sensitivity analysis tries to ascertain how sensitive an investment is to changes that affect the forecasts by calculating different outcomes based on levels of risk.

Illustration 7: Sensitivity analysis and net present value

The directors of Hunterfeld plc are considering expanding their operations by opening a new plant. The capital investment will be $24m and a net present value analysis based on a discount factor of 10 per cent has shown a positive result of $3.2m. The finance director has asked for a sensitivity analysis based on the likelihood that the cost of capital could be higher or lower. The following summary has been prepared.

Discount factor	Risk	Net present value $m
8.5%	60%	5.8
9%	70%	5.3
9.5%	75%	4.8
10%	80%	3.2
10.5%	75%	1.1
11%	65%	(0.8)
11.5%	50%	(2.4)

The summary illustrates that the project is worth carrying out on the current assumption about the cost of capital and for a range of discount factors close to this assumption. However, there is 50–65 per cent chance that the cost of capital would be too high for the project to be worthwhile, causing a negative net present value.

Writing a report on a potential capital investment

You may be required to write a report on a potential capital investment project, assessing whether the business should invest in the project or not. When evaluating a capital investment project, you will be expected to give a balanced answer of the benefits and the limitations of investing in the project, considering both financial and non-financial factors.

Illustration 8: The contents of a report on a potential capital investment project

Using the information on Jacklyn Ltd plus the additional information below it is possible to draw up a report on the potential financial and non-financial considerations of the investment project.

Additional information:

Jacklyn Ltd will have to borrow the money to pay for the new machine. This debt has to be paid back over three years. It is also expected that the workforce will have to be trained how to use the new machine. The carbon footprint is expected to be larger with this machine.

Report contents should include, among other factors, the following.

Financial considerations

- The payback and discounted payback periods are in a short period of time and before the debt has to repaid to the bank.
- The training of the workforce will cost time and money.
- There will be interest to pay on the debt. Was this included in the outflows? If not it is an extra cost that needs to be considered.
- Borrowing for this machine may reduce the opportunities for borrowing to fund other areas of the business (e.g. health and safety).
- How long is the machine expected to last – will it need replacing not long after the payback period?
- Can the machine be leased and not purchased? This may be a cheaper option which will mean that there is no need to borrow from the bank. This will aid cash flow as no interest charges are paid.
- The NPV is positive at a cost of capital of 10 per cent.
- The ARR is 50 per cent for this investment project.
- The IRR is higher than the cost of capital, so the project should be selected.

Non-financial considerations

- Some of the staff may feel threatened by the introduction of a new machine and may resist change by not wanting to be retrained.
- Staff may fear being replaced by the machine and may be demotivated by the lack of money put into other areas of the business.
- Staff may be concerned at the lack of liquidity within the business and may be concerned that there will be no future wage rises or productivity bonuses. This could cause a fall in morale.
- How much disruption will there be while the machine is being replaced?
- Can the production process continue without the machine being replaced? If not, then unless there are cheaper alternative replacement machines, this machine must be purchased.

Getting it right

In all reports there should be an evaluation process, with a balanced view whereby both sides of the argument are given and a final recommendation is made with a summarised justification.

- Will the increase in carbon footprint result in action by outside pressure groups, including government agencies, which may disrupt production?

Final recommendation

The machine appears to have a relatively quick payback and a positive NPV so if it lasts for at least several more years, and staff can overcome their concerns, then it is recommended that the business purchases the machine.

End-of-chapter questions

1 **Payback method**
Explain two possible reasons why a business may be interested in a quick payback period.

2 **Comparing the investment appraisal methods**
Identify the advantages and disadvantages of using each of the following methods of capital investment appraisal:

a payback
b the ARR
c the IRR
d NPV.

3 **Calculating payback and ARR**
The managers of Stanley Standen Ltd are considering the purchase of either machine Elpha or machine Fettan. The following information applies to these machines.

	Elpha $	Fettan $
Purchase price	400 000	500 000
Net cash inflows		
Year 1	140 000	80 000
Year 2	140 000	120 000
Year 3	140 000	180 000
Year 4	140 000	220 000
Year 5	140 000	280 000

Both machines are expected to last five years. They are depreciated using the straight-line method and are expected to be sold at the end of their life: Elpha for $30 000 and Fettan for $80 000.

The machine Fettan creates toxic waste. This waste would be disposed of using lorries which would travel through the local town.

Required

a Calculate the payback period for each machine.
b Calculate the ARR for each machine.
c Which machine do you recommend that the managers of Stanley Standen Ltd should purchase? Justify your recommendation.

4 **Calculating the internal rate of return (IRR)**
The cost of capital for Patel plc is 14 per cent. The managers are considering a three-year project that will cost $100 000.

The net cash flows for the project are expected to be:

Year 1	$40 000
Year 2	$45 000
Year 3	$50 000

The extracts from the present value tables for $1 are:

	12%	14%	16%	18%	20%
Year 1	0.893	0.877	0.863	0.847	0.833
Year 2	0.797	0.769	0.743	0.718	0.694
Year 3	0.712	0.675	0.641	0.609	0.579

a Calculate the discounted payback period for the project.
b Calculate the IRR for the project.
c Should the managers of Patel plc undertake the project? Explain your answer.

5 Calculating NPV

The main cutting machine of Gawain Wilkins Ltd needs to be replaced. A replacement machine will cost $300 000.

The current machine cuts 40 000 units a year. The number of units cut is expected to be reduced by 10 per cent in year 1 due to the time taken to install the new machine. The number of units cut is expected to increase to 42 000 units for both year 2 and year 3, respectively.

Additional information:

- The cost of capital is 10 per cent.
- The following is an extract from the present value table for $1.

	10%
Year 1	0.909
Year 2	0.826
Year 3	0.751

- It is assumed that revenues are received and costs are paid at the end of the year.
- Each unit of production costs $12 to manufacture.
- Each unit is expected to sell for $15 in years 1 and 2, increasing by 5 per cent in year 3.
- It is assumed that everything produced is sold.

Required

a Calculate the annual net cash flows for each year, which are expected to result from the purchase of the machine.

b Using the expected annual net cash flows, calculate the NPV for the replacement machine.

c State whether or not the managers of Gawain Wilkins Ltd should purchase the machine. Give reasons for your answer.

6 Calculating payback, IRR, ARR and NPV

One of the assembly machines at Roberts Ltd needs to be replaced.

A replacement machine will cost $200 000, which is payable on purchase. The replacement machine is expected to last four years, and will be depreciated using the straight-line method. It will need a complete maintenance check-up in year 3 at a cost of $50 000.

The existing machine assembles 4000 units a year. The number of units assembled by the replacement machine in year 1 is expected to be 35 per cent lower than the existing machine due to the time lost during installation and testing. In year 2 it is expected that 4500 units will be assembled, and this will increase by 20 per cent each year compared to the previous year.

The existing machine produces units at a cost of $26 each whereas the replacement machine will produce units at a cost of $24 each. The selling price is currently $42 per unit, but with the improved quality provided by the replacement machine this will increase to $45 per unit. From year 3 it is expected that the cost of manufacture will increase by 25 per cent each year and the selling price will increase by 30 per cent each year compared to the previous year.

The cost of capital is 14 per cent.

The following is an extract from the present value tables for $1.

	12%	14%	40%
Year 1	0.893	0.877	0.714
Year 2	0.797	0.769	0.510
Year 3	0.712	0.675	0.360
Year 4	0.636	0.592	0.260

It is assumed that all production is sold.

a Calculate the expected net cash flows for each year for the replacement machine.

b Calculate both the payback period and discounted payback period for the replacement machine.

c Calculate the ARR for the replacement machine.

d Calculate the NPV for the replacement machine using the expected net cash flows. Assume that revenues are received and costs are paid at the end of each year.

e By selecting a relevant discount factor, so that you have both a positive and a negative NPV, calculate the internal rate of return. Use the 12 per cent and 40 per cent columns in the table provided.

f Should the managers of Roberts Ltd purchase the new machine? Give reasons for your choice.

Topic 2: Cost and management accounting

Exam-style questions

1 **Investment appraisal**

Rex Limited manufactures plastic storage boxes. The directors are considering buying a new, more efficient moulding machine to replace the existing machine. The new machine will increase output by 25 per cent. The company's profit for the year ended 31 December 2014 was $45 000.

The new machine will cost $160 000, it will have an estimated useful life of four years and will have a residual value of $40 000 at the end of four years.

The company's bank has agreed to provide a loan to purchase the machine, repayable over four years. Annual loan repayments, including interest of $15 000, would be $55 000 per annum.

If the company purchases the new machine:

- staff training at a cost of $8000 will be required in the first year
- fixed costs will be $80 000 per annum, including straight-line depreciation of $30 000 per annum
- maximum capacity of 10 000 storage boxes per month will be achieved immediately
- maintenance of the new machine is expected to cost $2000 in the first year and is expected to increase by $1000 in each subsequent year
- contribution per storage box will be $1.35.

The company's cost of capital is 12 per cent and the following discount factors apply.

Year 1	0.893
Year 2	0.797
Year 3	0.712
Year 4	0.636

Required

a Calculate the profit for year 1 if the directors purchase the new machine. [6 marks]

b Calculate the annual cash flows for each of the four years. [4 marks]

c Calculate the payback period of the new machine in years and days. [3 marks]

d Calculate the net present value of the new machine. [6 marks]

e Advise the directors whether or not they should purchase the new machine. Justify your answer. [4 marks]

f State two other capital investment appraisal techniques that the directors could use to aid their decision. [2 marks]

[Total: 25 marks]

2 **Standard costing**

Chang Limited manufactures one item of kitchen furniture known as Excon.

The following standard cost data is available for one unit of Excon.

Direct materials	4 metres @ $6.25 per metre
Direct labour	3.5 hours @ $8 per hour

During March 2015, the budgeted production was 240 units.

The actual data for March 2015 was as follows.

Production	210 units
Direct materials	852 metres at a total cost of $5 010
Direct labour	770 hours at a total cost of $6 468

Required

a Calculate the following variances for March 2015:

i direct material price variance [2 marks]

ii direct material usage variance [2 marks]

iii direct labour rate variance [2 marks]

iv direct labour efficiency variance. [2 marks]

b Prepare a statement reconciling the standard cost of production with the actual cost of production. [7 marks]

c Comment on the possible reasons for the variances calculated in parts (i)–(iv). [6 marks]

d State four advantages of using a system of standard costing. [4 marks]

[Total: 25 marks]

3 **Budgets and activity-based costing (ABC)**

Hatim Limited manufactures one product, an office chair.

Sales of the chair for the period April–July 2015 are expected to be as follows.

	Units
April	400
May	600
June	700
July	1 000

Hatim Limited plans to hold 1500 metres of wood in inventory in April and to increase this to 2000 metres in May and then maintain it at this level.

Each chair uses 12 metres of wood at a current cost of $1.80 per metre. It is expected that the price of wood will increase to $2 on 1 June 2015. Hatim Limited plans to hold 1500 metres of wood in inventory at 1 April 2015 and to increase this holding to 2000 metres at the end of May 2015.

The selling price of each chair at 1 April 2015 is expected to be $80. The directors plan to increase the selling price to $95 on 1 May 2015.

All sales are on credit and 80 per cent of customers pay in the month following sale and receive 5 per cent settlement discount. All remaining customers pay in full in the second month after sale.

Hatim Limited purchases 90 per cent of materials on credit and pays suppliers one month after purchase to receive a 5 per cent settlement discount. The remaining 10 per cent of materials are paid in cash in the month of purchase.

Required

a Prepare a production budget for each of the four months April–July 2015. [4 marks]

b Prepare a raw materials purchases budget for each of the four months April–July 2015. [4 marks]

c Prepare a trade receivables budget for each of the two months June and July 2015. [8 marks]

d Prepare a trade payables budget for each of the two months June and July 2015. [3 marks]

Hatim Limited currently operates a system of absorption costing. The directors are considering changing to a system of activity-based costing (ABC).

Required

e Discuss the advantages to the company of operating a system of ABC. [6 marks]

[Total: 25 marks]

4 Cash budgets and budgetary control

Baku Limited is a manufacturer of ladies' clothing. The following information has been extracted from the company's budgets for the six months ending 30 September 2015.

	April $000	May $000	June $000	July $000	August $000	September $000
Sales	40	36	42	50	48	40
Purchase materials	16	18	24	22	18	16
Wages and salaries	6	7	8	10	8	6
Overheads	11	12	12	16	14	12

Additional information:

- All sales are on credit. Forty per cent of customers pay in the month of sale and receive 5 per cent settlement discount. Fifty per cent of customers pay in the month after sale, 5 per cent pay two months after sale and the remaining 5 per cent of sales become irrecoverable debts.
- Purchases of materials are all on credit and suppliers are paid in the month following sale. One half of all suppliers allow Baku Limited to deduct a settlement discount of 2.5 per cent.
- Wages and salaries are paid in the month they are incurred.
- Overheads include $2000 per month depreciation. Of the remaining overheads, 40 per cent are variable and are paid the month after they are incurred. The remainder of overheads are fixed and these are paid in the month they are incurred.

- Taxation of $5000 is payable in August.
- The company plans to pay for additional non-current assets of $15 000 in July and $9000 in September.
- The bank has agreed to provide an overdraft facility to the company of $15 000.
- The bank balance at 1 April 2015 is expected to show an overdraft of $2100.

Required

a Prepare cash budgets for each of the four months June–September 2015. [13 marks]

The directors of Baku Limited are aware that they may suffer a shortage of cash resources in the coming months.

b Advise the directors of actions they could take to improve the cash position of the company over the four months of the cash budget prepared in part (a). [4 marks]

c Explain two benefits to a business of preparing budgets. [4 marks]

d Explain two drawbacks to a business of preparing budgets. [4 marks]

[Total: 25 marks]

Index